U.S.–SOVIET RELATIONS

THE NEXT PHASE

U.S.–SOVIET RELATIONS

THE NEXT PHASE

EDITED BY

Arnold L. Horelick

A BOOK FROM THE RAND/UCLA CENTER FOR THE
STUDY OF SOVIET INTERNATIONAL BEHAVIOR

CORNELL UNIVERSITY PRESS

ITHACA AND LONDON

CONTENTS

[5]

PREFACE

After a decade of stagnation and deterioration, U.S.-Soviet relations have begun in the middle of the 1980s to move into a new phase of political and diplomatic reengagement. This new phase centers on the resumption of nuclear arms control negotiations, and it is symbolized by the first summit meeting of the two countries' leaders in six years. But whether this reengagement can be sustained long enough to alter substantially the political environment of the relationship, what concrete results it can produce, particularly in arms control, and what shape the U.S.-Soviet relationship will ultimately assume, all remain highly uncertain.

Expectations on both sides are tempered by the failures and disappointments of the past ten years. The much-heralded Soviet-American detente of the 1970s began to lose momentum within months of the second Nixon-Brezhnev summit of 1973, which produced the U.S.-Soviet Agreement on the Prevention of Nuclear War. The second half of the 1970s witnessed detente's steady decline and then its abrupt plunge in 1980 after the Soviet invasion of Afghanistan. During the first half of the 1980s the relationship was frozen in a posture of almost unrelieved hostility and acrimony. With two major exceptions, virtually all of the contacts and arrangements laboriously established and institutionalized during the 1970s were discontinued, dismantled, or emptied of substantive content.

Those two exceptions, however, suggested the boundaries within which the two rivals were prepared to play out the tensions of the new, postdetente phase of the relationship. The first exception was the Soviet-American grain trade. Its revival early in the Reagan administration—indeed, during the administration's otherwise most militantly anti-Soviet phase—displayed the domestic political limits beyond which the American political system would not permit "ordinary" (or "non-acute-crisis") confrontation with the Soviet Union to be pushed. Also, it demonstrated how persisting economic disabilities gave Soviet leaders a stake in preventing political deterioration so grave as to interrupt essential economic intercourse with the West.

[7]

The second exception was nuclear arms control negotiations. These were resumed during 1981–82 despite President Reagan's rejection of the unratified SALT II treaty signed by the Soviet Union and his own predecessor, and despite deep Soviet suspicions of the new American administration's "seriousness" about the entire arms control enterprise. Although the Soviets broke off the negotiations at the end of 1983, when their campaign against the deployment of U.S. intermediate missiles in Europe failed, they agreed to resume them at the beginning of Reagan's second term in 1985. Whatever the tactical considerations that have motivated the two sides, however ambivalent or even reluctant both sides may still be, the return of the superpowers to arms control negotiations also reflects a mutual awareness of the boundary that defines their rivalry—their shared interest in regulating the strategic relationship so as to avert general nuclear war.

The abrupt Soviet walkout from the Geneva arms control negotiations in November 1983 marked the final act in the phase of postdetente decline ushered in by the Soviet invasion of Afghanistan and the American reaction to it. Thereafter underlying geopolitical conditions and competing strategic interests remained unchanged, but after a one-year hiatus the tactical interests of both sides began to coincide sufficiently to warrant restarting the disrupted diplomatic process.

Washington and Moscow both opted in early 1985 for diplomatic reengagement, but for different reasons and with divergent expectations. The U.S.-led success of the Western alliance in the Euromissile crisis and the resounding reelection victory of the president instilled in the Reagan administration at the start of its second term a greater confidence than it had in 1981 in the U.S. bargaining position and a sense that the correlation of forces in the world was now changing in the West's favor. Meanwhile the experience of the first term had demonstrated that a credible arms control effort was essential to preserve allied cohesion and to maintain domestic support for the administration's continuing military buildup. Some in Washington saw diplomatic reengagement with the Soviets as purely a tactical requirement for managing allied and domestic nuclear angst; others, however, saw promising new opportunities to conclude agreements with the Soviets on better terms than had previously been available.

For Moscow, diplomatic reengagement recommended itself because the previous policy had proven so counterproductive. The Soviet walkout had served only to isolate the Soviet Union, reducing pressures on the U.S. administration to make concessions and abandoning the diplomatic high ground to Washington, which responded adroitly by shifting to a markedly more conciliatory declaratory policy in 1984. Meanwhile the underlying concerns that had caused Moscow to seek relief from intensified U.S. competitive pressures remained unchanged—persisting economic stagnation, technological lag, and social malaise at home; imperial troubles in Eastern Europe; and overextension and setbacks in the Third World. The Soviet decision to resume the negotiations predated the formal investiture of Mikhail Gorbachev as Party General Secretary, but his accession on the eve of the new Geneva talks imparted to the opening of this new phase of U.S.-Soviet relations a new and unfamiliar verve and energy from the Soviet side.

It thus seems clear at the start of the second half of the 1980s that a new phase is unfolding in the oscillating U.S.-Soviet relationship. But the process of change is likely to be slow and uneven, and to occur within fairly narrow bounds. Political elites in both Washington and Moscow take a conservative view of the limits of the possible in the U.S.-Soviet relationship. In the coming years they are likely to explore only a limited portion of the spectrum of past relations, much less of what is theoretically possible. A replay of the halcyon years of detente is no longer in the cards. Yet to both sides, the political costs and risks of attempting to sustain prolonged, unalloyed confrontation may no longer seem commensurate with the meager benefits such a posture confers.

Between the detente of the early 1970s and the hostile deadlock of 1983–84 there is still a wide range of possibilities, each with rather different implications both for the security and well-being of the United States and the Soviet Union and for the quality of international life generally in the years ahead. The choices now before the American and Soviet leaderships could determine where in the spectrum of possibilities U.S.-Soviet relations will find themselves in their fifth post–World War II decade.

Anticipating the unfolding of this new phase in U.S.-Soviet relations, the Rand/UCLA Center for the Study of Soviet International Behavior invited a group of the country's leading scholars of Russia and the Soviet Union and analysts of Soviet-American policy making to join in a systematic effort to illuminate the underlying issues and to explore the policy alternatives. This volume had its inception in a national conference on U.S.-Soviet relations conducted in Los Angeles and Santa Monica on October 18–19, 1984, and keynoted by Secretary of State George P. Shultz. The approach of this book, incorporating policy-oriented analysis into a context of scholarly research on U.S.-Soviet relations, reflects the rich range of talents and extensive experience of the authors; among them are outstanding scholars and leading policy analysts, including some who have been senior government officials dealing with Soviet affairs. It also reflects the intensive interaction of the authors and editor with a broad cross-section of other scholars, analysts, and members of the U.S. policy community who served as reviewers and critics.

The resulting book traces the evolution of the U.S.-Soviet relationship to its present state and draws lessons from that history pertinent for today; assesses domestic and alliance constraints on policy making in each country vis-à-vis the other; analyzes the agenda of current major policy issue areas in the relationship; and finally, in the light of the foregoing, examines a range of broad alternative strategic frameworks for the conduct of U.S. policy toward the Soviet Union in the coming phase.

Major Themes

The continuing national debate on U.S.-Soviet relations revolves around two key issues that recur as major themes in this book. The first theme concerns the nature of the adversary that is the object of U.S. policy. The second concerns the broad U.S. strategic approach that is appropriate for dealing with such an adversary. The two issues are inextricably linked in analytical terms although they are not usually connected in systematic ways in policy debates.

At the most fundamental, philosophical level the argument is dominated by two polar views of the nature of the Soviet Union as a political entity and international actor. Both views are represented in this book. One view holds that the Soviet Union is by its very nature an aggressive, expansionist, imperialist power; that the roots of its international behavior are to be found deep in its domestic system; and that meaningful and enduring change in Soviet international behavior can come about only from the transformation of that system or from its collapse. Short of such basic, systemic change, external efforts to influence Soviet behavior, let alone efforts to affect basic Soviet propensities to expand and behave aggressively, can have only limited and temporary success. Because Soviet leaders are careful risk calculators as well as incurable expansionists, they can be deterred temporarily by sufficient displays of Western strength and resolve. In this view, however, Western policy must aim over the long term to foster processes of transformation inside the Soviet Union, at a minimum by denying Soviet leaders the external sources of sustenance and relief from growing domestic strains which could enable them to escape the necessity of risking potentially system-altering reforms.

The other view assigns far greater weight to the international environment in general and to Western policy in particular as factors determining or influencing Soviet international behavior. Acknowledging that the history, ideology, and political culture of the Soviet Union condition its international behavior and distinguish that behavior in important respects from that of other powers, adherents of this position nonetheless believe that considerations of *Realpolitik*, particularly those arising from the U.S.-Soviet nuclear superpower relationship, have come to dominate the foreign policy calculus of Soviet leaders. Accordingly, in this view, the external environment of Soviet policy making, not the domestic system of the Soviet Union, should be the primary if not the exclusive object of Western policy. A strategy aimed openly at forcing a transformation of the Soviet internal order has a high probability of backfiring, promoting not liberalization at home and cooperation abroad but domestic xenophobia and heightened external belligerence. Thus, it is argued, Western policy can contribute more effectively and reliably to an eventual shift in the balance between Soviet internal and external priorities by affecting the Soviet leaders' calculation of the external costs and risks of internal change. The West should seek to shape an external environment that is inhospitable to Soviet aggrandizement, while at the same time being receptive to and prepared to reciprocate Soviet self-restraint.

A second, related set of themes examined in this book concerns the broad U.S. strategy appropriate for dealing with the Soviet Union in the light of the present global power relationship and the strategic trends shaping its future. At issue here is what the Soviets call the correlation of forces—the balance of static and dynamic measures of strength across the full range of military, political, economic, social, and psychological dimensions. Beliefs about the fundamental nature of the adversary and of the East-West competition provide a context for elaborating a broad strategy framework. Specific sets of policies during particular periods of time are, however, shaped by the political leadership's assessment of the existing correlation of forces and the direction in which it appears to be moving.

In the mid-1970s the U.S. national debate on policy toward the Soviet Union revolved around differing assessments of the correlation of forces. Political forces behind the candidacy of Ronald Reagan argued that previous administrations had permitted the correlation of forces, particularly its central military dimension, to shift dangerously in favor of the Soviet Union, so much so that any effort to concert a new strategy for dealing with the Soviet Union required the completion on an urgent basis of a military buildup to restore American power. Only after sufficient power had been restored could a diplomatic strategy be implemented effectively. Though acknowledging that the 1970s had been a decade of relative U.S. decline from former positions of overwhelming superiority in most dimensions of geopolitical standing and power, opponents argued that this view greatly exaggerated Soviet strength and advantages and that, in particular, the strategic nuclear relationship continued to be dominated by a state of parity.

In the middle of the 1980s there is a gathering consensus in the United States around a strikingly different assessment of the correlation of forces and of the strategic trends moving it. The contemporary view is that the correlation of forces is now shifting against the Soviet Union—sharply in its economic, political, and ideological dimensions, and prospectively in key aspects of the military dimension as well. Moreover, there is evidence that this view of the correlation of forces is increasingly informing policy deliberations in both Washington and Moscow. In the United States, however, major policy differences are emerging with respect to the appropriate U.S. policy response to the altered circumstances. Some argue that the favorable shift now occurring in the correlation of forces, especially in its military dimension, is still in an early stage; it should be pressed further rather than squandered or dissipated prematurely in negotiated agreements that could at best yield only marginal benefits and that might collaterally diminish the West's will to compete effectively. Time, according to this view, works in favor of the United States. Sustained competitive pressure on the USSR during its time of domestic troubles will eventually shift the correlation of forces further to the West's advantage, putting before the Soviet leadership a choice between far-reaching concessions to relieve pressures and the risk of internal crisis.

An alternative approach would have the United States employ its improved bargaining position now to seek agreements, specifically in nuclear arms control, with a hard-pressed Soviet leadership. The Soviets, it is argued, may be more amenable than heretofore to making agreements that substantially reduce strategic forces and enhance stability in return for reduced competitive pressures. Adherents of this view are prepared to settle now for less than the outside chance of large unilateral U.S. gains, which only an improbable best-case extrapolation of present strategic trends could yield. And they attach higher potential costs and risks to the greatly intensified military-political competition that, they fear, would ensue in a totally unregulated environment. Both of these approaches are also reflected in chapters of this book.

Preferences as between these two alternative approaches tend to reflect both different understandings of the nature of the Soviet Union and different assessments of the current correlation of its forces and its likely future course. Particular policy prescriptions are further mediated by divergent estimates of what policies can be managed and sustained in the light of domestic and alliance constraints. The experience of the past fifteen years has had a sobering effect on most of the specialists writing in this volume. The domestic circumstances of the United States and of the Western allies seriously inhibit the formulation and implementation of a sensible long-term strategy by any American administration. Those more inclined to seek improvement in the cooperative aspects of the U.S.-Soviet relationship see the major domestic impediment from the American political right; those more preoccupied with strengthening the U.S. position in the competitive aspect of the relationship see the constraining influence of the European allies as the most important obstacle.

The book is organized in four parts. Part I explores how the United States and the USSR got to where they are in their relationship. It draws from the range of post–World War II experience some lessons about what works and what does not in attempts to regulate the relationship. Building on historical experience, Part II explores the domestic constraints on U.S. and Soviet policy making vis-à-vis the other superpower, as well as the influence of alliance considerations on U.S. policy toward the USSR. In Part III key issue areas that dominate the relationship as it moves into a new phase are analyzed. Finally, Part IV presents a range of alternative strategic frameworks and conceptual approaches for managing U.S. relations with the Soviet Union in the new phase ahead.

The Postwar Experience

In the first chapter of Part I, John Van Oudenaren traces the evolution of the strategy of containment from its origins in George Kennan's seminal 1947 article on the sources of Soviet conduct, through its "militarization" and "Americanization" in the 1950s, its blending with detente in the 1970s, and its reemergence in more militant form in the postdetente period, after 1979. Van Oudenaren sees the course of East-West relations in the postwar period largely as the interaction of Western and Soviet efforts, Western efforts to manage the costs and risks of containment by combining extended nuclear deterrence and varying doses of detente, and Soviet efforts to undermine these Western attempts, chiefly by undercutting extended deterrence and playing politically on the Western popular fears of nuclear war associated with it.

The West's abandonment early in the postwar period of serious efforts to mount a direct conventional defense of Europe, and the steady erosion of U.S. nuclear superiority thereafter, created for the Soviet Union a Western periphery that was seen to be at once vulnerable and threatening. Detente revealed to the USSR Western anxieties about the risk of containment and European eagerness to trade with the Eastern bloc, but it also seemed to Moscow a Western effort to undermine Soviet gains in Europe by political and cultural means under the umbrella of extended deterrence. Van Oudenaren sees U.S. policy since the end of the 1970s, and particularly after the election of Ronald Reagan, as moving back in the direction of "neocontainment": seeking to strengthen the weakened underpinnings of that strategy by shoring up the credibility of American nuclear guarantees, improving the conventional defense posture of Europe, and stabilizing vulnerable situations in the Third World. But Van Oudenaren argues that such progress in strengthening the instruments of containment can do little to correct the difficulties of that strategy, because the difficulties are structural. He concludes that, for the long run, "de-nuclearizing" and "de-Americanizing" containment should remain policy goals, both for the United States and for Europe, even though their full realization seems highly unlikely.

In the second chapter Harry Gelman analyzes the rise and fall of detente and the causes and consequences of its unraveling. To some extent, the demise of detente was caused by incompatible misconceptions on each side about the meaning that the other attached to it. Fortuitous events further complicated the inherently precarious arrangement. In Gelman's analysis, however, the dominance of competitive over cooperative aspects of U.S.-Soviet relations was inevitable, caused by the essentially adversarial nature of the relationship, the competing interests of the two sides, and the historically, geopolitically, and ideologically conditioned Soviet compulsion to expand at the expense of the United States.

Gelman sees the most important underlying cause of tension in the Soviet-American relationship, now as in the past, in the assertive dynamism of a Soviet regime straining to press outward on the world scene and in the distinctive Soviet view of the insatiable military requirements essential to Soviet security. Gelman sees both of these factors as internally generated. In his view, these two central aspects of Soviet behavior were the most important, although not the only, causes of the collapse of detente in the 1970s.

Gelman argues that neither the atmosphere of 1972 nor that of 1983–84 is "normal" for the Soviet-American relationship. The relationship is essentially adversarial, and this underlying reality is not subject to change by U.S. policy. However, the degree of tension in the early 1980s is highly abnormal, and it is possible that it can be reduced significantly. U.S. policy can make a difference; but the future of the relationship depends on many variables, some of which are beyond the control of any U.S. government. Insulating the arms control process from the political consequences of any advances by one of the parties at the expense of the other is especially difficult. Linkage, even if formally excluded from the negotiating process, is always likely to exercise a tacit but crucial role. Although no major Soviet geopolitical advance has in fact occurred in the 1980s, the state of relative Soviet acquiescence, in Gelman's view, stems more from happenstance than from Soviet intention. It could change abruptly at any time. So in addition to all the other impediments, the Soviet-American relationship will always be vulnerable to independent factors that may unexpectedly open avenues of Soviet opportunity. These, Gelman argues, Soviet leaders are likely to find irresistible.

In the concluding chapter of Part I Seweryn Bialer draws on the lessons of the past to define the limits of what is realistically possible in tempering the virulence of the superpower competition. The deep-seated sources of Soviet-American conflict in the postwar era bring Bialer to anticipate that the competitive aspects of the relationship will continue to predominate for the foreseeable future. He argues that, although both the United States and the USSR have displayed a healthy respect for the dangers of confrontation in the nuclear age, the ability of the two rivals to continue to manage their competition safely depends heavily on how their policy makers learn to cope with policy dilemmas that are rooted in their own political systems.

The key Soviet dilemmas center on the relationship between ambitious external aspirations and the weakened domestic base for realizing them; between opportunities for establishing new Soviet geopolitical beachheads in the Third World and the costs and difficulties of achieving politically reliable control; between the gains from incremental geopolitical advances or additional military deployments and the costs of provoking a backlash from more richly endowed opponents. In confronting these dilemmas, Soviet leaders are pressed to make a choice. Either they must concentrate on urgent domestic problems while moderating their international ambitions, or they must attempt to combine efforts to restore internal dynamism with the uninterrupted and possibly costly and distracting pursuit of global power ambitions.

American policy dilemmas in dealing with the Soviet Union reflect an interaction of specific characteristics of the U.S. political system, the structure of its alliance relationships, and the requirements of the Soviet-American conflict itself. Volatile American public opinion, obstacles to the conduct of a consistent long-term policy toward the Soviet Union, tendencies toward moralizing in foreign policy, and divergent U.S.-European perspectives on East-West relations, all are expressions of the structural dilemmas confronting U.S. policy makers.

For Bialer, the dilemmas confronting both the superpowers have a systemic character. They make it questionable whether either power will be able in the future to adapt its policies to avoid the errors of the past and prevent the emergence of new, and potentially fatal, errors of judgment.

Domestic and Alliance Constraints

Part II examines how each superpower makes policy toward the other, focusing upon the constraints imposed and the imperfections produced by distinctive domestic and alliance circumstances. Although domestic political constraints on U.S. policy making toward the Soviet Union have become more severe in recent years, in Chapter 4 Joseph Nye concurs with Bialer that these constraints are long-standing and rooted in the American political system. Similarly, as Robert Blackwill shows in Chapter 5, for geographic, historical, and cultural reasons, the West European allies have always approached relations with the Soviet Union differently from the United States; the need to manage these differences has constrained U.S. policy toward the USSR throughout the postwar era. By contrast, Soviet policy making toward the United States has historically been far less influenced by larger societal or alliance constraints. But, as Dimitri Simes argues in Chapter 6, it is highly sensitive to patterns of power distribution within the ruling elite and to the personality of the senior party leader.

In his analysis of U.S. policy making Nye sees an array of systemic features combining to generate oscillation and randomness in policy rather than consistency and coherence. Electoral politics promotes exaggeration in the articulation of issues in U.S.-Soviet relations, and new political appointments deep into the national security bureaucracy with each new administration encourage frequent policy shifts. Moreover, institutional fragmentation, including the heightened role of Congress in foreign policy decision making, complicates the pursuit of consistent policy.

Quiet, private diplomacy with the Soviets, so highly recommended by foreign service professionals, rarely survives the intrusions of the open American policy making process; similarly, a policy toward the USSR based upon fine tuning and nuance is difficult to sustain. Nevertheless, Nye argues, achieving consistent and coherent policy toward the Soviet Union, though difficult, is not impossible. It requires, however, presidential ability to work out a clear strategy, to control the tone of the administration's rhetoric toward the USSR, and to establish a smoothly functioning policy making process *within* the administration. But even with all these elements in place, in the end consistent and coherent U.S. policy will also remain contingent on a minimum degree of Soviet self-restraint, such that inevitably competitive Soviet behavior remains below the threshold of public tolerance. Like Gelman, Nye contends that egregious Soviet actions are destined to produce a wrenching turn in U.S. policy.

The basic principle for a durable strategy is to cut the foreign policy coat to fit our domestic political cloth. An appropriate strategy must be modest enough to fit our domestic capabilities; it must focus on indirect effects, through maintaining our alliance relationships, as much as on the direct bilateral relationship with the Soviet Union; and it should combine balancing Soviet power with economic engagement and continual communication. Over time, according to Nye, such a strategy may gradually increase the transparency in the relationship, reducing the dangers of miscalculation and increasing somewhat our understanding of what goes on within the opaque Soviet society. In short, he argues, our strategy should not only manage the current threat of Soviet power but also seek gradually to improve the conditions that make it so difficult for a society organized as ours is to manage the relationship with the Soviet Union.

Robert Blackwill in Chapter 5 traces the interaction between the attempts of U.S. allies to affect U.S. policies toward Moscow and American efforts to manage the opportunities and constraints resulting from European stakes in and influence on U.S.-Soviet relations. In Blackwill's view, unless Moscow wants it otherwise, Europe has largely established itself as an island of detente, mainly free from East-West tensions generated elsewhere. Structural U.S. and European differences make a unified Western strategy on a global basis impossible.

Blackwill cautions that any U.S. attempt to change quickly these deeply entrenched European attitudes toward East-West relations is more likely to lead to a rupture in trans-Atlantic relations than to modify European behavior. A long-term U.S. strategy toward the Soviet Union has to take this probability into account. Whatever the frustrations, Blackwill concludes that the importance of Europe remains so great—as an irreplaceable asset and the preeminent prize in the U.S.-Soviet competition—that living with constraints while trying to improve at the margin remains clearly preferable.

In Chapter 6 Dimitri Simes examines a strikingly different domestic environment of policy making in the Soviet Union. The top leadership in Moscow is not immune to internal considerations in foreign policy formulation, but it perceives them through the prism of its own parochial interests without the mediating influence of constitutional checks and balances, an independent press, or an official party opposition. Despite the lack of institutional constraints from outside the Party high command, however, bureaucratic constraints and the internal politics of the Soviet elite which developed during the long Brezhnev era have created a strong predisposition toward bureaucratic caution and procrastination among senior leaders, and a strong aversion to radical departures.

The accession of Mikhail Gorbachev and the accompanying generational change in Soviet leadership may now be altering that predisposition, according to Simes. The diffusion of power that marked the long interregnum is now ending. Simes believes that Gorbachev, who consolidated his power position in the Kremlin with unprecedented speed, may enjoy more personal control over Soviet foreign policy than any Soviet leader in years. On the tactical level Soviet policy has already displayed a notably greater flexibility and more rapid responsiveness than in the past.

However, Simes cautions, the same qualities that could make Gorbachev a promising partner for the United States when superpower interests overlap—his intelligence, creativity, and decisiveness—could also make him a more dangerous rival. Gorbachev and his cohorts have thus far revealed no inclination to change the basic directions of Soviet policy, which have put the United States and USSR consistently at odds. But Gorbachev's ultimate intentions remain unknown, perhaps at this early stage even to Gorbachev himself. Accordingly, Simes writes, the United States would do well to focus on pursuing its own interests and communicating them to Soviet leaders in terms they can comprehend. As long as Gorbachev and his colleagues are still in the process of shaping their long-term foreign policy, Simes suggests, the Reagan administration has a unique opportunity to contribute to Soviet deliberations.

Issues in U.S.-Soviet Relations

The experience of the postwar period suggests that economic relations, interactions in the Third World, and arms control have been especially salient in conditioning the overall character of Soviet-American relations. The chapters in Part III examine these issue areas and explore their likely significance in the emerging new phase of the relationship.

Although there is a broad range of views about preferred U.S. policy approaches in these issue areas, specialists share a fairly broad consensus on three general propositions. First, the economic arena is likely to be relatively less important in U.S.-Soviet relations than it was during the 1970s and early 1980s, either in providing inducements to a desired Soviet behavior or as vehicles of punishment or denial, or both. Second, U.S.-Soviet competition in the Third World will inevitably continue, but Soviet opportunities for advances are no longer as attractive as during decolonization; Soviet vulnerabilities in client states have grown; and informal, indirect efforts to reduce the risks of competitive interactions and to manage any crises that might threaten hostile involvement seem more promising approaches than efforts at comprehensive "settlements" of Third World disputes under joint U.S.-Soviet auspices or explicit codes of conduct to manage the competition. Third, the strategic military competition and attempts to manage it will continue to be the central issue of U.S.-Soviet relations.

In Chapter 7 Abraham Becker explores the economic dimension of U.S.-Soviet relations, focusing on U.S. efforts to employ economic policy as a political instrument. He argues that U.S.-led attempts to use Western economic strength to affect Soviet policy and behavior have been notably unsuccessful. Such attempts, Becker's analysis shows, have misconstrued or ignored both the requirements for success and the range of effective possibilities open to the West. A more realistic assessment, he contends, would suggest that economic policy can have only a modest role in future Western strategy.

The U.S. trade position, in Becker's view, is too weak for wholly unilateral action; the political process in this country and its major allies, and the trans-alliance gap in basic attitudes on East-West relations, preclude effective concerting of strategy and balancing of the tools of international leverage. Selective denial to impede Soviet military buildup will probably be pursued under Democratic and Republican administrations, although with different intensity and dedication. Strengthened controls on leakage of militarily relevant technology, limitation of subsidies and credits, perhaps even the rudiments of an alliance energy policy to avoid another Siberian gas pipeline controversy —these seem feasible policy goals. But they will represent a marginal use of economic instruments in comparison to the far-reaching leverage and denial efforts of the recent past, and they appear to be the limit of the alliance's capability.

In his analysis of U.S.-Soviet interactions in the Third World, in Chapter 8, Francis Fukuyama argues that in certain key respects the United States and the Soviet Union are in the process of reversing roles. Future superpower interactions are therefore likely to appear quite different from the past. In the last decade the Soviet Union and its allies developed the political and military instruments to help put into place and sustain a number of narrowly based Marxist-Leninist regimes—including Angola, Mozambique, Ethiopia, South Yemen, and Afghanistan—which have proven to be more susceptible than previous clients to Soviet influence and control but at the same time weaker and more vulnerable to internal challenges. To Fukuyama, these changes suggest a qualitatively different environment for superpower interactions in a variety of Third World theaters. In their vulnerable client states the Soviets may increasingly find themselves trying to defend the status quo while the United States and its associates offer challenges to it.

Paradoxically, these growing vulnerabilities of Soviet client states could create greater opportunities for cooperative measures and bargaining between the superpowers over the management of their interactions in the Third World. U.S. ability to challenge the existing Soviet-sponsored order could, if handled correctly, result in greater overall leverage for the United

States. The world could become a rather mixed place, with the United States holding advantages in some theaters and the Soviets in others, or both holding advantages in different countries in the same theater. This mixed pattern of advantage and disadvantage could then provide a basis for serious negotiations on ending mutual intervention or on "neutralization" of the area in question.

Fukuyama acknowledges that these possibilities will be reduced by the fact that U.S. and Soviet influence over clients is and will probably remain limited. And U.S. domestic constraints will militate against anything that smacks of horsetrading over spheres of influence with the Soviet Union. The key to a more permanent basis for American influence in the Third World, Fukuyama concludes, will therefore remain the finding of a satisfactory and sustainable formula for reforming recalcitrant right-wing allies and encouraging the development of liberal democratic societies in the Third World.

After a series of intermittent, inconclusive talks in the early 1980s, nuclear arms control, the focus of Chapter 9 by Arnold Horelick and Edward Warner, has resumed its familiar place at the center of the U.S.-Soviet relationship. But despite the resumption of negotiations in 1985 and their endorsement at the first Soviet-American summit in six years, prospects for the Geneva negotiations remain highly uncertain. In the authors' view, deeply contradictory positions, above all on space-based strategic defenses, threaten a prolonged deadlock leading perhaps to the final demise of the already tenuous arms control regime that survives from the 1970s.

Although neither side is likely to find any enduring advantage in a totally unregulated nuclear arms competition, neither side is prepared to accept the other's definition of the arms control requirements for promoting a stable strategic balance. Still, the authors see some signs of a growing convergence of views on offensive systems. At the end of 1985 both sides displayed evident readiness to negotiate very deep cuts in offensive forces and weapons, although large differences remained on the appropriate application of these cuts to the respective force structures. But on the matter of strategic defense and space weapons the positions of the two sides remained frozen in diametric opposition.

The authors argue that fundamental strategic choices must now be made both in Washington and in Moscow if the huge roadblocks that remain are to be removed. The United States finds itself in the mid-1980s in a much stronger bargaining position than it has enjoyed since the 1960s. In arms control, as in policy toward the Soviet Union generally, Washington must now choose between two strategies. The first would maximize competitive pressure on the USSR at a time of comparative Soviet weakness, in an effort to achieve a far-reaching shift in the global power balance. The second would seek to translate the improved U.S. bargaining position into an arms control agreement providing for deep cuts in offensive arms of greatest concern to the United States in return for restraints on high-technology development programs of greatest potential concern to the USSR. The Soviet leaders, in turn, must decide whether to accept the costs of trying to cling to existing marginal strategic advantages against a U.S. leadership no longer willing to concede them, or to trade off these advantages in order to ease the pressure of a costly and unpromising new phase of high-technology competition. Arms control, the authors conclude, is the central policy arena in which the debate in both countries will be waged over the coming months and years, as the United States and the USSR work out the strategies that will govern their behavior in the new phase of their relationship.

Alternative Approaches

In the final section of the book three chapters by William Hyland, Marshall Shulman, and Richard Pipes, senior officials in the Nixon/Ford, Carter, and Reagan administrations respectively, lay out sharply opposed alternative strategic frameworks for managing U.S. policy toward the Soviet Union in the years ahead. Shulman and Hyland both see near-term opportunities for the United States arising out of new American advantages and growing Soviet difficulties, but they express doubts about the ability of either the U.S. or the Soviet leadership to adapt constructively to the altered strategic situation. Both, however, argue for U.S. initiatives in an effort to restructure U.S.-Soviet relations and to open up a broader dialogue, particularly on arms control. Pipes, by contrast, cautions against the illusion that an overriding U.S. and Soviet interest in avoiding nuclear war exists which can provide the basis for anything more than a truce in their relations. He argues particularly that an activist policy of seeking dialogue and broadened diplomacy for its own sake can only play into Soviet hands.

Marshall Shulman in Chapter 10 sees the present situation in U.S.-Soviet relations as unusually fluid, ambiguous, and unstable, with both sides confronting critical choices likely to affect the character of their relationship, particularly the military relationship, for many years to come. He views the U.S. choice essentially as between a policy of maximum pressure against the Soviet Union, to press current U.S. advantages and Soviet troubles, and a renewed effort to manage the relationship at lower levels of tension.

Shulman sees the objective situation as logically moving Soviet leaders to seek an easement in their external situation. At the deeper strategic level, however, he holds that debate continues whether the broad political strategy laid down by Brezhnev in 1971 is still valid or has been proved bankrupt. That strategy rested on the assumption that arms control negotiations with the United States were possible and in the Soviet interest; that reduced tensions would yield economic benefits for the USSR; and that "businesslike" relations with the United States were compatible with political competition in third areas. He attaches particular importance to whether U.S. policy leaves room for Moscow to make choices acceptable to Soviet leaders or only for capitulation. On balance Shulman sees U.S. policy heading in the direction of maximizing pressure on the Soviet Union, but he argues that a more rational policy is possible.

Hyland in Chapter 12 views U.S. options similarly, but he treats "watchful waiting" as operatively a more plausible choice, given the dynamics in the shifting correlation of forces favorable to the United States. On balance, however, he concludes that waiting is probably not a politically sustainable position, domestically or in the alliance. Strategic trends, moreover, could turn against the United States once more.

The United States, Hyland argues, has put itself in a better position to carry out the containment side of its policy, but now it needs to organize the diplomatic side. U.S.-Soviet relations, in his view, have reached a point where a wholesale rebuilding is required. In arms control he favors the United States proposing a comprehensive scheme incorporating the general lines of the Scowcroft Commission's recommendation that strategic force modernization be channeled in more stable directions over the long term while leaving open for negotiation the outcome of the Strategic Defense Initiative. But for arms control to succeed, he argues, a change in the political atmosphere is required; efforts to improve U.S.-Soviet relations should therefore not be limited to the arms control arena. Attempts at reconstruction must involve a broad, ongoing dialogue and partial political settlements where possible.

Pipes takes a very different view, stressing in Chapter 11 the risk that a hyperactive diplomacy could squander recent U.S. gains in pursuit of a stability that is inherently not negotiable with the Soviet Union. Pipes attaches only secondary importance to the arms control dimension of U.S.-Soviet relations, relying primarily on unilateral U.S. and alliance efforts to maintain the necessary balance. Peace for the Soviet Union, he argues, means controlled violence; it aims not at genuine coexistence but at pacification. For this reason, he says, extravagant hopes for arms control are misplaced and certain to lead to disappointment. Shulman by contrast sees failure to break the impasse in arms control negotiations as leading inevitably to a steep rise in military competition. Such an outcome would infect everything else in the relationship and lead to dangerous tension. Hyland also warns that continuing stalemate might inadvertently drive the USSR into a dangerous corner.

Pipes's strategy relies for success in the long term on a modification of Soviet international behavior through the transformation of the Soviet system. To that end, he calls on the West to broaden the scope of its foreign policy instrumentalities to correspond to those the USSR employs. He would firmly exclude the Soviet Union from internal U.S. policy disagreements, aid resistance to the Soviet Union in the Third World, conduct more active propaganda, and deny the Soviet Union gratuitous economic benefits from the West.

The alternative strategic approaches set forth in this book diverge sharply from one another in many fundamental respects. The differing Soviet responses that their adoption would elicit and the U.S.-Soviet interactions that would ensue could have profound consequences for the peoples of both countries and for world peace and stability. The authors and the editor of this book have sought to illuminate the issues and to expose the range of assumptions and estimates of the situation that underlay divergent policy preferences. It is for our readers to absorb and evaluate these debates, and to judge for themselves which choices best serve the interests of their country and those of a more secure, just, and peaceful world.

ARNOLD L. HORELICK

Santa Monica, California
January 1986

ACKNOWLEDGMENTS

This book is the first major publication in a new series on various aspects of Soviet foreign and military policy to be issued by the Rand/UCLA Center for the Study of Soviet International Behavior (CSSIB). CSSIB, a new joint center for advanced research and training in Soviet studies, was established in October 1983 by the Rand Corporation and the University of California at Los Angeles with major grant assistance from the Rockefeller Foundation. The Center supports a broad program of analytic and policy-relevant research in Soviet international behavior, provides training leading to a doctoral degree at UCLA or the Rand Graduate Institute, and disseminates its research findings to the public.

The present book is a product of CSSIB's research program, which seeks a balance between research to enlarge the broad base of academic knowledge that supports the study of Soviet international behavior and research to address directly those aspects of Soviet behavior most critically related to the conduct of U.S. foreign, defense, and arms control policies.

Among the large number of persons who made useful suggestions and comments in shaping this project, I particularly thank the following individuals who served as formal readers and commentators on early drafts of the chapters: Jeremy Azrael, George Breslauer, Roman Kolkowicz, Robert Legvold, Dennis Ross, Helmut Sonnenfeldt, Strobe Talbott, Vladimir Treml, and Warren Zimmerman. I am especially indebted to Robert Nurick, associate director of CSSIB, who read and critiqued many of the chapters and offered valuable advice throughout the editorial process. I also express my appreciation to Roger Haydon, the Cornell University Press editor who worked with skill and tact to make often complex and sometimes highly technical prose more gracefully accessible to a broad as well as to a specialized readership.

For their unfailingly dedicated and efficient administrative and secretarial support, I am indebted to Carolyn Pierce, the Center secretary, as well as to other Rand secretaries, Joanna Campbell and Hester Palmquist, who helped both with the typing and the tracking of extraordinarily peripatetic authors.

I also acknowledge the generous support of Enid C. B. Schoettle and the Ford Foundation for the project that led to this book. To John Stremlau and the Rockefeller Foundation a special thanks is due for their help in launching the Center and its training and research program.

Finally, I express my deep appreciation to my fellow authors whose collaboration in this venture made this book possible. Their willingness to respond to the editor's sometimes insistent requests and proddings substantially lightened my own burden.

A.L.H.

I

The Evolution of
U.S.–Soviet Relations

I

Containment:
Obsolete and Enduring Features

John Van Oudenaren

"Containment" entered the vocabulary of American politics in July 1947 with the publication of George Kennan's "The Sources of Soviet Conduct."[1] As the title of the article implied, Kennan's focus was not policy but the analysis of Soviet motives. The policy prescriptions that followed from the analysis were in large part implicit and not spelled out in any detail. They were to become the object of endless debate in later years.

The containment that Kennan outlined was, as the very term suggests, less a policy for dealing directly with the Soviet Union than a call for the United States to promote an external environment that would indirectly constrain Soviet options. Arguing that Soviet conduct was motivated by a complex mixture of ambitions and insecurities which the outside world was powerless to change, Kennan was profoundly skeptical that any combination of threats or enticements, sticks or carrots, aimed directly at the Soviet leadership could influence its behavior. Faced with an adversary that was both aggressive toward the outside world and fearful of external hostility, the United States in Kennan's view had to adopt a policy that would bound Soviet behavior— that would foster an international order in which the Soviet Union would gain nothing by aggression but also lose nothing by lowering its internal and external defenses. If confronted with this prospect for an indefinite future, he believed, Soviet leaders would transform the USSR into a "normal" state with a less combative relationship to the outside world.

Two assumptions, though not spelled out, were clearly central to Kennan's concept of containment. First, he left little doubt that the Soviet Union was the essential problem facing those interested in global stability and world peace; it therefore could not be considered a partner in any joint effort to

---

[1] X, "The Sources of Soviet Conduct," *Foreign Affairs* 25, 4 (1947), reprinted in George Kennan, *American Diplomacy, 1900–1950* (Chicago: University of Chicago Press, 1951), pp. 107–28.

promote a secure international order. By stressing the deep internal roots of Soviet hostility toward the West (and the role of this hostility in maintaining Stalinist rule), Kennan was arguing against the still considerable number of U.S. officials who believed that conflict with the Soviets could be avoided by offering them reconstruction aid, trade, and full participation in the United Nations.

Second, containment as Kennan outlined it virtually presupposed superior Western strength relative to the Soviet Union. Kennan himself was convinced that "Russia, as opposed to the Western world in general, is still by far the weaker party. . . ." He was confident, moreover, that the Soviet leaders themselves had no illusions about their relative position, noting that they regarded the USSR as "an oasis of power" which had been "won for Socialism." The message of the article was that the West should be confident of its strength and should work to supplement its material advantages with a superiority that Kennan referred to as variously "ideological," "political," and "spiritual."[2] It was *this* superiority that Kennan believed would point up the chasm between Soviet claims and reality and in so doing promote the "breakup or the gradual mellowing of Soviet power."[3]

In retrospect it is clear that Kennan was far too optimistic about the costs and likely duration of the containment effort he was proposing. He underestimated the ability of the Soviet Union to marshal its resources in such a way as to negate the political and military significance of the West's greater wealth. He overestimated the effect that Western force of example would have in undermining the ideological foundations of Soviet power. But above all, Kennan erred in his basic assumptions about the postwar international political order.

Like other American officials at the time, Kennan seemed to expect a restoration, with modifications, of the pre-1939 international political order in which the major Eurasian states largely offset one another's strengths.[4] The United States would remain an "over-the-horizon" power with the ability to intervene—as in 1917 and 1941—to restore a threatened balance, but it would not be required to conclude peacetime military alliances or permanently de-

---

[2]"Sources," pp. 126, 127.

[3]The theme of "moral" and "spiritual" superiority also runs through NSC-68, the 1950 document that outlined U.S. strategy for the Cold War. According to a typical passage: "It is only by developing the moral and material strength of the free world that the Soviet regime will become convinced of the falsity of its assumptions and that the preconditions for workable agreements can be created." "NSC-68: A Report to the National Security Council," reprinted in *Naval War College Review* 27, 6 (1975), p. 57.

[4]In lectures to the National War College in 1947 and 1948, Kennan stated: "Any world balance of power means first and foremost a balance on the Eurasian land mass. That balance is unthinkable as long as Germany and Japan remain power vacuums." Further, "Our objective is . . . to make it possible for all the European countries to lead again an independent national existence without fear of being crushed by their neighbor to the east." Quoted in John Lewis Gaddis, *Strategies of Containment* (New York: Oxford University Press, 1982), pp. 39, 41–42.

ploy U.S. forces overseas. Its main contribution to Western security would be economic and political.

The expectation that a Eurasian balance could be restored was based on assumptions about individual countries which proved to be profoundly mistaken. Not until well into the 1950s did Kennan, indeed most U.S. officials, accept the division of Germany as a permanent feature of the postwar international order.[5] Nor did Kennan fully realize the extent to which World War II had weakened France and Britain, until recently regarded as great powers.[6] Although he was more realistic than other American officials in accepting that Eastern Europe (a term that in 1947 would have excluded eastern Germany and Czechoslovakia but included Yugoslavia and Albania) would remain part of the Soviet sphere of influence, even he regarded this situation, which was by no means unprecedented in European history, as more a misfortune for the East European peoples than a threat to Western security. Certainly he did not foresee the formation of the Warsaw Pact and East European contributions to a strategy of "coalition warfare."[7] Finally, Kennan, who nowhere in "The Sources of Soviet Conduct" mentioned nuclear weapons, did not foresee the rapid acquisition by the Soviet Union of a nuclear capability and the absolute gap in power that this would create between it and the non-nuclear states of Western Europe.

The freezing (with minor exceptions) of the international political order along the lines established in 1945 invalidated many of the basic assumptions upon which Kennan had based his initial scheme. Containment was originally premised on the restoration, with American help, of autonomous centers of strength along the Soviet periphery. After 1947 it was to become very much an American venture. The "Americanization" of containment in part resulted from and also further contributed to its "militarization," as the United States and the Soviet Union increasingly confronted each other with military power in the heart of divided Europe. Originally a strategy that called for the United States to assume responsibility for world economic conditions and to provide political support to like-minded countries, by 1950

[5]For early postwar thinking on Germany see John H. Backer, *The Decision to Divide Germany: American Foreign Policy in Transition* (Durham: Duke University Press, 1978). In a 1980 letter to Gaddis, Kennan recalled that he envisioned not only the withdrawal of U.S. and Soviet troops from Germany but a Soviet pullback from Poland as well. See Gaddis, *Strategies of Containment*, p. 76.

[6]This misperception was widely shared in Washington. According to Charles Bohlen, ". . . one of the most astounding features of the war and immediate postwar period was that literally no one in the American government foresaw the extent and rapidity of the decline of British power." Bohlen, *The Transformation of American Foreign Policy* (New York: Norton, 1969), pp. 85–86.

[7]Even NSC-68, which many contemporary historians regard as alarmist in its assessment of the Soviet military threat, was skeptical about Eastern Europe's military potential. "It might not be in the interest of the Soviet Union to equip fully its satellite armies, since the possibility of defections would exist" (NSC-68, p. 66).

containment was seen by policy makers to require a huge U.S. military buildup and the overseas deployment of American forces. Containment thus evolved, contrary to Kennan's expectations, into an expensive and potentially dangerous strategy. It was also a strategy that held out little hope for quick solutions to major East-West issues.

The expense and likely duration of the containment effort soon pushed policy makers to look for ways of lowering the effort's costs and risks. During the Truman administration, concern about costs had already led to discussion of two questions. First, could containment be selective rather than universal? Second, was it necessary, in practicing containment, to respond to Soviet probes "on the ground" or was it possible to induce Soviet restraint by direct appeal to the Soviet leaders (promise of reward, threat of sanction, or some combination of the two). Selective containment was likely to be less expensive than universal containment, and encouraging or compelling Soviet restraint was likely to be less expensive than shoring up every area that was vulnerable to probes by the Soviets or their proxies.

Kennan had provided two simple answers to these questions, and by implication to the question of costs. He believed that containment could be selective; indeed, he questioned the open-ended commitment to any country under communist attack which the Truman Doctrine seemed to imply. Moreover, he did not believe that containment could be conducted through Moscow. The very essence of the policy as he outlined it was that positive developments in the outside world eventually would have their effect on Moscow— not the other way around. In his 1947 article he portrayed the Soviet Union as implacable and impervious to direct appeal, but he argued that its expansive tendencies could be checked by "the adroit and vigilant application of counter-force at a series of constantly shifting geographical and political points."[8]

But because the basic assumptions about the postwar international order on which Kennan had based his outline of containment were invalid, it was virtually impossible for any U.S. administration to accept Kennan's answers to either question. As the Cold War became a struggle between global systems with competing ideologies, no U.S. administration could remain indifferent to communist gains—which at the time usually was assumed to mean Soviet gains—anywhere in the world, because these would be perceived as gains for the competing system and a blow to the morale of all political forces resisting communist pressures. Containment thus became universal rather than selective.[9]

[8]Kennan, "Sources," p. 120.

[9]According to NSC-68, "The assault on free institutions is worldwide now, and in the context of the present polarization of power a defeat of free institutions anywhere is a defeat everywhere. The shock we sustained in the destruction of Czechoslovakia was not in the measure of Czechoslovakia's material importance to us. In a material sense, her capabilities were already at Soviet disposal. But when the integrity of Czechoslovak institutions was destroyed, it was in the intan-

In practice, of course, the Truman administration chose not to try to stop the advance of communism in China, and the Eisenhower administration limited its support for the French in Indochina. But selectivity in these cases was not based on the assumption that U.S. security interests could be defined in finite terms and particular regions could be "written off" as of no intrinsic significance for U.S. interests. Rather, it was based on a calculation of relative costs and benefits in the context of a long-term, global struggle with the Soviet Union. Truman would have preferred to contain communism in China, but he could see no way to do so without endangering the containment effort in other regions deemed more important. This attitude was quite different from Kennan's genuinely selective view "that were only five regions of the world—the United States, the United Kingdom, the Rhine valley with adjacent industrial areas, the Soviet Union, and Japan—where the sinews of modern military strength could be produced in quantity . . ." and that "the main task of containment" was seeing to it that none of the four non-Soviet regions fell under Soviet control.[10]

It also proved impossible for postwar administrations to counter Soviet pressures mainly by building strength—military and nonmilitary—along the Soviet periphery. Because of geographical realities and the rapid demobilization of Western military forces after 1945, the United States often found its local position in confrontations with the Soviet Union extremely weak. As a consequence, it was forced to rely on inducements and threats directed at Moscow rather than on Kennan's "vigilant application of counter-force at a series of constantly shifting geographical points." Stalin withdrew from Iran in 1946 not because he feared a U.S. military action in Iran. He withdrew because he was concerned that a refusal to withdraw would lead to a further deterioration in U.S.-Soviet relations and to adverse consequences in other regions that he regarded as more important.[11]

In the Berlin crisis of 1948 the American position on the ground was again

---

gible scale of values that we registered a loss more damaging than the material loss we had already suffered" (NSC-68, p. 56).

[10]Kennan, *Memoirs, 1925–1950* (Boston: Little, Brown, 1967), p. 359. In any case, as Gaddis points out, Kennan himself supported U.S. aid to Turkey, Greece, and later South Korea, not because he was convinced of their intrinsic importance but because he believed that their loss would be a blow to the morale of Western Europe. See *Strategies of Containment*, pp. 109–10. Truman administration officials also hoped that Chinese nationalism would assert itself and assure China's independence from the Soviet Union. In 1949, as the collapse of China approached, Dean Acheson issued a white paper in which he urged that the United States "should encourage all developments" that would divide the Soviets and Chinese. See Robert J. Donovan, *Tumultuous Years: The Presidency of Harry S Truman* (New York: Norton, 1982), p. 83.

[11]Exactly what transpired between Truman and Stalin concerning Iran has been a subject of controversy. In his memoirs Truman appears to have overstated the forcefulness of his "ultimatum" to Stalin. But there can be little doubt that he did apply pressure of some sort. For details see James A. Thorpe, "Truman's Ultimatum to Stalin in the 1946 Azerbaidjan Crisis: The Making of a Myth," *Journal of Politics* 40, 1 (1978), and Hannes Adomeit, *Soviet Risk-Taking and Crisis Behavior* (London: Allen & Unwin, 1982), p. 135.

decidedly inferior to the Soviet, but again the United States ultimately induced the Soviet leadership to exercise self-restraint. Recognizing the weakness of the U.S. military position in Germany and the risks of a direct
response to the Soviet challenge, Truman refused General Lucius Clay's request to run the blockade with an armored convoy. Instead, Truman chose to
launch the Berlin airlift and thereby shifted the onus of escalation to Stalin.
He also ordered sixty additional B-29 bombers moved from the United States
to Britain, thereby sending a message to Stalin that resort to force in the local
setting where the USSR had superiority (a challenge to the airlift) might provoke a response at a level where the United States enjoyed greater strength.[12]

Despite—indeed, because of—its relative weakness in settings such as
Iran and Berlin, the Truman administration remained committed in principle
to building strengths along the Soviet periphery. Although in its emphasis on
the military aspect of the Soviet threat NSC-68 differed in spirit from Kennan's article, both shared a basic commitment to the application of counter-
force to Soviet probes—the exact nature of this counterforce (military or
nonmilitary) being a secondary question.[13] NSC-68 repeatedly stressed that
the American and allied failure to create "forces in being and readily available
to defeat local Soviet moves with local action" was incompatible with a containment strategy that could be sustained over the long term.[14] Weakness in
local settings would undercut containment in two ways. In a crisis it was certain to place the West in a dangerous position, severely testing the credibility
of the American nuclear commitments. In situations short of crisis it would
place the West in a weak political and "moral" position from which to wage
cold war on a long-term basis.[15]

NSC-68's call for a huge buildup of American and allied conventional
forces reflected a recognition of these weaknesses and a desire to overcome
them no matter what the cost. For economic and political reasons, however,
the West never did acquire the capability to mount a successful conventional
defense in Western Europe or elsewhere along the Soviet periphery. Indeed,
after 1952 it largely abandoned even the pretense of local counterpressure
against Soviet moves. With NATO's dropping of the ambitious Lisbon force
goals—and, perhaps more important, with the French Assembly's rejection

[12]For details of the Berlin crisis, see Adomeit, *Soviet Risk-Taking*, pp. 97, 138.

[13]In later years Kennan regarded his choice of the term "counter-force" as unfortunate and
claimed that "counter-pressure" better conveyed his meaning. The difference between the two
terms has no bearing on the basic argument presented here.

[14]NSC-68, p. 99.

[15]According to NSC-68, "it is clear that our present weakness would prevent us from offering
effective resistance at any of several vital pressure points. The only deterrent we can present to
the Kremlin is the evidence we give that we may make any of the critical points which we cannot
hold the occasion for a global war of annihilation. . . . The risk of having no better choice than to
capitulate or precipitate a global war at any number of pressure points is bad enough in itself, but
it is multiplied by the weakness it imparts to our position in the cold war. Instead of appearing
strong and resolute we are continually at the verge of appearing and being alternately irresolute
and desperate . . ." (NSC-68, p. 80).

in 1954 of the planned European Defense Community—the basis of Western security shifted from direct defense in Europe to extended deterrence based on "massive [nuclear] retaliation."

This shift to an explicit reliance on extended deterrence was one of the most decisive developments of the postwar era. It had two long-term effects: it changed the *nature* of the power on which the West would rely to contain Soviet pressures, and it shifted the *source* of that power. Henceforth the United States would extend its strategic "umbrella" over countries in the shadow of Soviet power while devoting relatively fewer resources to conventional military power buttressed by stable economic and political conditions. The shift from reliance on strength at the periphery to "strength at the center"[16] in turn entailed a gradual transfer of ultimate responsibility for the security of Europe from the West Europeans themselves to the Americans.

Containment and Deterrence

The simultaneous "nuclearization" and "Americanization" of Europe's defense, and of containment in general, were to have enormous implications for the future of West-West and East-West relations. Within the West the active U.S. role gradually encouraged leaders and publics in countries along the Soviet periphery to see themselves as having less stake than the United States in countering the Soviet threat. In time at least some West Europeans came to regard themselves as bystanders, caught in a competition not of their own making and from which they might extricate themselves. It did not, however, lead to the kind of strength along the Soviet periphery which the architects of the Marshall Plan, NATO, and other early postwar initiatives had expected.

Americanization and nuclearization also gradually changed the nature of the East-West rivalry. Once containment was nuclearized, the West's posture toward the East became both weaker and more threatening than what Kennan had envisioned. Instead of bounding Soviet behavior with external strength (political, economic, and military) that was overwhelming but not threatening, nuclear deterrence did the opposite: it presented the Soviets with a Western periphery that was simultaneously vulnerable and menacing. In the 1950s the United States first deployed tactical nuclear weapons in Western Europe to compensate for NATO's conventional deficiencies. Initially Soviet leaders probably saw only the added threat that these weapons posed, but in time they came to realize that NATO's dependence on nuclear weapons was as much a source of weakness as a sign of strength.

The combination of threat and weakness which characterized the West's posture toward the East created incentives on the Soviet side to undercut deterrence as the weak link in Western strategy. The potential rewards for doing

[16]Ibid.

so were enormous—hegemony in Europe—while the potential costs of not doing so would be unacceptable to any Soviet leader. The Soviets were quick to realize, moreover, that reliance on nuclear deterrence was politically and morally problematic not only in its own right but also because of its exclusively American character. It was precisely what made NATO's shift to deterrence possible, nuclear weapons, that Western European publics found most objectionable about the U.S. connection. In time the Soviets also realized that by acquiring a capability to hit the continental United States with nuclear weapons, they could undermine the credibility of the American deterrent and thereby convince at least some Europeans that alliance with the United States created added dangers for Europe but produced no real security.

Although an integral part of Cold War containment policy, then, extended nuclear deterrence was not really compatible with containment as Kennan had articulated it or even as it was originally understood by officials in the Truman administration. U.S. policy makers, recognizing the difficulties inherent in excessive dependence on the extended deterrent, began a partial retreat from "massive retaliation" almost from the moment the concept was adopted, mainly by pressing for greater European conventional efforts. But it was impossible fully to return to the 1952 option. Although in the 1960s the European allies were pressured to accept flexible response, one component of which was "direct defense," West German and other European governments continued to argue against the admissibility of unequal zones of security within the alliance and hence against any retreat from nuclear "coupling" as the basis of alliance policy.[17]

West German and general West European resistance to conventional defense can be explained in part by the division of Europe in 1945 and the persistence of that division into the postwar era. While they could hardly have foreseen it at the time, Soviet policy makers in insisting that Germany remain divided not only took care of their major defensive concern in Europe—the resurgence of a powerful Germany—but also severely limited the West's options for a military defense against Soviet attack.[18] The narrow range of

[17]"For the Federal Republic of Germany, there can be no national defense and consequently no national military strategy. . . . No less secure zones or zones of differing risk must be allowed to exist in the Alliance or in the Federal Republic of Germany" (Federal Ministry of Defence, *White Paper* [Bonn, 1983], p. 154). It would of course be unfair to blame the abandonment of the Lisbon goals and the nuclearization of containment solely on the continental Europeans and the West Germans in particular. The cost-conscious American and British governments of the 1950s were no more eager than the West Germans to purchase an expensive conventional defense when they could rely on a cheaper nuclear deterrent. But it was only the continental Europeans—the West Germans and to an even greater extent the French under de Gaulle—who developed a *principled* opposition to conventional defense in Europe.

[18]Overtly nationalistic West Germans have argued that the West German refusal to consider conventional defense is based not only on practical grounds but on legal and political grounds as well. As long as Germany remains divided, they argue, it is not fully sovereign, and as such not responsible for its own security. Responsibility for the latter rests with the four occupying pow-

options available to NATO in turn provided opportunities for an offensive Soviet strategy toward Western Europe. This strategy was largely political, although it was underwritten by superior conventional and eventually theater nuclear power. By impressing upon the West Germans that their territory was inherently indefensible, Soviet leaders ensured that NATO's security would depend on the politically weak nuclear link. This link would become the focus of the USSR's offensive political strategy in Europe, which involved nuclear-free zones, no first use, pledges not to attack states that refused to host nuclear weapons on their soil, and so forth.

No matter how robust the U.S. strategic forces may be at a given moment, the Soviets are likely to regard the West's dependence on them to maintain the security of regions on the USSR's periphery as essentially a position of weakness that can be undercut over time. In the absence of a U.S. nuclear monopoly, or at least an overwhelming superiority, reliance on a nuclear deterrent is doubly weak. In peacetime it can be eroded by Soviet "peace" appeals, and in crises it may not prove credible, especially if the other side has taken steps to deter the deterrer.

The shift to reliance on nuclear deterrence rendered obsolete much of the early postwar thinking about containment, invalidating both of the basic assumptions upon which Kennan's strategy had been based and which were reflected, in somewhat different form, in NSC-68. These initial assumptions were that the Soviet Union was the main international security "problem," and that the West had to assert its material and "moral" superiority in order to deal with this problem. By the mid-1950s publics in Western countries were split over what was the greater threat, Soviet aggression or the strategy that NATO had adopted to counter that aggression. As Hans Speier wrote in 1957, "the fact that NATO is unable to meet conventional aggression by conventional means gives the Soviet Union a political advantage in peacetime. . . . The Soviet Union may be threatening war . . . , but the fear of war in consequence of Soviet aggression turns into a fear of the weapons that will be employed in that war, and the responsibility for aggression becomes less important in European eyes than the responsibility for the nature of the war."[19] By the 1960s the view was being increasingly accepted in the United States that nuclear weapons were a problem in their own right, and that any solution to the nuclear problem would require cooperation with the Soviet

---

ers. See the attack on flexible response and the call for a return to massive retaliation by the left-wing Social Democrat Guenter Gaus, "A Peace Policy for Germany," in Rudolf Steinke and Michael Vale, eds., *Germany Debates Defense* (Armonk, N.Y.: Sharpe, 1983), and in the same book Egon Bahr's attack on NATO strategy, "Bearing Responsibility for Germany: Twenty Years of the Wall." For a rare American analysis of this aspect of German thinking, see Horst Mendershausen, *The Defense of Germany and the German Defense Contribution* (Santa Monica: Rand Corporation, P-6686, September 1981).

[19]Hans Speier, *German Rearmament and Atomic War* (Evanston: Row Peterson, 1957), pp. 103–4.

Union. This line of argument provided the main impetus to the initial efforts of the Kennedy administration to achieve negotiated arms control.

The second assumption—that containment would operate against a background of Western material and "moral" superiority—was also invalidated by the shift to a reliance on nuclear weapons to deter the Soviet Union. In the moral realm, reliance on a strategy of mass annihilation was itself a powerful factor undercutting Western and especially American pretensions to superiority over the Soviet Union. Soviet propaganda was quick to advance—and Western peace groups eager to echo—the charge that the United States was endangering the planet's survival for the sake of its political objectives. In the material realm, nuclear weapons rendered the concept of military superiority increasingly problematic and, according to some observers, completely obsolete. Long before the Soviet Union approached a position of parity with the United States, its ability to hit the United States with even a few nuclear weapons was raising severe doubts about the credibility of the U.S. commitment to Europe, even though for much of the period the United States retained a massive nuclear and, on a global basis, conventional superiority over the Soviet Union.

The obsolescence of these early postwar assumptions—identification of the USSR as the problem and the need for Western superiority—is nowhere more apparent than in the contemporary arms control process, which is now not merely one aspect of East-West relations but in fact the dominant aspect. By its nature, arms control shifts the focus of the East-West competition from the behavior of the protagonists to the size and quality of their nuclear arsenals. By its nature, arms control generates pressure for codification of parity in these arsenals and, as argued below, for a gradual enlargement of the number of areas in which the parity principle is applied—from central strategic systems to all nuclear weapons, and from all nuclear weapons to political relations between the two sides.

Containment and Detente as Process

If deterrence was alien to containment as Kennan has outlined it, so was detente as it was pursued in various forms after Stalin died in early 1953. Kennan, who personally was appalled both by Soviet propaganda and by emotional anticommunism, was not opposed to detente in the literal sense of the term—"relaxation." But it is necessary to distinguish between detente as an objective state of affairs, a "relaxation of tensions," and detente as a policy or process that is expected to lead to concrete outcomes. Kennan did not believe in detente in the latter sense. He was skeptical that relaxation and atmospherics could lead to even minor convergences of views, much less to the reunification of Europe or the fundamental transformation of the Soviet system.[20]

But just as the costs of containment drove the Eisenhower administration to embrace deterrence, so the economics and the politics of the 1950s (and even more so those of the 1960s) encouraged Western leaders to look to detente as a way of lowering the costs and risks of containment and ultimately as a way of solving the political problems at the heart of the East-West conflict. For the United States, particularly in the activist Kennedy years, the major cost of containment was the potential cost of nuclear war, driven home by the Cuban missile crisis. American leaders therefore sought to keep containment intact but to launch a limited detente with the East, a detente centered around arms control and the lowering of the risks of nuclear war. At the same time as it was revitalizing many elements of containment (the conventional buildup in Europe, foreign aid, and competition in space), the Kennedy administration, in what was to set a pattern for the future, began to separate arms control from other issues in the bilateral relationship with the Soviet Union and to accord it unique status as an East-West issue.

For Western Europe—particularly for Konrad Adenauer and Charles de Gaulle, the two European conservatives with whom Kennedy had to deal—the major cost of containment was not the risk of war, which neither leader rated very highly, but the continued division of Europe and Western Europe's continued dependence on decisions made in Washington and Moscow.[21] U.S. arms control efforts initially dismayed the West German government, which clung to the hope that cold war with the USSR could lead to a solution of the German problem. But as the shock induced by the change in U.S. policy wore off, German governments began to see detente as potentially a vehicle for rather than an obstacle to movement on intra-German issues. De Gaulle also opposed the arms control and defense reform initiatives of the Kennedy administration, and his opposition in time led him to take France out of the integrated NATO command and denounce American nonproliferation policy. But de Gaulle's disputes with the United States led him not back to a cold war posture toward the Soviet Union but rather to his own detente with the East.

In the 1960s, then, all the major Western countries saw detente not as an

---

[20]Kennan's convictions on this question were categorical: the Soviet leaders "are not likely to be swayed by any normal logic in the words of the bourgeois representative. Since there can be no appeal to common purposes, there can be no appeal to common mental approaches. For this reason, facts speak louder than words to the ears of the Kremlin; and words carry the greatest weight when they have the ring of reflecting, or being backed up by, facts of unchallengeable validity" ("Sources," pp. 117–18).

[21]De Gaulle's reaction to the Cuban missile crisis was different from the worried responses of official Washington. According to Arthur Schlesinger, de Gaulle told Dean Acheson, "If there is a war, I will be with you. But there will be no war." Quoted in Schlesinger, *A Thousand Days* (Boston: Houghton Mifflin, 1965), pp. 815–16.

abandoning of containment but as an attempt to build on containment's achievements. Detente aimed to preserve Western positions while peacefully whittling away at those of the East. The West enjoyed, or at least seemed to enjoy, a "position of strength" relative to the Soviet Union, and containment had taught that strength would allow the West to reach a settlement of differences on advantageous terms. The United States, while mainly concerned with stability and arms control, proclaimed its policy of "bridgebuilding," the Federal Republic its "small steps," and France its goal of transcending the "Yalta order" through *détente, entente, coopération.* Many in the West were hopeful that the Soviet Union was undergoing internal changes ("deideologization") that would make it more amenable to accommodation and assure the success, on Western terms, of the various detente initiatives.

This turn to detente raises the thorny question of the role of negotiations in dealing with a "contained" Soviet Union. The architects of containment in the Truman administration were ambivalent and divided about the role of negotiations in implementing containment. Kennan opposed efforts to improve relations merely to engender trust in the Kremlin leaders. But Kennan did believe in exploring possibilities for genuine bargaining with the Soviets on outstanding territorial and political issues. Indeed, Kennan's long-standing hope, very much alive in 1949 and even in the 1950s when he put forward his disengagement proposals, was that negotiations could lead to mutual Soviet and American withdrawal from Europe and the restoration of a European equilibrium.

Other leading officials, notably Acheson and Nitze, did not believe that one could bargain with the Soviets on fundamental issues. In an era of ideological politics and of conflict between democratic and totalitarian states, the compromises that had characterized traditional diplomacy were no longer possible. Instead, they placed primary emphasis on building up Western "positions of strength" while pursuing what might be called "pseudo-negotiations."[22] The purpose of such negotiations, apart from helping to maintain Western solidarity, was to give the Soviet Union what amounted to an opportunity to effect a unilateral surrender in an orderly fashion. According to NSC-68,

> The objectives of the United States and other free countries in negotiations with the Soviet Union . . . are to record, in a formal fashion which will facilitate the consolidation and further advance of our position, the process of Soviet accommodation to the new political, psychological, and economic conditions in the world which will result from adoption of [NSC-68's recommended] course of action and which will be supported by the increasing military strength developed as an integral part of that course of action. In short, our objectives are to record, where desirable, the gradual withdrawal of the Soviet Union and to facilitate that

[22]See Fred Charles Iklé, *How Nations Negotiate* (New York: Harper & Row, 1964), pp. 17, 21–22, for a discussion of this term.

process by making negotiation, if possible, always more expedient than resort to force.[23]

Dulles's attitude toward negotiations combined elements of both the Kennan and the Acheson-Nitze positions, and he often vacillated between the two. On the one hand, Dulles stressed that there was little if anything to negotiate with the Soviets: if they would cease their propaganda activities, agree on the West's terms to the reunification of Germany, and conduct free elections in Eastern Europe, the Cold War would be over. Reflecting this view, Dulles regarded summits as "tests" that were useful only in helping to determine whether the Soviets had at last come around to accepting Western positions. On the other hand, Dulles sometimes recognized that it might be advantageous for the United States to offer genuine concessions to the Soviet side in exchange for counterconcessions. It was this recognition which enabled him to negotiate the Austrian State Treaty of 1955.

Dulles hoped that the agreement on Austria would be a first step toward an across-the-board Soviet retreat, but it soon became clear that Austria was an exception. After 1955 events increasingly conspired to deepen the division of Europe and to rule out negotiated changes in the postwar political order. By the time the West turned to detente, in the 1960s, the differences between those who like Kennan advocated genuine bargaining with the Soviets and those who like Acheson favored building "positions of strength" had become irrelevant. The Soviets had made it clear that they were not open to explicit bargaining with the West on the territorial and political status of East Germany. And the Western position of strength, though much in evidence in the recent Berlin crisis and the more recent Cuban missile crisis, had proved useless in securing changes in the European political order.

The only choice that seemed open to the West was, as Willy Brandt expressed it, to "accept the status quo in order to change it." The West Europeans, and the Germans in particular, remained interested in mitigating the effects of the political division of Europe and in creating a mechanism for eventually overcoming this division. The European version of detente therefore sought to balance the requirements of containment, at least in Europe, with positive elements such as the promotion of trade and political change which, it was argued, would promote a long-term political solution to the East-West conflict in Europe. This "solution" would have to become acceptable to some future Soviet regime. Under contemporary circumstances, however, it was recognized by all as completely unacceptable to the Soviets. Detente thus became a strategy for pursuing cold war goals by other means — using "relaxation" for conflictual purposes.

The alliance's new approach to detente was formulated in the 1967 Harmel Report, in which the allies pledged to pursue the dual goals of deterrence and

---

[23]NSC-68, p. 90. The Soviets, of course, pursued their own variety of pseudo-negotiations under the doctrine of "peaceful coexistence."

detente. According to the report, the alliance's first function "is to maintain adequate military strength and political solidarity to deter aggression and other forms of pressure and to defend the territory of member countries if aggression should occur." Its second function is "to pursue the search for progress towards a more stable relationship in which the underlying political issues can be solved. Military security and a policy of detente are not contradictory but complementary."[24]

Whatever its merits in holding together the alliance, the Harmel approach was completely antithetical to containment as it had been understood earlier in the postwar period. Where containment sought to bound Soviet behavior by simultaneously confronting the USSR with overwhelming external strength and remaining sensitive to Soviet defensive concerns (hence the rejection of "rollback" and "liberation"), the Harmel strategy, at least as it was implemented by European governments after Brandt, did precisely the opposite: it made a virtual fetish of not aspiring to military or political superiority over the Soviet Union, while at the same time openly proclaiming the West's revisionist intentions toward the USSR's most vital sphere of interest, Eastern Europe and the German Democratic Republic.

Detente as process, like deterrence, could be perceived by the Soviets as both weaker—in the sense that it could be undercut and turned against the West—and more "provocative" than containment as Kennan had outlined it. Whenever Soviet leaders have concluded that the basic "correlation of forces" was moving in their favor, they have not taken very seriously Western and especially West German statements about long-term political change—including the unilateral letter that the West Germans addressed to the Soviet Union at the time that the FRG-USSR treaty was concluded.[25] Throughout the 1970s the Soviets interpreted West German acceptance of the postwar borders in Europe as a triumph for Soviet diplomacy. That triumph, they believed, had set in motion a process that would lead not as the West Germans claimed it would, to an overcoming of the division of Europe on terms favorable to the West, but to the eventual creation of an "all-European order" on Soviet terms. Whenever the Soviets have concluded that the correlation of forces was unfavorable or becoming less so, on the other hand, they have reacted harshly and all but halted detente. The Soviet "antirevanchism" campaigns of the mid-1960s and the early 1980s, both of which were launched when the USSR confronted a weak and unstable situation in Eastern Europe and a

[24]The text of the Harmel Report appears in *Department of State Bulletin*, January 8, 1968, pp. 50–52.

[25]The August 12, 1970 letter from Foreign Minister Scheel to Andrei Gromyko states: "Dear Mr. Minister, In connection with today's signature of the Treaty between the Federal Republic of Germany and the Union of Soviet Socialist Republics, the Government of the Federal Republic has the honor to state that this Treaty does not conflict with the political objective of the Federal Republic of Germany to work for a state of peace in Europe in which the German nation will recover its unity in free self-determination." The text of the letter appears in *Survival* 12, 9 (1970), pp. 327–28.

more assertive United States, suggest a Soviet insistence that detente as process be pursued either on Soviet terms or not at all. Under no circumstances can it be allowed to lead to an attenuation of the division of Europe on Western and especially West German terms.[26]

In short, West European detente policies, to the extent that they succeed in accomplishing their stated objectives of weakening Soviet control in Eastern Europe and "leavening" the Soviet system, are certain to provoke a repressive reaction in the East. To the extent that they fail to accomplish these objectives, the same policies contribute to an image of Western weakness in Soviet eyes. They do so for two reasons. First, detente effectively neutralizes much of the West's and especially Western Europe's economic potential in the competition with the Soviet Union. It does so because West European political leaders regard military superiority not only as difficult to achieve in *practice* but, in view of its perceived effect on relations with the East, as undesirable in *principle*. Second, detente creates mechanisms—trade, institutionalized summitry, contacts with Social Democratic parties, and so forth—by which the Soviets can hope to gain increasing and ultimately decisive influence over Western Europe. This hope may well be illusory. But to the extent that the existence of these mechanisms feeds this hope, it undercuts the long-range objective of compelling the Soviets to scale down their global objectives and to revise their concept of international order.

Containment through Detente

The Nixon-Kissinger policy of what has been called "containment through detente"[27] differed from its European counterpart both in the assumptions on which it was based and in the objectives that it aimed to achieve. With its emphasis on improving international stability, American detente policy actually downplayed the prospects for political change in Europe, focusing instead on arms control and functional cooperation. As Raymond Aron observed, Nixon, like every American president since Kennedy, was seeking "to remove direct relations between the two superpowers from the scope of

[26]According to the 1985 CPSU draft program, "Respect for territorial-political realities which came about as a result of World War II is an inalienable condition for the stability of positive processes [i.e., detente] in this and in other regions. The CPSU is resolutely opposed to attempts to revise these realities on any pretexts whatsoever and will rebuff any manifestations of revanchism." *Pravda*, October 26, 1985. It also should be noted that the Soviets use the term revanchism in a specifically Marxist-Leninist sense. Any Western attempt to reverse Soviet and socialist gains is *ipso facto* "social revenge." According to the draft program, "Imperialism offers severe resistance to social progress and makes attempts to halt the course of history, undermine socialism's positions, and take social revenge on a worldwide scale." In the Soviet view, the overall campaign by "imperialism" to take "social revenge," which is led by the United States, reinforces allegedly West German "territorial-political revanchism."

[27]See Stanley Hoffmann, *Dead Ends* (Cambridge, Mass.: Ballinger, 1983).

the hazards of local conflicts and inopportune interventions by the small powers."[28]

On the level of grand strategy, Nixon's detente can be considered an effort to contain the Soviet Union along lines similar to those suggested by Kennan, but under vastly changed circumstances.[29] Like Kennan's containment, it aimed to bound Soviet behavior by creating an order—a "stable structure of peace"—that was both strong and nonthreatening. The United States would adopt a nonthreatening posture by eschewing strategic superiority, not openly questioning the legitimacy of the Soviet system, not engaging in economic blockades, not exploiting turmoil in Eastern Europe, and by assuaging the personal insecurities of Soviet leaders. But by drawing back from its own active role in the world and highlighting the emergence of multiple centers of power, which Nixon argued neither the Soviet Union nor the United States could dominate, the United States would point up the futility of any Soviet effort to achieve global domination or even condominium with the United States.[30]

Within the framework of this grand strategy, the Nixon administration hoped to moderate Soviet behavior by using diplomatic and economic levers to induce Moscow to rein in its clients and proxies. With regard to trade and other forms of functional cooperation, Nixon rejected both the pure Cold War pattern that aimed to isolate the Soviet Union and the bridge-building approach that posited that such cooperation led in itself to moderation on the Soviet side. Nixon and Kissinger, although they occasionally referred to the long-term effects of trade, mainly wanted to be able to use credits and other economic exchanges as instruments to influence Soviet behavior from day to day and crisis to crisis.

[28]Raymond Aron, *The Imperial Republic* (Englewood Cliffs: Prentice-Hall, 1973), p. 123.

[29]John Lewis Gaddis, perhaps the leading U.S. authority on containment and an enthusiast of Nixon's policies, also argues that there is a basic similarity between the Kennan and the Nixon-Kissinger approaches to containment. He does so, however, for reasons different from those offered here. Gaddis argues that Kennan's containment could have worked but was never tried during the Cold War and that Nixon and Kissinger finally attempted to put Kennan's ideas into practice, only to be sabotaged by domestic political factors. Here I argue that Kennan's containment, while based on valuable insights into the nature of the Soviet Union, was never tried because it could not have worked, based as it was on assumptions about the outside world that were totally obsolete. See Gaddis, "The Rise, Fall and Future of Detente," *Foreign Affairs* 62, 2 (1983–84). For a third view of the relationship between Kennan and Kissinger, see Hoffmann, *Dead Ends*, who argues that Kissinger's policy "was a bold attempt to combine universal containment, à la Eisenhower and Dulles . . . *and* the Rooseveltian concept (or conceit) of enticing and ensnaring the Soviets into cooperation on America's terms" (p. 16).

[30]Nixon's second annual foreign policy report to the Congress is instructive: "If we have had to learn the limitations of our own power, the lessons of the last two decades must have left their imprint on the leadership in the Kremlin—in the recognition that Marxist ideology is not the surest guide to the problems of a changing industrial society, and most of all in the foreign policy dilemmas posed by the spread of Communism to states which refuse to endure permanent submission to Soviet authority—a development illustrated vividly by the Soviet schism with China." Richard M. Nixon, "The Second Annual Report to the Congress on U.S. Foreign Pol-

The United States continued to respond directly to Soviet and proxy probes as it had throughout the postwar period, although under the Nixon doctrine it hoped to limit the commitment of U.S. ground forces. (That detente had not eliminated the need for such responses was evident as the Nixon-Ford-Kissinger era came to an end, with Kissinger calling for U.S. responses to the final North Vietnamese push against the south and to the Soviet-Cuban action in Angola.) These responses required the same means that had been used in the 1950s and 1960s: military and economic aid, covert operations, and direct involvement of U.S. forces, preferably air and naval. They were, however, undertaken for a different or at least an additional purpose. Under containment the United States had worked to create sources of strength in third areas, to confront the USSR with "situations" precisely because its leaders were impervious to rational appeals and blandishments; under the Nixon detente the United States found it necessary to respond to challenges less to achieve actual results on the ground (if they were achieved, so much the better) than to convince the Soviets that the United States was able to maintain its part in the complex bipolar relationship. Because policy focused on maintaining credibility in Moscow, winning while desirable was perhaps less important than demonstrating the will and the ability to respond to Soviet probes.

As a strategy of containment the Nixon detente was clearly a failure. It did not head off a series of Soviet and proxy gains which began with the fall of South Vietnam and continued with the Cuban move into Angola. In addition, a strong case can be made that for all the superficial compatibility between European and American detente policies in the early 1970s, those policies actually undercut each other. By the end of the 1970s it was clear, at least from the Soviet perspective, that the U.S.-Soviet detente had opened the way to greater Soviet influence over Western Europe even as Soviet–West European detente weakened the cohesiveness of the U.S. alliance system and thereby undercut U.S. global power.

Kissinger stresses tactical factors in explaining the failure of detente, and above all the refusal of the Congress to give the president the instruments he needed to manage the relationship with the Soviet Union.[31] Undoubtedly there is some merit in this view. But the fundamental premises of detente were also problematic.

Nixon and Kissinger based their policy on the recognition of two basic facts. First, they concluded that the Soviet Union was determined to achieve strategic nuclear parity and that for technological and political reasons the United States would not be able to recover overwhelming superiority. Sec-

---

icy," February 25, 1971, in *Public Papers of the Presidents: Richard Nixon, 1971* (Washington, D.C., 1971), p. 304.

[31] See Henry A. Kissinger, *White House Years* (Boston: Little, Brown, 1979), p. 1255.

ond, they recognized the diffusion of economic power and political influence throughout the world since the height of the Cold War.[32]

Although these two developments were recognized and widely discussed in the early 1970s by American, Soviet, and West European commentators, their implications were by no means unambiguous. Some in the West argued that parity would give the USSR a new sense of security, transforming it into a more status quo–oriented power and thereby lowering the costs and risks of containment. But others argued that the Soviet achievement of parity would further weaken the U.S. alliance with Europe and embolden the Soviet Union in the Third World.

Similarly, some in the West believed that the emergence of Japan and Western Europe as economically stronger and politically more self-confident centers of power would render them less vulnerable to Soviet political pressure. China's breakaway from the Soviet bloc could also be seen as introducing a new, independent power center to the international system and hence another source of resistance to Soviet expansionism. From this perspective, the diffusion of nonstrategic power could be seen as creating the elements of a stable order in which the opportunities for Soviet aggression would be limited. But others in the West pointed out that the loss of overwhelming economic and financial preponderance by the United States had generated domestic political and international financial pressures (in "Mansfieldism" and persistent U.S. balance-of-payments difficulties) for a scaling back of U.S. commitments overseas. From this perspective, the diffusion of economic and political power, even if in large part from one "imperialist center" to its two rivals, was bound to weaken containment, which had always been a primarily American responsibility.

In retrospect it is clear that the United States and the Soviet Union were in fundamental—if unexpressed—disagreement about the implications of the Soviet Union's rise to strategic parity and the rise of Western Europe, Japan, and China to new positions of economic strength and political influence. More important, they disagreed about the relationship between these two developments. American officials seemed to assume that "strategic bipolarity and political multipolarity," to use Kissinger's phrase, both of which could be seen as aspects of the "leveling" process that had occurred throughout the world with recovery from World War II, were mutually offsetting and therefore would not result in dramatic changes in international alignments. The United States expected in effect to preserve the substance of containment, first by recognizing the Soviet Union's increased power and seeking to constrain that power through bilateral mechanisms such as SALT and economic

---

[32]The idea that the world had entered a new era of strategic bipolarity and political, economic, and conventional military bipolarity was by no means an invention of the Nixon administration. It was widely discussed in the early 1970s. See, for example, Alastair Buchan, *Power and Equilibrium in the 1970s* (New York: Praeger, 1973), and Aron, *Imperial Republic*, for European views.

relations, and second by promoting—or at least claiming to promote—a "multipolar" or "pentagonal" international order in which increased Soviet power would confront not only American power but non-American power centers as well.

For the Soviets, however, the emergence of U.S.-Soviet strategic parity and the diffusion of economic and political influence were not offsetting but mutually reinforcing. Both could be interpreted as different aspects of the same general phenomenon: American decline. The Soviets expected major global changes to ensue from the relative American decline in both areas —changes of which they would be the chief beneficiary and the United States the chief victim. From the Soviet perspective, there was an inherent contradiction in a policy that sought to preserve containment by conferring on the Soviets a form of equality—strategic parity—that they regarded as the very antithesis of containment. As Strobe Talbott observed, the Soviets felt they had "achieved the permanent and internationally acknowledged status of a superpower coequal to the United States" and that a superpower "cannot, by definition be contained, isolated or encircled."[33]

In trying to separate the nuclear component from other aspects of the U.S.-Soviet relationship, the Nixon administration was following a pattern established by earlier administrations in emphasizing the unique nature of nuclear weapons, not the special political status of the United States and the Soviet Union as possessors of these weapons. For the Soviets, however, SALT could not be separated from politics with mere phrases like "strategic bipolarity and political multipolarity." SALT had to express the special political status of the two superpowers. Having achieved a recognized nuclear parity, the Soviets saw themselves finally in a position—militarily and politically—to make good on Khrushchev's claim, premature in 1961, that "with equal forces, there must be equal rights and opportunities."[34]

Neither the American nor the Soviet interpretation of the relationship between strategic bipolarity and political multipolarity can be said to have been "objectively" correct. As objective assessments, both contained elements of truth. U.S.-Soviet relations in the 1970s were therefore destined to become a struggle to determine which interpretation—the one biased in favor of the United States, the other more favorable to the Soviets—would prove more accurate. Much of this struggle centered on arms control and how each side perceived its relationship to the East-West political rivalry.

Containment and Arms Control

U.S.-Soviet differences over the implications of strategic parity were most

[33]Strobe Talbott, *The Russians and Reagan* (New York: Vintage, 1984), p. 29.
[34]Khrushchev, speech in 1961, quoted in Arnold L. Horelick and Myron Rush, *Strategic Power and Soviet Foreign Policy* (Chicago: University of Chicago Press, 1966), pp. 87–88.

clearly reflected in how each side chose to interpret the principle of "equality," which both had accepted as the basis for detente. According to the "Basic Principles of Relations between the United States and the USSR," signed in 1972 by President Nixon and General Secretary Brezhnev, "the prerequisites for maintaining and strengthening peaceful relations between the USA and the USSR are the recognition of the security interests of the Parties based on the principle of equality and the renunciation of the use or threat of force."[35] Exactly what the American delegation thought it had accepted when it pledged to respect Soviet "equality" is uncertain.[36] But there can be little doubt that Soviet leaders attributed far-reaching significance to the term, claiming that the United States had acknowledged as valid the Soviet claim to "equality and equal security." In the Soviet view, equality and equal security implied in turn a challenge to NATO strategy and a change in the relationship between the United States and its allies. As a prominent West German specialist has observed: " 'Equal security' with the United States, as demanded and sought by the Soviet Union, largely denies security to the West Europeans and the other allies of the United States. In case of war, their territory would be destroyed and overrun by Eastern forces, if the Soviet concept worked out as intended. There would be no security whatsoever for them."[37]

In addition to claiming that strategic parity entitled the Soviet Union to a more favorable balance of power in Europe, Soviet officials also laid claim to a right to greater influence in the Third World. As Seweryn Bialer has written:

> Soviet expansion in the Third World is based on the idea that the achievement of strategic parity with the United States should be translated into visible gains in Soviet influence and power in the Third World. The key term in the Soviet vocabulary of political goals is "political equality" with the United States. It is not always clear what the term "equality" means in terms of foreign policy or whether the model is the optimistic and dramatically active United States of the 1950s and 1960s or the sober United States of the late 1970s and early 1980s. I be-

---

[35]*Department of State Bulletin*, June 26, 1972, p. 899. The Russian version of the "Basic Principles" appeared in *Pravda*, May 30, 1972.

[36]As Vernon Aspaturian has noted, "it is not entirely clear that President Richard M. Nixon and his national security adviser, Henry Kissinger, anticipated, much less intended, that the principle of strategic parity and equal security should or would invest the Soviet Union with global power status." See "Soviet Global Power and the Correlation of Forces," *Problems of Communism* 49, 3 (1980). Other points in the Basic Principles would seem to deprive the term of much of its practical significance. For example, Points Eleven and Twelve state: "The USA and the USSR make no claim for themselves and would not recognize the claims of anyone else to any special rights or advantages in world affairs. They recognize the sovereign equality of all states . . .;" and "The basic principles set forth in this document do not affect any obligations with respect to other countries earlier assumed by the USA and the USSR."

[37]Gerhard Wettig, "Germany, Europe and the Soviets," in Herbert J. Ellison, ed., *Soviet Policy toward Western Europe* (Seattle: University of Washington Press, 1983), p. 37.

lieve, however, that it is the earlier model on which the Soviet goal of equality in the 1970s and 1980s is based.[38]

The Soviets have to stretch a bit to argue that "equality and equal security" are in fact enshrined in the Basic Principles.[39] They are on firmer ground with respect to SALT I and SALT II. Although SALT I contains no explicit reference to the concept, the "Basic Principles of Negotiations on Further Limitation of Strategic Offensive Arms," signed by Brezhnev and Nixon at the June 1973 Washington summit, states that "both Sides will be guided by the recognition of each other's equal security interests and by the recognition that efforts to obtain unilateral advantage, directly or indirectly, would be inconsistent with the strengthening of peaceful relations. . . ." The preamble to SALT II states that the parties were "guided by the principle of equality and equal security." Finally, the "Joint Statement of Principles and Basic Guidelines for Subsequent Negotiations on the Limitation of Strategic Arms," which presidents Carter and Brezhnev signed at the 1979 Vienna summit, twice pledges the sides to be guided by "equality and equal security."[40]

Soviet leaders now charge that the United States has rejected the concept of equality and equal security as a basic guideline to U.S.-Soviet arms control. In a literal sense their charge is correct, as was demonstrated at the Geneva INF talks where chief negotiators Paul Nitze and Yuli Kvitsinsky were involved in several exchanges over the concept.[41] But the Reagan administration rejects "equality and equal security" not, as the Soviets charge, because it has broken radically with the views of its predecessors but because it has been forced to negotiate on issues where U.S.-Soviet differences about what constitutes equality cannot be postponed or glossed over, as they were in SALT I and II. Even if President Carter had been reelected in 1980, it is unlikely that the substance of U.S. proposals at Geneva would have been significantly different.

[38]Seweryn Bialer, "The Soviet Union and the West in the 1980s: Detente, Containment, or Confrontation?" *Orbis* 27, 1 (1983), p. 42.

[39]According to the Soviet *Dictionary of International Law*, equality and equal security "was recognized as just by the American side and made the basis of the document 'Principles of Relations Between the USSR and the United States,' the SALT I and the SALT II accords, and, subsequently, other acts relating to disarmament and arms limitation. The same principle, formulated as 'nondetriment to the sides' security,' was made the basis for the Vienna talks on Mutual Reduction of Armed Forces and Arms in Central Europe, which have been conducted since 1973. The principle of equality and identical security has become an organic part of international law, and no question relating to disarmament can be resolved under modern conditions without observing it." Quoted in Aleksei Ivkin, "Printsip razoruzheniia" (Principle of disarmament), *Pravda*, September 17, 1984, my translation.

[40]The texts of these agreements can be found in United States Arms Control and Disarmament Agency, *Arms Control and Disarmament Agreements* (Washington, D.C.: ACDA, 1980).

[41]After an exposition of the concept by the Soviet side, Nitze is reported to have asked his Soviet counterpart: "Is that your idea of equality? If so, then it illustrates the underlying problem. What you're demanding is nuclear forces equal or superior to the aggregate of nuclear forces of all other countries. That amounts to a demand for absolute security for yourselves, which means absolute insecurity for everyone else." See Strobe Talbott, *Deadly Gambits* (New York: Knopf, 1984), p. 110.

The key issue on which Soviet and U.S. interpretations of equality clash is that of U.S. nuclear weapons in Europe—the so-called forward based systems (FBS) and, since 1979, the Pershing II and ground-launched cruise missiles. Forward based systems had always been an issue in SALT, where the Soviets demanded from the outset that these systems be counted in U.S. central strategic system totals and where the United States insisted that they be excluded from explicit consideration in the talks. According to Gerard Smith, the chief U.S. negotiator at SALT I, "the Soviet delegation played skillfully and often on this FBS theme. We heard more about it than any other subject."[42]

The weapons in question are militarily less significant than the central strategic systems that figured in SALT. But politically they play an important role in "coupling" the United States and Western Europe and in maintaining, for West Europeans, the credibility of flexible response and American extended deterrence. Soviet objections to FBS and INF must be seen, therefore, in the context of a long-standing Soviet effort to undercut extended deterrence and the crucial role it plays in American containment strategy. As one American official stated in 1981, "the Soviet Union is insisting that Western Europe does not have a right to call upon American strength to counterbalance Soviet power and geographical advantage."[43] Not only do the Soviets dispute Western Europe's "right" to call on American assistance, but they interpret American support of this right as a covert attempt to subvert the strategic parity negotiated in the early 1970s and to achieve superiority "on the backs of others."[44]

The dispute over American weapons in Europe therefore reflects fundamentally opposed views in East and West about the legitimacy of the Atlantic alliance and its basic strategy. For the NATO countries, U.S. nuclear weapons in Europe are a partial compensation for the conventional imbalance created by the presence of Soviet forces in central Europe. For the West European countries, U.S. nuclear forces in Europe also compensate for the nuclear imbalance in Europe—an imbalance that was initially brought about by self-imposed restraint on the Western side and later given international codification in the Non-Proliferation Treaty, which the United States joined with the USSR to press upon reluctant allies and especially the Federal Republic. In effect, the West argues that extended deterrence is a substitute for a regional balance to which Western Europe is in principle entitled, but which it is unable or unwilling to achieve at the conventional level and which it has denied itself at the nuclear level.[45]

[42]Gerald Smith, *Doubletalk: The Story of the First Strategic Arms Limitation Talks* (Garden City, N.Y.: Doubleday, 1980), p. 93.

[43]Richard Burt, director of politico-military affairs, speech to the Arms Control Association, Brussels, November 23, 1981, in *Department of State Bulletin*, November 1981.

[44]Speech by Ambassador Stefan Chervonenko, Paris, reported in *New York Times*, April 16, 1980.

[45]West European officials explicitly invoke the Non-Proliferation Treaty to support the West's right to depoy American nuclear missiles in "forward" positions. According to Alois

The Soviets clearly reject such arguments. In Soviet writings, extended deterrence by the United States is often associated with terms such as "blackmail," "pressure," "diktat," and so forth. One need not be sympathetic to Soviet objectives or accept the Soviet characterization of U.S. motives to acknowledge the grain of truth in the Soviet view. Nuclear deterrence *is*, especially in regions where the countervailing conventional power is extremely weak or even deliberately neglected as a matter of policy, a way of extending influence and guarantees to regions that the United States and its allies do not have the will or resources to defend on the ground.[46]

In theory a situation in which the U.S., the Japanese, and most NATO governments hold one view of the relationship between nuclear balances and political "opportunities" (to use Khrushchev's phrase) and the Soviets another could persist indefinitely. But in practice the current Soviet attitude on extended deterrence and American weapons in Europe and Asia represents a major threat to the Western alliances. In 1979–83 the NATO governments won the battle to deploy Pershing II and cruise missiles, thereby repudiating the Soviet demand for "equality and equal security." But the INF debate showed that many individuals and some of the major European parties, although by no means sympathetic to Soviet objectives, now accept Soviet definitions of equality and favor acceptance of Soviet proposals on key security issues. With its diplomatic "peace programs," propaganda, and demonstrative arms control policy, the Soviet Union has inserted itself into the Western security debate and convinced many in the West of the essential fairness of its positions.

On the American side, there is a double danger. If, on the one hand, the United States adopts a tough policy toward the Soviet Union, failing to conclude arms control agreements and improving its strategic deterrent in ways that suggest an American striving for superiority, it will fuel West European

---

Mertes, parliamentary state secretary in the Foreign Ministry, the Federal Republic "signed the nuclear non-proliferation treaty in the expectation that Moscow would adhere to the call for sincere disarmament efforts and to respect German needs. The Soviet Union had taken note of and not questioned the argument that the Federal Republic depends on the U.S. security guarantee. Bonn would regard a refusal to negotiate on certain categories of weapons as a grave violation of the treaty." Remarks paraphrased in DPA, December 10, 1984. European officials also are critical of the American tendency to downplay the significance of the NPT. In a sharply worded reply to Henry Kissinger's 1984 proposals for restructuring NATO, Mertes stated: "The treaty on the nonproliferation of nuclear weapons has since 1968, in accordance with the common wishes of the United States and the USSR, cemented the imbalance of power between Western Europe and America. The treaty banning nuclear weapons prevents the establishment of a multilateral European nuclear power, and this means every direct or indirect co-responsible power of European non-nuclear states over the nuclear potential of the allies. . . . Many Americans have forgotten: the fundamental basis of the German acceptance of the nuclear Non-Proliferation Treaty was the ever-present nonviolability of the nuclear security guarantee of the United States for the Federal Republic, including Berlin, *and the agreement to take all necessary military and political steps for the credibility of this guarantee*." "Das Buendnis hat sich bewaehrt," *Die Zeit*, March 16, 1984, my translation, my emphases.

[46]For a typical restatement of this position see R. G. Bogdanov, "Paritet ili 'ustrashenie'?" (Parity or "intimidation"?), *SShA: Ekonomika, Politika, Ideologiia* no. 10 (1984), pp. 3–14.

sentiment for a semineutralist "security partnership" with the Soviet Union. On the other hand, either out of conviction or under pressure from the powerful domestic arms control constituency, U.S. administrations may negotiate bilateral arms control agreements that undercut American nuclear guarantees and that prejudice relations with allies in Europe and Asia. American sensitivity to the effect of arms control on alliances may have improved somewhat since the middle 1960s, when the director of the Arms Control and Disarmament Agency could write in *Foreign Affairs* that the United States was prepared to accept the "erosion of alliances" which would result from U.S.-Soviet sponsorship of the Non-Proliferation Treaty.[47] But the strength of sentiment favoring arms control has increased as well.

In the 1970s European governments were disturbed by American handling in SALT II of the cruise missile and Backfire bomber issues. The prospect of public or private understandings between the United States and the Soviet Union on the nuclear systems of France and Britain could complicate relations with those countries. And negotiations on INF could pit U.S. relations with Japan against the preservation of ties with Western Europe—or vice versa. However these issues are handled, arms control will remain at a minimum a complicating factor for U.S. administrations seeking to manage the nuclear competition with the Soviet Union while at the same time trying to uphold the nuclear guarantees that have become the very basis of the West's containment strategy.

Containment: Obsolete and Enduring Features

The failure of the Nixon-Kissinger detente and of its continuation, in modified form, by the Carter administration set the stage for a far-reaching discussion in the United States of the need to revitalize containment.[48] In the late 1970s this discussion focused on the Third World where the Soviet Union, with gains in Vietnam, Angola, Mozambique, Ethiopia, South Yemen, Cambodia, Nicaragua, and Afghanistan, decisively breached containment for the first time since the late 1940s. After 1979 the momentum of Soviet gains in the Third World slowed dramatically, but another threat came to the fore: the systematic, long-term Soviet effort to undercut extended deterrence and to sever the basic security links between the United States and its European and Asian allies. By the early 1980s it was clear that the United States needed to fashion a strategy of containment which would respond

---

[47]William C. Foster, "New Directions in Arms Control and Disarmament," *Foreign Affairs* 43, 4 (1965), p. 600.

[48]See, for example, Robert E. Osgood, "The Revitalization of Containment," *Foreign Affairs* 60, 3 (1982), and Robert Legvold, "Containment without Confrontation," *Foreign Policy* no. 40 (1980).

both to Soviet threats in the Third World and to Soviet efforts to undermine American alliances.

In discussing the requirements of such a strategy, it is useful to recall the history of containment, both as it was outlined by Kennan and other early postwar policy makers and as it was then implemented after 1947 by successive U.S. administrations. As a prescription for dealing with the real world, Kennan's containment was virtually obsolete the moment he unveiled it. He hoped to fashion a policy based on the continued existence of multiple, autonomous centers of power, including a reconstituted German state. By the late 1940s, however, the division of Europe and the almost complete dependence of its western part on the United States had become the dominant reality facing American policy makers.

Recognizing the changed realities, officials in the Truman administration —sometimes resisted but more often encouraged by their European counterparts—transformed containment. They adopted Kennan's language and to some extent his view of the USSR, but they "Americanized," "militarized," and "nuclearized" containment in ways that Kennan had not envisioned. This new version of containment was basically successful in halting Soviet territorial advances until the mid-1970s. It had numerous potential difficulties, however, most of which Kennan had foreseen and tried to avoid. It relied too heavily on American advantages that could not last forever, and it failed to hold out the promise of solutions to political problems that Western publics would not tolerate indefinitely.

By the late 1960s the Nixon administration recognized that the premises upon which the Truman, Eisenhower, and Kennedy-Johnson administrations had based their strategies of containment were no longer valid. A containment that was largely American, military, and nuclear was workable only as long as the United States maintained strategic superiority over the Soviet Union, conventional superiority at sea and in many regions outside Europe, and a high degree of credibility with and support from its overseas allies. By the late 1960s the United States had lost or was in the process of losing all of these advantages.

Nixon's response to these new and decidedly less favorable circumstances led him back, as many commentators noted, to a strategy that in some (although by no means all) respects had more in common with Kennan's containment than with the policies pursued after 1947. But Nixon's strategy was based on assumptions that proved to be illusory. By the Arab-Israeli War of October 1973, if not earlier, it was clear that to speak of multiple power centers and a pentagonal world was to overstate the contributions that China, Japan, and Western Europe could make to global stability. The rhetorical effort to downplay the significance of the strategic nuclear competition also failed. If anything, arms control confirmed nuclear competition as the centerpiece of superpower relations.

With the failure of Nixon's detente, U.S. policy began to drift back, albeit slowly, to containment as it had been pursued from Truman to Johnson. During the last year of the Carter administration "neocontainment" was accepted as "the new orthodoxy"[49] in American foreign policy. This orthodoxy, which was seen even more strongly after President Reagan's inauguration in 1981, called for a wide range of efforts aimed at restoring containment to what it had been prior to the 1970s.

These efforts focused on three areas. They looked to shore up the credibility of American nuclear guarantees through major improvements in U.S. strategic nuclear forces. They continued efforts to improve conventional defense in Western Europe. Finally, they worked to stabilize situations in the Third World by improving American capabilities to intervene with light, mobile forces, by granting increased military and economic aid, and by forging bilateral agreements with friendly states in unstable regions.

Although specialists frequently lament the lack of an American foreign policy consensus since Vietnam, action in all three of these areas seems to attract fairly strong support across the political spectrum. The Reagan administration may be forced by political pressures to scale down its Strategic Defense Initiative and perhaps part of its strategic offense program, but there seems to be a large body of political support for strategic force modernization. Similarly, public opinion and most of the Congress support the improvements in conventional defenses which began during the Carter administration and were stepped up under Reagan.

Less of a national consensus has emerged about such complex regional issues as Central America, the Middle East, and Southern Africa. Americans remain divided over the role that the United States should play in supporting friendly but nondemocratic regimes in the Third World, over the circumstances in which the United States should use military force overseas, and over the admissibility of attempts to subvert communist regimes in Nicaragua and elsewhere. This lack of consensus to some extent reflects the breakdown that occurred during the Vietnam War. But it also reflects the inherent complexity of these regional crises and the seemingly "no win" character of many situations in the Third World. The lack of national consensus notwithstanding, the United States has made strides in improving its capabilities for overseas intervention, in training the armed forces of friendly countries, and in raising the level of its security cooperation with countries in the Middle East, Central America, and elsewhere. Disaster may yet strike in such places as Saudi Arabia, the Philippines, or Pakistan, but on balance the outlook for containing the Soviet threat in the Third World has probably improved in the last several years.

In summing up the results of the post-1979 turn to neocontainment, it can be said that the United States has made progress in strengthening the *instruments* of containment which served so well in the 1950s and early 1960s. With

[49]Hoffmann, *Dead Ends*, pp. 85–151.

current programs it is likely to continue to do so. But a strengthening of the instruments of containment, while it may be desirable, will do little to correct those weaknesses which are inherent in containment. Because containment depends heavily on strategic deterrence, a robust deterrent is clearly preferable to a weak one. Similarly, because containment remains very much an American venture, a strengthening of American capabilities is also desirable. But improvements in the instruments of containment will not overcome problems that were already apparent in the 1950s and early 1960s, when in relative terms American capabilities were far greater than they are today.

Over the long run, "denuclearizing" and "de-Americanizing" containment should remain a policy goal, not only for the United States but for its allies. De-Americanization would not only spread the costs of containment more evenly between the United States and other countries, but it might over time make more of an impression on the Soviet leadership than would a further intensification of the U.S.-Soviet rivalry.[50] As long as Soviet global ambitions are sustained by a belief that the Soviet Union can achieve these ambitions by isolating the United States—a prospect that to at least some Soviet leaders probably appears deceptively feasible—the building of alternative centers of power should remain an American objective.

But however desirable the denuclearization and de-Americanization of containment may be, their realization is unlikely. With its size, wealth, and importance in Soviet calculations, Western Europe could do more than any other region of the world to further both objectives. But Western Europe will remain concerned with its own prosperity and its competitive position in world markets and with mitigating the division of Europe through its detente policies. Building up its military power in order to constrain Soviet power will be at best one of many priorities. If intermediate objectives such as scaling down the American role in containment and lessening the West's dependence on nuclear weapons are likely to remain elusive, Kennan's ultimate objective of promoting the "breakup" or "mellowing" of Soviet power is even more remote. In contrast to the situation even as recently as the early 1970s, when "deideologization" and a "leavening" of the Soviet system were much discussed, contemporary policy makers now speak of virtually open-ended conflict with the Soviet Union.[51]

As long as the Soviet Union strives to remain competitive with the West, it is likely to cling tenaciously to the two factors that enabled it to frustrate

---

[50]As Zbigniew Brzezinski has written with regard to Europe, "the historic balance in Europe will be changed gradually in the West's favor only if Russia comes to be faced west of the Elbe rather less by America and rather more by Europe." See his "The Future of Yalta," *Foreign Affairs* 62, 2 (1984–85), p. 294.

[51]Typical is the recent comment by former undersecretary of state Lawrence Eagleburger, who when asked if the Soviet system would change in ways that would allow for a less hostile relationship with the United States, answered: "Not in my lifetime. And I tell you that if we were sitting here 40 years from now having the same discussion, the answer would be the same: Not in my lifetime." Quoted in *U.S. News and World Report*, June 11, 1984.

Kennan's original scheme for containment: the division of Europe (and of the German nation), and the possession of nuclear forces powerful enough to destroy both the United States and its allies. As long as it does so, containment is likely to remain what it has been since the 1940s: expensive, risky, and at times politically divisive, both within the United States and between the United States and its allies.

To manage the costs and risks of containment, Western leaders will rely, as they have to one degree or another since the 1950s, on two instruments of policy. They will rely on deterrence, by which they mean extended deterrence from the United States to allies and the deterrence of non-nuclear attacks by nuclear means; and they will rely on detente, by which they mean, at least as far as detente in Europe is concerned, a policy of trying to change fundamental political realities by long-term processes. But as argued above, both deterrence and detente are flawed as instruments for dealing with the Soviet Union. In periods of relative Western weakness the Soviets will see these instruments as vulnerable to Soviet countermeasures. When the West enjoys or is perceived to enjoy a relative position of strength, by contrast, the Soviets will see deterrence and detente as instruments of pressure and provocation, against which they will react as they did in the mid-1960s and, to a certain extent, in the early 1980s in their dealings with the United States and West Germany. In the long run, then, neither deterrence nor detente is likely to dilute the insecurities and ambitions that remain, as in Kennan's day, the basic sources of Soviet conduct toward the outside world.

2

The Rise and Fall of Detente: Causes and Consequences

HARRY GELMAN

For many Americans, the contours and assumptions of the detente era have already come to seem somewhat blurry, indistinct, remote. In part they have done so because of a kind of temporal insularity: our perceptions inevitably tend to be dominated by the concerns of the present and the immediate past. It is difficult to recapture the state of mind of most of the U.S. elite between the spring of 1972 and the autumn of 1973, when there was a widespread inclination toward optimism about the prospects for a steadily broadening Soviet-American relationship, periodically reinforced by major agreements, in which cooperation would increasingly replace competition.

These assumptions were initially much more widely shared than some conservatives are now prepared to admit.[1] By the same token, regardless of whom we blame for the recent condition of Soviet-American relations, in this decade an atmosphere of pessimism has conditioned the expectations of most of the U.S. elite about the long-term feasibility of good relations with the Soviet Union.

At the same time the foreshortening of perspective leads many to exaggerate the differences between the recent past and the middle distance. It is obvious that Soviet-U.S. relations sharply deteriorated during the Reagan administration. It should be equally clear, however, that the relationship had already been deteriorating for a much longer period—and that by the mid-1980s the downward slide had already lasted four or five times as long as the relatively brief period when a consensus of Americans thought that cooperation was predominant. It comes as something of a shock in 1986 to be reminded that it is not only six years since the invasion of Afghanistan but also a decade since the Soviets began their interventions in Africa, eleven years

---

[1]It is instructive, for example, to recall the role that William J. Casey played in 1974 as chairman and president of the Export-Import Bank, in defending the principle of extending large credits to the Soviet Union when this principle first began to lose support in the Congress.

since the passage of the Jackson and Stevenson amendments and the Soviet renunciation of the trade agreement with America, and twelve years since the Soviet-American crisis during the Yom Kippur War. There have been several ups and downs along the way, but the element of continuity in what has been happening to the relationship is difficult to ignore.

This is not to deny that something qualitatively new was added in the 1980s, after the invasion of Afghanistan and particularly during the first term of President Reagan. In this chapter I shall explore the extent of the difference in the 1980s. But it should be clear at the outset that I am speaking of a change in the slope of an already long-descending curve.

Against this background, four general questions raised by the detente experience and our present predicament seem to me particularly important. First, was the decay of detente inevitable? Did detente collapse because the two elites held opposing assumptions about the goals of the relationship from the outset? If so, to what extent were these conflicting notions merely avoidable exaggerations and mistakes—illusions and misunderstandings, as is often suggested? To what extent, on the other hand, were the contrasts in perspective the inescapable product of incompatibilities of national interest?

Second, to what extent do the changes introduced into the relationship since the end of the 1970s represent a sharp break with what went before? What aspects of the postdetente era are completely different from those of the late 70s, and suggest the passing of a watershed, and what aspects are merely the culmination of a long, incremental process of erosion?

Third, what remains today from the wreckage? What features introduced into the relationship in the early 1970s have endured into the postdetente era?

Finally, what shall we consider "normal" for this relationship—the atmosphere of 1972 or that of 1984? If the answer is "neither," then we must ask what *mixture* of attributes is normal—which features of the postdetente era must be expected to last indefinitely, and which features might, in principle, be changed for the better?

The Long Transition from Detente

The Two Sets of Motives

Although there were some points of symmetry in the motives that drew Washington and Moscow into detente, yet on the whole the practical inducements that each side perceived differed considerably.

On the Soviet side, the Brezhnev leadership's approach to the United States in the early 1970s was impelled by a mixture of considerations, all of which were gravely affected by the subsequent evolution of events. From the outset, four of these factors were probably dominant in persuading the Politburo that it had an interest in expanding bilateral dealings with the United States. The first was the leadership's extraordinary anxiety about China at the start of the decade. The second was the Politburo decision that the problems of the Soviet economy, made manifest by the disappointing results of 1969, required a much more vigorous effort to expand importation of Western, and particularly American, technology and capital. The third was the emergence in 1969–70 of *Westpolitik*, which made more feasible the Soviets' long-held hopes for a European security conference that would legitimize their gains from World War II and that might possibly open the way for insinuation of greater Soviet influence into Western Europe. By the early 70s, however, the Soviet campaign for this conference had reached a stage at which it could go no further without specific new Soviet negotiations with the United States. The fourth and final reason was the Soviet discovery of an interest in reaching strategic arms agreements with the United States, agreements that would constrain U.S. deployment in areas of U.S. technological advantage, provided that Soviet strategic programs in areas of priority were adequately protected. In each of these realms, Soviet hopes and expectations about what might be obtained from the United States experienced a sharp rise in the first years of the decade, and a long decline thereafter.

On the American side, meanwhile, the impulse to expand relations with the USSR was also channeled by a set of specific circumstances, many though not all of which have also now long since vanished.

Perhaps the most important of these conditioning factors was the Vietnam War, which had envenomed American society, destroyed the American foreign policy consensus, increasingly hemmed in the presidency, created growing political constraints on all U.S. military programs, and offered the Soviet Union an irresistible opportunity to seize on the negative worldwide reaction to promote the erosion of American influence and the advancement of Soviet influence. At the same time, not the least important consequence of the war was to strengthen the illusion—adhered to with astonishing tenacity by distinguished Americans from Harriman to Kissinger—that given sufficient inducement the Soviet Union both could and would extricate the United States from its Vietnam predicament on terms short of total defeat. This bipartisan craving for a diabolus ex machina, rather pathetic in retrospect, was therefore one of the leading impulses that led the United States into detente and of course subsequently faded away.

A confluence of other, specific considerations also guided the American leadership into more intimate dealings with the Soviets. Negotiated constraints on Soviet strategic nuclear programs seemed increasingly desirable as U.S. concerns over the Soviet third-generation ICBMs grew; they also seemed increasingly possible as Soviet concerns over the U.S. advantage in antiballistic missile technology became more evident. A geopolitical windfall at the turn of the decade—Sino-Soviet military confrontation and the opening of Sino-American dealings—simultaneously seemed to offer another major negotiating lever upon the USSR. The creation of a broad, incrementally growing arms control regime with the Soviet Union, building on earlier partial agreements such as the Test-Ban Treaty, also seemed to offer an opportunity to counteract the enervating domestic effects of the Vietnamese war by appealing to a latent tradition of bipartisan support for efforts to reduce tensions.

The prior movement of the Brandt government of West Germany into dealings with the East since 1969–70 meanwhile created both increased opportunities that the United States could seek to exploit through negotiations with the USSR on European issues and increased political penalties in Europe for not doing so. Some sections of the U.S. business community anticipated substantial profits from investment in and trade with the Soviet Union, although on the whole this economic motive was much less important for the United States than it was for the Soviet Union. And finally, there was Kissinger's well-known vision of remaking the Soviet perception of self-interest, of enticing the USSR into a network of relationships with the United States which would inhibit Soviet expansionism around the world.

The Process of Mutual Disillusionment

Detente progressively unraveled as each of the two sides incrementally discovered that it could not obtain from the other the really enormous concessions needed to realize its own list of hopes. The two sets of discoveries involved in this process of mutual disillusionment went on simultaneously from as early as the autumn of 1973, and increasingly reinforced each other thereafter.

The Soviets found, above all, that the United States was unwilling to make the huge transfers of capital and technology which the Soviet leaders had apparently envisaged at the onset of detente. In addition, the Politburo learned that the United States was unwilling to side with the USSR against China; that important elements in the U.S. polity viewed detente as sanctioning a degree of U.S. intrusion into the internal control practices of the Soviet dictatorship which the Soviet oligarchs regarded as threatening their legitimacy and therefore intolerable; and that the United States was unwilling to accept as consistent with detente those specific Soviet military advantages in the central and regional matchups which the Soviets regarded as both natural and essential to their interests.

Finally, the Politburo also found that the United States was unwilling to legitimize under detente what the Soviets regarded as the natural process through which they intended to strive to supplant American influence wherever possible and incrementally to reverse the many geopolitical advantages that the United States retained over the Soviet Union as a great power on the world scene. On the other hand, the Soviet leaders themselves regarded as illegitimate and deeply resented the U.S. role in supplanting their influence in Egypt after 1973, as well as the subsequent U.S. refusal to shore up Soviet regional weakness by accepting the Soviet Union as coarbiter in the Middle East.

The Americans, meanwhile, were gradually finding that the Soviets, despite long-held hopes to the contrary, lacked the leverage on Vietnam to bring about a lasting compromise settlement, had no intention of spending their political capital in Hanoi in pursuit of this chimerical purpose, and in fact were unwilling to refrain, even at the height of detente, from supplying Hanoi with the military matériel used to cast aside the supposed settlement and to bring about the eventual humiliating U.S. defeat. This American discovery during the first half of the 1970s would be followed, at the decade's end, by the discovery that the Soviets had ensconced themselves in certain former U.S. military facilities in southern Vietnam.

The Americans also discovered, again despite hopes foolishly encouraged by some U.S. leaders, that the SALT I Interim Agreement did not resolve the threat to U.S. retaliatory capability originally perceived as latent in certain of the Soviet third-generation ICBMs. Instead, this agreement was eventually found to have allowed the replacement of these weapons with a fourth generation of ICBMs which posed an even greater threat. The disruption of the U.S. arms control consensus which resulted from this belated discovery gave impetus to the subsequent growth of disagreement in the United States over the acceptability of a SALT II treaty that also failed to resolve the threat posed by increased Soviet missile accuracy and throw-weight.

In addition, the Soviet achievement in the first half of the 1970s of what is generally called a "robust" parity in strategic capabilities was followed, in the second half, by what turned out to be a sustained and successful unilateral Soviet effort to build a more decisive regional nuclear superiority in Europe, supplementing the substantial existing Soviet advantage in conventional forces. Concern over trends in the European military balance therefore tended to reinforce U.S. anxieties about the purposes behind the Soviet central strategic buildup.

The net result, by the end of the decade, was a profound schism in the U.S. elite, placing in question what had previously been fairly broadly shared assumptions about the efficacy and legitimacy of arms control agreements with the Soviet Union. The political effects of this disillusionment were greatly magnified by disappointment with Soviet conduct in other policy realms, so that the ratification of SALT II was ultimately defeated by a mixture of factors, some of which had little directly to do with arms control or the nuclear force balance. By the time that America entered the postdetente era of the 1980s, the arms control process with the Soviet Union had thus become not only far more problematical in its own right but also far more isolated from surrounding sources of mutual confidence. The role of arms control had been transformed, from the centerpiece of a broadening relationship with the Soviet Union to an increasingly precarious vestige of stability in a widening sea of mutual hostility.

The Soviet Offensive in the Third World

One major factor, in particular, coincided with the growth of the arms control debate in the United States in the latter half of the 1970s and ultimately helped to prevent the ratification of SALT II. This was, of course, the major expansion of the Soviet military and political presence in different parts of the world that took place in this period. This expansion came about partly through an incremental widening of the scope of Soviet naval and air operations to more and more distant areas, and partly through the associated provision of Soviet arms assistance to radical nationalist movements or to newly independent states formerly dominated by the West.

Such Soviet efforts to expand the Soviet geopolitical position around the world could be interpreted in three ways. On one level, this behavior could be seen as nothing more than the natural endeavor of a late-coming, newly emerging power to catch up with earlier rivals. The obvious analogy was the behavior of imperalist Germany in Africa prior to World War I. On another level, it could be interpreted as reflecting an equally natural desire on the part of the Soviet Union to achieve real equality in stature with the other superpower, the United States, which had long enjoyed (and for that matter, still enjoys) a world presence and power projection capability not matched by the USSR. These two interpretations might be termed the "secular" explanations for Soviet conduct. During the 1970s they were repeatedly adduced in some U.S. quarters to demonstrate the nonthreatening nature of successive Soviet actions and the compatibility of those actions with detente. Those who took this view tended to see little in the way of pattern in Soviet efforts to exploit instability in Africa, Asia, and Latin America; rather, they saw isolated, regional events, each of relatively minor concern to the United States.

However, superimposed on these two interpretations was a third, suggested both by the rhetoric and by some of the actions of the Soviet leaders. Under the impact of events, this view became fairly widely held in the United States by the end of the decade of detente. It saw the Soviet impulse to expand as part of an internally driven, perpetual contest with the West, and especially the United States, a struggle to which all other purposes and relationships were subordinated and which was impelled by the central myth under which the Soviet leaders seek legitimacy. This Soviet impulse ruled out in principle the acceptance of any point of final equilibrium or settlement with the main opponent. In this view, the purported Soviet quest for equality was in fact a never-ending drive to supplant.

The existence of such a quasi-religious impulse was suggested and advertised among other things, by Soviet rhetoric proclaiming an unalterable and inevitable duty to come to the aid of "revolutionary and national liberation movements." To be sure, the Soviets never behaved as though they meant this literally, and they always displayed a highly selective sense of this obligation, which in practice was measured almost exclusively in terms of *Realpolitik* and the net Soviet advantage in the struggle with the USSR's main rivals. Nevertheless, successive American governments recognized this reiteration of Moscow's alleged obligation to help promote revolutionary change as suggesting a deep-seated Soviet intention—indeed, compulsion—to keep striving to erode the position of the West and the United States around the world, whatever the state of the Soviet-American bilateral relationship. A decade before the onset of detente President Kennedy had reacted strongly to Khrushchev's enunciation of this doctrine. At no point in the evolution of Soviet-American bilateral dealings during the 1970s did the Soviets change their view that detente and peaceful coexistence could not be allowed to halt their effort to change the world at the expense of the detente partner.

Like Mr. Reagan, but unlike many others in the United States, the Soviet leaders apparently took for granted a zero-sum relationship in the world arena. Evidently they did not see how their position in the world could possibly be improved unless that of the opponent were whittled down. Evidently also they saw American behavior in Egypt and the Near East in the mid-1970s as confirming a similar U.S. view of the underlying incompatibility of Soviet and American interests. U.S. behavior, they seemed to feel, furnished tacit justification for assertive actions that the Politburo felt compelled to take in any case.

Although the possible consequences for the bilateral relationship with Washington were surely a factor in the leadership's consideration of Soviet moves in the Third World, they were apparently never allowed to become a dominant factor. It is difficult to believe that the members of the Politburo were oblivious to the effects of this Soviet behavior upon the trend of opinion in the United States, and were totally unaware that their conduct had something to do with the rightward evolution of the American polity late in the decade. But insofar as they considered restraint at all, they apparently saw inadequate recompense for sacrificing opportunities for potential Soviet gains—inadequate, that is, because tradeoffs in benefits from the American relationship became increasingly incommensurate as the decade went on. I shall return to this point shortly.

The Soviet solution was to attempt to impose on the United States a separation between the bilateral relationship and the interaction of the two powers in the world arena. Throughout the 1970s Soviet leaders sought to maintain a wall between the two sets of phenomena, and to induce the United States to acknowledge the legitimacy of a mutually profitable bilateral relationship even as they went forward with efforts to supplant the United States around the world. They repeatedly made it clear that acceptance of this separation was an essential aspect of their conception of detente. Accordingly, throughout the Nixon, Ford, and Carter presidencies, the Politburo consistently rejected American attempts at "linkage"—that is, efforts to hold aspects of the bilateral relationship hostage to Soviet behavior elsewhere.

In retrospect, however, preservation of the wall the Soviets sought to erect was out of the question. If Soviet behavior could not adapt to the conception of detente held by the American public, then those aspects of detente which the Soviet leaders did wish to preserve could not survive. This was especially true because of the wounded state of the American presidency from 1973 on, which rendered all dealings with the Soviet Union vulnerable to attack, both from the left (in 1974) and from the right (thereafter).

In addition, the spectacular Soviet advances in Africa, Southeast Asia, and Southwest Asia between 1975 and 1979 were particularly traumatic for much of the American public because they coincided with a series of extraordinary American humiliations, from the evacuation of Saigon to the seizure of the U.S. Embassy in Teheran. Although the Soviets were certainly not responsible for all the American misfortunes, they exulted in them and openly sought, with varying degrees of success, to profit from them.[2] These Soviet efforts were therefore increasingly linked with the American humiliations in the world's perceptions; much of the American public, and the Soviets themselves, seemed to share the Chinese judgment at the time that the United States was a "retreating wave" on the world scene, the Soviet Union an "advancing wave." In consequence, by the end of the 1970s a sizable majority in the United States had come to see detente as having opened the way for an explosion of Soviet efforts to wrest advantages, in several different spheres simultaneously, from an inernally and externally stricken America.

In sum, I would suggest that Soviet behavior in the Third World in the late 1970s was the most important single factor in the destruction of the American consensus supporting detente, in the sense that it served as a catalyst for all the others. While some bilateral negotiating initiatives undertaken early in the Carter administration—notably the conventional arms transfer and Indian Ocean talks—were undermined as a direct result of the clash of the interests of the two powers in the Third World, the more profound effects of this clash were indirect. Concern over Soviet strategic and European deployments, resentment of U.S. humiliations, and anger at the obstacles created for Jewish emigration from the USSR all were given focus in the public mind by a series of specific, dramatic, readily perceived events around the world. These events seemed cumulatively to confirm hostile Soviet intentions, creating a pattern sensed much more vividly by a wide audience than the abstruse calculations and complex allegations of defense analysts about the military balance.

---

[2]Particularly striking was Soviet behavior in response to the seizure of the American Embassy in Teheran. Lacking a good opening to the new Iranian regime, the Soviet leadership apparently felt that it needed to seek one by fanning the flames of Iranian hostility toward the United States. It therefore hailed the takeover of the U.S. Embassy, at first quite explicitly, in the broadcasts of an "unofficial" radio station based in the USSR and under Soviet control. See the discussion in Harry Gelman, *The Brezhnev Politburo and the Decline of Detente* (Ithaca: Cornell University Press, 1984), pp. 36, 229 n.16.

The China Factor

Could U.S. policy have caused events to evolve differently in the late 1970s? It has been suggested, for example, that the growth of Soviet efforts to expand their presence and influence in the Third World after 1975 was prompted, in part, by Soviet chagrin over the failure of their efforts to prevent or to break the new American relationship with China. In this view, disappointment with the U.S. unwillingness to forgo its China connection was instrumental in disillusioning the Soviets with the results of detente, thus helping influence Moscow to launch an offensive in the Third World. This view seems to me implausible on several grounds.

It was, of course, evident from the outset—that is, from the time of the extended crisis on the Sino-Soviet border, in the spring and summer of 1969—that U.S. attitudes toward China would be a paramount Soviet concern. The Soviets were intent on avoiding excessive difficulties with the United States during the period of military confrontation with China, and thereafter they sought to accomplish three defensive and offensive purposes: to minimize the U.S. ability to derive leverage in Soviet-American dealings from Sino-Soviet difficulties; to head off any U.S. movement toward military alignment with China against the Soviet Union; and, if possible, to induce Washington instead to align itself with Moscow against the interests of the People's Republic.[3]

Soviet anxieties produced a variety of reactions in the 1970s. At the outset, when the U.S. detente with the USSR and the American opening with China were developing together, the Soviets were apparently sufficiently exercised about the possibility of Sino-American collaboration to make some marginal concessions in negotiations with the United States, notably by accelerating conclusion of the Berlin Quadripartite Agreement in 1971. After the summer of 1971, however, the situation in the Sino-Soviet-American triangle never again had a demonstrable effect upon Soviet willingness to make tactical concessions.

Instead, the Soviets presented a long series of warnings and appeals to the United States—warnings against U.S. conclusion of a "military alliance" with China and appeals to Washington to reach some sort of understanding with Moscow, formal or informal, against Beijing. The appeals for cooperation against China seem to have been concentrated in the first half of the decade, when a large measure of detente still existed. Two requests for formal written agreements with anti-Chinese intent were particularly notable; one was made in 1970, during the SALT I negotiations, and the other in 1974, in the waning weeks of the Nixon presidency. Warnings about U.S. collabora-

[3]See Harry Gelman, *The Soviet Far East Buildup and Soviet Risk-Taking against China* (Santa Monica: Rand Corporation, R-2943-AF, August 1982), pp. 46–52.

tion with China against the Soviet Union, on the other hand, went on spasmodically throughout the decade as detente dwindled, and indeed into the present decade and the Reagan presidency. Toward the end of the 1970s, when the United States, in reaction to Soviet behavior on other matters and to the general decay of detente, finally did begin to seek a significant degree of security cooperation with the PRC, the Soviet Union went so far as to warn publicly that arms control negotiations could be adversely affected.[4] Here the Soviet leaders professed, at least for a time, to believe in "linkage."

But it is anachronistic to suggest this turn in American policy late in the decade had stimulated Soviet behavior in the Third World after 1975. Although Washington would not accept a security relationship with the USSR directed against China, Brezhnev's warnings against a U.S. "military alliance" with the PRC addressed a contingency that was never a real possibility during Kissinger's tenure in office. Although extensive Sino-American exchanges of information and opinion went on during the Nixon and Ford administrations, it does not appear that such security measures as U.S. arms sales to the PRC, naval port visits, and joint contingency planning—let alone the creation of an "alliance" with the PRC[5]—were under active consideration in this period. American policy did not begin to move in this direction until the later half of the Carter administration, and this shift from 1978 on—the incremental triumph of Zbigniew Brzezinski's perspective on the strategic triangle over that of Cyrus Vance—was itself propelled in large part by the American reaction to the Soviet offensive in the Third World.

It is reasonable to suppose that despite the repeated and vehement expressions of concern about the Sino-American relationship which the Soviets made in private, the Soviet leaders were well aware that the Kissinger-Nixon policy toward China was a limited one, amply balanced by American concern to reach agreements with the Soviet Union. Indeed, the bulk of Soviet published comment between 1972 and 1975—particularly after the signing of the SALT I agreement in May 1972—suggests a growing inclination to assume that the United States would not wish to jeopardize the arms control process and other overriding American interests by entering a close security relationship with Beijing. Even as late as November 1974, moreover, when detente had already begun to decline, the Chinese leaders were themselves highly chagrined when the United States consented to hold a summit meeting with Brezhnev at Vladivostok, adjacent to China. The Soviets had chosen this site with precisely that effect in mind, and can only have been gratified and reassured by the Ford administration's acquiescence in this slight to Beijing.

It could be argued, to be sure, that the Politburo was disturbed in this pe-

---

[4]*Pravda*, June 17, 1978. In January 1979 the Soviets did briefly hold up the final stages of the SALT II negotiations in response to Deng Xiaoping's visit to the United States.

[5]In addition, of course, it must be remembered that at no point in the Sino-American relationship has the PRC indicated any willingness to accept a relationship with the United States approximating a formal "alliance."

riod not by an expectation that the United States would line up with China against the Soviet Union, but rather by the repeated confirmation that Washington would not consent to an arrangement with Moscow directed against China. It would be far-fetched to conclude, however, that Kissinger's refusal to depart from the course he steered between China and the USSR was sufficient provocation to incite the Soviet leadership to undertake more active measures in the Third World to counter American interests.

The Stevenson Amendment and the December 1974 Watershed

It seems likely to me that a more more potent factor in reinforcing the Politburo's inclination to seize on the opportunities that began to open up in the Third World after 1975 was a bilateral event that occurred in Washington in December 1974. At this time, Soviet hopes that America might furnish decisive help to the Soviet economy were abruptly ended, and this was, from the Soviet perspective, a real turning point.

This watershed was passed when the U.S. Congress approved the Stevenson Amendment to the Export-Import Bank bill. The amendment limited to $300 million the total that the bank could guarantee in loans to the Soviet Union over the next four years without seeking further congressional approval, and it banned the use of any of this money for energy development and production. The immediate issue was the prospect of extremely large U.S. loans to the Soviet Union over the next few years for the Yakutsk/North Star Siberian energy development projects. These capital transfers and the associated technology inputs were probably the biggest single dividend that the Politburo had anticipated from the detente relationship. The passage of this legislation under the nose of a preoccupied Secretary Kissinger rendered moot an elaborate tripartite compromise, which Kissinger had worked out with Gromyko and Senator Jackson, granting the Soviets most-favored-nation status under the Trade Act in return for certain Soviet concessions on Jewish emigration. The Soviet response was to disavow the emigration compromise and to abrogate the October 1972 Trade Agreement with the United States, indignantly proclaiming that the USSR could never be bribed to permit interference in Soviet internal affairs. In fact, however, the problem was that henceforth the bribe would always be too small.

The reasons that the Congress took this step in 1974 are of larger interest today because they vividly suggested that Soviet and American expectations from the relationship are likely always to be out of phase. The American executive leadership had wished, in effect, to make large credits available promptly to the USSR as an inducement to *subsequent* Soviet good behavior. The American legislature, in addition to being influenced by certain more ignoble considerations,[6] was fundamentally opposed to this sequence of

[6]Major sections of the Congress and the press were, in addition to all else, interested in using the occasion as part of a more general campaign to attack and constrict the powers of the presi-

tradeoffs. Various sectors of the coalition[7] in the American elite that forced through the Stevenson Amendment were disturbed by Soviet behavior in the Arab-Israeli crisis before and during the October 1973 war, or angry at Soviet encouragement of and applause for the Arab oil embargo, or annoyed at continued heavy arms shipments to Vietnam, or concerned that large credits to the USSR would give the Soviets political leverage over American creditors. In general, this coalition was determined to ensure that all future credits to Moscow somehow be made contingent upon *prior* good Soviet behavior in all arenas.

It seems unlikely, however, that the Soviet leadership, for its part, has ever been willing to contemplate such a bargain, either explicit or tacit, with the U.S. elite. The Soviets apparently expected large-scale American economic assistance as a down payment on a relationship that Soviet leaders would, at most, evaluate on an ad hoc basis to determine what, if any, acts of political restraint the returns from that relationship might from time to time justify. The members of the Politburo apparently never dreamed that the documents signed with the United States in 1972 implied a general commitment to desist from the perpetual struggle for competitive advantage over the Americans. They therefore saw nothing inconsistent between the sweeping ritualistic promises recorded in May 1972[8] and their public and private efforts the following year, for example, to induce the Arabs to wield the "oil weapon" against the West. They were evidently surprised that American resentment of this behavior contributed to Washington's withdrawal from what the Soviets saw as its side of the bargain.

Even if the Stevenson Amendment had not passed, however, the economic benefits at stake might not have sufficed to bring the Soviet leaders to a different course of action in the Third World. Even if the Soviets had not been disappointed in the hopes they entertained in 1972 for massive American investments that would bring magical increases in Soviet productivity, the Politburo might in any case not have persuaded itself to refrain from exploiting those qualitatively new opportunities which emerged in Africa and elsewhere after 1975. But in any case, of course, this contingency never arose.

The 1970s in Retrospect

In sum, I believe that initial misconceptions on both sides did indeed play a role in fostering the eventual demise of detente. Misconceptions were by no means the only factor, however, nor necessarily the most important one.

---

dency in the immediate aftermath of Watergate. For some of those involved, the pros and cons of the Soviet-American relationship were secondary to this endeavor.

[7]I stress that this was a coalition in which *liberal* forces played a major if not unique role, enforcing their will to defeat an essentially conservative effort to hand over large sums of money to the Soviet Union. Readers who find this comical reversal of roles in the mid-1970s to be, from today's standpoint, incredible are referred to the discussion in Gelman, *Brezhnev Politburo*, pp. 148–51, 250 n.68, 251 n.69.

[8]It will be recalled that a document on the "basic principles" of Soviet-U.S. relations, signed at the 1972 summit, pledged both sides to refrain "from efforts to obtain unilateral advantage at

Brezhnev for his part fundamentally misconstrued the ability of the U.S. presidency to deliver on the American side of the tacit bargain reached in 1971–72.[9] He underestimated the capacity of a rampaging American pluralism to veto executive commitments, operating first from the standpoint of the left and then from that of the right. For this reason, he misjudged the willingness of the United States either to provide the kind of economic help envisioned by the Soviet Union at the start of the 1970s or to accept the kind of strategic arms agreement tolerable to the USSR at the close of the decade. At the same time he greatly overestimated the willingness of the U.S. public to accept with equanimity the successive challenges and injuries to American interests—in the Third World and in the strategic and regional military balances—which he and his colleagues regarded as essential to Soviet interests and a legitimate part of the detente understanding.

American leaders, for their part, erred in supposing that the Soviet Union could or would deliver to the United States as part of the detente bargain an acceptable and lasting compromise in Vietnam. They also erred in supposing, or at any rate in suggesting to the U.S. Congress, that SALT I could prevent the growth of the Soviet threat to American land-based retaliatory capabilities. They erred in their hopes that the construction of a network of relationships with the United States could induce Soviet leaders to display restraint in the Third World. And finally they erred, most decisively, in assuming that the construction of such a network of inducements would be politically possible in the United States in the absence of far more prior Soviet restraint than the Politburo was willing to consider.

In addition to these initial errors on both sides, historical accident played a role in undermining detente which should not be underestimated. A long list of fortuitous developments unforeseeable in 1970—Watergate, the death of Salazar and its consequences in Africa, the revolutions in Addis Ababa and Kabul, the fall of the shah, Pol Pot's disastrous pugnacity toward Vietnam after 1975—affected the relationship between the superpowers during the 1970s, progressively exacerbating their underlying conflict of interests.

Finally, in view of the extent to which those interests did and do conflict, one should not entertain illusions about the possibilities for the relationship in the 1970s, even if the two sides had not begun the decade with separate sets of faulty assumptions. Had mutual expectations had been significantly lower,

---

the expense of the other, directly or indirectly." The context had seemed to refer to behavior of all kinds, not merely weapons deployments.

[9]It is difficult to estimate with confidence Brezhnev's perception of the quid pro quo he was offering to the United States as the Soviet side of that bargain, particularly since elements of that quid pro quo emerged and then vanished incrementally. One may surmise, however, that in 1972 he may have seen four such elements as most important: those limited constraints on existing Soviet deployment programs for third-generation ICBMs which he accepted in SALT I; the embarrassments that he was forced to accept in dealings with Vietnam and Egypt in the spring and summer of 1972, as a result of his dealing with the United States; his temporary consent to expand Jewish emigration from the Soviet Union; and his temporary moderation of the customary vehemence of Soviet propaganda attacks on the United States.

the ultimate disillusionment and bitterness would have been less intense, but by the same token far less would have been attempted. What attitude would the American leadership have taken in 1970 had it known with certainty that any attempts to induce Soviet restraint in the Third World were foredoomed? What attitude would Brezhnev have taken in 1970 had he known that his hope of decisive American help for the Soviet economy was illusory?

In short, given the objective outside factors that impinged on the relationship during the 1970s, and given the inescapable asymmetries in the attitudes and goals of the Soviet Union and the United States—especially Soviet assumptions about the military requirements of Soviet security and about the Soviet right and duty to change the world in the USSR's favor—it seems highly probable that the competitive aspects would have strongly predominated over the cooperative aspects of the relationship in this period, whatever the circumstances. Even if illusions about detente had not flourished and then withered, the atmosphere by the end of the decade would probably have been rather harsh in any case—perhaps analogous to that which prevailed in the late 1960s. The relationship need not, however, have deteriorated as far as it did.

The Postdetente Era

The Change in the Bilateral Atmosphere

Given all that has gone before, what has changed since late 1979? The first, most obvious difference is of course the further exacerbation of bilateral conflicts. Here the preponderant trends ran strongly in one direction after 1980, beginning with the American reaction to the invasion of Afghanistan and the decisive victory of the point of view represented by Zbigniew Brzezinski over that championed by Cyrus Vance and Marshall Shulman, deciding the long guerrilla struggle for Mr. Carter's oscillating soul. As earlier suggested, there seems little doubt that this tipping of the scales within the Democratic administration coincided with the culmination of a broader shift that had been going on within the American polity throughout the late 1970s. This polarization of popular perceptions of Soviet behavior in turn contributed, along with many other factors, to the election of Carter's successor. The increasing Soviet pessimism about prospects for the bilateral relationship evident in Moscow as the Reagan administration went on thus derived as much as anything else from a sense that an underlying shift had occurred in the center of American political gravity, a shift at least as important as questions of political personality.

This shift was reflected from the start—that is, from 1980—both in demonstrative American gestures and in more basic, secular changes that became increasingly important as time went on. Some of the punitive steps taken against the USSR in 1980, while regarded as infuriating and injurious by Moscow, did not themselves represent fundamental and long-lasting changes in U.S. behavior. The announced rationale for many of the more notable moves against Soviet interests in President Carter's last year was that of imposing "sanctions," that is, ad hoc responses with the avowed aim of punishing specific Soviet acts. These responses were based on an extremely faint hope of getting the Soviets to undo what they had done (i.e., to get out of Afghanistan) and a somewhat stronger hope of inhibiting future Soviet behavior. Many of these steps either were one-time by nature (the boycott of the Moscow Olympics) or were at least posed as theoretically reversible upon evidence of better Soviet conduct (the rescission of Aeroflot landing rights, the grain boycott).

At the same time the political reaction that the invasion of Afghanistan evoked in the Carter administration and in the U.S. public also tended strongly to reinforce certain longer-term shifts in U.S. policy which had already begun. These secular trends, strengthened by the events of December 1979, were hostile responses to cumulative trends in Soviet behavior, and the added impulse they received in 1980 was, in the long run, much more serious than the "sanctions" for Soviet interests. They included, among other things, the collapse of support for the ratification of SALT II, the trend toward heightened U.S. military spending, and the seeking of security cooperation with the PRC.

It seems likely that one of the chief Soviet grievances against Ronald Reagan was that he sought to institutionalize this broad, underlying shift in the American posture which began under his predecessor. Reagan carried the shift much further and systematized it. The late-Carter rationale of "punishing" specific Soviet acts in an empirical spirit was subsequently overlaid by assumptions about an unending struggle against the Soviet Union and what were now judged to be the long-term requirements dictated by the eternally hostile essence of the relationship. These assumptions bore a strong resemblance to those which for many years have impelled Soviet competitive behavior against the United States in the world arena. In the postdetente era the posture of the United States has thus become somewhat more symmetrical with that of the Soviet Union, both in broad outline and in certain specific respects.[10]

[10]Specific examples of the tendency of the Reagan administration to strive to reduce asymmetries that appear to give the Soviet Union an advantage include the reciprocal decay in American adherence to the doctrine of mutual assured destruction, considered by many to have been previously rejected by the Soviet Union; the effort to impose a sharper strategic focus upon control over trade with the USSR, in response to Soviet central coordination of foreign trade activities for strategic purposes; the effort to enforce greater secrecy upon the American government and upon American research, in emulation of Soviet practice; the effort to compete more vigorously with the KGB by allowing a longer leash to covert action; and the sporadic effort to enforce greater reciprocity in the access of Soviet spokesmen to the United States and to the American media. Many of these endeavors have encountered great resentment and resistance in the United States as running counter to American traditions. Critics are often led to indict the "Manichean" view of the Soviet Union which Reagan has used to justify the quest for greater symmetry. The

One characteristic of this new American posture, particularly in the first two years of the Reagan administration, was a degree of sustained stridency not heard from the American leadership for many years. The Soviet leaders may have expected more reserve in propaganda emanating from the highest level, but they were affronted by Reagan's rhetoric not so much because they were personally insulted but primarily because this rhetoric appeared to be consciously employed as part of a broad effort to undo the gains that the Soviets had registered over the United States in the 1970s. On the one hand, attacks on the Soviet Union were used to muster U.S. public support for large increases in spending on strategic and conventional weapons programs that were openly advertised, at least initially, as intended to restore American superiority. On the other hand, the same attacks were used, in effect, as tacit justification for a new American refusal to accept as a basis for future agreements on strategic arms control certain of those Soviet partial advantages which in SALT I and SALT II had been previously accepted and, in the Soviet view, legitimized.

In addition, the United States in the postdetente era has sought to impose this new zero-sum view of the relationship with the Soviet Union upon Washington's European allies. First, an unsuccessful attempt was made to compel the West Europeans to abandon their gas pipeline deal with the Soviets; more generally, efforts were greatly intensified and sustained to induce the West as a whole to constrict the flow of technology and scientific ideas to the East. At the same time the impulse to impede Western inputs to the growth of Soviet military strength has merged with a much vaguer and inconsistently applied desire to minimize Western help to the Soviet economy as a whole, on the general grounds that any easing of Soviet economic dilemmas must also ease constraints on Soviet military resources.[11] In broadest terms, the Reagan administration conveyed to the Soviet leaders an aspiration to wage economic warfare against them, albeit on a scale that has greatly exceeded its political capabilities. In this as in some other cases, the administration provided a stimulus to Soviet paranoia without obtaining a commensurate payoff.

The first half of the 1980s has also seen three American regional efforts against Soviet interests abroad. All three have, in effect, merely carried through initiatives begun under the Carter administration. These efforts have

---

central dilemma in judging how many of these measures are acceptable for America, however, is compounded by the fact that this Manichean view is already deeply implanted in the Soviet Union. It gives the USSR certain very important tactical advantages in the competition with the United States.

[11]One reason why this goal is not often avowed explicitly—in addition to the impossibility of getting America's allies to accept it—is its incompatibility with the U.S. domestic political realities that induced Reagan first to abandon the Carter boycott on grain shipments to the USSR and then to conclude a new, "boycott-proof," long-term grain agreement with the Soviet Union.

consequently enjoyed a broader consensus in the United States than have some other features of the Reagan program.

In Europe, the Reagan administration carried to its logical conclusion the train of events inaugurated with the NATO double-track decision of December 1979. The Atlantic alliance had resolved to deploy intermediate-range nuclear missiles, to restore the linkage to the U.S. strategic deterrent which the Soviet SS-20 deployments in Europe threatened unless negotiations could remove that threat. The Soviet Union, in the first half of the decade, proved unwilling to give up the military and political advantages inherent in the SS-20 deployments and, despite an enormous Soviet political campaign and great domestic tumult in Western Europe, was ultimately unable to prevent the start of the Western counterdeployment of intermediate-range missiles.

In Japan, the Reagan administration has found it possible to continue and enlarge the trend, begun by Carter, of heightened Japanese military cooperation with the United States. This trend significantly helps U.S. military capabilities against the Soviet Union in the Western Pacific. It has been assisted by the Soviets' continued militarization of the southern Kuriles claimed by Japan and by the threat that the Japanese perceived in Soviet SS-20 deployments in Asia.

And with China, despite an initial crisis in Sino-American relations occasioned in part by Reagan's ideologically motivated inclinations toward Taiwan, the Reagan administration ultimately found it possible to reestablish the trend of limited and unacknowledged security cooperation inaugurated by its predecessor. The United States was able to do so partly because Reagan shifted his priorities but more importantly because the Soviet Union's policies attacking Chinese geopolitical interests in Asia made it impossible for Beijing, despite its desire to reduce tensions with Moscow, to abandon its loose security connection with America. In all three cases, therefore—with Europe, Japan, and China—the postdetente era has witnessed specific American achievements in the regional competition with the Soviet Union, achievements greatly facilitated by Soviet military priorities and heavy-handed behavior.

The Soviet leadership's immediate response to all these developments was to reaffirm the policies that each of its various adversaries perceived as threatening and to assert heightened defiance of all adversaries, beginning, of course, with the United States. Until the autumn of 1985 the oligarchy deployed against the United States a degree and volume of vituperative propaganda not seen since the 1950s and far surpassing Reagan in rhetorical extravagance. The American president was repeatedly compared with Adolf Hitler and incessantly charged with leading the world toward "the flames of nuclear war." This rhetoric was not moderated, but on the contrary further elevated, after Reagan began to moderate his own attacks on the USSR in 1983. It is clear that this Soviet language was intended, at least in large part, to frighten

Western publics and thereby place pressure on Western governments for concessions to the Soviet Union. In addition, the Soviet propaganda campaign
about the allegedly increased danger of nuclear war and Reagan's alleged resemblance to Hitler was evidently pressed by certain segments of the Soviet
elite, particularly in the military establishment, as tacit justification for claims
in resource allocation which may be controversial.

At the same time, however, the exceptionally noisy and savage Soviet rhetoric of the early 1980s also seemed to reflect the heightened stresses, internal
and external, on the leadership. A prolonged, enervating succession crisis was
superimposed on the grave secular problems of the Soviet economy just as
those problems were being exacerbated by the heightened challenge of the
Reagan military program. Meanwhile the Soviet oligarchs have been compelled since the start of the postdetente period to deal with an apparently
unendable war in Afghanistan, a severe challenge to the stability of their position in Poland, and the previously mentioned setbacks to Soviet hopes of
blocking INF deployment in Europe and drawing China away from its unacknowledged orientation toward the United States. The tensions created by
these multiple pressures were dramatized in both the confusion and the pugnacity displayed by the leadership after the Soviet Union shot down a Korean
commercial airliner in September 1983. In addition to all else, the adoption of
this posture of vehement defiance and vilification of the main antagonist may
be regarded as the normal reaction of a Soviet leadership that has come to see
itself as beset from many sides.

The Soviet Interregnum

Most of these diverse stresses are likely to be long-lasting, but the internal
disarray that they produced in the Soviet leadership during the first half
of the 1980s appears to have been only a transitory phenomenon. Until the
spring of 1985 there was a noticeable deterioration in the effectiveness of Politburo leadership. The semiparalysis of policy characteristic of Brezhnev's
last years, as his health worsened, was followed after his death by an interregnum of two successive ailing general secretaries and an increasing perception,
both at home and abroad, of policy deadlock, inertia, and vacillation. In particular, the perceived physical and political weaknesses of the general secretary chosen in February 1984, Konstantin Chernenko, engendered in the
Soviet Union a growing malaise associated with a sense of weakness and division at the center. Many Soviets, particularly in the military, appeared to
regard this prolonged dearth of vigorous leadership as damaging to the national interest. In the early 1980s the Kremlin entered this "time of troubles"
just as the American presidency partially recovered its status, which had been
seriously weakened in the 1970s by the effect on American society of the
Vietnam war and the Watergate crisis.

Prolonged disarray in the Politburo came to an end, however, with the death of Chernenko in March 1985 and the election of Mikhail Gorbachev as general secretary. Since then the Soviet leadership, although still confronted with extremely difficult internal and external problems and by no means unanimous about how to resolve them, has evidenced more vigor, adroitness, and coherence in confronting the United States, both in bilateral dealings and in political competition in the world arena.

The Arms Control Impasse

A more fundamental change since late 1979 has been a prolonged impasse in the arms control process, the principal remnant of detente which had endured through the latter 1970s. The decay of this process is by now a familiar story, unfolding in stages long before the signing of SALT II in June 1979. Ratification of this treaty was threatened from the outset by the unwillingness of major sections of the U.S. elite to accept aspects of the bargain concluded—particularly the failure to place greater constraints upon Soviet land-based ICBMs, to eliminate the Soviet advantage in throw-weight, to obviate what was consequently perceived as a growing threat to U.S. retaliatory capabilities, and to avoid what some saw as intolerable ambiguities in provisions regarding verification. Political opposition on these strategic grounds was reinforced, as already suggested, by resentment on other grounds, particularly the cumulative reaction to various Soviet military adventures in the Third World and to simultaneous U.S. humiliations. This accumulation of grievances undoubtedly contributed to the vehemence of the reaction of the American public as a whole to the invasion of Afghanistan. That event, in the closing days of the decade, put an effective end to the already dwindling chances of ratification of SALT II. Simultaneously it contributed to the eventual advent to power of a man who had termed that treaty fatally flawed.

Meanwhile the NATO dual-track decision on INF deployment in Europe, adopted in the same month that Soviet airborne forces began landing in Kabul, set in motion decisive changes in Soviet arms control priorities. After having reluctantly persuaded themselves that the alliance was serious and that there was a real possibility that the Pershing IIs and cruise missiles would some day arrive, the Soviets during the first half of the 1980s shifted their negotiating efforts to focus upon preventing these deployments.

This momentary shift in priorities was facilitated by the long delay in the presentation of a U.S. negotiating position in START and by the eventual Soviet discovery that this position encompassed large projected cuts in Soviet land-based missile capabilities, cuts that Soviet leaders, at the time at least, considered out of the question. Expecting little from START over the short term, the Soviets became increasingly inclined to make these negotiations temporarily hostage to satisfaction of their demands regarding INF. When they were at last defeated on the INF front, late in 1983, their immediate reaction was to suspend both sets of negotiations. Nuclear talks regarding both central strategic weapons and intermediate-range weapons thus remained in abeyance in 1984, ostensibly awaiting satisfaction of the Soviet demand that Western INF deployments be undone but in fact awaiting a Politburo decision on how and when to climb down from this untenable position.

This in fact began to happen in the last six months of the Chernenko regime when the Soviets established high-level bilateral contacts with the United States after Reagan's reelection. The Soviets then resumed arms negotiations with the United States in March 1985, in a three-ring format dealing separately but simultaneously with strategic offensive arms, strategic defense, and intermediate-range nuclear issues. The Soviets made this tactical retreat back to the negotiation table for several reasons. They were confronted first with the fact of Reagan's reelection; thus, they could hope for no early radical changes in U.S. arms negotiation positions. They realized that their 1984 boycott had been counterproductive for their political campaign in Western Europe. They recognized that their effort to block NATO's INF deployment was essentially lost; at the same time the issue of blocking Reagan's Strategic Defense Initiative had become more pressing for them because of the political priority newly assigned to it by the United States, and there was little hope of bringing pressure to bear on Washington over this issue while the Soviet Union was refusing to attend a negotiating forum. Finally, Chernenko's increasing incapacitation in the autumn and winter of 1984–85, the growing ascendancy of Gorbachev in this period, and Gorbachev's election as general secretary in March signified a shift in the balance of forces in Moscow which facilitated the jettisoning of failed tactics.

In the meantime, however, the existing arms control regime, established through the series of agreements signed in the detente era of the 1970s, had long since begun to erode. Although both sides unilaterally undertook to observe the provisions of the unratified SALT II treaty, the United States has begun planning a second new ICBM—the Midgetman—which if eventually deployed would require either abandonment of the treaty or its renegotiation. The Soviets, for their part, have already begun to diverge significantly from both the spirit and letter of the existing, unratified treaty. They have done so by declining to make certain reductions specified by the treaty while it remained unratified; by developing and beginning to deploy two new ICBMs, contrary to the treaty's provisions; and perhaps most strikingly, by displaying an ever more cavalier attitude toward the ludicrously ambiguous provision of the treaty regarding telemetry encryption.[12] At the same time the viability of the ABM treaty, long ago ratified by both sides and for a de-

---

[12]The SALT II "Common Understanding" on this subject is one of the best examples to date of an arms control provision setting forth criteria so inherently ambiguous as virtually to dictate contemptuous circumvention in the absence of good political reasons, outside the treaty itself, not to do so. This provision, that is, because of its exceptional ambiguity, was peculiarly dependent on an atmosphere of goodwill which would induce a degree of Soviet voluntary compliance in interpretation sufficient to satisfy the United States. In June 1979, therefore, it was already becoming an anachronism and shortly would become much more anachronistic.

cade regarded as the more successful half of SALT I, was being increasingly threatened, both by American plans for the future and by present Soviet transgressions. The American prospective challenge is inherent in U.S. plans for space defense and was made manifest in 1985 in efforts to reinterpret the treaty to legitimize testing in the future, a right that most observers had long believed the treaty denied. The more immediate nibbling at existing ABM treaty obligations by the Soviets is implicit in the USSR's development of new surface-to-air missile systems that may have capabilities against strategic ballistic missiles, in Soviet development of rapidly deployable components for a new ABM system, and especially in the Soviet construction of a large new radar of a kind and in a place apparently banned by the treaty.[13]

Whatever implications this gradual, mutual preparation to jettison commitments and understandings reached in the 1970s may have for the military balance, this feature of the postdetente era is likely to be increasingly nerve-wracking for Western populations unless some new arms control structure is created in the second half of the 1980s. Moreover, the threat to stability perceived in the growing shakiness of the arms control structure is generally seen as being greatly exacerbated by new technological developments that hold grave implications for arms control—most notably, in the short run, the advent of the cruise missile with the possibly insoluble problems that it poses for verification.

On the other hand, the experiences and revelations of the postdetente period have probably made it quite difficult to assemble an American consensus adequate to support whatever new arms control structure the U.S. government may seek to create with the Soviets. The evidence suggesting that the Soviets are in fact already violating the ABM treaty is likely to become very important in future U.S. political struggles over the acceptability of new arms control formulas reached with the Soviet Union. This is all the more likely because many (although far from all) in the United States hold the strong conviction that the Soviet Union has flagrantly violated at least one earlier arms control agreement, the 1972 Bacteriological Weapons Convention ratified by Moscow in 1975, by manufacturing mycotoxins for use in Indochina and transferring them to Vietnam. Thus one of the striking new features of the postdetente era has been a considerable enlargement of that portion of the U.S. elite and public which is inclined to believe that the Soviet Union does, in fact, violate arms control agreements.

In short, the fact that the issue of violations remains a matter of bitter contention in the United States itself clouds the prospect for the resurrection of a broad consensus on arms control. There is no common understanding in the United States, much less in the West, about how unambiguous a Soviet violation would have to be to trigger a significant response; nor how significant

[13]See Michael Krepon, "Both Sides Are Hedging," *Foreign Policy* no. 56 (Fall 1984), pp. 153–72; also James A. Schear, "Arms Control Treaty Compliance: Buildup to a Breakdown?" *International Security* 10, 2 (Fall 1985), pp. 141–82.

such a violation would have to be, nor, indeed, what an appropriate response might be. Thus, although one of the prominent results of detente is a heightened determination in the United States to seek "verification" of arms control agreements, the United States has yet to establish a consistent rationale for the purpose of verification efforts.

Against this background, the chief pressure on the Soviets to reach a new compromise arrangement with the United States is likely to come from the Soviet perception of technological inferiority to the United States in the new realm of space defense. The situation repeated that of the early 1970s: the United States again had the potential to use Soviet awareness of an American advantage in strategic defense as a lever with which to press for Soviet concessions on strategic offense. Meanwhile the chief pressure on the American side, as before, is likely to come from the growth of apprehensions within the U.S. and allied publics.

At the end of 1985 it remained unclear whether these two factors would be sufficient eventually to produce a viable new agreement. During Gorbachev's first nine months, his apparent desire to secure a breathing space for the Soviet Union to address its economic difficulties led him to take two small steps back from the Soviet posture of intransigence after returning to arms negotiations with the United States. The first was the tabling, in the autumn of 1985, of a new Soviet proposal on offensive strategic arms, a proposal that while still grossly inequitable and unacceptable to the West, contained some elements—notably regarding the size of force cuts which the USSR might now be willing to entertain—that might at last serve as a basis for further negotiation. The second was Gorbachev's willingness, despite the absence of immediate concessions on strategic defense from President Reagan, not only to hold a summit meeting with the president in November but also to allow that meeting to inaugurate a period of some moderation of Soviet public attacks on the American leadership. But the prognosis for the continuation of such Soviet restraint remained highly uncertain in view of the huge difficulties still confronting an arms control agreement: on the Soviet side, reluctance to surrender the relative force gains of the 1970s; on the American side, both Reagan's reluctance to abandon strategic defense and the profound distrust of the Soviet Union created by the events of the past.

The Slowdown of Soviet Advance in the World Arena

A fourth distinctive new feature of the post-1979 era has been a noticeable slowdown in the previously rapid multiplications of Soviet military and political footholds around the world. This phenomenon has varied considerably from region to region. In general, the Soviets have been principally concerned to defend and consolidate the main geopolitical advances that they had staked out in the late 1970s, notably in Angola, Ethiopia, Afghanistan, and Indochina. In Africa their position has been somewhat weakened, at least for the time being, by their inability to offset the leverage exercised by South Africa over its Black African neighbors, a situation that compelled Marxist regimes in Angola and Mozambique to sign diplomatic agreements with Pretoria in the early 1980s to seek relief from South African pressures. In the Middle East, where the Soviets' political base had already been rendered narrow since their estrangement from Sadat's Egypt and the signing of the Egyptian-Israeli treaty, the Soviets for a time seemed humiliated by their inability to prevent the Israeli conquest of South Lebanon or the temporary arrival of the Western powers in Beirut. In Afghanistan they are widely perceived to have become bogged down since 1980 in a seemingly endless punitive war against the local population. In the Far East, despite a steady increase in their theater nuclear advantage and a gradual expansion in their new military position in Cam Ranh Bay, the Soviets have been forced to deal in the 1980s with increasingly adverse reactions from local states to these very military advantages, notably in the case of Japan, China, and the ASEAN countries. Even in the Caribbean and Central America, where since 1979 they have contemplated the prospect of risk-free advances in Soviet influence as a result of Cuban exacerbation of U.S. difficulties, by mid-decade this prospect, while still fairly promising, had become much less of a sure thing. Meanwhile, regimes sponsored by the Soviets or their clients have themselves come under long-term insurgency challenge in the 1980s, notably in Nicaragua, Angola, Afghanistan, and Cambodia.

As in the past, many Americans have overemphasized voluntaristic explanations for what has seemed to be a sudden change in Soviet fortunes around the world. Observers who in the late 1970s had persisted in seeing evidence of a "master plan" in the succession of Soviet advances in Africa, Afghanistan, and Southeast Asia now perceived evidence of a deliberate Soviet decision to hold back from efforts to advance. Some who in the immediate wake of the invasion of Afghanistan had conjured up visions of imminent further invasions, in the crude style of Hitler, now saw a Politburo newly and mysteriously inhibited from executing such plans. President Reagan did not hesitate to cite the Soviet failure to add to their sphere as evidence of the success of his policies; and even some Americans who are not supporters of Mr. Reagan have seemed to believe that the general posture of his administration has dissuaded the Soviet leadership from adventurist initiatives it would otherwise have taken. The Soviet failure to take action to halt the 1982 Israeli advance to Beirut and the expulsion of the Palestine Liberation Organization from that city was sometimes cited as an example of unwonted Soviet caution.

Such interpretations appear to me to exaggerate considerably both the extent of the Reagan administration's inhibiting influence upon Soviet behavior and the extent to which the stagnation of Soviet fortunes in the Third World over the last few years can in fact be attributed to Soviet inhibitions. This is not to say that Reagan's demeanor has had no influence, nor that the Soviets have seen no new reasons for caution.

It is plausible to suppose that Soviet behavior since 1980 has indeed been constrained to some degree by the USSR's multiple preoccupations, although this has probably not been the most important reason for the Soviet failure to make large new advances. Soviet military manpower, particularly in ground forces, has been increasingly stretched by the competing demands created by the recent growth in the list of adversaries. The Soviet leaders, in addition to satisfying the ongoing requirements of their buildup against China in the east and NATO in the west, felt obliged to hold very large forces perpetually in readiness to crush the Poles during 1980 and 1981. Also, of course, they have believed it necessary to allocate more than one hundred thousand troops on a permanent basis for the war against the Afghans. It is possible, as some Chinese analysts contend, that the Politburo has considered itself "pinned down" by the Afghan war, in the sense that it has been constrained more than hitherto against large new commitments of Soviet ground force resources in additional theaters.

In addition, some propaganda evidence suggests that since Brezhnev's death the Soviet regime has become at least somewhat more pessimistic about the balance of economic and political cost and benefits of commitments to Third World regimes in marginal situations.[14] Charles Wolf and some Rand colleagues have also produced evidence suggesting that the effective burden on the Soviet economy of supporting the Soviet empire—including the cost of subsidizing Cuba and Vietnam for strategic and political reasons—has at last grown to proportions that are likely to give Soviet leaders reasons for caution about assuming large additional burdens.[15]

But although these considerations may play some role in Soviet thinking, particularly where large costs or risks are in prospect, there is little reason to doubt that the primary cause of the recent slowdown in Soviet fortunes has been the same factor that was the primary cause of the rapid Soviet advance in the late 1970s: the scope of perceived opportunities. A tide of favorable circumstances that began a decade ago permitting decisive Soviet exploitation —for example, the death of Salazar and the dissolution of the Portuguese empire, the Ethiopian revolution, the Kabul April 1978 coup, Pol Pot's pugnacious behavior toward Vietnam—has now ebbed. The last few years have perforce been devoted largely to efforts to defend and consolidate the advances of the past.

Soviet leaders probably assume, however, that the recent slowdown in Third World opportunities is not likely to persist to the end of the decade. They are well aware that past Soviet advances have been predicated upon openings created by civil and international instability and violence and that in the absence of such turmoil the Soviet Union is at a great disadvantage in

---

[14]See Stephen Sestanovich, "Do Soviets Feel Pinched by Third World Adventurism?" *Washington Post*, May 20, 1984.

[15]See Charles Wolf, Jr., et al., *The Costs of the Soviet Empire* (Santa Monica: Rand Corporation, R-3073/1-NA, September 1983).

competing with the West in economic dealings with the Third World states. But they have some reason to expect instability and new opportunities to be generated somewhere in Asia, Africa, and Latin America before the 1980s are finished. In such countries as the Philippines and Pakistan, where severe threats now exist to the stability of the American position, Soviet leaders may already see the seeds of such future opportunities. There is little reason to assume that the Politburo believes that the long-term effort to expand Soviet presence and influence on the world scene at the expense of the West and the United States must come to a halt, or that it has ceased to pay dividends, or that it need necessarily involve unacceptable costs or risks.

Until the next dramatic evidence of Soviet advance materializes, however, the perception of near-stagnation of Soviet fortunes around the world is likely to cause a gradual dilution of the American consensus that the Reagan administration has sought to mobilize against the USSR. As suggested earlier, the hardening of U.S. opinion in the years immediately prior to Reagan's election had been accelerated by the widespread perception of a rapidly expanding Soviet presence around the world; this sense of a dangerous global political trend was to many observers as alarming as adverse trends in the force balance. Brzezinski's suggestion that the impulse of the 1970s toward cooperation with the Soviet Union finally perished in the "sands of the Ogaden" is therefore undoubtedly correct. By the same token, however, the slackening of the tide of Soviet opportunities since 1980 has contrasted ever more vividly with the intensification of American offical rhetoric; this contrast is in turn slowly eroding the large majority that had supported Carter's new posture toward Moscow in his last year as president. In sum, the very lack of notable new Soviet gains has become a factor gradually adding to the pressure on the Reagan administration to find ways to come to agreements with Moscow.

The Lasting Legacies of the 1970s

These, then, are the changes in the five years of the postdetente era. But what has endured from the preceding decade? Which of the leading developments of detente are likely to remain with us indefinitely? I shall cite five such developments.

First, several new Soviet-American institutional relationships that came into existence in the last decade survive, although their value remains limited by present circumstances. Perhaps the one with the greatest potential importance for the future is the joint Standing Consultative Commission, which since SALT I has dealt with matters of arms control interpretation and compliance. Virtually paralyzed in the early 1980s, like many Soviet-American forums, by the intensity of mutual distrust and the impasse in the arms control process, this institution is nonetheless an important structural innovation. It could be useful to both sides in the future.

In addition, certain other arms control-related venues established as a consequence of initiatives taken in the 1970s continue to exist, notably the Mutual and Balanced Force Reduction (MBFR) negotiations in Vienna and the talks on "confidence-building measures" (CBMs) in Stockholm. Both of these are now little more than propaganda battlefields—in the case of the Vienna talks, largely because the Soviets are unwilling to abandon their existing conventional force advantages in Europe, and in Stockholm, because of the Soviet preference for generalized mutual pledges with asymmetrical effects on Western interests rather than for concrete and intrusive CBMs. Nevertheless, both of these empty vessels remain available to be filled should the Soviet perspective some day be modified.

Beyond them, an important remnant remains from the network of informal contacts between the United States and the Soviet Union that expanded enormously in the late 1970s. This network has in recent years been constricted by the worsening of the bilateral atmosphere, by the Reagan administration's attempts to impose reciprocity on some mutual contacts, and by certain recent Soviet efforts to tighten security controls over all Western communications and contacts with the Soviet population. In addition, it should be recognized that the effects of informal contacts upon the two countries were always highly asymmetrical, because the Soviet Union was always far more interested in using such contacts to press the Soviet viewpoint upon the American elite than in allowing American views to reach Soviet policy makers. Nevertheless, the continued existence of some such contacts remains a modest factor making for political stability in the relationship.

Finally, it is noteworthy that one aspect of the Soviet-American trade relationship of the 1970s has endured and, indeed, become more firmly institutionalized in the postdetente era. That aspect is of course American grain exports to the USSR, evoked in the last decade by the Soviet incremental discovery that Soviet agriculture was unlikely for the foreseeable future to supply the feed needed to expand meat production. A long-term grain agreement negotiated during the Carter administration was partially breached by the Carter boycott of 1980, but it has now been succeeded by a "boycott-proof" agreement with Moscow. Although an extraordinary anomaly in the overall posture of the Reagan administration in the first half of the 1980s, this permanent grain trade also imparts a modest element of stability in the relationship.

Second, two trends of the 1970s adverse to Soviet interests have endured into the postdetente era. They hamper Soviet competitive efforts against the United States. One I have previously mentioned: despite the improvement that has taken place in the atmosphere of Sino-Soviet relations, Soviet encirclement of China has continued to fuel Sino-Soviet rivalry in Asia. Notwithstanding some important recent advances in bilateral dealings—including expansion of trade, the signing of a long-term trade agreement, and mutual agreement to allow the USSR to reequip a few old Chinese factories—the

Soviet Union has declined to make any concessions to larger Chinese geopolitical demands for Soviet retreat from actions around the Chinese periphery hostile to Chinese national interests. Thus the Soviets have refused to halt or reverse the force buildup they have long been conducting along China's northern frontiers, they have refused to cease their support for Vietnam's effort to consolidate its hold on Cambodia, and they have also refused to abandon their own military effort to consolidate their hold over Afghanistan. In consequence, China has been impelled to continue to maintain a loose, unacknowledged security association with the United States. The net effect is that a considerable portion of Soviet military efforts continues to be directed against China and away from the United States and its European allies.

The other adverse trend that has continued in the 1980s is the malaise in the Soviet economy, the first symptoms of which had originally helped impel the Soviet leadership to seek a remedy in association with the United States. The secular decline in the rate of growth of the Soviet economy—a decline that began to gather speed not long after the Soviets in effect lost hope for an American remedy, in December 1974—today impinges on three major aspects of the Soviet competition with the United States. Soviet economic difficulties render the burden of military spending increasingly onerous and make the prospect of heightened arms competition with the Reagan administration a grim one. Soviet technological backwardness in most nonmilitary areas of production helps make the Soviet Union a marginal factor in the world economic system dominated by the capitalist industrial powers, and also makes it difficult for the USSR to consolidate some of those Third World gains it initially staked out with security assistance. Finally, as suggested earlier, Soviet economic constraints are apparently increasing the effective burden of supporting the Soviet empire, and may be making Soviet leaders somewhat more cautious about assuming large new burdens for political and strategic reasons in marginal cases.

The fourth and fifth legacies of the 1970s are two major countervailing trends that the Soviets consider highly favorable to their competitive interests against the United States.

Despite all of the problems noted, the qualitative change in the late 1970s which saw the Soviet Union's emergence as a much more visible competitor to the United States around the world has not been undone. Despite some ebbing of Soviet fortunes from the high tide of advance in the last decade, the Soviet geopolitical presence remains much more far-flung than before. It is likely to remain so. The Soviet Union has not been forced to abandon the most important of the new bridgeheads established in the 1970s—in Ethiopia, Aden, Afghanistan, and Indochina—and there seems little reason to expect it to do so in the 1980s. The USSR continues to strive to consolidate these positions and, where possible, to improve on them.

All of these places, along with the bridgehead earlier established in Cuba, are linked to the gradual deployment of Soviet military and naval strength into new regions, from the South China Sea to the Red Sea, from the Khyber Pass to the Gulf of Mexico.[16] The effort to continue this process is in turn linked to very extensive building programs for naval and other weapons. Although in all major respects the Soviet Union's political presence, geopolitical weight, and power projection capabilities in distant regions around the world remain inferior to those of the United States, this very fact provides a continual incentive to Soviet leaders to persevere in efforts to build on what was accomplished in the 1970s as prudent opportunities permit.

These realities seem to ensure that whatever fortunes befall Soviet efforts in the future, the United States and the Soviet Union will remain geopolitically engaged across a broader canvas than was the case before the 1970s. This worldwide interaction will remain an essential aspect of the bilateral relationship.

The final legacy is this: the Soviets thus far also appear to have retained the essence of the advances they registered in the central strategic and regional nuclear balances. In the 1970s the Soviet Union attained what is generally termed a "robust" overall parity with the United States in strategic nuclear capabilities; it also established and enlarged an important advantage in theater nuclear capabilities in both Europe and Asia. All of these changes have endured since 1980, and all seem likely to survive for a long time. Although the Soviets are undoubtedly concerned at the prospect of the United States using its technological advantages to seek to undo their central strategic gains of the 1970s, they seem grimly determined to make every sacrifice necessary to prevent this from happening. In Europe, despite the vehement Soviet objections to the limited INF deployments begun in 1983, the Soviets have every reason to believe that they will retain a considerable advantage in intermediate-range nuclear delivery capability even after these deployments are completed. In Asia, where the Soviet nuclear advantage has always been much greater, the Soviet SS-20 building program and bomber deployment program appear designed to guarantee to the USSR a decisive theater nuclear edge, whatever contingencies may emerge in future Chinese or American deployments.

These present realities reflect the Soviet sense of what is required in each of the three spheres adequately to protect Soviet security. They seem to guarantee continued tension between the Soviet Union and those of its adversaries—notably the United States and China—which find this degree of Soviet insurance unacceptable and threatening. Beyond this, the evident Soviet desire to retain simultaneously the existing force ratios in strategic nuclear weapons and in theater nuclear weapons both in Europe and in Asia is likely to come into increasing conflict with the exigencies of a revived arms control process.

---

[16]Symbolic, in this regard, was the arrival of Badger medium bombers at Cam Ranh Bay in November 1983.

Conclusions

The panorama surveyed suggests the following conclusions.

1. Neither the atmosphere of 1972 nor that of 1984 is "normal" for the Soviet-American relationship. That relationship is likely to be highly competitive for the foreseeable future, and there is little ground for hope that bilateral cooperation can diminish that competition to secondary importance or make the relationship, on the whole, a "friendly" one, as was being suggested in 1972. This generalization will probably hold true regardless of the personalities who lead the United States and the Soviet Union over the rest of the 1980s. This relationship is essentially adversarial, and the underlying reality is probably not subject to change by U.S. policy. At the same time the degree of tension seen in the first half of the 1980s was abnormal, and it may be possible to reduce it significantly. Whether this does in fact happen will depend upon the interplay of many variables, some of which can indeed be affected by the U.S. posture and negotiating position but some of which will be beyond the control of any American government.

2. The most important underlying cause of the tension created in the past has not been the behavior of the Reagan administration, although it can be criticized on several grounds, but rather the assertive dynamism of the Soviet regime (reflected in Soviet efforts to press outward on the world scene over the last two decades) and its associated view of military requirements essential to Soviet security. Both of these factors are internally generated by a combination of historical, geopolitical, and ideological considerations. These two central aspects of Soviet behavior were the most important causes, although not the only ones, of the destruction of detente in the 1970s and the sea change in American public opinion which helped bring the Reagan administration to power.

3. Consequently, although the willingness of the American leadership to compromise—particularly regarding space defense—will certainly affect the evolution of the Soviet-American relationship over the rest of the 1980s, the emerging priorities of the new Gorbachev leadership will probably be even more important. With continued intense rivalry between the superpowers in the world arena virtually certain, much will depend upon the weight that Gorbachev assigns to a Soviet need for a "breathing space" in the relationship with the United States, as a prerequisite for his efforts to impart new life into the faltering Soviet economy. The overriding issue is whether Gorbachev will be willing—and can enforce upon his colleagues—a modification of the past Soviet view of acceptable compromise in the broad geopolitical competition, a view that proved fundamentally unacceptable to the majority in both American political parties in the 1970s.

4. The content of the Soviet-American arms control agreements concluded in the 1970s appears, on balance, to have played at best only a marginal role in restraining strategic nuclear competition. However, the arms control

process—the ritual sequence of negotiate-sign-negotiate—appears to have played a much larger role as a talisman of stability for the multitudes. Whereas the implications of the agreements reached became a matter for increasing disputation within the U.S. elite, the fact that agreements were being reached remained the essential matter for millions in the United States and in the West who had neither knowledge of nor interest in the minutiae of what was being disputed. The momentary halt in this cycle of negotiation— signaled by the U.S. failure to ratify SALT II at the close of the 1970s and then confirmed by the Soviet walkout from negotiations four years later —was thus a traumatic political event of major proportions quite apart from its concrete consequences for the strategic balance. Although the cycle of talks was restarted in 1985 with the Soviet return to negotiations, the prospects of a long-term impasse in those talks and a continued decay in the arms control regime remain unacceptable to the American consensus. The Reagan administration is therefore likely to come under growing domestic pressure during its second term to reach some agreement in talks with the USSR.

5. At the same time the political viability of any future nuclear negotiations that the two powers may undertake will always remain highly vulnerable to the political consequences of a successful advance in the world arena by one of the parties at the expense of the other. In the United States this generalization appears especially likely to be true, and to be relatively independent of the preferences of any particular American government. Whatever the degree of urgency attributed to arms control and despite the desire of part of the U.S. elite to protect this process at almost any cost, it is unlikely that any American nuclear agreement with the Soviet Union, whatever its terms, would be ratified in the next few years if the USSR in the same period somehow found it possible, for example, to move into dominant influence over the government of Pakistan, or of the Philippines, or of Iran. Linkage, even if it is formally excluded from the negotiating process, is always likely to exercise a tacit but decisive role in the confirmation process. All major Soviet-American bilateral negotiations should therefore be understood to have an unstated global political aspect.

6. No such major Soviet geopolitical advances have in fact occurred since 1980. This state of relative Soviet quiescence, however, appears to stem much more from happenstance than from Soviet intention, and it could change without notice at any time. Although the Soviet leaders feel somewhat burdened by their war in Afghanistan, and are also likely to be reluctant to assume major new economic burdens for the sake of new Third World clients, there is still no evidence, and little reason to believe, that they are willing to accept the status quo in the overall division of political forces in the world, which still greatly favors the United States. They therefore continue to await major new geopolitical opportunities, and thus far they seem unlikely to be willing to sacrifice one, should one present itself at acceptable risk, for the

sake of any bilateral agreement with the United States. In addition to all other impediments, therefore, the Soviet-American relationship will always be vulnerable to independent factors that may unexpectedly open avenues of Soviet opportunity.

3

Lessons of History: Soviet–American Relations in the Postwar Era

SEWERYN BIALER

To write about the lessons of post–World War II Soviet-American relations is to distill the essence of a forty-year history. This chapter, of course, does not aspire to fulfill such an enormous task; it intends to be analytical rather than prescriptive and selective rather than comprehensive, focusing on what the author considers to be the most important lessons of the superpowers' postwar conflict.

A Spanish philosopher suggests that whether we like it or not, human life is a constant preoccupation with the future. Yet we should display a healthy dose of skepticism that "lessons of history" can serve as prescriptions for the future. First of all, the potential for historical discontinuities is always present. Moreover, analyses of historical events and trends can differ as greatly as can judgments of current events. Finally, there is no way of knowing whether the perspectives of a historian or a political scientist are shared by decision makers, or whether the "lessons" have been learned in the same way by the political leadership of the two protagonists. All this suggests the need for restraint and caution in generalizing about the not-too-distant and not-too-clear past.

Most important, however, lessons of history are limited in their applicability and reliability because of another factor—they provide only one element in attempts to shape the present and the future. Even the most accurate diagnosis of the past and the best learning process do not automatically or directly translate into suggestions about the present and future. In themselves they do not teach us what adjustments in the political and economic realm are possible or probable in order to take advantage of the lessons of history.

The teaching of history, or for that matter political science and sociology, is almost without exception a distillation and abstraction of the past. Yet the application of the "lessons of the past" to the present and the future cannot be abstract. Those who apply them have to consider the current social, political, and economic realities of the political systems that are expected to benefit. This juxtaposition of an abstract past and a very specific present almost always creates dilemmas for policy makers. These dilemmas represent the disparity between what the policy-making elites *want* to do in shaping the real world and what they *can* do—between what should be done and what is possible in the system the policy makers have inherited, a system that has largely been shaped by the past.

This chapter is divided into three parts. The first part draws conclusions from past Soviet-American relations as a means of defining the limits of what is realistically possible in tempering the virulence of the superpower conflict. The second and third parts seek to define the systemic nature of policy dilemmas faced by Soviet and American policy makers. These dilemmas leave open the question of whether the United States or the USSR will be able to adjust their respective policies toward each other so as to prevent the repetition of past mistakes and avoid the emergence of new and possibly fatal errors of judgment.

I

The four decades of postwar Soviet-American relations, and particularly the 1970s and early 1980s, have produced a rich body of experiences upon which academic analysts and policy makers alike can draw. Five elements of this history seem especially relevant. They are the balance of conflict and cooperation in the overall Soviet-American relationship; the superpowers' experience with strategic deterrence; the superpowers' experience with conflict management; the counterproductive results of their attempts to take temporary advantage of each other's weakness; and the tendency of each superpower to exaggerate what is necessary for its national security.

Competition and Cooperation

The elementary lesson from the past is that the sources of the Soviet-American conflict are so deep and many-sided that for the foreseeable future, the competitive and antagonistic dimension of U.S.-Soviet relations will predominate over the cooperative elements.

The conflict with the Soviet Union, which will undoubtedly endure through the remainder of this century and beyond, has many sources. Its principal roots, however, are basic, obvious, and simple: the Soviet Union and the United States represent qualitatively different political systems and subscribe to basically different values and divergent social, economic, cultural, and political priorities. Moreover, the Soviet Union and the United States are pursuing and promoting their diverse values and the policies that stem from them in the international arena. They perceive what is a clash of values as a basic, worldwide clash of vital national interests.

Even as they engage in relentless competition, neither the United States nor the Soviet Union can avoid striving to manage the relationship. Never before have great powers in conflict felt the same imperative. Today the nuclear revolution has made it unthinkable for them to play out their differences to what in the past would have been their natural, logical conclusion—war. The specter of nuclear annihilation has rendered such logic absurd.

Both superpowers face the imperative need to manage and deescalate the arms race in such a way as to stabilize and then gradually reduce their nuclear arsenals. The danger of a nuclear holocaust lies not in one superpower's deliberate, all-out nuclear attack against the other but rather in accidents and, even more important, in an unintended escalation of regional, peripheral confrontation beyond the control of either superpower. Accordingly, the entire range of Soviet-American relations must be managed. It is thus important for both groups of leaders to prevent situations from arising where, through lack of communication or through misperception of goals and behavior, neither side feels able to compromise or back down.

Although both superpowers recognize the need to manage their conflict, both sides experience major difficulties in doing so. The Soviet Union and the United States are out of phase in their roles and aspirations in the international arena. The Soviet Union has only recently reached the status of a global power and has gained military equality with the United States, and it is eager to take full advantage of this; in the international arena it is still a "hungry" country, unwilling to accept the status quo and highly ambitious. The United States, a long-established global power, wishes to preserve the status quo; though recognizing the need for change, it wants the process to be gradual and moderate, not revolutionary and radical. This contrast is especially relevant in the Third World, where ever-increasing social, economic, and political turmoil creates many opportunities and temptations for the Soviet Union to exploit. Moreover, the USSR's foreign policy resources are highly unbalanced, with the military constituting its most important and sometimes even its only major international asset. Consequently, the Soviet Union has an interest in seeing that domestic and regional conflicts in the Third World reach the military threshold, and it is trying to gain greater power and influence in the international arena by military means.

The entire history of Soviet-American relations demonstrates clearly that it is unwise to expect that any agreement or "atmospheric" improvement in Soviet-American relations can be a stable counterweight to the divergence of values and interests dividing the two superpowers. We should squarely face the fact that in the last decades of the twentieth century, competition and conflict between the Soviet Union and the United States will continue to overshadow areas of agreement and the imperative to cooperate.

Those who see the state of Soviet-American relations in the last five or six years as "normal" may be unnecessarily gloomy, although the second half of the 1980s may still prove their pessimism justified. Yet those who look back with longing to the heyday of detente can have little hope that the exceptional circumstances of that period will recur in the foreseeable future. In light of past experience, what both superpowers can most optimistically expect in the coming years is a *military* detente, to stabilize if not reverse the escalating arms race, combined with more regular and substantive communications on political issues. Those issues, however, will remain in the shadow of intense competition in the strife-ridden Third World.

Strategic Deterrence

Nuclear deterrence is effective. It has succeeded in preventing direct military confrontation between the superpowers. Though the present state of Soviet-American relations is potentially dangerous, neither today nor in the past decades has there really been an imminent danger of nuclear war or even limited employment of nuclear weapons.

In its general magnitude and intensity the Soviet-American competition is unique in the modern world. It is, literally, "global." No peacetime arms race or political conflict has ever been as all-consuming as this one has been since the end of World War II. But magnitude aside, the U.S.-Soviet relationship has another key peculiarity: the introduction of a vast array of nuclear weapons as a fundamental *political* factor in the rivalry. The level of sheer potential destructiveness of these weapons has prevented their actual military use, and nuclear weapons have therefore dominated the international environment in the postwar years primarily as a political factor. Nuclear weapons have prevented the intense conflict and arms race of the two superpowers from leading to a war, which would very probably have been unavoidable before the nuclear era; they have increased sharply the importance of the regional balance of conventional forces between the two superpowers and the importance of their alliances; and they have made the psychological—rather than the military— consequences of the nuclear balance of terror the central factor in international relations. Nuclear weapons are the foremost factor shaping the psychology of U.S.-Soviet relations. After all, deterrence, the key strategic concept of the nuclear age, is a psychological one, depending on each side's perceptions of its adversary and its self-image.

The American and Soviet leaderships of the post–World War II era proved to be sane in that they were determined to avoid nuclear war. There is no evidence to indicate that this sanity on both sides of the Soviet-American conflict will evaporate. Each side's sanity was and is based on its recognition of the reality of nuclear deterrence. In this sense "deterrence" was, and for the foreseeable future will remain, the only rational concept of the nuclear revolution in warfare.

However, the size and level of destructiveness of the superpowers' nuclear arsenals have moved far beyond the necessities of rational deterrence. Pressure on both superpowers is growing to break the cycle of an unending arms race and to move in the direction of a finite deterrence, which the Geneva negotiations may offer the last chance in this century to achieve. Such finite deterrence would involve nuclear arsenals that are greatly reduced in size and destructiveness, balanced despite the asymmetry of force mix and geopolitical situation of the two superpowers, and, most important, stable in denying a first-strike capability to either side.

Conflict Management

Although the 1972 written agreements on "rules of behavior" between the United States and the Soviet Union are very ambiguous, the actions of both superpowers in crises have in fact followed tacit rules of prudence that prevented their confrontations from escalating dangerously.

Since the Soviet Union achieved strategic parity with the United States, there have been a number of occasions when the clash of the two superpowers' interests could have escalated out of control. In each case, however, a potentially dangerous escalation was defused by prudent behavior on both sides. In the early days of detente the 1973 Yom Kippur Arab-Israeli War provided an example of such behavior. On the one hand, because of the strong American response the Soviets quickly abandoned their threat, implicit in a high-level alert of Soviet airborne forces, to intervene on the side of Egypt. On the other hand, strong American pressure on Israel prevented the total destruction of the Egyptian military after it had been surrounded on the west bank of the Suez by Israeli forces.

The potentially dangerous involvement of both superpowers in Lebanon in 1984 provides a more recent example of their prudence. In 1983, during the invasion of Lebanon, the Syrian air force suffered a disastrous defeat at the hands of Israel. In response the Soviets deployed SAM-5 and SS-21 missiles operated by Soviet personnel in Syria, their last and only ally in the Middle East. In 1984 the United States, while trying to resolve the Lebanese civil war peacefully, brought two major naval and air task forces to the shores of Lebanon and deployed a contingent of Marines in Beirut itself. The Soviet and American forces were separated by only a few dozen miles. The Soviets contributed to defusing the potential danger of the situation by promising to employ their forces only in case of an Israeli attack on Damascus. The United States contributed to defusing the danger by withdrawing its forces at the first face-saving opportunity.

From the experience of Soviet-American relations in the postwar era it is possible to identify tacit "rules of prudence" that both sides have observed and, one hopes, will continue to observe. The most important of these rules seem to be the following:

avoid extreme behavior, especially direct military intervention in the other's declared or recognized spheres of influence (e.g., American behavior regarding the Hungarian revolution of 1956 or during the period of "dual power" in Poland in 1979–81; the highly limited Soviet engagement in Central America);

act with restraint where the "vital interests" of either superpower are involved (e.g., the Soviets' caution in their involvement in the Persian Gulf; American caution in developing military cooperation with the People's Republic of China);

avoid direct confrontation or contact of military forces, and disengage when such confrontation or contact seems probable (e.g., Lebanon in 1984);

avoid "cornering" the other side, and leave open to it a face-saving way out when a direct confrontation occurs (e.g., the Cuban missile crisis, which started because Khrushchev initially broke the rules of prudence but in which both sides showed prudence in ending the crisis);

avoid inflicting a defeat on a superpower's ally so catastrophic as to humiliate the superpower itself (e.g., the aforementioned outcome of the 1973 Arab-Israeli war);

avoid even the most limited (i.e., tactical) use of nuclear weapons against any opponent;

engage in nonpublic consultations, even at times of highly strained relations, about the superpowers' intentions with regard to areas or issues of high confrontational potential (e.g., Lebanon in 1984, Iran in 1984–85, and the question of nonproliferation);

continue, except for short intervals, to negotiate on arms control even in the face of great difficulties in the overall political relationship between the superpowers;

reach explicit agreements creating mechanisms that would contribute to the de-escalation of potential confrontational incidents (e.g., the Incidents at Sea Agreement and the "hot line" communications link).

With rare exceptions, the two superpowers have tacitly observed these and other rules of prudence because the rules serve each side's self-interests. The durability of those interests provides the strongest argument that the rules of prudence will continue to be observed; if general relations should improve, some rules may even become more explicit and institutionalized (as, for instance, an agreement not to intervene directly with one's own or proxy forces in regional conflicts). Incidentally, with notable exceptions, the tacit rules of prudence have also been associated with tacit "rules of mutual respect," where the two sides toned down their harsh deprecatory rhetoric and recognized the legitimacy of each other's global interests. It is quite probable that these rules of mutual respect will again be adhered to in the second half of the 1980s. This is more likely to be the case if regular summit meetings, serving as a vehicle to reinforce the rules of prudence and respect, become a normal part of the superpower relationship.

Temporary Advantage

The behavior of the superpowers toward each other in the last decades leads to a blunt conclusion: it is unwise and counterproductive for either superpower to "kick" the other whenever the "correlation of forces" moves in the adversary's disfavor.

Soviet-American relations in the last fifteen years have gone through two periods—detente, and then a period of high tension and very limited negotiations and communications. In each period one of the superpowers tried to take advantage of the other, exploiting its period of weakness. In each, one of the superpowers engaged consciously or unconsciously in actions and rhetoric humiliating to the other. And in each, the harsh and dominating attitude of one superpower provoked the other, quite predictably, to respond unwisely and disproportionately.

In retrospect detente, ushered in by the 1972 Soviet-American agreements, began with the United States in a position of weakness that only grew in the ensuing years. The debilitating Vietnam war, with its inglorious ending, was the key symbol of American weakness as the United States entered the detente era; the constitutional crisis of Watergate, which undermined the credibility of the American executive, became the key symbol of American weakness during detente. The post-Vietnam and post-Watergate syndromes almost paralyzed the American decision-making process in foreign and military affairs in the late 1970s.

It is still unclear whether the Soviet Union entered detente conscious of the basic weakness of the American position. What is clear, however, is that by the mid-1970s the Soviets had begun to interpret detente as license for a continuous Soviet military buildup and for a cost-free hunt for targets of opportunity in the Third World. In this respect it is not really important whether Soviet assertiveness of the 1970s brought significant and lasting gains to the Soviet Union. The important truth is that in the course of their military buildup and "neocolonial" adventures, the Soviets humiliated the United States and created in America a decisive mood of "present danger."

The American reaction was not long in coming. The post-Vietnam and post-Watergate syndromes proved to be to a large extent passing phenomena. The last two years of the Carter administration were already characterized by commitment to an American military buildup and to an increasingly activist attitude in foreign policy. Yet the real reaction to the Soviet behavior of the 1970s and the accompanying American impotence came with the election of Reagan and the popularity of his program to restore American strength.

The rhetoric emanating from the Reagan administration during its first term in office was unnecessarily humiliating to the Soviet leadership. The attempts at large-scale military buildup, especially when combined with President Reagan's announcement in March 1983 of the Strategic Defense Initiative as a national goal, were and continue to be perceived by the Soviets as American attempts to regain strategic superiority.

The process of succession in the Soviet Union complicated the response of Soviet leaders to the growing perception of the danger represented by President Reagan's policies to their security and aspirations. Yet the basic Soviet line, which took clear shape in the fall of 1983, was unequivocal. Domestically, the Soviets countered Reagan's rhetoric and the perception of danger from America by vicious propaganda campaigns not much different from the Stalinist prototype. In fact, something resembling a state of siege was declared inside the Soviet Union. Conscious of their grave domestic and imperial problems, the Soviets defiantly responded to the U.S. stance by adopting an extremely hard line, which remained unyielding even to President Reagan's concessionary offers and attitudes in 1984. At the same time the Soviets seemed ready to respond to any and all of Reagan's military initiatives to strengthen America with their own programs of similar magnitude.

With the reelection of President Reagan at the end of 1984 and the early 1985 succession of Mikhail Gorbachev in the Soviet Union, the United States and the Soviet Union entered a new phase in their relations. Even if we assume that there has been a positive learning process by both leaderships and that the domestic situations in both countries leave open broad policy choices —both are big assumptions—it is still not clear whether the stalemate in their relations can be broken and the intensity of their confrontation substantially reduced. It is an open question whether President Reagan's conciliatory overtures to the new Soviet leadership can convince the Soviets of U.S. sincerity, goodwill, and reasonableness in searching for a Soviet-American modus vivendi. Relations between great powers are not spigots to be turned off and on at the whim of either side. Soviet agreement to resume comprehensive arms control negotiations in Geneva should not obscure the enormous chasm that still divides the two nations.

Americans and Soviets remain locked into their proclaimed positions. They do not seem ready to rescind their past actions. They are slow to suggest new and more equitable negotiating positions. Domestic circumstances, anger, pride, and suspiciousness on the part of both countries have diminished the flexibility and the willingness of the leaderships to take major steps toward easing their conflict. The lesson of this experience for both the American and the Soviet leadership is, however, clear: Don't kick a great power when it is down. Whatever the temporary satisfactions and gains, there will eventually be a heavy price to pay.

In the 1980s the trend in the international correlation of forces has shifted in favor of the West and particularly the United States. In today's circumstances it would be wise for the American leadership to present to the Soviets a negotiating offer that, in Arnold Horelick's words, "will require Moscow to make concessions to relieve pressing U.S. strategic concerns that accumulated in the 1970s. But such an offer must also be sensitive to Soviet strategic anxieties, which are growing; it must promise Moscow a more acceptable outcome in the mid-term than the Soviets could expect from a totally unregulated strategic competition. It should communicate U.S. determination to shape an international environment that is increasingly less hospitable to Soviet aggrandizement, but that is not so implacably hostile as to signal that Soviet self-restraint would remain unreciprocated."[1]

Definitions of National Security

To an increasing degree the chimera of national security as defined and pursued by both superpowers is unattainable under the conditions of the nuclear revolution.

The experience of the Soviet-American conflict in the nuclear age suggests strongly that both superpowers subscribe to a false and unrealistic concept of national security. The two most security-minded types of countries, it has been said, are those which have been invaded frequently and those which have never been invaded. In the second half of the twentieth century the Soviet Union and the United States confirm the truth of the remark. The Soviet preoccupation with national security has a very long history, dating back to the Czarist empire. It took the nuclear revolution in warfare to make security issues an American preoccupation. But once this security concern was introduced into the thinking of American leaders and the political public, it assumed a position of central and even overwhelming importance.

The Russian and Soviet heritage, reinforced by a messianic Marxist-Leninist ideology, has driven Soviet leaders to pursue what can only be described as *total security*. No amount of arms, no level of military expenditure, no panoply of international security agreements seems sufficient to provide the Soviets with a sense of security they find adequate. The psychology of Soviet leaders, then, leads them to pursue an elusive goal — military strength surpassing that of all opponents combined. This attitude obscures from Soviet leaders the elements of redundancy in their military projects and almost always makes them inclined to identify large numbers of more powerful weapons with a higher degree of national security. It is an attitude that ultimately, although not necessarily intentionally, makes the Soviets secure only if other nations are insecure. However logical in theory, in practice this course has been deeply counterproductive to Soviet security interests. It has evoked powerful reactions from adversaries who feel endangered by the Soviet military buildup and respond with their own, seeking to restore what they consider to be a more equitable military balance.

---

[1]Arnold L. Horelick, "U.S.-Soviet Relations: The Return of Arms Control," *Foreign Affairs* 63, 3 (1985), pp. 511–37.

It is a sign of rather remarkable Soviet-American convergence that the American approach to national security is beginning in important respects to resemble that of the Soviets. American leaders have been engaged in a major military buildup to overcome what they have perceived as growing Soviet advantages. Soviet leaders, maintaining that strategic parity between the two superpowers exists, see in the American buildup of the 1980s clear evidence of a U.S. attempt to attain strategic superiority. So goes the spiral of nuclear arms escalation, with the likely final result only an increase in the insecurity of both superpowers.

The reason for the futility of the Soviet and American search for security is that the concept on which they base their policies is fundamentally flawed. First and foremost, it is anachronistic. The nuclear revolution has made unattainable the level of national security that great powers, and particularly the United States, have known in the past. Nothing will change the fact that the fate of our country is in the hands of Soviet leaders and that the fate of the Soviet Union is in the hands of American leaders. Now that both superpowers have achieved the capacity for mutual assured destruction, no action on either side can in any way change the fundamental condition of security, or rather insecurity, in which they find themselves.

The course of an unending nuclear buildup, intended to serve as a deterrent to the other side, depends on a notion of protection and safety which is no longer viable. Through their overwhelming and virtually unlimited destructiveness, nuclear arms, while immensely increasing the security preoccupations of the two superpowers, have at the same time made it impossible, finally and irreversibly, to achieve the degree of safety and security which great powers possessed in the non-nuclear past. Yet neither the Soviet nor the American political-military leadership seems willing to recognize this paradox.

One of the clearest lessons from the past is that any effort by either the Soviet Union or the United States to break out from the condition of strategic parity is ill-conceived, expensive, and futile. As the American reaction to the Soviet buildup of the 1970s has shown, the Soviets will not be permitted to tilt the balance in their favor. Nor will the United States be permitted to do so. A high level of national security can be achieved by each superpower only if it is a common security, one that addresses the anxieties of both superpowers.

Well beyond the end of this century both we and the Soviets will remain on the firing line. We both must accept this reality. We both must learn how to live with it. And most important, we both must seek to minimize, through agreements, the vulnerability of our positions—a vulnerability that will not decline as a result of a new arms race. As Robert Jervis remarks, the Soviet Union and the United States have "to come to grips with the unfortunate fact that no strategy can provide the kind of protection that was possible in the past. Only by understanding and accepting the implications of nuclear weapons can we develop a more appropriate policy. But even such a policy, we must realize, cannot meet all the standards we normally require of rationality."[2]

II

Even if absorbed theoretically by the policy makers and political publics of both countries, the lessons of the forty-year history of postwar Soviet-American relations will have no major impact on policy so long as the systemic characteristics and ideological pressures in both countries do not adjust to the realities of the nuclear age. These realities require from the superpowers a modicum of cooperation with each other, even while each at the same time pursues its own interests and promotes its own values. For each of the two superpowers, these contradictory goals of cooperation and competition can be depicted in terms of foreign policy-making dilemmas that involve both the domestic and international situations and the predilections of the two sides.

The dilemmas that influence the direction and effectiveness of Soviet foreign policy will influence Soviet-American relations both directly and indirectly in the remainder of the 1980s. Most of these dilemmas are systemic in nature. This is to say that in most cases they do not stem from the predispositions of particular Soviet leaders, or from their errors of judgment. Rather, they stem from the ideological or experiential predilections and biases of the leadership and elite strata and from the structural characteristics of the contemporary domestic system, which is tradition-bound and resistant to modernization. For analytical purposes, these dilemmas of Soviet foreign policy may be grouped into three distinctive sets of relationships: between internal resources and internal aspirations, between central and peripheral foreign policy goals, and between expansionist aspirations in the Third World and the realities of the Third World.

Without doubt the first set of dilemmas, concerning the relationship between internal resources and external aspirations, is the most important in its consequences and the most difficult for the Soviets to resolve.

The Soviet domestic system has entered a period of secular decline that can be characterized as a systemic crisis of effectiveness (though not a crisis of survival). The elements of this crisis are economic, political, social, ideological, and cultural. Meanwhile the Soviet Union externally remains in an aggressive, dynamic period of expansionist aspiration and potential international ascendency. Moreover, while fighting an uphill battle to revitalize their domestic system, in the coming decade Soviet leaders will certainly be facing an international situation that will provide many strong temptations to intervene and expand in the unstable Third World and, if present trends continue, to gain greater influence over the policies of America's European allies.

[2]From an unpublished paper by Robert Jervis, June 1985.

Soviet ambitions in the international arena require a large commitment of resources that can be employed in support of a dynamic foreign policy. Yet the domestic crisis limits the resources that the Soviet leadership can devote to external purposes. In turn the pursuit of ambitious external goals contributes to the deepening of the internal crisis. In contemporary circumstances, international expansionism is not a solution to internal difficulties, as it has been for many previous empires, but rather an added burden.

Moreover, the foreign policy resources available to the Soviets are predominantly military in nature; they possess far fewer political, ideological, cultural, and economic resources than the West does. Soviet assets are, and are likely to remain, even more skewed in the military direction than they were in the 1970s. The paucity of nonmilitary alternatives sets an effective limit on Soviet ambitions to expand its role as a global power, and it puts a premium on situations susceptible to the direct or indirect employment of military resources. This in turn increases the importance of American military capabilities and raises the chances for Soviet-American military confrontations.

The Soviet empire in Eastern Europe poses an additional problem, which to a large extent can be considered an integral part of the Soviet domestic crisis, and clearly also creates a Soviet foreign policy resource burden. The Soviet commitment to the control of its East European empire is absolute and undiminished. The key source of this commitment is not only Soviet security interests but also the legitimization of Party rule at home. Yet from the point of view both of Soviet "returns" on imperial investments and of the internal situation in the East European states, the Soviet empire has entered a period of secular decline. The basic stability of Eastern Europe requires either increased economic contributions by the Soviets or closer economic, and therefore political, relations with the West. The Soviet Union is hardly ready to commit itself to the first course (and as a matter of fact Soviet subsidies to Eastern Europe have been cut dramatically), nor to permit the second. In addition, the political-economic situation in Poland, the key country of the Soviet East European empire, has not been resolved in any way: the uneasy truce between the government without a people to lead, and the people without a government, could at any time be shattered by a disastrous explosion of popular discontent.

Finally, in the highly centralized Soviet party-state a strong and purposeful leadership constitutes a key domestic resource necessary for the energetic pursuit of foreign policy goals. The paralysis of the last years under Brezhnev, and the prolonged process of successions after he died, created a partial power vacuum in the Kremlin that is only now being filled. The selection of Gorbachev as General Secretary signals a domestic change in the direction of a strong and unified leadership. Yet the full consolidation of Gorbachev's power will require a number of years to achieve. Meanwhile the conduct of Soviet foreign and security policies will continue to be constrained by the internal need to achieve consensus within the ruling oligarchy. Negotiations with the United States requiring substantial Soviet concessions are thus less likely to succeed in the face of the strong opposition that vested Soviet interests may put up against such concessions. More broadly, the need for consensus limits the flexibility of the Soviet leadership in dealing with the United States.

All these problems can be reduced to one primary choice facing Soviet leaders: Should the Soviet Union concentrate on its domestic problems and those of its empire while moderating radically its *active* foreign policies and international ambitions, or should it continue on a course that combines efforts to restore internal dynamism with the pursuit and expansion of its ambitions as a global power? Of course, such historically decisive choices are never so clear-cut but instead involve a change in stress, in intensity of commitment, in degree of preference. Yet it is exactly such a change in degree— sometimes dismissed as merely marginal—that can reverse a trend and prepare the groundwork for new opportunities for compromise agreements between the Soviet Union and the West. The way in which the Soviet leadership will resolve the conflicting policy priorities—or its conscious decision not to resolve them, or its inability to do so—will decisively influence the international situation in the 1980s.

The second dilemma of Soviet foreign policy—the incongruity between primary and secondary goals—has been brought into sharp focus by the Soviet experience with detente in the 1970s and early 1980s. The Soviet leadership was convincingly shown that detente is not "divisible"; a linkage between the various responsibilities of detente and the benefits it offers is absolutely unavoidable because of the domestic political realities of a populist democracy such as the United States.

Military, political, and, to a lesser extent, economic relations with the United States constitute the central axis of Soviet foreign and security policy. The experience of the late 1970s and early 1980s has shown, however, that stable and beneficial relations on this central axis cannot be reconciled with Soviet external aggrandizement by military means and with an unrelenting buildup of Soviet military might. The Soviet leadership is encouraged to be cautious, limited in its pursuit of peripheral expansion, by the necessity of at least some accommodation with the United States; the Soviet leadership is tempted to exploit targets of opportunity, by turmoil in the Third World and the possibly transitory opportunities for Soviet expansion which turmoil creates.

At the same time, although detente with Western Europe survived the break with the United States, Soviet policies in Eastern Europe nevertheless have weakened the West European commitment to detente. Furthermore, as the INF issue and conservative political trends in West Germany and Great Britain have shown, the Soviet Union cannot count on a decisive weakening of the American–West European–Japanese relationship if the USSR pursues aggressive military and foreign policies. The Soviets have also found that detente with Western Europe, though highly gratifying and economically profitable, is not a substitute for stable relations with the United States. The United States, when it chooses to oppose the Soviet Union, is the only decisive obstacle to Soviet international ambition.

Here again the Soviet leadership is facing a difficult choice. Either it must sacrifice the Soviet Union's central relationship in order to gain marginal and probably temporary advantages, or it must adjust its military and foreign policies in such a way as to restore a balance in its relations with the United States.

The third set of issues plaguing Soviet foreign policy concerns activity in the Third World. The central Soviet goal in the postwar era has been the attainment of global military power equal if not superior to that of the United States. The Soviet leadership believed that military parity with, or superiority over, the West would produce a dominant political position for the Soviet Union in the international arena. Yet in practice the Soviet leadership has found it very difficult to translate its military capabilities into greater and lasting international power and influence. It is finding not only that attempts to do so carry an increased risk but that its successes are transient.

In its quest for expansion in the Third World the Soviet Union vacillates between two goals: increased influence without control, on the one hand, and expanding Soviet power, which requires that Soviet control be secure, on the other. The "payoffs" in growing influence seem more and more ephemeral; the quest for power—that is, control—seems more and more expensive and dangerous.

Well into Brezhnev's tenure the Soviet leadership came increasingly to recognize that the "profits" from its "investments" in the Third World were temporary and that the costs were rising. The Soviets' conclusion, it seems, was to opt wherever possible for actual power rather than for ephemeral influence. Although the Soviets did not abandon efforts to achieve low-cost influence over many Third World regimes, they probably decided that enduring power over those regimes could be attained only through a substantial, highly visible presence of their military and security forces or those of their client states. This partly explains the Soviet pattern of military intervention of 1975–79, with their own or proxy forces engaged directly in such places as Afghanistan, Ethiopia, and Angola.

It may be that in the long run this Soviet pattern of acquiring power through military intervention will prove temporary. Yet the danger that the pattern will be repeated is quite high, and it poses three dilemmas for the Soviet leadership—of central vs. secondary goals; of foreign policy resources; and of anticolonialism vs. "hegemonism."

The first two components have already been discussed. The third, anticolonialism vs. hegemonism, requires elaboration. When the Soviets' presence in the Third World was virtually nonexistent, it was very easy for them to act as a champion of anticolonialism. Today, however, Third World states expect not only vocal support from their Soviet friends but also major economic aid with no strings attached, and a Soviet willingness to take political-military risks without the recipient country becoming a mere client state. The Third World perceives the Soviet Union as an industrial power that—like the Western democracies—has the responsibility to respond actively to demands for global redistribution of wealth. Soviet rejection of Third World claims on a share of its own national wealth makes the USSR appear not much different from the Western states.

Furthermore, the increased military presence of the USSR and its allies in the Third World evokes an enmity toward the Soviet Union among Third World neighbors of Soviet clients. Other Third World countries react with unease about the Soviet political-military presence, which acts as a reminder of their colonial experience, complete with notions of white supremacy. Still others respond with active struggle against Soviet-supported regimes. At present, and probably increasingly in the future, "national liberation movements" will no longer automatically be anti-western but will be directed against Soviet-leaning regimes as well (e.g., UNITA in Angola, MNR in Mozambique).

These dilemmas of Soviet foreign policy are clearly conditioned by the experience of Soviet-American relations, past and present. Gorbachev's actions after he consolidates his power will show how much of this experience has been absorbed by the new generation of Soviet decision makers, and how much the systemic moving forces of Soviet foreign policy can be adjusted to new realities. The Soviet leadership's foreign policy choices are more than ever intertwined with the country's domestic and imperial situation; they are complex, difficult, and troubling. Western policies in the 1980s will be an even more crucial factor in Soviet decisions about their own foreign policies than they were in the 1970s.

III

But if the experience of post–World War II Soviet-American relations has illuminated the dilemmas of Soviet foreign policy, it also suggests dilemmas for American foreign policy, dilemmas that result from the interaction of specific characteristics of the American system with the requirements of the Soviet-American conflict.

The nuclear revolution, as discussed above, requires a redefinition of many concepts from the prenuclear ear. The Clausewitzian formula that "war is the continuation of politics by other means" is one such concept. To be rational for the United States today, this formula must be rephrased to read "politics is the pursuit of avoiding a nuclear war without surrendering one's core values and interests." The difficulties that the United States faces in implementing this new formula became particularly clear in the last decade. It is against the background of these difficulties that the systemic issues or dilemmas of American policy toward the Soviet Union should be formulated. The most important of these have to do with the difficulties of preparing America for a prolonged contest with the Soviet Union; the role of ideology in American foreign policy making; the quest for consistency; continuity and flexibility in American policy toward the Soviet Union; and the question of the unity of the Western alliance in opposing Soviet expansionism. In all of these areas the nature of the American system, politics, and psychological profile plays a decisive role.

The first issue of U.S. policy making toward the Soviet Union concerns Washington's capacity to mobilize the American public by measured means to achieve the long-term support necessary to conduct an active foreign policy and to check Soviet expansionism. President Reagan's attitude and policy toward the Soviet Union, especially during 1981–83, have been widely regarded as a "gut response" of the representative of the American right. Indeed, there is no doubt that the administration's approach reflected deeply held beliefs about the inadequacy of previous American policy. Yet one should at least consider an additional explanation as well: the rhetoric of the Reagan administration, the tone of its behavior and its entire public relations management, also had the calculated aim of sensitizing and arousing American opinion to the Soviet danger. The administration was singularly successful in this regard and so created irresistible pressures on Congress to provide what Reagan viewed as the necessary funds to confront the Soviet Union with a new military and political reality. It is very doubtful whether, in the absence of Reagan's rhetoric and the sense of danger stemming from Soviet behavior which he conveyed, it would have been possible to pass a significant and largely necessary increase in the military budget at a time of recession, when simultaneous cuts in welfare spending were also being made and budget deficits were immense.

Future Soviet international behavior will in all probability continue to generate an imperative need to mobilize the support of the American public for sacrifices to preserve the balance of power with the Soviet Union. It is an open question whether in an atmosphere of normalization of Soviet-American relations, let alone "managed rivalry," the American public and its representatives will have the staying power to confront Soviet competition. To put it simply: Would it be possible in the American system to raise military expenditures very substantially even in times of recession, as President Reagan was able to do, without his efforts to rekindle the Cold War? Will it be possible for the American leadership to be interventionist, without inflammatory rhetoric and exaggeration and an atmosphere of imminent danger, when competition with the Soviet Union requires it? The question stems largely from an important element of American reality: the attention span of the American public and its support of particular policies that require sacrifices are very short. Moreover, U.S. politicians, particularly in Congress, are highly responsive to the shifting winds of public opinion, probably much more so than their counterparts in other industrial democracies.

Closely related to this problem of the nature and changeability of American public opinion and the responsiveness of its representatives in the American populist democracy is the second dilemma of American foreign policy: the consistency and staying power of American political leadership. There is something to the common argument that whatever policy toward the Soviet Union an American president adopts, it should at least be consistent and given sufficient time for its effectiveness to be tested, rather than oscillating wildly and sending conflicting signals to the Soviets, to the allies, and to the home audience.

The Reagan administration is far from being an exception to this mode of behavior. President Reagan's prolonged campaign against the Soviet–West European pipeline project was a case in point. This campaign, for the first time in the history of the Atlantic alliance, was widely perceived in Europe as an American attempt openly to infringe on the sovereign rights of West European countries; moreover, the campaign was obviously doomed to defeat from the beginning, as even its proponents recognized. It harmed the alliance and achieved nothing for its authors.

Of course the pipeline case can also be cited as an example of Reagan's consistency (or even principled obduracy), even if it was misguided and politically counterproductive. Yet shortly after this campaign President Reagan's aides engaged in an intensive effort to increase the level of annual American grain sales to the Soviets. While in Moscow, Reagan's secretary of agriculture not only criticized President Carter for imposing the grain embargo after Afghanistan but also the concept of embargoes in general. He declared that America would never again use this tool against the USSR.[3] And this occurred under ideologically the most anti-Soviet administration in memory.

Frequent and poorly argued changes in U.S. policy toward the Soviet Union during the tenure of an American administration, major and continuing clashes of opinion within it, the tendency for each new administration to start almost from scratch in formulating its Soviet policy—these are by now well-known patterns of U.S. behavior. Under these conditions how can American policy be consistent and reflect a long-range view of a preferred course of action? In the past the level of American material superiority was so high that it could compensate for much else that was lacking. This is no longer the case. Moreover, in the past the bipartisan foreign policy elite of people inside and outside the government provided an important steadying influence on presidential foreign policies. As a coherent entity, this elite no longer exists.

The third dilemma of American foreign policy concerns its lack of flexibil-

---

[3]*New York Times*, August 26, 1983.

ity and consequent tendency toward stark, "either-or" prescriptions. To express this dilemma differently, one can say that too often in foreign policy, tactical flexibility is sacrificed in the service of strategic rigidity, or that strategic goals are not served well because of rejection of a broad range of tactical moves. The typical case here concerns American use (or, rather, nonuse) of incentives and disincentives in its policy toward the Soviet Union.

In conceptual terms a broad range of instruments is now available to influence Soviet foreign policies. It includes escalating the costs and risks of Soviet expansion, manipulating the Soviet fear of confrontation with the United States, preserving an equitable balance of military power, offering rewards in economic, political, and status fields, and so on. But no combination of those instruments and the policies they serve will miraculously resolve our conflict with the Soviet Union. There are no "quick fixes." Rather, the conflict can be regulated only through flexible and effective use of those tactical instruments as disincentives and incentives. Here a key lesson of the 1970s and early 1980s is that the use of incentives and disincentives must be interrelated: only when disincentives are credible, strong, and continuous can incentives have any effect; and when incentives are offered, the effect of disincentives will be magnified.

However, from the beginning of detente the United States has been unable to offer much in the way of positive incentives to influence Soviet behavior (e.g., trade and credit agreements) and unable to make its disincentives credible (e.g., increased military spending and a meaningful response to Soviet adventures in Africa). As Richard Lowenthal characterized the situation in the 1970s, the Soviet Union had nothing to fear from the United States and nothing to lose because of the United States.[4] Therefore, during the detente period the tactical instruments available to American policy went largely unused—seemingly offering to the Soviet Union an almost total and costless freedom to choose its own behavior in the international arena. During the Reagan administration's first term the United States completely abandoned incentives in its policies toward the Soviet Union and left the Soviet Union no choice at all. Until the election year of 1984 one had the impression that the American leadership feared "contamination" of the ideological purity of its strategy by any display of tactical flexibility.

Reconciling American policy toward the Soviet Union with the attitudes and policies of the Atlantic allies constitutes the fourth difficult set of issues in America's Soviet policy. We have of course learned that the unity of the Western alliance is essential in formulating policy toward the Soviet Union, crucial in particular to the effectiveness of policy instruments chosen to influence Soviet international conduct. Without doubt, this quest for unity is frustrating. When the United States moves closer to the Soviet Union, its Eu-

---

[4]"The Shattered Balance: Estimating the Dangers of War and Peace," *Encounter*, November 1980, p. 12.

ropean allies fear a Soviet-American "deal" or Soviet-American "condominium." When the United States moves away from the Soviet Union, its European allies fear that Europe will be dragged into a superpower confrontation, or that there is an increased risk of a war being fought on European soil.

The problems of achieving unity in the Western alliance, finding the acceptable or desirable levels of American leadership within the alliance, and reconciling divergent American and West European (particularly West German) perspectives and prescriptions with regard to policies toward the Soviet Union have grown increasingly more difficult for American administrations. Soviet aggressive actions, which in the past so often unified the allies behind a common policy, produced deepening fissures within the alliance during the Carter and Reagan administrations. The Soviet invasion of Afghanistan, for instance, constituted a turning point in Soviet-American relations but provoked only token opposition in Western Europe; similarly, the imposition of martial law in Poland in 1981 was perceived by the United States as a Soviet challenge but in Western Europe was often met with tepid condemnations combined with unconcealed relief that the Soviet Union had not been compelled to invade Poland and that the Polish "embarrassment" would not spoil Soviet–West European relations. The most recent example is the first phase of deployment of American intermediate-range missiles in Europe, which the European allies—whose concerns had sparked the NATO decision to deploy those missiles in the first place—accepted with a notable lack of enthusiasm as an unavoidable political necessity, if not a concession to the United States.

It is quite easy and comforting to the conscience of many West European leaders to ascribe the differences within the alliance to American aggressiveness and lack of sophistication on the one hand (under Reagan), and American vacillation and indecisiveness on the other (under Carter). It is as easy for the American "right" to proclaim an alleged Finlandization of Western Europe or for the American "left" to embrace without reservation the European left's characterization of American foreign policy. Yet in reality the alliance's problems reside in the fact that, with regard to the "Soviet question," American and European perspectives are different and can hardly be homogenized in the future. These differences have to be acknowledged as "normal" now and in the foreseeable future, and they must be negotiated within the alliance from case to case without undue pressure.

The European perspective on the conflict with the Soviet Union is to a dominant degree shaped by the realities of the European continent and by a *Realpolitik* approach to international relations. The American perspective on East-West relations, by contrast, is that of a global and ideological superpower. It would be surprising, given the different magnitude of U.S. resources, different scale of its military power, different history, and different geopolitical situation, were the American perspective on relations with the Soviet Union to be identical with that of the Europeans.

But though the differences are real, so are the overwhelming common interests. If these differences are not accepted by the United States as legitimate in an alliance of free nations, and if the American reaction to them is not flexible and pragmatic, then the fissures in the alliance will grow. (Needless to say, the West Europeans must show a much greater sensitivity to American global interests and commitments as well. If Western Europe is the front line of the defense of America itself, the Persian Gulf, for instance, is a front line of the defense of Western Europe and Japan to which they both contribute little.)

The high level of ideologization of American foreign policy, particularly toward the Soviet Union, constitutes its fifth dilemma. On the one hand, the Soviet Union is perceived as an evil country with an immoral and despicable leadership. On the other hand, the safety and security of the United States and other democratic nations depend—as American policy makers well realize—on our ability to reach a modus vivendi with the "Kremlin gangsters."

The source of this ambiguity, and of the dilemma it poses for American policy makers, lies in the mixture of idealism and realism with which Americans approach foreign countries in general. The ethos of the American system is belief in social, ethnic, and especially political pluralism. Similarly with regard to the world political system, the explicit American attitude is tolerant, indeed supportive, of pluralism. Yet this toleration is in fact restricted to exclude some communist regimes—those that are our adversaries in the global competition.

With regard to those countries which support our global conflict with the Soviet Union, we are, or at least we try to be, pragmatic and realistic, often ignoring their antidemocratic nature and invoking in defense of our position our belief in a pluralistic world order. With regard to the Soviet Union, we are idealistic, shocked by the excesses of its regime and its antidemocratic nature, and do not apply in our assessments of it our recognition of the legitimacy of pluralism in the world order. We still consider the Soviet system—which has been in existence for nearly seventy years—some bad dream that will go away, an unnatural growth on the global body politic.

We deeply dislike the Soviet system, we abhor the past crimes and the present excesses of its leaders, we are convinced of the superiority of democratic systems. Through both governmental and private channels we aim to influence the Soviet leaders' attitudes toward human rights. But because of nuclear weapons, we have to coexist with the Soviet Union, now and in the decades to come, even if the Soviet system does not change significantly. Neither we nor the Soviets have any choice in this respect.

Were our policy one of *Realpolitik*, modeled on European tradition and example, we would be concerned only about the effectiveness of our opposition to the Soviet threat and our success in defusing or minimizing the worldwide nuclear danger. As matters stand, however, our foreign policy toward our main adversary, the Soviet Union, is confusing.

We are constantly oscillating between the imperative of managing the in-

ternational environment of our relations with the USSR and our desire to
help transform the Soviet Union. On the one hand we must seek to regulate
and manage the superpower conflict so as to prevent war and oppose Soviet
expansionism. On the other hand, we would like to change the Soviet system
(or see the downfall of Soviet power), to make Soviet-American agreements
contingent on internal Soviet developments, and to inhibit by any means
available the growth of Soviet great-power influence. Today more than ever
we are constantly torn between what our minds dictate as possible and necessary and what sentiments and our ideology portray as desirable and just.

The American preoccupation with the way other nations and states rule
themselves is well-intentioned, but it can be harmful to our interests and is almost always disruptive to the U.S. foreign policy process. The reformist zeal
to change the Soviet Union's system, though present in many former American administrations, has been especially pronounced under Reagan.

The reformist impulse in U.S. foreign policy has deep and varied historical
roots, going back to the formation of the American nation-state. At bottom,
however, lies what, by contrast to Europe, is a peculiarity of the American
historical experience—namely that the United States is what Seymour Martin Lipset calls the "First New Nation," a nation that was created and deliberately shaped rather than one that evolved in a slow, long historical process.[5]

This special characteristic of American history accounts to a large extent for
the differences between the American approach to the role of foreign policy
and those of other industrial democracies. Americans are predisposed to look
at social, economic, and political systems not as the result of organic historical processes, but rather as creations of man, which can therefore be manipulated, restructured, rearranged, and readjusted. The outlook is "mechanistic"
in that it views political systems as an engineer might look at a machine, considering all the ways it could be improved. In the sociopolitical field, in the
best tradition of the Enlightenment, the model for the improvement of other
nations is provided for Americans by America itself. In this view all nations
can and will be democratic and capitalist, if only goodwill is present and "evil
forces" are destroyed or controlled. It is therefore perfectly logical that foreign policy, America's instrument for influencing other nations, should serve
the high purpose and the commendable goal of shaping, nurturing, reinforcing the democratic instincts present in all peoples.

Other democratic capitalist nations with more "natural" origins are infi-
nitely more aware of the role that historical conditions and evolution play in
shaping the political culture, institutions, and processes of contemporary nations. Their view of others is organic, not mechanistic. Institutions evolve but
are not created. The body politic resembles a living organism rather than a
machine; and the number of and relationship among its component parts is

[5]Seymour Martin Lipset, *The First New Nation: The United States in Historical and Comparative Perspective* (New York: Basic Books, 1963).

quite limited. Hence any reforming impulse in European or Japanese foreign policy is more symbolic than real. Although such a view is often branded in the United States as cynical and unprincipled, it reflects the international reality more closely than does the marriage of American idealism and its foreign policy.

There is still another deeply rooted historical cause that has survived through two centuries and makes American foreign policy different from that of other Western democracies. As we all know, the American founding fathers believed that in the United States they were creating a superior instrument of human betterment. They counterposed what they created to decadent, old Europe and advocated an isolationist foreign policy as necessary and positive. In his Farewell Address, George Washington stated: "The great rule of conduct for us in regard to other nations is in extending our commercial relations to have with them as little political connections as possible. . . . There can be no greater error than to expect, or to calculate upon real favors from nation to nation. 'Tis an illusion which experience must cure, which a just pride ought to discard."

I would like to suggest that the isolationism of the past and the reformism of American foreign policy now are two sides of the same coin. The isolationism characteristic of the United States until this century began was, among other things, an expression of American feeling that our system is superior to all others. American foreign policy reformism is based on an identical premise. Isolationism was intended to preserve America's purity and prevent its contamination through political intercourse with old and corrupt powers. American foreign policy reformism intends through political intercourse to bring other nations to appreciate the glory of American democracy and to foster the inculcation of American values abroad. The belief in one's righteousness which underlay American isolationism for so long also constituted the basis of American interventionism and foreign policy reformism from their beginning. Wilson's "making the world safe for democracy," FDR's "Four Freedoms," Carter's human rights campaign, Reagan's struggle against the "evil empire"—all have a common theme, that national interest alone is *not* a sufficient basis for American foreign policy. They all convey a sense of mission and an optimistic faith in the results of a reformist foreign policy. In all probability we are all morally richer because of that missionary streak and outright defense of decency. We should not, however, have illusions about how effective such a crusading policy can be, how well it really serves American vital interests, or how practical and safe it is in the era of nuclear revolution.

It is not at all clear that a carefully managed policy toward the Soviet Union, with limited, realistic aims, can be sustained under the American system. Will the moods of the electorate and the media inevitably lurch from one extreme to another? It is clear, however, or it certainly should be, that the American political leadership in both parties has a duty to present to the public the grim reality of the prolonged conflict we face and the need for flexibility in the use of our foreign policy resources in the decades to come. To the end of this century, and probably beyond, democratic nations have no alternative but to face the conflict with the Soviet Union while at the same time striving to cooperate in areas of mutual interest. There is no precedent in human history for that kind of danger we now face and for the complexity of issues that we must resolve. Knowing our adversary and ourselves is indispensable to our search for an effective and safe policy toward the Soviet Union.

II

Domestic and Alliance Determinants
of U.S. and Soviet Policy Making

4

The Domestic Environment
of U.S. Policy Making

JOSEPH S. NYE, JR.

Which American president complained about the difficulty of cooperating with the Russians because they were "so corrupt, so treacherous and shifty, and so incompetent"? The answer is not Ronald Reagan; it was Theodore Roosevelt. And it was in 1911, not 1974, that the Congress first ignored warnings from the State Department and tried to use trade legislation to encourage the Russians to treat their Jewish citizens better—only to find that the Russians treated them worse.[1] These historical footnotes remind us that difficulties in formulating U.S. policy toward the Soviet Union have roots that go deeper than the past decade.

Part of the problem in formulating policy toward the Soviet Union lies in the secretive and repressive nature of that society. The Soviet Union is a black box to us. We see what comes out, but not what goes on inside. For example, we have to construct estimates of Soviet defense expenditures as best we can from the military outputs we observe, because the published Soviet defense budget is designed to conceal more than it reveals. In the absence of reports from a free Soviet press, and lacking informal access to the country's decision-making elite, we try to understand Soviet motives on the basis of their observed actions. Since more than one interpretation is possible, it is not surprising that Americans can appeal to the same "facts" to support widely divergent interpretations of Soviet reality and attendant policy prescriptions. The Soviet Union is a particularly difficult society for us to deal with.

American Foreign Policy:
Cultural and Institutional Roots

Another part of the problem, however, lies in American society. To some extent the Soviet case is merely one instance of a general American problem.

[1] John L. Gaddis, *Russia, The Soviet Union, and the United States* (New York: Wiley, 1978), pp. 41, 46.

[111]

American foreign policy making is a notoriously messy process, for reasons rooted in our political culture and institutions. The U.S. Constitution is based on the eighteenth-century liberal view that power is best controlled not by centralization and socialization but by fragmentation and countervailing checks and balances. In foreign policy the Constitution establishes an open invitation to the executive and legislative branches to struggle for control.[2] This struggle is complicated by the federal and, in geographic terms, relatively dispersed nature of the political elite; the weakness and poor discipline of the national political parties; the strength and legitimacy of economic, ideological, and ethnic pressure groups; the depth and frequency of political turnover in the executive branch after elections, and the role of the press, almost constitutionally entrenched as a virtual fourth branch of government. All these features are familiar to Americans, but they are strange to most governments.

Not only are U.S. institutions rare and complex, but they are embedded in a distinctive political culture that stresses American exceptionalism, moralism, isolation, and quick solutions to problems. As Dexter Perkins once observed, this political culture gives American foreign policy unique characteristics of moralism and publicity.[3] In addition, U.S. foreign policy, as he also noted, tends to oscillate between inwardly and outwardly oriented attitudes; between realistic and moralistic approaches, and between executive and legislative domination of the process.

There have been various explanations of such swings. The cultural explanation stresses the optimism and innocence of an isolated, Lockean liberal culture that successively encounters and withdraws from a harsh outside reality. The geopolitical explanation stresses the extent of the freedom that location in the Western Hemisphere (plus the British navy) allowed us, except on rare occasions when intrusion or encirclement looked possible and stimulated us to respond. The institutional explanation turns to the pluralism and separation of powers enshrined in our eighteenty-century Constitution, with its invitation to struggle for control of foreign policy.

A key institutional factor is the constitutional fragmentation and geographical dispersion of power in the United States. With a far broader and more dispersed political elite than the Soviet Union (or most European countries), the United States takes longer to develop or to change a consensus on policy. Such lags accentuate oscillation. To try to shorten them, the political leadership often exaggerates the degree of external threat.

One particular instance of institutional fragmentation is the division of foreign policy powers between the executive and the legislative branches. Not

[2]Edwin S. Corwin, *The President: Office and Powers* (New York: New York University Press, 1940), p. 200.
[3]"What is Distinctly American about the Foreign Policy of the United States?" in Glyndon Van Dusen and Richard Wade, eds., *Foreign Policy and the American Spirit* (Ithaca: Cornell University Press, 1957).

only does this division itself contribute to incoherence, but the executive has to simplify and exaggerate to overcome the inertia of a diverse and loosely structured body of 535 individuals with weak party loyalties. Another institutional factor that contributes to oscillations and inconsistency is the practice of political appointments deep in the executive branch. Not only does this practice weaken the ability of career civil servants to pursue a constant policy, but many members of this "government of strangers" hold office for only a few years.

Electoral politics also contribute to inconsistency and oscillation in American foreign policy. Because political power must be defended at the polls every four years, elections affect U.S. policy toward the Soviet Union. One effect is a simply "outs vs. ins" proposition. So central is the Soviet Union to American security that mishandling of the relationship is a handy stick with which to beat incumbents, particularly if they appear to be insufficiently strong against the Soviet Union. The years 1952, 1960, 1976, and 1980 follow this pattern. Then the ensuing administration, at least in the beginning, makes an effort to differentiate its new policy from that of the defeated predecessor before it returns to a central tendency.

A second variant of this electoral hypothesis draws distinctions between Republicans and Democrats. John Lewis Gaddis has argued that until the Reagan administration, the fiscal orthodoxy of Republican presidents (Eisenhower, Nixon, Ford) made them more cautious in their assessment of the economic costs of containment, and thus they followed a more selective approach to containment. The particular strategy of containment altered with partisan success at the polls rather than in response to changes in Soviet behavior.[4] Others argue that Republican presidents are better protected politically on their right flank and so have more leeway to reach accommodation with the Soviets.[5] Whatever the merits of these explanations, it is clear that the interaction between a highly secretive society and a highly fragmented one creates a context that renders a coherent U.S. foreign policy difficult to develop and implement.

A variety of devices has been suggested to improve the coherence, consistency, and efficacy of American policy toward the Soviet Union. At the cultural level, better education about the Soviet Union and the incorporation of more expertise in the policy process might help. At the institutional level, new legislative committees and executive-legislative interactions could be tried. In the executive branch, different organizational procedures can be attempted for handling such issues as trade, intelligence, and so forth. But our political culture is not likely to change quickly; our Constitution is difficult to amend; the effect of "iron triangles" of bureaucrats, congressional committees, and interest groups (for instance in agriculture) cannot easily be over-

[4]John L. Gaddis, *Strategies of Containment* (New York: Oxford University Press, 1982).
[5]Alan Wolfe, *The Rise and Fall of the Soviet Threat* (Washington: Institute for Policy Studies, 1979).

come; and the oscillation caused by electoral campaigns are unpredictable and unavoidable. These aspects of our domestic environment, virtually unchangeable, limit our choices. It makes no sense to design a strategy that requires secrecy or fine tuning if we know these requirements cannot be satisfied. We will have to settle for simpler, more robust approaches that accommodate the domestic American reality described below.

Key Factors and Changing Determinants

American foreign policy can be thought of as a pyramid. At the apex is the presidency; the base is public opinion and groups; the Congress forms the intermediate layer. The public may be some distance from the apex of policy, but the democratic nature of the culture and constitutional limitations make a firm public base critical. Shifts at that level can easily topple presidential policy.

Public Opinion

Public opinion in the United States has frequently been characterized as isolationist, but William Schneider points out that "non-internationalist" is a more accurate term.[6] Only a small minority of the American public regularly pays close attention to foreign affairs. The large majority is a nonattentive public that prefers not to be bothered. This does not mean that broad public views are irrelevant, however. The nonattentive public can be aroused by major events and mobilized to vote when foreign affairs affect it directly. Foreign policy has played a significant role in several elections, such as those of 1952, 1960, 1964, and 1968 (with Korea, Cuba, and Vietnam as focal points).

The nonattentive public is not particularly ideological in its foreign policy attitudes. It can be pulled left or right by current concerns. In regard to the Soviet Union, opinion polls show, the nonattentive public wants a policy that reflects both strength and peace. In that sense, broad public opinion supports a two-track approach toward the Soviet Union. But if at any particular moment the nonattentive public perceives a threat to one or the other of those values, it will focus on that concern.

In 1980, when the nonattentive public felt that the Carter administration had let American strength lag, it could be readily recruited to support conservative elite positions. By 1982, when it felt that the Reagan administration was neglecting the peace issue, the general public showed strong support for the nuclear freeze movement. In the absence of a policy that meets both symbolic concerns simultaneously, then, nonattentive public opinion can be

---

[6]This section follows the discussion in William Schneider, "Public Opinion," in J. S. Nye, ed., *The Making of America's Soviet Policy* (New Haven: Yale University Press, 1984).

quite volatile, quickly pulled from pole to pole by dramatic events and elite campaigns. But even so, it has been less volatile than elite opinion. The major changes in mass opinion over the past three decades, as Daniel Yankelovich has argued, have been a diminished optimism about the benefits of nuclear weapons and a less virulent anticommunism in viewing the Soviet Union.[7] The balanced concern of nonattentive public opinion serves as an anchor that limits elite opinion from excesses in one direction or the other.

Public opinion that is attentive to foreign policy tends to be better educated and, until the last decade, tended to follow presidential leadership. The attentive public was more willing to accept arguments about why we should be involved in entangling alliances, send our youth abroad, and spend tax dollars on foreign aid. Until the late 1960s both liberal and conservative internationalists tended to share a common, Cold War consensus on Soviet issues. That elite consensus fragmented in the late sixties and seventies over Vietnam and detente.

By the 1970s the attentive public was split left from right, with activists on both sides expressing their policy criticisms in highly moralistic and ideological terms. Each wing competed for the votes of the inattentive public; the left succeeded better in the early seventies, when Vietnam loomed large, and the right later in the decade, when Vietnam faded and concerns arose about Soviet advances in the strategic balance and the Third World.

Though the Cold War consensus broke apart over Vietnam, that fragmentation also reflected deeper changes in American politics. One change was in the political parties, and involved gradual party realignment and voter de-alignment.[8] Beginning with the Goldwater candidacy of 1964, Republicans gradually moved rightward and Democrats leftward. Activist elites began to care more about controlling the soul of the party than about winning elections. Foreign policy, particularly toward the Soviets, became a tool in the ideological struggles that split attentive elites and party activists. In the 1970s, moreover, the New Deal coalition eroded because of such domestic social changes as blue-collar suburbanization and the civil rights movement. At the same time, many voters were dealigning from strong party identification. With political parties split and weakened, support for a bipartisan approach to foreign policy became more difficult to assemble.

A second major change in American politics was the rise of antiestablishment politics. Divisions within the attentive elite led to less deference to presidential leadership. Responding to Vietnam and Watergate, the press became more active and adversarial, with the effect of further eroding "followership." The old establishment of East Coast bankers, lawyers, and businessmen who had tended to dominate foreign policy positions was being replaced by a

---

[7]Comments at Rand/UCLA Conference, October 18, 1984. See also Public Agenda Foundation, *Voter Options for Nuclear Arms Policy* (New York, 1984).

[8]See Gary Orren, "The Changing Style of American Parties," in Joel Fleischman, ed., *The Future of American Political Parties* (New York: Prentice-Hall, 1982).

younger and more professional foreign policy elite, an elite more oriented toward publicity and ideology and itself internally divided.[9] Finally, the rise of
television news meant that even the inattentive public was continually being
faced with foreign news it neither understood nor wished to tolerate. The net
effect was increased frustration and reduced toleration and consensus.

Public opinion also affects foreign policy through the political lobbying of
specific groups and through elections and opinion polls. By and large, more
groups seem to press negative than positive concerns on Soviet policy. There
is very little in the way of a supportive constituency for the USSR. In a nation
of immigrants, ethnic groups have long had important effects on U.S. foreign
policy,[10] but there are few Russian-Americans. On the contrary, concerns
for East European ethnic groups constrained Roosevelt, and more recently,
concerns over Jewish emigration set limits on Nixon's use of trade as an instrument of detente. Business groups have sometimes pressed for more trade
with the Soviet Union, but with the exception of agriculture, trade levels are
too low to generate strong pressures. The defense industry has close ties to
the Defense Department, and both have a general interest in worst-case analyses of Soviet policy which help increase defense budgets. But the experience
of the early 1970s, when the defense budget was repeatedly cut, shows that
theories of an iron grip on Soviet policy by the "military-industrial complex"
are greatly exaggerated.

Finally, there are groups with a specific focus on Soviet policy per se,
among them the Committee on East-West Accord and the Committee on the
Present Danger. By and large, the influence of such groups is limited. The
Committee on the Present Danger was an effective lobbyist against SALT II
in the late seventies, but its general influence may be exaggerated—it was, after all, swimming with the conservative tide in American politics at that time.
In general, groups may play an influential role on specific issues and for limited purposes, but their long-term influence depends upon the parameters set
by broad public opinion.

Congress

No legislature in a major power plays so significant a role in foreign policy
as does the U.S. Congress. Its role is enshrined in the Constitution. But how
it plays that role has varied over time.[11] The formal sources of its power over
foreign policy include the authority to declare war, to ratify treaties, to provide funds, and to confirm executive branch appointments. But the degree to

[9]See I. M. Destler, Leslie Gelb, and Anthony Lake, *Our Own Worst Enemy* (New York: Simon
& Schuster, 1984), chap. 2.

[10]Paul Y. Watanabe, *Ethnic Groups, Congress, and American Foreign Policy* (Westport, Conn.:
Greenwood, 1984).

[11]Thomas Franck and Edward Weisband, *Congress and Foreign Policy* (New York: Oxford
University Press, 1979).

which it asserts separate policy preferences depends strongly on less formal factors.

The first two postwar decades have been dubbed the period of the "imperial presidency" in part because of congressional deference to executive leadership in foreign policy.[12] This does not mean Congress was irrelevant. On the contrary, Truman was greatly concerned about garnering congressional support for his initiatives, and Senator Vandenberg was a key player in shaping policy. Moreover, bipartisanship on European and Soviet policy did not protect the administration from severe attacks on its Asian policies. Nonetheless, the existence of a broad Cold War consensus in attentive public opinion together with strong leadership in the Congress allowed the executive branch a freer hand than it has today.

The increased prominence of the Congress in U.S. foreign policy since the 1960s reflects both the Vietnam-related fracturing of the consensus in public opinion, discussed above, and the reform movement in Congress. Reform weakened the seniority system and the powers of older, more conservative committee chairmen. The net effect was to make it more difficult for the executive branch to obtain congressional acquiescence by working with a few key leaders. Some younger congressmen rejected the style of "going along with the club" and adopted an entrepreneurial approach to developing issues which would gain them attention in the media. In this they were abetted by the burgeoning of congressional staffs. The Congress has gained a more important role in foreign policy as a result, but it is a more fragmented and unpredictable role.

As I. M. Destler has pointed out, the Congress has no central machinery or committee structure that can adopt a consistent, long-term view of the Soviet Union.[13] The Congress tends to be regularly involved with competitive aspects of the U.S.-Soviet relationship which come up in programmatic form (e.g., the defense budget) but only sporadically involved with cooperative aspects (e.g., approval of agreements). In addition, Congress is responsive to group pressures, many of which focus on the conflictual aspects of the relationship.

The Congress rarely takes a leadership role in U.S.-Soviet policy. It is hard for 535 individuals, subject to differing constituency pressures, to agree on a leadership role. Rather, the Congress tends to be responsive, and in the absence of a broad bipartisan consensus it tries to constrain the executive with legislative restrictions on aid, trade, human rights reports, and so forth. The possibility of congressional leadership is not precluded: a handful of key congressmen (Aspin, Gore, Dicks) and senators (Nunn, Cohen), for example, played a leading role in stimulating a presidential commission and working with it to alter the Reagan administration's arms control proposals in 1983.

---

[12]Arthur Schlesinger, Jr., *The Imperial Presidency* (Boston: Houghton Mifflin, 1973).
[13]This section draws on I. M. Destler, "Congress," in Nye, *Making of America's Soviet Policy*.

But there are limits to the attention that a congressman can lavish on any one issue. Overall, the Congress remains extremely sensitive to the trends it senses in the public opinion to which it must turn for votes every two years.

The Executive

The single most important actor in formulating U.S. policy toward the Soviet Union is the president, but he is heavily constrained by public opinion, party activists, interest groups, and the Congress. In addition, he has to manage a complex executive branch bureaucracy that officially works for him but whose members also have interests of their own. Foreign policy is not the exclusive purview of the State Department; in fact the State Department's control over foreign policy has gradually eroded over the past few decades. Increased interdependence has blurred the lines between domestic and foreign policy. Each of the major domestic departments develops little foreign offices of its own, and pursues its own interests. Defense and intelligence are obvious examples. The former can use its vast budgetary resources and the latter its control over information to influence foreign policy. Press accounts indicate they have increasingly done so in recent years. Agriculture and Commerce also represent strong constituencies that often wish to deal directly with the Soviet Union; farm and business lobbies frequently use these departments to press specific agendas. Executive branch bureaucracies are repositories of necessary expertise, but they also exert centrifugal strains on presidential policy.

Bureaucratic conflicts do not concern simply the overall interests of the executive departments. Very often specific interest groups will work with a part of an executive department and with a congressional subcommittee to promote a particular interest, whether it be a weapons program, a trade license, or a human rights case. These "policy whirlpools" or "iron triangles" as they are sometimes called, are most effective on issues that do not receive much publicity or high-level attention. While a president can often curb such interests when he devotes full attention to them, such an effort is costly in terms of time and political capital. The smaller the amount of attention by the public and the White House, the greater is the influence of such groups on policy.

No president can expect to manage all the details of policy toward the Soviet Union—or any other of the multitude of issues that crowd his desk. The key tasks for the president are to inform the public, work with the Congress, manage the bureaucracy, and lead our alliances. These tasks establish the legitimacy of his foreign policy.[14] There are two keys to the effectiveness with which presidents have been able to cope with these tasks: first, development

[14]Alexander George, "Domestic Constraints on Regime Change in U.S. Foreign Policy: The Need for Policy Legitimacy," in Ole Holsti, Randolph Siverson, and A. George, eds., *Change in the International System* (Boulder: Westview, 1980).

of a coherent strategy toward the Soviet Union; second, establishment of a smooth policy process within the executive branch. Different presidents have performed differently on both accounts. Truman and Nixon were most explicit in their strategy; Eisenhower and Kennedy had effective processes. Carter and Reagan have not scored particularly well on either count.

A strategy, as Robert Bowie argues, is not a detailed blueprint, but it does communicate an image of the Soviet problem in terms of basic American interests, and it communicates instruments to pursue those interests at levels of cost that are acceptable to and sustainable in democratic public opinion.[15] Without a sense of strategy, policy will be pulled off course by current crises, bureaucratic forces, and congressional and interest group pressures. Given the fundamental role of public opinion in determining foreign policy, a president's ability to communicate his strategic vision to the public is an important determinant of the degree of freedom he will experience when the time comes to implement policy.

Equally important to a president's ability to determine policy toward the Soviet Union is the quality of his foreign policy process. For Truman, Eisenhower, and Ford the State Department worked relatively effectively with the White House. Kennedy, Johnson, and Nixon had White House–centered processes. The Carter administration was plagued by tension between the two. In an effort to avoid such problems, President Reagan came into office determined to curtail the growth in the influence of the National Security Council adviser within the White House, but his first Secretary of State, Alexander Haig, soon ran into difficulties with other White House staff members. And with the NSC adviser's role diminished, the White House found it difficult to mediate disputes between the secretaries of state and defense.

Some tension between White House and State Department is inevitable. A president is a political leader whose staff is closely attuned to his domestic political constituency. The State Department tends to deal with and understand the problems of foreigners. Thus the idea of simply handing foreign policy to the State Department is implausible for political reasons, not to mention the blurring of domestic and foreign policy which gives other departments legitimate roles in foreign policy formulation.[16] The National Security Council and the White House staff (including the NSC's chief) are therefore bound to play important roles in advising the president and managing the process. Difficulties arise when the NSC adviser plays a public or negotiating role, which will necessarily conflict with the secretary of state's role as spokesman. The resulting impression will be one of incoherence—which proved a serious

---

[15]This section follows Robert Bowie, "The President," in Nye, *Making of America's Soviet Policy.*

[16]Graham Allison and Peter Szanton, *Remaking Foreign Policy* (New York: Basic Books, 1976).

constraint on the effectiveness of the Carter administration.[17] Even when these two key roles are properly delimited, improvements can be made within both the State Department and the NSC staff to bring expertise about the Soviet Union to bear on policy formulation more effectively than is now the case.[18]

A smooth process and an effectively communicated strategy do not guarantee a president success in shaping his Soviet policy. Accidents and crises may drive him off course. Soviet behavior also shapes his performance. In many ways Soviet actions in the 1970s reinforced rightward tendencies in U.S. domestic politics by "confirming" the conservative interpretation. Though a smooth process and a coherent strategy may be necessary for a president, therefore, they are probably not sufficient to make him the major determinant of U.S.-Soviet policy.

When Has the System Worked?

No foreign policy can be fully consistent. By its very nature, foreign policy involves balancing competing objectives in a frustrating and changeable world. The Soviets have not always been consistent or coherent in their policies, but incoherence in American foreign policy is deeply rooted in our political culture and institutions. The eighteenth-century founders of the Republic deliberately chose to deal with the dangers of tyranny by fragmenting and balancing power rather than centralizing and socializing it. In a sense, a degree of incoherence and inconsistency in foreign policy is part of the price we pay for that choice. For better and worse, ours is a government of "separated institutions sharing powers."[19]

The executive branch has certain natural advantages over the Congress in the constitutional "invitation to struggle" for control of foreign policy. Even so, the Congress has a broad set of legitimate means to block, divert, or confuse foreign policy initiatives if it so chooses. The system has worked most coherently when the president has had a relatively coherent strategy and executive branch process, and when there was a general executive-legislative compact symbolized by "bipartisanship" in foreign policy.

By and large, this was the situation during the Cold War period. Three conditions contributed to the relative harmony between the branches of government in that era: deference to the president on the important matters; sufficient centralization in the Congress to allow congressional leadership; and a

---

[17]Compare Cyrus Vance, *Hard Choices* (New York: Simon & Schuster, 1983), with Zbigniew Brzezinski, *Power and Principle* (New York: Farrar, Straus, & Giroux, 1983).

[18]See J. Nye, "Can America Manage Its Soviet Policy?" in Nye, *Making of America's Soviet Policy*. Also Richard Pipes, *Survival Is Not Enough* (New York: Simon & Schuster, 1984), pp. 274ff.

[19]Richard Neustadt, *Presidential Power* (New York: Wiley, 1980), p. 26.

general consensus on the Soviet threat and how to meet it as the engine of postwar American internationalism.

It is important, however, not to idealize the Cold War policy process. Coherence is not the same as effectiveness: coherent policy based on a faulty appraisal of Soviet behavior will not be effective. Even when the process provided conditions favorable for making coherent policy, problems still occurred with the management of our relations with the Soviet Union. The executive branch's need to develop sustained support from Congress and the public often produced oversimplification in the description of Soviet behavior. Exaggeration is, after all, an important way of collecting power in a polity characterized by fragmented institutions and a dispersed political elite. Nuances, fine tuning, and small adjustments in course are difficult to sustain. Overstatement and militarization of the Cold War in 1950 followed an earlier understating of the problem as the strategy inherited from Roosevelt eroded in the early postwar period.

The Cold War era was also marked by difficulty in framing and maintaining support for a strategy that established a consistent, effective relationship between ends and means in American policy. This difficulty was exacerbated by our liberal political cultural reaction to the harsh reality of Soviet expansion and the resulting excoriation of the Soviets in our electoral competition. Stalin was portrayed as Hitler. As Wolfe argues, there was a consistent tug to the right in the competition between the political parties.[20] Such circumstances made it difficult to maintain support for George Kennan's conception of containment by limited means, because such an approach depended on "the ability of national leaders to make and maintain national distinctions between vital and peripheral interests, adversary capabilities and intentions, negotiations and appeasement, flexibility and direction."[21]

The threat described (and exaggerated) in NSC-68 in 1950 called for means far in excess of what was domestically feasible. A gap developed between election rhetoric and policy implementation. Eisenhower spoke of "rolling back" communism in 1952, but within six months he adopted more modest goals, and his fiscal conservatism led him to reduce the demand for military means. Excessive reliance on nuclear weapons was a means to bridge the gap between an exaggerated threat and insufficient conventional means to cope with it. Similarly, Kennedy came into office sounding like an echo of NSC-68, but later, in 1963, tried to adjust goals and means in a more modest direction in some aspects of policy (though not in Vietnam). In short, even in the Cold War era, when the parts of the political system worked relatively harmoniously with one another, that harmony had to be purchased at considerable price.

[20]Wolfe, *Rise and Fall*, p. 36.
[21]Gaddis, *Strategies of Containment*, p. 88.

Nixon and Kissinger developed a strategy that was more effective in relating ends and means. An opening to China was to encourage better Soviet behavior. Arms control agreements codified Soviet parity but were also to constrain further Soviet growth at a time when our defense budget was under domestic attack. Trade and a web of agreements on cooperation were tacitly linked to improved Soviet behavior in relation to Third World crises. The approach to detente was dictated not by goodwill or naïveté toward the Soviet Union but by the need to adjust to changes in Soviet military power and in American domestic conditions.

Nonetheless the Nixon-Kissinger strategy failed. If an effective foreign policy strategy must set forth a general, long-run vision that combines a reasonable and persuasive account of Soviet intentions and capabilities with an account of our long-term goals and the feasibility of achieving them with the means we have available, then Nixon's may have been the best strategy we have produced for the management of the Soviet relationship in the postwar period. But a successful strategy must include a third dimension—domestic political acceptance that the strategy is desirable and feasible. In that area Nixon and Kissinger were less successful.

The usual explanation is that the accident of Watergate derailed the strategy. While Watergate certainly had an effect in sapping executive strength, the Nixon-Kissinger strategy was inherently difficult to implement in our political system. It relied on fine tuning where fine tuning is difficult to manage. It relied on secrecy in a system where the media are virtually a fourth branch of government. It depended upon a personal control which worked when things went well but which left few congressional and bureaucratic allies to share the burden when things went poorly.

Nixon also succumbed to the typical American pressure to exaggerate as a way of building and maintaining consensus. His was not the exaggeration of the scope of threat, however, but of the extent of change. Pressed by Vietnam and domestic turmoil, Nixon compensated by exaggerating the new structure of peace which was being created. Moreover, as Stanley Hoffmann has written, the appetite for detente grew with the eating; detente was oversold to the American public.[22] The net effect was a sense of deception and disillusion which accentuated the ensuing turn of the cycle of attitudes in the direction of renewed hostility.

The 1970s would have been a difficult decade in which to implement any strategy of relations toward the Soviet Union, let alone one that depended upon fine tuning, linkage, secrecy, and personal control. As the decade wore on and the conservative trend in the cycle of American politics strengthened, the domestic climate for detente worsened. The period of renewed hostility at the end of the decade resulted from the coincidence of a conservative trend in American politics interacting with a Soviet military buildup and the exten-

[22]Stanley Hoffmann, "Detente," in Nye, *Making of America's Soviet Policy.*

sion of Soviet-Cuban military influence in several Third World countries. This should remind us of the important effect of Russian behavior on American domestic politics. The American political process may exaggerate and amplify Soviet actions, but the Soviets have often done themselves a disservice by their seeming failure to take into account the effects of their actions on American politics.

The oscillation in American opinion and policy toward the Soviet Union since the mid-1970s is quite striking. The high point of detente in the Nixon administration was soon followed by growing skepticism as President Ford was challenged by conservatives for his party's nomination in 1976. Jimmy Carter's presidency reflected the ambivalence in public opinion in the latter seventies. Although Carter tried to reconcile the harder and softer approaches of his NSC adviser and his secretary of state, the result was speeches (and policy) in which the different views often appeared to be held together more by staples than by overarching strategy. Moreover, Carter gradually moved from the softer to the harder approach in response to public opinion changes and aggressive Soviet behavior over the four years of his presidency. Where Carter had run in 1976 on a platform urging cuts in defense expenditures, in 1980 both Carter and Reagan advocated increases in the defense budget. Reagan's early pronouncements about the Soviet Union were particularly harsh, and arms control negotiations were put on a back burner. Yet by 1984 President Reagan had markedly softened his rhetoric and placed a high priority on renewed arms control negotiations. Whether such oscillations will lessen or continue in the future will depend on the interaction of American politics and Soviet behavior.

Prospects for the Future

The domestic environment provides four main determinants for U.S.-Soviet policy: a coherent presidential strategy and policy process; an executive-legislative compact; a relatively stable period in public opinion and political alignments; and Soviet behavior that does not stir up American public opinion. For the future there are mixed prospects along these four dimensions.

Projecting Soviet behavior is beyond the scope of this chapter, but the relative quiescence of the past few years may be a hopeful sign. If the indigestion of Afghanistan and a preoccupation with internal political and economic issues mean that the Soviets will avoid any dramatic or adventuresome acts, then a condition necessary for an improved domestic climate will have been fulfilled. Of course, such scenarios are not totally within Soviet control. Events in Poland, the Middle East, or Central America could present nasty shocks to American opinion even without Soviet instigation or significant exploitation, just as in 1980 the Iranian hostage crisis reinforced the American public's sense of impotence and negatively influenced U.S.-Soviet relations.

As for domestic sources of instability in public opinion, there may be cause for some optimism. While Reagan's elections in 1980 and 1984 did not represent a profound realignment of parties, as the elections of 1932 and 1936 did, they may have marked the consolidation of the gradual realignment that occurred in the 1960s and 1970s and that in ideological terms tore each of the parties apart. The new foreign policy professionals and the activist press still create problems for presidential followership, but there are some signs that the extreme antiestablishment fervor of the 1970s is cooling. Moreover, basic inattentive public opinion remains fixed in its interest in a two-track approach that pursues both peace and strength with regard to the Soviet Union.

If the ideological battles of the seventies have tapered off somewhat, it may be more possible to work toward some sort of executive-legislative compact or some semblance of bipartisanship in Soviet policy. One can imagine several devices, such as presidential-legislative commissions, that could help foster such a development. Thoughtful congressmen have also begun to realize that some of the congressional restrictions of the 1970s may have gone too far. The Supreme Court's striking down in 1983 of the legislative veto reinforces this trend.

On the other hand, the fragmentation of congressional leadership is largely unchanged, and the rise of ideological congressmen who appeal to the media rather than follow the style of "the club" does not augur well for efforts at bipartisanship. In the absence of presidential leadership that reaches into the middle of the opposition party (rather than skimming off a few ideological sympathizers, as Reagan did in his first term), it is hard to see very encouraging prospects for a real revival of bipartisanship.

Last but far from least is the question of presidential strategy and policy process. Given the current conservative trend of American politics and the historical record of politicians using the Soviet threat as a political weapon, Republicans have more leeway than Democrats in their ability to formulate a strategy. As Samuel Huntington argues, "Administrations that adopt an unbalanced but more consistent posture . . . are likely to come under significant pressure to moderate their stance and may be led to a middle-of-the-road, balanced policy in practice. By talking like Ronald Reagan, in short, Ronald Reagan may end up acting like Jimmy Carter wanted to act but could not. Moderation, especially in practice, may be the child of extremism, particularly in rhetoric."[23]

The Carter administration started with a two-track approach but was highly susceptible to being driven off course by Soviet behavior, by the conservative trend in domestic opinion, and by the need to mobilize two-thirds

[23]Samuel P. Huntington, "Renewed Hostility," in Nye, *Making of America's Foreign Policy*, p. 289.

of the Senate for the ill-fated SALT II negotiated with the Soviet Union. Had Carter moved more quickly or articulated his strategy more clearly (and with a single spokesman), he might have escaped these pitfalls. His potential strength was in appealing to the basic structure of American public opinion that favors a two-track approach. But the experience of the Carter administration showed that the absence of a clearly articulated strategy and a messy policy process can turn this asset into a liability as at any particular moment the public leans toward the pole that it fears is being neglected. Only a president who educates the public about the equal importance of long-term military strength and peaceful engagement is likely to escape the problem that Huntington describes.

Will the second Reagan administration be able to build more successfully on the pillars of American domestic opinion? The answer will depend on three conditions. First, there must be a clear strategy, a sense of where we want to go and how to get there at acceptable cost. Second, the rhetoric must be controlled by a strategy that gauges its effects on three audiences: domestic, allied, and Soviet. Third, there must be a policy process that is capable of formulating and implementing such a strategy.

The evidence from the first Reagan administration was not encouraging on any of these counts. While the administration policy process did settle down somewhat after its first stormy years, it did not develop a capacity for strategic formulation. In the absence of a coherent strategy and close presidential attention, it was easy for bureaucratic conflicts to paralyze the policy process. The general climate made obstruction a particularly easy tactic for those who wished to cut trade or avoid arms control.[24] As William Hyland described the situation in 1984: "Tactics dominated. Strategy has virtually disappeared. Platitudes substitute for policy. Despite occasional forays (Project Democracy) we are excessively defensive. We seem content, even smug, when some Soviet thrust is parried. As a consequence, we have rarely thought about the terms of a settlement with the Soviet Union."[25] And the problems of controlling the effect of rhetoric on multiple audiences were clearly not solved. On the other hand, the public attention devoted to these flaws during the 1984 election campaign made the president more aware of the critical domestic requirements for an effective Soviet policy.

The first year of Reagan's second term was marked by a continuation of the milder rhetoric that was introduced in 1984, culminating in the symbolism of the "fireside summit" with a new and physically competent Soviet leader. But the open disagreements among major advisers continued. The administration's strategy remained rather opaque, and the immediate results of the summit did little to clarify it, except to suggest that the administration was edging

[24]See Alexander Haig, *Caveat* (New York: Macmillan, 1984); Strobe Talbott, *Deadly Gambits* (New York: Knopf, 1984); William Root, "Trade Controls That Work," *Foreign Policy* 56 (Fall 1984), pp. 61–80.

[25]William Hyland, "Paging Mr. X," *New Republic*, June 18, 1984, p. 37.

back to the two-track mainstream of postwar American policy toward the Soviet Union.

In conclusion, the formulation of a strategy will always be crucial. This is not to deny that process matters, and a number of measures can be taken to improve the process by which America manages its relations with its principal adversary. But there are strict limits to what such changes can achieve. We can alleviate the tendency to oversimplify and exaggerate which tends to amplify the oscillations in our policy. We can improve executive and legislative procedures; we may be able to reduce the incoherence that results when different parts of our polity speak with different voices or take contradictory actions. And we can hope that the tides of political realignment will eventually ebb sufficiently to allow a centrist orientation, bipartisan policy, and cooperation between the branches to reduce the excesses that otherwise grow out of our constitutional structure.

But our political culture and institutions do not change quickly or easily. The implications of this simple-sounding proposition are very significant: there will always be limits to the types of strategies that we can successfully follow. And our ability to manage our Soviet relationship is a matter less of organization than of choosing an appropriate strategy. The basic principle for a durable strategy, therefore, is to cut our foreign policy coat to fit our domestic political cloth.

This does not mean appeasing the Soviet Union or failing to balance Soviet power. Quite the contrary. What it means is that if we pick an inappropriately ambitious strategy, we will fail in the long run because the American domestic politics will produce oscillations and inconsistency. In a nuclear age, we ignore such reality at our peril. An appropriate strategy (1) must be modest enough to fit our domestic capabilities; (2) must focus on indirect effects through maintaining our alliances as much as on the direct, bilateral relationship with the Soviet Union; and (3) should combine a balancing of Soviet power with economic engagement and continual communication. Over time such a strategy may gradually increase the transparency in the relationship, reducing the dangers of miscalculation and increasing somewhat our understanding of what goes on within the opaque Soviet society. In short, our strategy should not only manage the current threat of Soviet power; it should also seek gradually to improve the conditions that make it so difficult for a society organized as ours is to manage its relationship with the Soviet Union.

5

European Influences and Constraints on U.S. Policy toward the Soviet Union

ROBERT D. BLACKWILL

"I have always thought about American Presidents that the great thing is
to get them to do what we want."
Prime Minister Harold Macmillan to Queen Elizabeth II, 1961.

On March 5, 1946, in Fulton, Missouri, Winston Churchill, with President
Truman at his side, warned that the leaders of the Soviet Union were intent
on bringing about "the indefinite expansion of their power and doctrines."
Anticipating by thirty-five years the view from Ronald Reagan's White
House, Churchill had an immediate impact on U.S. policy toward the USSR,
an impact that many contemporary European leaders would envy in its dramatic effect if not in its judgments. As Lord Halifax, the British ambassador
in Washington, wrote to Churchill in April 1946, "there has been a steady
movement of understanding [in America] what your Fulton speech was
about and appreciating it. Many people of a kind that I hardly have expected
to take that line, have said to me what an immense service you rendered by
stating the stark realities and what an effect that had upon the thinking and
policy of the Administration. I have very little doubt that is true."[1] Even allowing for ambassadorial exaggeration and fractured English, it was.

Contrast this with the scalding reaction from Washington in the spring of
1980 to another European leader's attempt to influence U.S.-Soviet relations.
Helmut Schmidt was interested in Moscow's call for a joint moratorium on
INF deployment. After the chancellor had made several public references to
the subject, President Carter sent Schmidt a blunt message in June stressing

The author thanks his faculty colleagues at the Kennedy School, Gregory Treverton, Ernest
May, and Albert Carnesale, for their comments on drafts of this chapter and Philip Zelikow for
his research assistance. The opinions expressed here are solely the responsibility of the author.
[1]Quoted in Daniel Yergin, *Shattered Peace: The Origins of the Cold War and the National Security State* (Boston: Houghton Mifflin, 1977), p. 177.

that none of the allies should retreat from the NATO consensus. Schmidt replied defensively with an assertion that Churchill would have found unexceptionable in principle but perhaps peculiar in Schmidt's particular practice: "It has been my habit for 20 years to voice my ideas without asking anybody else. . . . It is a false conception to believe European governments don't have a right to voice their concern, don't have a right to make their proposals."[2] Yes, but if Schmidt had any objective other than addressing his immediate domestic political constituency—if, for instance, he had the longer-term goal of altering the U.S. position in intermediate-range nuclear forces—he might have remembered that he had an attentive audience on Pennsylvania Avenue in addition to the one at an SPD party congress in Essen.

Between these two polar episodes rests the body of postwar European experience. The allies have attempted to affect U.S. policies toward Moscow, and the Americans have tried to manage the opportunities and constraints that result from European stakes in and influence on U.S.-Soviet relations. The painful archetypes from these four decades are familiar. The Europeans have complained about American unilateral pronouncements, policies, and actions concerning Moscow: NSC-68, McNamara's 1962 Ann Arbor speech, the 1973 U.S. nuclear alert, the Olympic boycott, the Carter Doctrine, the Strategic Defense Initiative.

And the United States has been irritated with perceived European weakness or allied unwillingness to follow the American lead in issues relating to the Soviet Union: the 1947 U.K. withdrawal from Greece, Vietnam, the Yom Kippur War, Afghanistan sanctions, East-West trade and the gas pipeline, Central America today. At the same time these disagreements should not obscure the periods of relative harmony and cooperation from European governments in the making of U.S.-Soviet policy: the Marshall Plan, the Berlin blockade, the Korean War, the creation of NATO, the Cuban missile crisis, the Berlin Agreement, SALT II, and INF arms control and deployment.

This chapter attempts to go beyond the generally accepted if somewhat murky proposition that Western European attitudes play a part as Washington makes its Soviet policy. It surveys historical episodes of influence by the British, French, and Germans, as the most important and broadly representative of the NATO allies, on U.S. policy toward the USSR, and it identifies trends that may be relevant for the period beyond 1985. It briefly describes how Western Europe was viewed by Washington policy makers in the immediate postwar period and how that U.S. perspective and allied preoccupations affected the Marshall Plan, the 1947 British withdrawal from the Near East, and the first Berlin crisis. The chapter then examines in turn the European impact on U.S. policy vis-à-vis the Soviet Union with respect to the German question, defense and arms control in Europe, strategic weapons and arms control, Eastern Europe, East-West economic relations, and the Third

[2]Quoted in Leon Sigal, *Nuclear Forces in Europe* (Washington, D.C.: Brookings, 1984), p. 80.

World. In conclusion, it discusses the policy consequences flowing from this allied dimension for the United States as it prepares for the post-Geneva summit phase of U.S.-Soviet relations.

The Prize Is Europe

That Europe was the preeminent prize in the Cold War was an article of faith for U.S. policy makers in the immediate postwar period. Few at the time would have quarreled with George Kennan's view of August 1948, that in meeting the Soviet challenge "We should select first those areas of the world which . . . we cannot permit . . . to fall into hands hostile to us, and . . . we [should] put forward, as the first specific objective of our policy and as an irreducible minimum of national security, the maintenance of political regimes in those areas at least favorable to the continued power and independence of our nation."[3] The Atlantic community headed Kennan's list. In the same year President Truman approved NSC 20/4, which determined that "Soviet domination of the potential power of Eurasia, whether achieved by armed aggression or by political and subversive means, would be strategically and politically unacceptable to the United States."[4]

The reasons for this perspective in Washington were obvious to those involved. The countries of Western Europe represented America's cultural and intellectual parentage and the most realistic hope for a sustained community of democracies in which the U.S. experiment could thrive. A rebuilt Europe, free from communist influence, would make an irreplaceable contribution to the new international economic order that emerged from World War II. Only in a vigorous and democratic Western Europe could West Germany transcend its terrible past and become a constructive member of the international community. The military potential of a reinvigorated Western Europe would both ease the burden of America's new global responsibilities and strengthen deterrence against Soviet aggressive designs on the Continent.

The converse was seen to be equally—and frighteningly—true. A Western Europe under Soviet sway or even neutralist in orientation would deeply compromise U.S. national interests. Such a Europe would inevitably require a much greater U.S. defense establishment and a significantly increased defense budget. And twice in the twentieth century the United States with its allies had fought and defeated attempts by hostile nations to dominate Europe. To forget that Europe was in the first instance what the U.S.-Soviet competition was all about would call into question those extraordinary earlier sacrifices. The notion would have struck Truman, Marshall, Acheson, and their colleagues as an odd lapse of memory.

[3]Quoted in John Lewis Gaddis, *Strategies of Containment* (New York: Oxford University Press, 1982), p. 30.
[4]Quoted in ibid., p. 57.

With this U.S. preoccupation with the geopolitical importance of the Continent naturally came allied influence and leverage on Washington's policies relating to the Soviets, especially in Europe. In the early years after the Fulton speech, Europeans often practiced a strategy of influencing Washington by playing on their own weakness, their vulnerability to Soviet inroads. The Marshall Plan was, of course, predicated on the nightmare of European collapse. And although in a manner typical of postwar American practice the Europeans were not consulted before Marshall's speech announcing the plan, they were as usual quick to affect its implementation. Prime Minister Attlee remarked, "it was in very general terms and there were quite a lot of the Americans who didn't want to go anything like so far. They'd have been glad to see it die. But Ernie [Bevin] got on to the French and the others right away and gave it life, and that encouraged America to go ahead."[5]

The Marshall Plan not only produced this cooperation among the allies to sway Washington, it also produced an early example of allied efforts to sensitize the United States to the domestic European effects of U.S.-Soviet relations that directly affected the Continent. The Truman administration had no desire to include the Soviet Union in the Marshall Plan, but the Labour government in Britain felt differently. In the United Kingdom there was broad backing across the ideological spectrum for what Leon Epstein called an "economic bridge over the East-West ideological gulf."[6] So as Dean Acheson notes, the United States, despite its instincts, included Moscow in the Marshall Plan offer rather than "assume the responsibility of dividing Europe."[7]

The hasty British withdrawal from the Near East in February 1947 was another example of an allied weakness conferring leverage on U.S. policy vis-à-vis the USSR. It did not escape Marshall that only the United States could replace Britain in maintaining the balance of power in the region, thus stopping a Soviet advance. As he told Defense Secretary Forrestal, the British decision was "tantamount to British abdication from the Middle East with obvious implications as to their successor."[8] Clement Attlee thought so too: "By giving notice at the right moment that we couldn't afford to stay and intended to pull out we made the Americans face up to the facts in the eastern Mediterranean. As a result we got the Truman Doctrine, a big step."[9]

In the 1948–49 Berlin crisis, too, the British pushed Washington to "face up to the facts." At the outset of the crisis the British position was probably more intractable than that of the United States. As W. Phillips Davison later noted, "The parliamentary debate on June 30 makes it clear that the British recognized their vital interests to be at stake, and face the prospect that a

[5]Clement Attlee, *Twilight of Empire: Memoirs of Prime Minister Clement Attlee*, "As Set down by Francis Williams" (New York: Barnes, 1962), p. 173.

[6]Leon Epstein, *Britain—Uneasy Ally* (Chicago: University of Chicago Press, 1954), p. 45.

[7]Dean Acheson, *Present at the Creation: My Years in the State Department* (New York: Norton, 1969), p. 232.

[8]Quoted in Bruce Robellet Kuniholm, *The Origins of the Cold War in the Near East* (Princeton: Princeton University Press, 1980), p. 409.

[9]Quoted in ibid., p. 407.

showdown might lead to war. Even Aneurin Bevan, the fiery Labour Party leader who later became known as an advocate of neutralism, is said to have been in favor of dispatching an armored column up the highway to Berlin."[10] Or, as Attlee observed, "it wasn't, I think, until the Berlin air-lift that American public opinion really wakened up to the facts of life. Their own troops were involved in that, you see. Before that there'd been a lot of wishful thinking. In spite of everything I don't think they really appreciated Communist tactics until Berlin."[11]

Interestingly, the French reaction differed from that of the British. While in a sense the United Kingdom was reaching back to Fulton for its position, in Paris one saw a recalcitrance that was the shape of things to come. In a conversation between the U.S. ambassador to France and the chief of the Central European division at the Quai d'Orsay, the French diplomat said that he "personally believed that a serious error had been committed by the Western powers when the Berlin crisis first arose by overstressing the importance of remaining in Berlin and announcing that we would remain there at all costs." Expressing the opinion that "the prestige of the Western powers in Berlin could only decline whether they maintain their military and governmental forces in Berlin, or not,"[12] the official seemed to support Robert Murphy's conviction expressed to Marshall at the time that "most of the French . . . would not go into mourning, I am sure, if Berlin were abandoned."[13]

From these early episodes in Europe several themes emerge which have been repeated throughout the postwar period. Consultation on issues relating to the Soviets was not always a particularly strong suit on Washington's part. The allies had more success in getting what they wanted from Washington by working together and through professing weakness than they did by manifesting strength. As the years passed, the reality of Soviet military presence and political pressure began to alter allied perceptions—first in Paris —of how to deal with the Soviet threat in Europe. It would produce growing differences on the two sides of the Atlantic on that score. And the United States was forced to take into account allied perspectives, including those emanating from domestic European politics, in its political and military policy toward the USSR, especially with respect to Europe.

The German Question

In the last forty years U.S. political strategy in Europe vis-à-vis the Soviet Union has to a large degree centered on Germany's future. But it was not

---

[10]W. Phillips Davison, *The Berlin Blockade: A Study in Cold War Politics* (Princeton: Princeton University Press, 1958), p. 151.
[11]Attlee, *Twilight of Empire*, p. 172.
[12]*Foreign Relations of the United States, 1948, Volume II* (Washington, D.C., 1973), pp. 916–17.
[13]Ibid., p. 894.

only Moscow that troubled the West: John Foster Dulles, a good friend of the Federal Republic, warned Willy Brandt, "we shall never permit a reunited and rearmed Germany to roam around in the no man's land between East and West."[14] And twenty years later President Giscard d'Estaing told his National Assembly, "I consider that it is important for the military balance of our continent that French forces should not be inferior in number to those of the other continental military power, namely Germany."[15]

So since 1945 the allies—first primarily Britain, then France, and later still the Federal Republic—have had a major influence on U.S. policy. The American decision to proceed with the creation of a West German state was supported by the British because of a conviction in Whitehall that the United Kingdom could not afford the costs of supporting the German economy. It was opposed in Paris both because of a fear of German revanchism and because of concern about Soviet retaliation against France. But France persistently lost the early arguments about the future of Germany. French foreign minister Georges Bidault ruefully noted in December of 1946 that when France speaks of Germany, "it is a little like a voice crying in the wilderness and up to now the wilderness has not replied."[16] The inability of Paris to overcome Anglo-American agreement on German issues persisted through the Berlin airlift (France was not needed to make the airlift work) and German rearmament. And when in March 1952, in a note delivered to Britain, France, and the United States, Stalin offered a reunified Germany, neutralization, withdrawal of all foreign troops, and a small indigenous German army, once again it was Whitehall whose counsel weighed most heavily in Washington.

The Truman administration immediately saw this Soviet initiative as a ploy to divide the West, to frustrate the European Defense Community, which at that point still held some promise, and to prevent German rearmament. Bonn and Paris were equally negative, though for somewhat different reasons. Adenauer thought that the Stalin plan would ensure a weak Germany vulnerable to Soviet pressure; Schuman worried about precisely the opposite prospect, because the Soviet initiative allowed for an independent German military capability. But again it was the British argument that had the most force in Washington. Cautioning against an automatically negative U.S. reaction, Anthony Eden urged a "cleverer" Western response. The ensuing "battle of notes" between Washington and Moscow was designed by Eden to explore Stalin's offer, to see how much the USSR really would concede, and to place the blame for the continued division of Germany squarely on the Soviets.

This pattern of differing views of the United States and United Kingdom

---

[14]Quoted in Ernest May, "Soviet Policy and the German Problem," *Naval War College Review*, 1983, p. 35.

[15]Quoted in Josef Joffe, "Europe's American Pacifier," *Survival*, July–August 1984, p. 178.

[16]Quoted in Edgar S. Furniss, *France: Troubled Ally. De Gaulle's Heritage and Prospects* (New York: Harper, 1960), p. 18.

on the one hand and France, this time joined by the Federal Republic, on the other, carried on through the Berlin crises of 1958–59 and 1961. On November 10, 1958, Khrushchev proposed that the four-power occupation of Berlin should end, that Berlin should become a free city, and that henceforth all issues concerning access to the city should be the responsibility of the German Democratic Republic. If the West was not responsive within six months, Khrushchev threatened, the Soviets would sign a treaty with East Germany, with whom the three powers would then have to deal. Partly because of Dulles's fatal illness, the United States responded with confusion.[17] With both the French and the Germans contending that the Soviet threats should be ignored, Macmillan visited Moscow to arrange a four-power meeting of foreign ministers. The ensuing Geneva conference met the British objective of talking with Moscow about the problem, but it produced no result. With weak leadership from Herter and differing views among the allies, the West was in disarray.

Perhaps reacting to Western disunity, perhaps to test the new and young American president, Khrushchev delivered another ultimatum concerning Berlin on February 17, 1961: East Germany should control access to West Berlin, which must become a free city. And on June 15 he announced that if the four powers had made no diplomatic progress by the end of the year, the Soviet Union would conclude a treaty with the Democratic Republic. Again Paris and Bonn favored a strongly negative response: de Gaulle in part because he feared U.S. unreliability and U.S.-Soviet condominium, and Adenauer, who was also suspicious of Washington, because the Federal Republic could accept no legal recognition of the division of Germany or Berlin.

Macmillan saw matters differently. Worrying that the crisis could evolve into a war, he thought that "public opinion both in France and the United States was moving not toward negotiation but towards intransigence; 'anyone who talks sense is called a coward and a traitor.' "[18] Whether because of the strength of British argument or because of other factors, as the weeks passed the United States did indeed increase its interest in negotiating with the Soviets. Macmillan reassured the Queen that the Americans were "getting off their high horse."[19] But to Paris, U.S.-Soviet bilateral discussions on Berlin confirmed that, as de Gaulle had already argued, the Americans could not be trusted to defend Europe's security interests in talks with Moscow. Thus it was no surprise that the four Western foreign ministers, meeting in Paris in early August, were unable to work out a common approach to the Soviet initiative.

A week later the Berlin Wall went up. Adenauer demanded a vigorous and tangible U.S. response, and the mayor of Berlin, Willy Brandt, blamed

---

[17]See Adam B. Ulam, *The Rivals: America and Russia since World War II* (New York: Viking, 1971), pp. 299–301.
[18]Harold Macmillan, *Pointing the Way, 1959–61* (New York: Harper & Row, 1972), p. 389.
[19]Ibid., p. 391.

America for allowing the intolerable to happen. In Brandt's words, "a curtain was drawn aside to reveal an empty stage. . . . Ulbricht had been allowed to take a swipe at the Western superpower, and the United States merely winced with annoyance."[20] De Gaulle pronounced that nothing strategic was at issue. The United States seemed alarmed but uncertain, and Macmillan yearned to negotiate: "Partly because the Americans have got very excited, the situation is tense and may become dangerous. . . . The Americans wanted to issue a great and rather bombastic 'declaration' but this has been shot down . . . partly by our insistence on combining a willingness to negotiate with any declaratory reaffirmation of Allied rights and obligation. . . . The President sent me a message about sending more troops into Berlin. Militarily, this is nonsense."[21] Thus the Western powers, in the aftermath of the erection of the Berlin Wall did all they could do—which was nothing much except argue among themselves.

A decade later the 1971 Quadripartite Agreement on Berlin marked a new and more cooperative phase among the Western powers in the evolution of the German issue. Henry Kissinger was satisfied that with Washington in control of the process, the agreement would give *Ostpolitik* "a constructive direction and ensure Western unity with respect to the U.S.S.R."[22] The Heath government was acutely preoccupied with internal economic difficulties. In Paris, Pompidou was pursuing a less ambiguous foreign policy and courting the Federal Republic. In sum, and unlike the past, both the allies and the United States were committed to better relations with Moscow, and "coordination among the Western powers and with the Federal Republic [was] remarkably good."[23]

Several generalizations emerge from this brief historical review, generalizations that may be of some help as we look ahead. In the first two decades after 1945 the Europeans usually could reach no consensus on how to deal with Moscow during conflicts related to the German question, including those on Berlin. This failure came about partly because the rest of the Europeans and the United States were worried about the German danger as well as the Soviet one. For more than ten years after the war British views were paramount among the allies on the German question, but as time passed British influence receded and, especially after de Gaulle left office, the Federal Republic began to assert itself as the most powerful influence on the United States on these issues. When this occurred, and with the rise of Social Democratic governments in Bonn which reversed Adenauer's harsh policies toward the East, agreement among the Western powers was finally possible—agreement not on how to respond to aggressive Soviet actions or pronouncements, how-

[20]May, "Soviet Policy," p. 28.
[21]Macmillan, *Pointing the Way*, p. 393.
[22]Henry A. Kissinger, *White House Years* (Boston: Little, Brown, 1979), p. 530.
[23]William E. Griffith, *The Ostpolitik of the Federal Republic of Germany* (Cambridge: MIT Press, 1978), p. 197.

ever, but instead on how to promote East-West accord in central Europe. (This last point was equally true, despite Henry Kissinger's reservations, during the trans-Atlantic Conference on Security and Cooperation in Europe [CSCE] negotiations, which culminated at Helsinki in 1975.)

Thus Western consensus on handling the USSR's German policy was possible largely because of a change in approach, a desire felt first in Bonn and Moscow for accommodation. Because it is difficult to conceive of a constellation of political forces in the Federal Republic which would choose to disrupt the present stability anytime soon, a future chill would have to be triggered by the Soviets. If this is so, it seems likely that any U.S. decision to introduce instability into Central Europe, for whatever reason, would produce a grave crisis in U.S.-German relations and perhaps even a cooperative effort by Bonn and Moscow to frustrate American designs. As we shall see, this German perspective has had its most anxious expression in recent times in matters concerning European arms control and defense.

Defense and Arms Control in Europe

U.S. defense arrangements in Europe have always been shaped to a large degree by European attitudes and constraints. American administrations pay attention to allied views because the United States has little choice. Despite the judgment of some maritime strategists, Europe cannot be defended without the Europeans. To reverse Gertrude Stein's observation about Oakland, they're the there there.

In the early postwar period, as we have seen, it was the British whose influence was paramount on the Potomac, and the talk from the United Kingdom was often tough when it came to dealing with Moscow. That the United States should participate formally through treaty commitments in the defense of Europe was Ernest Bevin's visionary idea. In 1948 British views triumphed over French ones as Anglo-American cooperation was decisive in producing the decision to proceed with the creation of a West German state. The French were again losers in the argument in the early 1950s over German rearmament. With Bevin cautiously acceding to the U.S. initiative to establish a credible conventional defense of Europe which would include the Germans, and Adenauer skillfully extracting political concessions concerning German sovereignty as a quid pro quo from Washington, Paris failed in its effort to thwart the creation of a West German army.

Indeed, we can see emerging from this period a pattern that persisted until recently. From French rejection of U.S. medium-range ballistic missiles (MRBMs) in 1958, to its angry opposition to McNamara's Ann Arbor speech, from de Gaulle's rejection of Kennedy's offer after the 1962 Nassau summit with Macmillan to sell the French the Polaris system to the Multilateral Force (MLF), from France's withdrawal from NATO's integrated military structure in 1966 to the Yom Kippur War, France persistently opposed efforts by Washington policy makers to forge a unified Western policy toward the East.

If the late 1940s and early 1950s saw British dominance in allied efforts to mold Washington's calculations concerning Moscow and the mid-fifties to early seventies produced the height of French intransigeance in this respect, the past fifteen years have seen West Germany become the most influential allied voice in U.S. deliberations on relations with the Soviet Union. Largely freed from its past, West Germany possesses the most powerful and successfully sustained economy in Europe and a major political voice within the European Community. It is the largest contributor of allied troops to the defense of Europe. A war on the Continent would likely begin with a Soviet invasion into the territory of the FRG, thus making West Germany most vulnerable to attack and most crucial to defend. Recent political trends in the Federal Republic—the rise of the Greens and the SPD in opposition—have raised for some observers the question of its enduring commitment to Western security policy. And, finally, the United States must pay greatest attention to Bonn while forming and implementing its policy toward the USSR, because Bonn is the principal target in the Soviet Union's European strategy.

The United States defends forward in Germany without fortifications, therefore, because the Germans want it that way, not because of military criteria. The controversy raised by Presidential Review Memorandum 10 (PRM-10) in 1977 over whether to revise the concept of forward defense reminds us of quivering sensitivities in the Federal Republic in this regard. That the alliance is by its essence defensive is almost a law of nature in all NATO capitals, but it finds its most extreme expression in Bonn. The painful budgetary requirements of a plausible conventional defense—from the 1952 Lisbon force goals through the 1977 Long Term Defense Program to SACEUR General Rogers's current efforts—are felt most acutely in the Federal Republic. West Germany also has the most to gain from raising the nuclear threshold just far enough to strengthen deterrence, but it has the most to lose immediately if the threshold is raised so high that a third conventional war in Europe this century can be fought beneath it. Germany's recent past, its geographic location and the special vulnerability of Berlin, its historic trade and human contacts with the East, its desire for eventual reunification, and its domestic political preoccupations, all give it the highest stake among the allies in good U.S.-Soviet relations.

This is particularly true in European arms control. In the early days of MBFR, German concerns about the creation of a special arms control zone in the center of Europe were an important part of NATO's discussions on the subject. Later, after President Giscard d'Estaing had unveiled his idea of a Conference on Disarmament (COD) in Europe, Bonn was as insistent as Paris that the conference go forward despite reservations in parts of Washington. (Some in the United States believed that nothing important could be accomplished in a thirty-five-nation forum; conventional arms control in Europe should be the province of MBFR; it would be hard to keep NATO together in such a gathering; and such a conference would reduce European awareness of the Soviet threat.) In the end, and although it took years, the United States bowed to the strength of European and especially German feeling that the conference would help the Federal Republic manage the INF issue. Washington concluded that agreement on a CDE would also help maintain allied support for the human rights elements of CSCE.

It was in INF that the full force of German influence and importance was most dramatically revealed. Helmut Schmidt raised the problem first in London in 1977. The initial reaction of the Carter administration was cool, both because Washington recognized that the problem Schmidt had voiced about the Eurostrategic balance had no obvious answer and because it was an initiative born not on the Potomac but on the Rhine—and without prior consultation. And having advanced a proposition that in the end produced a hardware solution, the chancellor then insisted that a parallel arms control track would have to accompany any NATO decision to deploy INF weapons. Again, parts of the Carter administration recognized the danger that pressure would build in Europe, especially in Germany, to reach an arms control result—among some Europeans, almost any arms control result—that would make deployment unnecessary. They also recognized that the four-year period between the decision to deploy and first deployment would invite the Soviets to become a major player in the evolution of allied public and parliamentary opinion on the issue. But unlike in the neutron bomb fiasco, in which to Schmidt's consternation President Carter stunningly reversed himself at the last moment, this time the chancellor, as in the ancient Chinese curse, got his wish.

The Reagan administration inherited both elements of the INF decision but obviously, at least in its first year, regarded the negotiating track without enthusiasm. This attitude was not lost on European public opinion, which also was deeply troubled by occasional comments from administration officials who seemed to dream boldly of U.S. strategic superiority and casually to acknowledge the possibility of a limited nuclear war in Europe. The ensuing years have seen the initial phase of INF deployment, at the end of 1983. They have also seen U.S. exchanges with the Soviets which moved from the "zero option" in late 1981, through Paul Nitze's "walk in the woods" in 1982 and the U.S. offer in September 1983 for an interim INF agreement, to new INF proposals presented in 1985, when nuclear negotiations resumed in Geneva, and again in early 1986. As the allies and the Soviets well knew, all these proposals were developed with an eye to the European and, in particular, to the German public.

Thus the allies have had a major impact on the European security policies of the United States. The size, configuration, location, and military strategy of NATO forces have been decisively determined by allied considerations; what the Europeans refuse to accept is not possible, no matter what its virtues. The same is true of European arms control, both conventional and nuclear. For more than a decade MBFR has been under the microscope of allied influence, and the Conference on Disarmament in Europe might well never have occurred without strong European lobbying with Washington. As for INF, it is Helmut Schmidt more than U.S. policy makers who should take responsibility for identifying the problem, as well as for the present solution and its enduring consequences.

None of these historical patterns is likely to change fundamentally in the years ahead, although all will be under some pressure from one or both sides of the Atlantic. One constant in postwar allied military relations has been European unwillingness or inability to create, along with the United States, a credible conventional defense against the Warsaw Pact. There is no sign that the European economies in the latter 1980s will generate the funds required to make anything near the 4 percent real annual growth in defense expenditures which General Rogers indicates is necessary for credible conventional defense. And nowhere in sight on the Continent are there political forces that would give higher priority than is currently given to the defense budget at the expense of social programs. Indeed, given the complexion of most European opposition parties, quite the opposite is true.

Although technological advance will bring some improvements in NATO conventional defense, its high cost plus its made-in-America label will limit the degree to which Europeans will purchase these new items. Moreover, some of this technology alarms European politicians because of its impressive capabilities against forces closer to or even within the Soviet Union. And, finally, allied governments, parliaments, and publics simply regard the Soviet military threat to Europe as less palpably serious than does the United States, and they did so even before the Geneva summit of 1985. All this suggests that at least through the 1980s, unless the United States begins to withdraw from the Continent, NATO's conventional defense will look much like that of the past—not good enough by itself to give Western policy makers sufficient confidence but, along with nuclear weapons, perhaps good enough to deter war.

This extension of current trends is likely to hold also in the area of conventional strategy. Romantic notions that some Europeans hold of territorial defense or a "European peace order" are not likely to be sufficiently plausible in military terms or sufficiently compelling in political terms to move the present allied consensus. European governments, especially the FRG's, fear that any departure from present strategy will destabilize their delicate domestic situations. The same European conservatism will also resist Samuel Huntington's proposal for a new retaliatory offensive strategy, a conventional attack on Eastern Europe if the Soviets invade NATO territory.[24]

---

[24]See Huntington's arguments in "Conventional Deterrence and Conventional Retaliation in Europe," *International Security*, Winter 1983–84, pp. 32–56.

Whatever the military merit of Huntington's dynamic concept, the idea embodies several elements that any German chancellor in the 1980s would find decisively disabling. It alters the status quo controversially with respect to NATO military strategy in a divisive domestic political environment in the Federal Republic. It raises in West Germany, especially among the young, the sinister ghosts of 1938–39. It requires the Bundeswehr to plan and exercise for offensive operations rather than for counterattacks, a difference of major and negative significance across the political spectrum in the Federal Republic. And implicitly it accepts the initial loss of West German territory while allied forces are attacking elsewhere.

The picture with respect to NATO's nuclear doctrine is not much different. We all recognize the reasons for the eroding credibility of extended deterrence and flexible response. To address the problem, some circles in the United States have called for an effort to regain strategic superiority; others on both sides of the Atlantic wish to experiment with no-first-use declarations, nuclear-free zones, more robust European nuclear forces, or even Franco-German nuclear cooperation. Nonetheless, in my judgment we will probably see no important changes in the near future unless Washington tries to force an alteration. Although many recognize the weaknesses and paradoxes of flexible response, no alternative in sight could come close to meeting the differing military and political prerequisites on the two sides of the Atlantic. We should reduce the dangerous vulnerability of our nuclear weapons in Europe and follow the Soviets in expeditiously modernizing shorter-range systems (no easy task in itself). But U.S. policy makers most likely will have to continue to live with forward defense, conventional inferiority, and flexible response—for all the flaws and ambiguities inherent in such positions.

European arms control is also likely to see more of the same. NATO's Special Consultative Group (SCG) mechanism invented for the INF negotiations kept the allies behind the U.S. negotiating position; it also produced an increasing desire in allied capitals to have a major voice in designing American arms control proposals to the Soviets. As we know, mainstream sentiment in Europe is fiercely in favor of arms control. The allies believe that arms control holds the cheerful promise of reducing East-West tensions, especially in Europe; moderating domestic political disagreements; lowering the numbers and capabilities of weapons on the Continent; cutting defense expenditures; and, most important, avoiding nuclear war. Whatever one may think of their merits, these European preoccupations are unlikely to abate. We can therefore anticipate fervent allied pleas, particularly in the post–Geneva summit atmosphere, for U.S. flexibility in European arms control negotiations in order that a somewhat fragile European consensus on defense issues might hold. U.S. policy makers will have to manage this particular allied constraint as best they can, but at least they will face European pressures less effective in the area of strategic forces than on conventional forces.

Strategic Weapons and Arms Control

In the early postwar era the allies played an important part in American strategic weapons policy. The British, it is true, failed to persuade Washington to continue nuclear assistance to the United Kingdom while the Baruch Plan was being put forward in 1946. But in 1953–54 the Churchill government's arguments for a nuclear emphasis in the defense of Europe had, along with the difficulty of making good on the Lisbon force goals, a telling impact on the development of Eisenhower's "New Look" strategy and NSC 162/2.[25] At the time the U.S. strategic force was made up of aircraft located at foreign bases or at sea. And it was Europe (and Japan)—not the American homeland—that we were principally defending. This, too, gave the allies a more immediate link to American nuclear deployments than was later to be the case after the B-52 and the ICBM were introduced into the U.S. force.

The current trend on this issue began with Defense Secretary McNamara's speeches of 1962, at Athens in May and Ann Arbor in June. With no advance consultation with the Europeans, McNamara confidently announced that the U.S. strategic deterrent should be based on multiple employment options and a counterforce emphasis. Theater nuclear forces, he proclaimed, including those of France and Britain, were destabilizing. Harold Macmillan's later comments capture the fiery essence of the allied reaction: "Earlier in the year, from the best of motives but using the worst of all possible methods, the heavy boots of the American Secretary of Defense had trodden firmly and repeatedly on sensitive French toes. . . . He could hardly have done anything more calculated to upset his French and British allies. . . . The President . . . claimed that his Government was actively engaged in reeducating NATO, which was one of the purposes of McNamara's speech. But unhappily, while most of the boys in the NATO school contented themselves with a mild protest against the clumsiness of the master, the French . . . were almost speechless with indignation."[26] Indeed, it was only after five years had elapsed and France had withdrawn from the integrated NATO military structure that the United States could convince its allies to accept an alliance manifestation of the doctrine of flexible response, the doctrine that McNamara had unveiled in the summer of 1962. (We can assume this pattern continued at least up through PD-59, concerning U.S. nuclear targeting, in 1980. If Secretary of State Muskie was not consulted, the same was probably true of the allies.)

Later still in the 1960s the French rejected the Non-Proliferation Treaty as they had flexible response and the Limited Test Ban Treaty (TBT), thus in Washington's eyes weakening the nonproliferation regime and allied solidarity. It was also during the mid-1960s, first with MLF and then with the NPT,

[25]See Lawrence Freedman, *The Evolution of Nuclear Strategy* (New York: St. Martin's, 1983), pp. 78–81.
[26]Harold Macmillan, *At the End of the Day, 1961–1963* (New York: Harper & Row, 1973), pp. 334–36. Also see Freedman, *Evolution of Nuclear Strategy*, pp. 227–39, and David Schwartz, *NATO's Nuclear Dilemmas* (Washington, D.C.: Brookings, 1983), pp. 165–73.

that the Federal Republic began to lobby on the Potomac about nuclear issues, with an effective national position. But here, as in other early examples,
the prevailing winds of influence blew across the Atlantic from West to East.

Waning U.S. interest about allied views on strategic nuclear questions became evident again in the first Nixon administration. In SALT I, both the Interim Agreement and the ABM Treaty were negotiated without important allied contribution. One observer sounded a familiar European lament: "Some
NATO members found . . . that the United States government's eagerness to
consult turned out to mean little more than a willingness to inform others of
what it had already decided to do."[27] At the time it was perhaps enough, because in the final stages of the SALT I negotiations there was no disagreement between the U.S. and the Europeans that U.S. forward-based systems
should not be counted. And the decision by Washington to sign an ABM
treaty with Moscow fitted neatly with British and French desires.

The heated argument at the end of 1973 between Henry Kissinger and
French foreign minister Michel Jobert about the U.S.-Soviet Agreement to
Avoid Nuclear War showed again Washington's disinclination to consult (as
opposed to inform) the Europeans about strategic nuclear issues. It also
showed the allied incapacity to do anything except complain from time to
time about the matter. This pattern seems to have continued with respect to
the Ford-Brezhnev agreement at Vladivostok in 1974 and Secretary Vance's
ill-fated visit to Moscow in March 1977.

With SALT II the allied dimension was somewhat more prominent, because a proposed treaty protocol banned the deployment for three years of
ground-launched cruise missiles (GLCMs) and sea-launched cruise missiles
(SLCMs) with ranges over six hundred kilometers. Although it may seem remarkable after the 1983 "Year of the Missile" political environment in Europe,
at the time both the British and the Germans were worried that these limits
would be extended beyond three years, rendering long-range cruise missiles
unavailable for deployment in the European theater. Nonetheless, despite additional European concerns about the treaty's noncircumvention clause and
Schmidt's comment at one point that "the SALT compromise does not strike
us as being satisfactory in every respect,"[28] most allied governments lined up
strongly behind the treaty. But as Josef Joffe pointed out at the time in *Die
Zeit*, "the Bonn government has praised SALT II so compulsively not because it is wildly enthusiastic about the substance of the agreement, but because it is obsessed with the political consequences of its rejection. . . . First,
there is Berlin. . . . Secondly, there is East Germany. . . . Third, and most tangibly, there is the human aspect."[29]

This German preoccupation more with the political than the military ele-

---

[27]Ian Smart, "Perspectives from Europe," in Mason Willrich and John Rhinelander, eds.,
SALT: The Moscow Agreements and Beyond (New York: Free Press, 1974), p. 190.
[28]Quoted in David S. Yost, "SALT and European Security," in Yost, ed., *NATO's Strategic
Options: Arms Control and Defense* (New York: Pergamon, 1981), p. 123.
[29]Quoted in ibid., pp. 122–23.

ments of strategic weapons and arms control continued into the 1980s. But there is no public evidence that allied views figured in any significant way in the Reagan administration's choice of MX basing modes, in the decisions to build the B-1B or deploy nuclear SLCMs, in any of the START proposals, or indeed in the president's general conviction that the United States should build up its military forces first and then, negotiating from a position of strength, proceed with more credible arms control.

Finally, the president's Strategic Defense Initiative apparently reached allied leaders after the American people had heard it from the Oval Office. Unable to influence the concept before the speech, some allies expressed their views, often not for attribution, in the months after the event: U.S. ballistic missile defense could bring the return of Fortress America, leaving Europe perilously vulnerable; a similar Soviet effort would threaten the penetrability of British and French strategic forces; and an eventual abrogation of the ABM Treaty would pull down the last remaining pillar of detente. Nonetheless, President Reagan's determination to pursue SDI, as expressed at the Geneva summit, clearly reflects both some carefully defined European governmental support in 1984–85 (especially by Britain and Germany) for strategic defense research and the general limits of allied influence in this area.

Looking back at the historical experience, the extent of allied influence on U.S. decisions concerning its strategic offensive forces, and recently its possible strategic defenses, seems mostly marginal. When the matter of U.S. forward-based systems has been raised in U.S.-Soviet negotiations in the past fifteen years, the majority view of the Europeans—to exclude those systems from the talks—has been identical to that of successive U.S. administrations. No singular allied influence is apparent. On nontransfer and noncircumvention clauses, too, the Europeans have had strong views, but again these have differed little from those of the United States. In most U.S. decisions regarding the makeup of strategic forces and research into strategic defense, as well as its positions in the SALT I, SALT II, START, and the nuclear and space negotiations, in sum, the allies were not consulted in any effective way and played a negligible role in the formulation of these particular U.S. policies toward the USSR. (One exception may have been the allied role during the fall of 1985 in the Reagan administration's decisions to continue to observe SALT II provisions as long as the Soviets do likewise and to abide by a restrictive interpretation of the provisions of the ABM Treaty.) Only in the LTBT, NPT, and Comprehensive Test Ban negotiations did various European governments take a direct and important part in U.S. deliberations and then only because their cooperation or participation was indispensable to Washington.

The reasons for this usually faint allied influence are not likely to change significantly anytime soon. The composition of U.S. strategic forces and the issue of strategic defense are now driven by Soviet military developments, Service and civilian preferences in the Department of Defense, arms control implications, congressional and public attitudes, and high U.S. domestic politics. The Europeans are both too remote from this complex process and have too little to offer to buy themselves into the game. And in trying to influence American strategic arms control policy toward the Soviet Union, the Europeans suffer from essentially the same liabilities as they do with regard to decisions concerning weapons systems.

But there is a possible allied opening here. Were the START and INF negotiations ever to merge, one European objective would surely be to penetrate the hard U.S. shell surrounding strategic arms talks, not least because of the growing importance of "gray area" systems. Precisely because of that likelihood, future U.S. administrations will try to avoid such a merger. Even less likely, it seems to me, are cuts in U.S.-Soviet strategic weapons sufficiently deep to bring French and British forces even indirectly into the negotiations as Gorbachev proposed in Paris in October 1985. Were that to happen, however, Paris and London would probably insist that they participate in the development of the U.S. negotiating position.

Eastern Europe

The Europeans may not have had an irresistible interest in and influence on U.S. strategic weapons issues, but American policies toward Eastern Europe are another matter. After Churchill had failed to persuade Roosevelt to adopt a military strategy that would reduce the likelihood of Soviet postwar domination of Eastern Europe, the allies had no desire to intervene there to support anti-Soviet elements. At the time of the Czech coup in 1948, George Marshall noted his concern "at the probable repercussions in Western European countries of a successful Communist coup in Czechoslovakia without challenge or consequences. We feel that there is a real possibility that such a development in Czechoslovakia would stimulate and encourage Communist action in Western European countries, particularly in Italy."[30] However, Marshall's search for "tangible steps" went for naught. Bevin concluded that "we were impotent in the matter," and Bidault told the American chargé in Paris that any "demarche in Prague was useless."[31] With this fatalistic conviction rife among the allies, the United States, the United Kingdom, and France contented themselves with a declaration of protest.

Despite calls for rollback by the Eisenhower administration, the Soviet invasion of Hungary in late 1956 produced another limp Western response. The British and French were distracted by Suez, and although Adenauer's distrust of Moscow was confirmed, the Federal Republic too had nothing to suggest. As for the United States, it announced it would act only within the United Nations and through humanitarian appeals.[32]

---

[30]*Foreign Relations of the United States, 1948, Volume IV* (Washington, D.C., 1974), p. 736.
[31]Bevin and Bidault are quoted from ibid., p. 737.
[32]Ulam, *The Rivals*, p. 265.

It was more of the same when the Red Army crushed Czechoslovakia in August 1968. Wanting a summit with the Soviets, Lyndon Johnson in essence looked away. Richard Crossman, who was in the Wilson cabinet in Britain at the time, reported that the Foreign Office "which only wants to keep in with the Americans . . . [is] anxious to accept a Russian-imposed *fait accompli*." (As a sign of things to come, the British Board of Trade warned against upsetting the country's improving trade relations with the USSR.)[33] French foreign minister Michel Debré called the Soviet invasion a "traffic accident" on the road to detente. And in Bonn Chancellor Brandt, in a theme that was also to become familiar from the SPD as the years passed, hastened to argue that the Soviet invasion made improved East-West relations more important than ever. "Gritting my teeth," he later recalled, "I clung to the realization that we had, even now, to maintain a course aimed at reducing tension—partly, if it ever became possible, in order to prevent tragedies like the one in Prague. . . . We could not accept this as the end of Ostpolitik."[34]

We will look later at the imposition of martial law in Poland in the context of East-West economic relations. Once again there was no willingness on the part of the Reagan administration or of the allies to challenge in any fundamental way the status quo in Eastern Europe. As Secretary Haig observes in his memoirs, Washington warned against outside intervention but did nothing to "encourage futile Polish resistance."[35] And although the Europeans were willing verbally to caution the Soviets before the crackdown, after December 1981 the allies stubbornly opposed those in the Reagan administration who wished to force Poland into debt default and stop the gas pipeline. Prime Minister Thatcher carefully explained to Haig in January 1982 that "the United States must understand that the continental Europeans profoundly believed that they needed the pipeline and would desert the United States on this issue rather than abandon it."[36]

Later in the year the bitter allied reaction to the president's June 18 sanctions against them confirmed both Mrs. Thatcher's forecast and the continuation of a pattern of passive European behavior regarding Soviet power in Eastern Europe which stretched back nearly forty years. When Soviet suppression of Eastern Europe has been both egregious and public, the allies have been willing publicly to condemn such action on Moscow's part, but little more. For most of the period U.S. policy has been essentially the same as that of the Europeans. When the Reagan administration tried to depart from the pattern, in 1982, it partially turned the brutal suppression of Solidarity from an East-West into a trans-Atlantic conflict.

[33]Richard Crossman, *The Diaries of a Cabinet Minister,* vol. 3: *1968–1970* (New York: Holt, Rinehart & Winston, 1975), pp. 171–72.
[34]Willy Brandt, *People and Politics: The Years 1960–75* (Boston: Little, Brown, 1976), pp. 217–18.
[35]Alexander M. Haig, Jr., *Caveat: Realism, Reagan, and Foreign Policy* (New York: Macmillan, 1984), pp. 240–41.
[36]Quoted in ibid., p. 255.

With the passage of time and the growing European commitment to (and investment in) East-West stability in Europe, one would have to guess that this deep allied reticence will continue well into the next phase of U.S.-Soviet relations. Any U.S. effort to organize stronger reactions to future Soviet crackdowns in Eastern Europe will therefore probably meet the same fate as President Reagan's attempt with the Europeans in 1981–82. Only a bloody military intervention by the Red Army might lead the allies to consider mild retaliatory steps, such as briefly suspending arms control talks and high-level political contacts.

East-West Economic Relations

It should follow that the allies are also highly unlikely to agree to significant constraints on Western trade with the East. This commerce is centuries old for the northern Europeans, especially the Germans. In addition, for the allies trade with the Soviet Union now represents jobs, entrenched domestic political interests, and a concrete manifestation of improved East-West relations in Europe.

Thus it was that after Afghanistan and in the wake of the partial grain embargo by the United States, the European Community increased its grain sales to the USSR. Nor was this all. In gross violation of what President Carter believed were personal commitments by Schmidt and Giscard d'Estaing, Germany and France filled in for U.S. companies and contracted to build aluminum and steel plants in the Soviet Union. This was quite apart from the European view, held with special intensity in Bonn, that Western economic sanctions against the USSR might provoke Soviet retaliation against Berlin, the Eastern Treaties, or the arms control process. As Cyrus Vance reports, "insofar as trade sanctions and export credits were concerned, they [the Europeans] refused to take strong steps."[37]

With respect to Poland in 1981–82, the European response was similar, and for similar reasons, to an even more ambitious idea emanating from parts of Washington. Haig records the following exchange with the British prime minister: "The President was thinking of doing more. It was possible, I said, that he would impose a total embargo on the Soviet Union. . . . At these words, a silence fell over the luncheon table. Mrs. Thatcher gasped."[38] It does seem, therefore, that with these fruitless attempts in 1980–82 by the Carter and Reagan administrations, the allies essentially won the argument. European influence, along with other factors, has now turned the tide decisively against serious Western constraints—including constraints by the

[37]Cyrus Vance, *Hard Choices: Critical Years in America's Foreign Policy* (New York: Simon & Schuster, 1983), p. 392.
[38]Haig, *Caveat*, p. 256.

United States—on trade with the Soviet Union, except in the case of narrowly military technology transfer or when war seems likely. The apparent absence of any serious attempt by the Reagan administration to persuade the allies to include economic sanctions in the Western reaction to the Soviet shooting down in August 1983 of Korean airliner 007 appears to confirm unyielding European hesitation to use economic instruments in response to Soviet transgressions on the Continent or in the Third World.

The Third World

Although U.S. frustration over European unwillingness to resist strongly Soviet inroads outside Europe had its most recent and painful manifestation after the Soviet invasion of Afghanistan, it is not a new phenomenon. Britain's refusal in 1946−47 to match Soviet support for the Communists in the Greek civil war and its general withdrawal from the Middle East forced the United States to assume Western responsibility for the geopolitical future of Greece, Turkey, and Iran. During the Korean War the British worried both about the effects on the defense of Europe of the commitment of so many U.S. troops to such a remote location and about the possibility that Moscow would escalate the crisis horizontally, into Europe.

And although the Cuban missile crisis provided an extraordinary example of allied support for the United States in a crisis with the Soviets, Macmillan did ask himself, "Was it not likely that Khrushchev's real purpose was to trade Cuba for Berlin? If Khrushchev were stopped with great loss of face in Cuba, would he not be tempted to recover himself in Berlin? Indeed, might not this be the whole purpose of the exercise—to move forward one pawn in order to exchange it for another?"[39] (Twenty years later, in 1981, press reports that Alexander Haig wished to "go to the source" and confront Cuba excited similar concerns in Europe, and after the Soviet invasion of Afghanistan a prominent German strategist asked if President Carter wished to trade Kabul for Berlin.)

A phrase in Macmillan's first message to Kennedy at the outset of the Cuban crisis also makes one wonder how the Europeans would have reacted even to the unambiguous Soviet challenge that a second Cuban missile crisis would represent: "Many of us in Europe have lived so long in close proximity to the enemy's nuclear weapons of the most devastating kind that we have got accustomed to it. So European opinion will need attention."[40] That, for the post−Geneva summit phase of U.S.-Soviet relations, is putting it mildly.

The Europeans, of course, had no taste for America's involvement in Vietnam. The Wilson government supported Johnson at considerable do-

---

[39]Macmillan, *At the End of the Day*, p. 187.
[40]Ibid., p. 189.

mestic political cost, not least because of U.S. support for sterling and Rhodesian sanctions, but it brought no real conviction to the task. The Germans gave reluctant and modest political assistance, and Erhard maintained a good relationship with Johnson until the dollar-drain crisis of 1966. De Gaulle told Harold Wilson that "the U.S. should leave Vietnam. The U.S. paid no attention, of course. . . . [France] was not going to be drawn into someone else's war. The French were not so rich that they could afford to ruin themselves for this kind of reason. They were too fond of life. They would not go down this road with the United States."[41] Most decisively, the United States requested troops from the European allies in 1965–66; it got none.

The Europeans appeared to feel the same way during the 1973 Middle East war. Even as Washington was stressing that the war's strategic importance stemmed from the dangers of advances by Moscow or its radical Arab clients and even Soviet military intervention, the allies publicly disassociated themselves from U.S. objectives and actions, especially the airlift in support of Israel. According to Kissinger's account, the British made it clear that they would not allow the use of U.S. bases in the United Kingdom for intelligence gathering in the Middle East. France banned U.S. aircraft from resupplying Israel from its airspace and worked to protect its relations with Moscow and the Arab world. The Federal Republic refused to allow Israeli ships to use its ports to pick up U.S. equipment, and for a time it denied use of its airspace to the United States for the resupply effort.[42] As for the U.S. "DefCon III" alert of its military forces near the end of the war, Willy Brandt, the German chancellor at the time, concludes conveniently in his memoirs, "It is fair to assume that the stand-to ordered by Kissinger and secret service Chief William Colby on the President's authority was attributable to a false evaluation of intelligence reports."[43] Kissinger seems not far wrong in his conclusion that the allies were determined "to opt out of any possible crisis with the Soviet Union."[44] Cyrus Vance, with his customary restraint, has put the allied reaction to Afghanistan well. "Because of their geographical propinquity to the Soviet Union and their understandable desire to protect the concrete gains of detente, our allies were reluctant to react as strongly as we did. Rather than risk the stability so slowly and painfully won in Europe, they preferred to leave to the United States the task of deterring Soviet adventures outside of Europe. This came perilously close to the mistaken idea that detente and Western European–Soviet relations can be isolated from events elsewhere."[45] Perilously close indeed, one might add.

While such episodes appear to suggest that the Europeans may well not

[41]As quoted in Harold Wilson, *The Labour Government, 1964–70: A Personal Record* (London: Weidenfeld & Nicholson, 1971), p. 404.

[42]Henry A. Kissinger, *Years of Upheaval* (Boston: Little, Brown, 1982), p. 709.

[43]Brandt, *People and Politics*, p. 463.

[44]Kissinger, *Years of Upheaval*, p. 710.

[45]Vance, *Hard Choices*, p. 393.

come to the direct aid of the United States in future Third World crises with the Soviets, another troublesome consequence of this allied attitude is not always sufficiently recognized. In a familiar war game the United States—having failed to stop a Soviet invasion of Iran through conventional means—considers the use of nuclear weapons to slow the Soviet advance and force a recalculation in Moscow. Even in so desperate a circumstance and even with the Gulf's oil at risk, what would be the reaction in European governments, parliaments, and publics to a possible U.S. first use of nuclear weapons against the USSR? Would a positive decision by the president save the oil only to shatter the alliance? The choice would not be an easy one for an American president to make, and similar contingencies might threaten in other parts of the world.

Policy Consequences for the Next Phase of U.S.-Soviet Relations

Some of the allies may worry in the future, as they have done periodically in the past, about U.S.-Soviet condominium. But from the record of the past twenty years it seems relatively safe to conclude that the Europeans will not soon call on Washington to be tougher on Moscow. Instead, historical review suggests that most allied constraints and influences on the United States in the years ahead will emanate from tension, not from cooperation, in the superpower relationship:

The Federal Republic of Germany will be at the heart of these allied constraints; this is largely because, as Ernest May has pointed out, "nothing —*nothing*—could so disturb and endanger international relations as a German state offering to play makeweight in the balance of power."[46]

The Germans will strongly oppose any U.S. action or policy that threatens to disrupt the status quo in Europe, especially in Berlin. The Federal Republic will be supported by most of the other allies.

The Europeans in general and the West Germans in particular will resist any direct U.S. attempt to promote instability in Eastern Europe, even if turbulence there initially results from indigenous attempts to loosen the Soviet grip.

Because they are unlikely to be replaced anytime soon, NATO's forward defense, flexible response, and inferior conventional balance, will continue to confront the United States with a now familiar prospect: it could lose a conventional war in Europe if it does not use nuclear weapons first, but if it does use them the escalatory consequences are uncertain. Neither Western conventional defense efforts, emerging technologies, nor schemes to change the alliance's nuclear doctrine are likely fundamentally to alter NATO's long-time dilemmas in this respect.

The Europeans will continue to find in arms control, especially in Eu-

---

[46]Ernest May, "American Forces in the Federal Republic: Past, Present and Future," in *The Federal Republic of Germany and the United States* (Boulder: Westview, 1984), p. 170.

rope, an activity ideal to their regional preoccupations and objectives. No U.S. administration will be able to resist for long, without strains in U.S.-European relations, allied arguments for frequent American flexibility in various arms control forums in order to promote East-West relations in Europe and to put the blame for lack of progress on Moscow. Similarly, any attempt by the United States to deemphasize arms control in the superpower relationship, however compelling the reasons for doing so, would have to anticipate significant collateral damage in Western Europe.

U.S. decisions regarding its strategic forces will continue to be made free from significant allied influence; much the same will also be true of strategic arms control, even though the Europeans will remain highly concerned about the impact of SDI on the Geneva negotiations concerning offensive nuclear weapons and about any U.S. challenge to the ABM Treaty. In addition, the allies will pay close attention to the effects of any American START or INF proposal on nontransfer and noncircumvention issues, "gray area" systems, and French and British forces. The allies would have to be directly involved in any renewed U.S. effort to seek further limits on nuclear testing.

The allies will oppose constraints on East-West trade in general, with the exception of narrowly defined technology with direct military applications, and economic sanctions against the Soviet Union in particular. In the case of sanctions, the United States would probably face the choice between adopting unilateral economic sanctions or no economic sanctions at all.

In most Third World crises with the Soviets, the United States should expect little tangible support from its allies. The Europeans, moreover, who want no part of horizontal escalation, will fiercely resist the attempt to import any such crisis into Europe.

These likely allied views should allow the United States to pursue more or less its current European security policy. In a crisis outside Europe, however, Washington cannot realistically anticipate allied assistance to any important extent in meeting the Soviet military challenge.

On the other hand, the Europeans will remain willing to try to reduce Soviet opportunities through moderating regional disputes (Zimbabwe, Namibia, Lebanon); through economic assistance (Portugal, Turkey, Pakistan, Egypt); or, in the French case, through protecting its interests in Africa by use of the Foreign Legion.

To put it another way, unless Moscow wants it otherwise, Europe has largely established itself as an island of detente, an area predominately free of East-West tensions generated elsewhere. The United States can choose to work with the Europeans within the central constraints dictated by this unhappy state of affairs while pushing hard at the margins for improvements; it can choose to challenge those central constraints, thus producing crises within the alliance like those of 1973, 1980, and 1982; or it can begin disengagement from the Continent.

Calls like those by Helmut Schmidt, Henry Kissinger, and Lord Carrington for Western agreement on a global strategy toward the Soviet Union are well intentioned but unlikely to be realized. For all the reasons developed above, no such unified U.S.-European approach to Moscow's strategic ambitions has ever existed, nor is one likely to exist in the next several years. In fact, from NSC-68 through the "New Look," the early Nixon National Security Study Memorandums (NSSMs), the Carter administration's PRM-10 and Presidential Directive 18 (PD-18), and the Reagan administration's 1982 strategic review, the allies seem to have been consulted by Washington superficially or not at all in the course of administration studies of U.S. global strategy toward the USSR. The same appears generally to be true of comprehensive presidential statements on the subject, from President Kennedy's 1963 speech at American University through President Reagan's televised address to the nation on January 16, 1984, and the president's clearly personal conclusions about U.S.-Soviet relations as he conveyed them on November 21, 1985, to the Congress and the American people following his private conversations with General Secretary Gorbachev at the Geneva summit.

Conclusion

To some Washington policy makers considering the European element in U.S. attempts to contain the USSR, the picture developed above may seem a bit grim. It may seem especially unpalatable in view of the unique nature of the American commitment to the defense of Europe. In historical terms, that U.S. treaty obligation is nothing less than a sustained unnatural act. Arthur Vandenberg had good reason to say at the time that, "if this North Atlantic Pact is going to take on the . . . character of a permanent military alliance . . . there just ain't going to be any North Atlantic Pact, because you won't get the votes for it."[47] But Vandenberg was wrong. Often it is the capacity of nations and alliances to evolve with changing circumstances which allows them to remain vigorous and effective. Nothing in the foregoing is meant to suggest that these allied trends are necessarily immutable. (In this connection I am mindful, incidentally, that for 40 percent of those with serious heart ailments, the first symptom is death.) Sudden changes do occur, in life and in alliances, but sometimes the results are even positive.

Nevertheless, American administrations should take seriously the lamentable fact that energetic U.S. efforts in the last decade to change engrained patterns of European behavior have not met with signal success. Why did those efforts fail? The enduring trans-Atlantic bargain does not include—nor did NATO's 1967 Harmel Report, the most successful review of East-West relations in alliance history—the propositions that the West might itself upset

[47] Quoted in ibid., p. 159.

stability in Eastern or Central Europe; that the West might apply economic sanctions against the Soviet Union; that the allies would give direct assistance to U.S. efforts to contain the Soviet military threat in the Third World; or that the arms control process might bring in its train some inherent liabilities for the West.

One can be confident, at a minimum, that these notions will continue to be extraordinarily tough to sell to European governments, parliaments, and publics, and that any progress from Washington's point of view will be slow. Indeed, any U.S. attempt to change these deeply entrenched allied attitudes in a hurry is much more likely to produce a rupture in trans-Atlantic relations than to modify European behavior. A long-term U.S. strategy toward the Soviet Union in the Gorbachev period might wish to take this probable reality into account.

At the same time the allies do contribute the bulk of NATO forces immediately available to meet a Soviet attack on Europe: 90 percent of the ground forces, 80 percent of the tanks, 90 percent of the armored divisions, 80 percent of the combat aircraft, and 70 percent of the fighting ships. In addition, the allies have three million men and women on active duty and another three million in the reserves. As INF deployment indicates, moreover, policies managed skillfully from Washington, as in 1982–83, and a bit of luck can sometimes overcome neutron bomb fiascos, untoward comments from Washington officials, peace movements, and allied reservations about the European nuclear issue. But influential U.S. politicians and strategists doubt that this tangible contribution from the allies is sufficient.

It is thus fair to ask whether the enormous growth of Soviet military power and the renewed prominence of U.S. interests in Asia should outweigh the importance of Europe and consequent allied constraints in Washington's calculations concerning the USSR. That complicated cost-benefit analysis is outside the province of this chapter, but one might begin by testing the assumptions held by U.S. policy makers in the early postwar years. Most crucially, does Western Europe remain the preeminent prize in the strategic competition between the United States and the Soviet Union? Is it still an irreplaceable asset as the United States seeks to protect its way of life and strengthen its global position in the next phase of U.S.-Soviet relations? I would wish the allies to make a substantially greater contribution to meet the Soviet threat inside and outside Europe, but in essence I would answer these questions no differently from Truman, Marshall, and Acheson.

6

The Domestic Environment
of Soviet Policy Making

DIMITRI K. SIMES

Mikhail Gorbachev's accession to power has had an immediate and profound impact on the way decisions are made in the Soviet Union. For years
observers assumed that the Soviet political system was dominated by institutions rather than by personalities. Bureaucratic compromise was perceived as
a principal tool in reaching key decisions in Moscow. This is no longer the
case.

In less than a year Gorbachev—while still not quite a dictator—established himself as a strong and undisputed leader. A product of the party apparatus, the new General Secretary is sensitive to the interests and the mindset
of the ruling elite. But unlike his predecessors—with the possible exception
of Yuri Andropov during his brief tenure—Gorbachev seems to act as the
master rather than as a servant of the bureaucracy.

Not only did Gorbachev, during his first months in office, succeed in
restructuring the Politburo in a fashion assuring his predominance, he also
proceeded with a virtual purge of the top echelon of the party-government
structure. By the end of 1985 there had been a personnel turnover in 22 (out of
more than 80) ministerial positions, 40 of the 157 first secretaries of regional
party committees (including a key post of the Moscow City Party Committee), and 4 of the 15 first secretaries of the Soviet republics.[1] The security and
stability of the cadres, which were taken for granted during the Leonid
Brezhnev era virtually regardless of performance, have quickly become a matter of the past.

Still, Gorbachev is not a free agent. Although the new General Secretary is
more vigorous, assertive, and creative than any Soviet leader since Nikita
Khrushchev, he still has to operate within a well-established political and organizational framework. Significantly, the campaign to replace the old guard

[1]*Washington Post,* December 25, 1985.

has not yet resulted in new blood being coopted from outside the system. On the contrary, like the general secretary himself, officials appointed by Gorbachev almost invariably come from traditional backgrounds in the party apparatus and heavy industry. The principal difference between them and those being retired is generational. People in their seventies are being replaced by individuals in their mid-fifties to early sixties who, during the stagnation at the top characteristic of the Brezhnev period, waited for their chance with increasing impatience. There is no evidence yet that this "Gorbachev generation" is fundamentally different in terms of its basic outlook and intentions. Nor is there evidence that Gorbachev is willing or able to introduce radical departures from the patterns of the past. It is the conduct rather than the substance of Soviet policies which has undergone an impressive change since the death of Konstantin Chernenko.

General Context

It is no wonder that the absence of reliable information, coupled with the difficulties of comprehending the alien Russian/Soviet political culture, causes even well-informed Western analysts to disagree on the very basics of how the Soviet system functions today. To illustrate the point, one much quoted American political scientist seriously argues that "the Soviet leadership almost seems to have made the Soviet Union closer to the spirit of the pluralist model of American political science than is the United States."[2] And this observation is presented, not as a comment on the deficiencies of the "pluralist model," but rather as a genuine insight into the way the Soviet Union is governed.

Conversely, a respected historian of Russia argues that "since 1953, the Soviet Union has been run by a Stalinist elite acting as a collective body, a bureaucratic oligarchy originally created to serve the interests of a despot but emancipated from despotic whim and dedicated to the pursuit of its own interests instead."[3] Little allowance is made here for the possibility of meaningful divisions within the elite. Nor is there a supposition that this privileged group may enjoy some domestic legitimacy and be interested in something other than the most cynical pursuit of self-serving interests—"it knows how to intimidate and manipulate people, but not how to govern them, inasmuch as government always entails some measure of persuasion and consent."[4]

The domestic context of Soviet policy making is not limited to the interests of the bureaucratic elite and particularly the party apparatus, but it is domi-

---

[2]Jerry F. Hough, *The Soviet Union and Social Science Theory* (Cambridge: Harvard University Press, 1977), p. 10.
[3]Richard Pipes, *Survival Is Not Enough: Soviet Realities and America's Future* (New York: Simon & Schuster, 1984), p. 39.
[4]Ibid., p. 46.

nated by them. Michael Voslensky, formerly a senior Soviet foreign affairs analyst, does not overstate his case when he claims bluntly that "power in the Soviet Union is the dictatorship of nomenklatura"[5]—referring essentially to a list of senior positions, an appointment to which requires a top-level clearance.

In the absence of Western-style checks and balances, independent media, or any officially sanctioned opposition outside the institutional framework, it is no wonder that the ruling bureaucracy tends to identify its own interests with those of the country.

Foremost on the list of these interests is using foreign policy to improve the stability and prestige of the regime. There is a continuing debate among Western students of Soviet affairs as to whether the very nature of the Soviet system presupposes the constant search for legitimacy through international expansionism. Surely conservative and cautious Soviet leaders are not likely, consciously, to engage in risky and costly adventures in the world arena just to prove that history is still on their side. Revolutionary zeal as practical policy guidance is clearly a thing of the past.

Still, the international status quo is plainly unacceptable. When the Soviet Union under Brezhnev engaged in the pursuit of detente with the United States and detente euphoria existed at the time—not only in Washington but also in Moscow—the general secretary still felt obliged to stress that there would be no modus vivendi with imperialists. Detente was portrayed as the newest, most sophisticated and effective form of class struggle.[6]

On the other hand, the same search for legitimacy which encouraged expansionism was simultaneously reflected in the other side of Soviet foreign policy—an attempt to gain at least a symbolic status of geopolitical equality with America. Being accepted as an equal of the United States was a long-time ambition of the Soviet ruling strata. Unfortunately, once given, the reward was difficult to take back. And as a result, its moderating impact on the Soviet's international behavior was likely to be tempered as Moscow acquired confidence in being viewed as second to none both at home and abroad.

The Soviet media coverage of the November 1985 Geneva summit has demonstrated, however, that although the Kremlin is not prepared to pay with serious, substantive concessions for the image of being a coequal superpower, the image itself has not lost its appeal. That is particularly true because during the last decade the Soviets—without ever admitting it publicly—appeared to be more and more embarrassed that their leaders were literally unable to walk and talk straight. Gorbachev's forceful and overall competent performance in Geneva gave the Russians a new sense of dignity. There was also a special ele-

[5]Michael Voslensky, *Nomenklatura: The Soviet Ruling Class* (Garden City, N.Y.: Doubleday, 1984), p. 312. The term is also used to describe a class of privileged officeholders.

[6]L. I. Brezhnev, *O Vneshney Politike KPSS i Sovetskogo Gosudarstva Rechi i Stati* (Moscow: Izdatelsvo Politicheskoy Literatury, 1975), p. 469.

ment of pride that even a "hostile" U.S. president such as Ronald Reagan eventually "found no alternative" to a constructive dialogue with the USSR.[7] The author's conversations with Soviet officials in Geneva suggest that one reason Moscow welcomed U.S.-Soviet consultations on regional issues was that those consultations allegedly represented a tacit recognition of the Kremlin's global relevance, of its status together with the United States as one of the two principal managers of the world order.

The temptation to use foreign policy to enhance the stability and prestige of the regime has important but contradictory implications for the Soviet willingness to allow domestic changes to satisfy Western concerns about human rights. On the one hand, the Soviets' relative flexibility during the seventies on Jewish and German emigrations, on granting slightly greater access to foreign journalists and foreigners in general, suggests that if the price is right, the Politburo is prepared to consider some adjustments at the margins even in the most sensitive area of internal political controls. On the other hand, even flexibility at the margins has encountered resistance from some influential political sectors in the USSR. And anything resembling a genuine shift under foreign pressure in the way Soviet subjects are treated is viewed as a humiliating and thus unacceptable surrender.

Maintaining and strengthening the economic foundation of the system is another key foreign policy consideration for the Kremlin. Economic cooperation with the West is highly desired, but only as it is compatible with preserving the basic totalitarian structure. And one key purpose of this cooperation is to narrow the gap between the Soviets' military power and their economic backwardness. Public pronouncements by Soviet officials, economists, and media commentators demonstrate a painful awareness that the economy cannot be divorced from foreign policy considerations. On one level, since the early seventies the Soviets have perceived an influx of Western credits and technology as a substitute for a much needed but politically unacceptable economic reform. They still emphasize the need for "the international division of labor with the world of capitalism" and admit that there can be no return to economic autarky.[8] But after an initial enthusiasm they have gradually and reluctantly come to realize that Western trade is not a panacea. Not only did economic cooperation with the United States sour, but trade with Western Europe and Japan, despite some highly visible projects such as the Siberian natural gas pipeline, also failed to live up to earlier, excessively optimistic expectations.

On another level, as Mikhail Gorbachev argued at a recent ideological gathering in Moscow, unless the state of the economy is thoroughly improved, the USSR will be unable to preserve its status as a world power capa-

---

[7] *Izvestiya,* November 21, 1985.
[8] Cf. *Izvestiya,* July 9, 1984.

ble of protecting its own security and living up to its international commit-
ments.⁹ Similar warnings were sounded on several occasions by the former
General Staff chief, Marshal Nikolai Ogarkov.

Soviet economic troubles influence foreign policy behavior, that much is
clear. But how do they do so? According to the CIA, the annual rate of increase in Soviet military expenditure declined in the late seventies from 4–5
percent per year to about 2–3 percent. Was this modest slowdown in the Soviet military buildup caused by a reduced economic pie; was it a belated consequence of detente and arms control; or was it both? In any case, in 1984 the
Soviets announced an increase in their defense budget. Though official figures of military expenditures must be used with great caution, the announced
increase may nevertheless suggest that economic difficulties have not yet
reached a level where the Politburo feels unable to enlarge the flow of resources to defense. To make the situation even more murky, Soviet official
data suggest that the prodiscipline, anticorruption drive initiated by Yuri
Andropov led to some improvement in economic performance. If the suggestion is true, greater defense allocations may be less a response to new U.S. assertiveness than a reflection of a slight improvement in Soviet economic
fortunes.

As far as economic reform is concerned, Gorbachev has talked a great deal
about the urgent need to restructure the Soviet economy. But his pronouncements have been short on specifics. Nothing is being said about deempha-
sizing central planning. On the contrary, the new Council of Ministers
Chairman, Nikolai Ryzhkov, aged 56, served until recently as a First Deputy
Chairman of the State Planning Committee. To deal with an inherently weak
Soviet agriculture, Gorbachev's Politburo has given priority not to encouragement for the private initiative of collective farmers but to the creation of a
new superagency—a huge state committee in charge of the agro-industrial
complex. And it appointed as chairman of this committee Vsevolod Mura-
khovsky, aged 59, a party apparatchik who served as Gorbachev's deputy in
the Stavropol region.

But even if later—once Gorbachev's incremental changes toward a more
efficient system have run their course—the General Secretary were to launch
a truly decentralizing reform, it is far from obvious that the military budget
will be seriously reduced. There is even less certainty that the preoccupation
with putting the Soviet economic house in order will lead to greater flexibility on matters of arms control.

As it is practiced today, arms control is not especially relevant to Soviet defense expenditure. Even 50 percent cuts in both sides' strategic offensive
forces would not save much revenue. Although no precise figures are available, there is a consensus that strategic nuclear forces take no more than 10

⁹*Pravda,* December 11, 1984.

percent of the total defense budget. Indeed, in the short run the restructuring of the Soviet strategic arsenal that a possible arms deal would necessitate might cost more rather than less. As far as the Strategic Defense Initiative is concerned, the Soviets (like the Americans) are bound to continue with research. Limits on SDI research short of field testing are unverifiable and, accordingly, non-negotiable. But at this point the SDI effort involves little but research. Thus, even if some agreement on constraining SDI were reached, Soviet economic savings—in the foreseeable future at least—would be minimal.

The politics of a potential economic reform also argues against major reductions in defense expenditures. A decentralizing reform is bound to be controversial and initially very painful. Is it likely that Gorbachev would be willing to aggravate resistance by antagonizing the powerful military-industrial complex and security services? Open Soviet sources, as well as Soviet officials in discussions, suggest that the real debate in Moscow is not so much about the size of the defense budget as, rather, about how it should be distributed. What should be given greater priority, conventional forces or nuclear forces? Should the Soviet Union continue investing in enormous quantities of weapons, or would it make more sense to channel funds into research and development? The disagreement appears to be not along hard and soft lines, but between those who want to build more hardware today and those preoccupied with the technology race for the exotic systems of tomorrow.

Under Gorbachev the Soviet leadership has been unusually outspoken about the USSR's economic weaknesses. Despite fears in the West, however, available evidence indicates that unlike Nazi Germany, the USSR is not attempting to solve its economic dilemmas through foreign aggression. No push to take over Persian Gulf oil fields is in sight. Soviet East European clients, as well as Vietnam, are increasingly being asked to contribute investment, technology, and labor to Soviet economic development. But in most cases such contributions are made either to joint projects or (as in the case of Vietnam) as a form of repayment for Soviet assistance. Maintaining the economic health of the empire (especially outside Eastern Europe) is more a burden than an asset for the USSR.

Finally, economic scarcity influences the Soviet attitude to Third World expansionism. This proposition cannot be proved on the basis of Soviet public statements, but some solid corroborating evidence does exist. The Soviet media voice an open disillusionment with the political payoff from some of the USSR's Third World engagements.[10] Privately, Soviet specialists reflect a growing sense of frustration about the "wasting" of limited resources on ungrateful and unreliable regimes in developing nations. And Soviet moderation in dealing with Third World contingencies is probably attributable not

[10]See, for example, *Pravda*, June 24, 1984.

only to the Reagan administration's assertiveness and the activities of local resistance movements but also to Moscow's reluctance to make further costly
commitments.

Bureaucratic constraints and the internal politics of the Soviet elite in general also affect the Soviet foreign policy-making process. The Soviet establishment is not a homogeneous body. Although the establishment puts a premium on developing consensus and avoiding conflicts between elite factions,
inherent tensions exist—between the party apparatus and the economic management, between the consumer industries and agriculture on the one hand
and the military-industrial complex on the other, between those with authority for maintaining rigid controls and indoctrination and those responsible
for promoting scientific and technological progress. Most rivalries are not antagonistic, and the composition of bureaucratic coalitions varies from issue to
issue. Officials allied on one subject in the morning may find themselves on
different sides of another issue in the afternoon. Nonetheless, the leadership
must engage in a delicate balancing act if it is to avoid unnecessary institutional rifts and prevent the alienation of influential interests.

The world of Soviet bureaucracy is a world of constant competition, cynical maneuvering for power, careful calculation, and ruthless suppression of
opponents at an opportune moment. Because there is nothing awaiting officeholders outside the institutional system, they perceive a fall from grace as
an unmitigated disaster. Accordingly, protecting one's back and avoiding
providing rivals with ammunition are principal preoccupations with Soviet
officials. Accomplishment is appreciated and rewarded. But on balance, careers are usually made by pacers rather than racers. It is better to fail while
following orders than to annoy superiors and make oneself vulnerable to
charges of "immodesty" by displaying excessive initiative and imagination—
even if they do pay off.

In the absence of a strong General Secretary, bureaucratic caution and procrastination became notorious. Starting in the mid-seventies, when Brezhnev's health and intellectual faculties began to decline, the Soviet Union lived
without a strong chief executive. With other senior Politburo members also
out of steam and younger members preoccupied with presuccession maneuvering for power, most decisions were delegated to staff.

The staffs included a number of competent and even talented people who
were able to run Soviet foreign policy without major disasters. Foreign Minister Andrei A. Gromyko's relative vigor and tremendous experience were obviously of help. Even more important, the very size and power of the Soviet
Union virtually assured that, short of some tremendous blunder, Moscow
would be able to conduct business as usual. But business as usual became increasingly inadequate. The advent of the Reagan administration in the
United States, the unexpected (for the Soviets) cohesion of the American system of alliances, despite a shift in U.S. foreign policy toward a greater assertiveness, a growing opposition to Soviet advances in the Third World, insta-

bility in Eastern Europe (particularly in Poland), and finally, the declining international appeal of the Soviets' ideology and their model of development, all required a change more profound than marginal tactical readjustments. And such a change was beyond the reach of the bureaucracy.

Even those who were aware that something had gone fundamentally wrong were reluctant to advocate an alternative strategy. The premium was still on caution and reliability rather than on imagination and effectiveness. After all, Gorbachev had made a brilliant career while presiding over a failing Soviet agriculture. His political success was a vivid illustration that performance mattered less than deferring to one's seniors. And if his example were not enough, there was the case of Marshal Ogarkov, who reputedly lost his position because he indulged in the bureaucratic indiscretion of arguing a case too assertively. The new defense minister, septuagenarian marshal Sergei Sokolov, on the other hand, was known primarily for his lack of candor and an unquestioning loyalty to whoever was in power at the moment.

According to Nikita Khrushchev, in the Soviet context "it requires considerable inner maturity and a well-developed understanding of the world not only to grasp the narrow bureaucratic aspects of defense policy, but also to see things in the broader perspective."[11] But what exactly is this broader perspective as far as the Soviet leadership is concerned? Taking the views of the bureaucracy into account is, as Khrushchev's demise illustrates, an absolute imperative.

But Khrushchev's long tenure in power also indicates something else: short of major failures, fundamental indiscretions, and a great insensitivity to the requirements of the nomenklatura, the General Secretary has very considerable room for maneuver. It took Khrushchev's insensitivity in dealing with the elite to create the political revolt that led to his ultimate undoing. Gorbachev can probably go a long way in reshaping the nomenklatura and introducing substantive change before he risks sharing Khrushchev's fate.

The Institutional Structure

The ultimate Soviet decision-making body is the Politburo. Officially the highest party organ, the Politburo in fact is the executive-legislative committee of the elite as a whole. It includes members who represent the Central Committee Secretariat (which presides over the party apparatus) and secretaries of party committees in major cities and republics, as well as top government officials. Formally the Politburo is responsible to the Central Committee as a whole. But the last time a Central Committee plenum overruled the Politburo was in 1957 when Khrushchev, with the support of the military, defeated the so-called antiparty group, which enjoyed a majority position in the Presidium, as the Politburo was called at that time.

---

[11]*Khrushchev Remembers: The Last Testament* (Boston: Little, Brown, 1974), p. 541.

Since then, Central Committee meetings have been essentially pro forma, and in a couple of instances when Politburo recommendations were allegedly challenged, the "dissidents" paid for the violation of the rules with their political careers.[12] The authority of the Politburo is in no doubt, but it is uncertain to what extent decisions are reached through official deliberations and to what extent through the preceding informal bargaining between appropriate party and state agencies. Politburo sessions take place usually once a week —on Thursdays—and are as a rule attended only by those members who are located in Moscow. The agenda is long—sometimes, as reports in the Soviet media indicate, including more than a dozen items. Under these circumstances, the Politburo has difficulty devoting much substantive attention unless a matter of great principle or something very controversial is involved.

Indeed, substantive attention may be absent even when major issues are on the table. Arkady Shevchenko provides a revealing account of a Politburo meeting at which documents for the 1972 summit with Richard Nixon were approved. According to the former Soviet diplomat, who accompanied his boss, Foreign Minister Andrei Gromyko, to the session, "Brezhnev asked whether all members of the Politburo had received the draft U.S.-Soviet documents in time and if they had studied them. Most of the members nodded assent. 'Can I assume that the draft is approved?' Brezhnev asked. No one spoke. 'The draft is approved,' said Brezhnev after a few moments of silence."[13] The matter was closed, and the Politburo moved to the next item. Remarkably, Shevchenko states that only one Politburo member raised any questions regarding the draft in advance of the meeting—the then chairman of the Council of Ministers, Aleksei Kosygin. And his intervention turned out to be "brief and mild."[14]

This is not to suggest that the Politburo is somehow unimportant—quite the contrary. But under ordinary circumstances, real business is conducted behind the scenes, through a sort of informal interagency process. Once a consensus has been reached, the Politburo gives its stamp of approval.

There are two arenas below the Politburo level for institutional deliberations on national security matters. One is the Defense Council. The other is the Military-Industrial Commission under the Council of Ministers.

The Defense Council is frequently portrayed by Western analysts as a very important body, and indeed, in a variety of ways, the Defense Council has a highly visible profile. Its existence is written into the new Soviet constitution. Its chairman is traditionally the General Secretary. And Soviet leaders, both in public speeches and in private negotiations with Americans, frequently re-

[12]In 1967 Moscow party Secretary Nikolai Yegorychev reputedly challenged Brezhnev's handling of the Mideast crisis; during the May 1972 Plenum, Ukrainian party leader Petr Shelest was rumored to have objected to Nixon's visit to the USSR in the aftermath of the U.S. bombing of Hanoi and mining of Haiphong harbor.

[13]Arkady N. Shevchenko, *Breaking with Moscow* (New York: Knopf, 1985), p. 207.

[14]Ibid.

fer to its role. Yet no members except the chairman have ever been identified. The Defense Council does not even have a permanent headquarters. Significantly, Shevchenko, who in his memoirs refers to numerous officials at the foreign and defense ministries as well as in the Central Committee Secretariat, does not even mention the Defense Council.

There thus may be less to the Defense Council than meets the eye. The Defense Council gained prominence in the Soviet media in the late 1970s, and always in one connection—the fact that it was chaired by Leonid Brezhnev and later by his successors, Yuri Andropov and Konstantin Chernenko. (It is generally assumed that Gorbachev has now taken on this role, though official confirmation may be some time in coming.) One gets the impression of a concerted effort to build up whoever occupies the post of General Secretary, by portraying this person not only as the head of the party but also as a kind of commander-in-chief of the Soviet armed forces and as a man responsible for the national security establishment in general. The Defense Council chairmanship has been a useful symbol of the general secretary's preeminence. At most, the Defense Council appears to be the Politburo's working group on national security affairs. In that capacity—as part and parcel of the Politburo rather than a separate entity—it may indeed be of crucial importance.

The Military-Industrial Commission operates under the auspices of the Council of Ministers. Its principal responsibility is to coordinate the work of the several ministries supervising Soviet defense production. The Commission until recently was chaired by deputy prime minister Leonid Smirnov, who took part in SALT I negotiations during the May 1972 Moscow summit. Kissinger describes him as "one of the ablest and most intelligent Soviet leaders" he dealt with.[15] Although officially affiliated with the Council of Ministers, the Military-Industrial Commission operates in close cooperation with the Central Committee Secretariat. Shevchenko states that he was present at the Commission's meetings "where Dmitri Ustinov, then Party Secretary, played a crucial role." According to his account, the commission served as a forum for "heated debates" between Gromyko and then Defense Minister Marshal Andrei Grechko regarding the "Soviet position on submarine-launched missiles."[16] He was recently replaced by Yuriy D. Maslyukov, 49, who came from the Defense Industry Ministry.

A number of government and party agencies are involved in preparing positions on national security issues. Their institutional relationships suggest more of a division of labor than a clear-cut dominance of the party apparatus over the government bureaucracy. Significantly, as Shevchenko states, "on most questions, the Foreign Ministry, unlike other ministries, is directly responsible only to the Politburo."[17] In fact, both the Ministry of Defense and the Committee of State Security (the KGB) seem to be in the same position.

---

[15]Henry Kissinger, *White House Years* (Boston: Little, Brown, 1979), p. 1234.
[16]Shevchenko, *Breaking with Moscow,* p. 205.
[17]Ibid., p. 187.

Various departments of the CC Secretariat are responsible for clearing top appointments in these state agencies. They monitor morale and discipline but do not supervise much substantive work.

The CC International Department, headed by CC Secretary and Candidate Politburo member Boris Ponomarev, plays only a limited role in both formulating and implementing policy vis-à-vis the United States. The department is primarily occupied with developing ties to nonruling Communist parties (contacts with parties in power are the responsibility of the Department on Liaison with Ruling Communist Parties) and to so-called national liberation movements. Officials from the International Department have important functions in dealing with countries where Communists or left-wing radicals enjoy considerable standing. The United States is obviously not in that category. Accordingly, the department's prerogatives are narrower in the American case than in the cases of, for instance, France or Italy.

The U.S. section at the International Department is considered among the weakest. When its former head, Nikolai Mostovets, used to come to the United States with Soviet delegations, his junior status was clear. Mostovets's replacement is a mid-level foreign ministry aide who was formerly with the Soviet Embassy in Washington. Soviet insiders explain that the main function of the section is to maintain links with the American Communist party. In state-to-state relations, the section's role is said to be limited. A more important function is performed by Ponomarev's principal deputy, Vadim Zagladin. But as Shevchenko claims, Zagladin's role is itself restricted, to appeals for greater emphasis on the ideological dimension in relations with the United States.[18]

The personal secretariat of the General Secretary, on the other hand, has become influential in formulating the Soviets' American policy. Until recently the role of Gorbachev's top foreign policy aide was played by Andrei Aleksandrov-Agentov, 68, who performed this function for every Soviet leader since Brezhnev brought him to the Central Committee in 1964. Aleksandrov's replacement, Anatoly Chernyaev, 66, worked for two decades in the CC International Department, eventually rising to a deputy chief level. His duties included speechwriting for Brezhnev and contacts with West European communist parties. Though Aleksandrov came from the foreign service and Chernyaev from academia, there are no identifiable differences between the two, except the new man's greater flamboyancy.[19]

Yet it is the Foreign Ministry that provides the leadership in preparing position papers for the Politburo on relations with the United States. Shevchenko reports that while he worked as an adviser to Gromyko in 1970–73, there was not a single case "when the Politburo failed to adopt the ministry proposal." More recently, of course, Gromyko's standing in the Politburo

---

[18]Ibid., p. 190.
[19]Dimitri K. Simes, "What's so Great about Gorbachev?" *Washington Post*, February 23, 1986.

rose dramatically. He was made a member only in April 1973 and for a while was constrained by Brezhnev's personal role and the tremendous influence of the party's chief ideologist, International Department supervisor, Politburo member, and CC senior secretary, Mikhail Suslov. With their deaths in 1982 and the death in February 1984 of Andropov (whose experience and activism were bound to increase the General Secretary's role), Gromyko found himself by default the Politburo's key voice on American affairs. The death of Defense Minister Marshal Ustinov in December 1984 and—in the short term at least—Gorbachev's relative inexperience in international affairs enhanced the Foreign Minister's standing even further.

Gromyko's prominence could well be among the main reasons why he had to be "kicked upstairs" to the chairmanship of the rubber-stamp Supreme Soviet Presidium. In his new capacity Gromyko still has to perform many ceremonial foreign policy functions. On occasion—for instance, when Iraqi president Saddam Hussein visited Moscow—he is given an opportunity to head the Soviet negotiating team.[20] His successor, Eduard Shevardnadze, lacks an international affairs background (he made his career as a Komsomol, police, and party official in Soviet Georgia), certainly giving the experienced Gromyko an edge during Politburo deliberations. The fact that Shevardnadze still relies on deputies who made their careers during Gromyko's twenty-eight-year tenure is also of relevance.

Yet there is little doubt that as far as the basic direction of Soviet foreign policy is concerned, Gorbachev is currently in control. The General Secretary did not even take Gromyko to the Geneva summit. In addition, Shevardnadze's record in Georgia does not conform with the image of a pushover. On the contrary, his performance, in terms both of substance and of personal advancement, can be characterized by risk taking and imagination—an unusual approach among Soviet bureaucrats. As Shevardnadze gains experience and confidence, Gromyko's role in foreign affairs is bound to decline further. And inevitably, his former protégés at the Foreign Ministry will either develop new loyalties or be replaced.

According to Soviet insiders, Shevardnadze is Gorbachev's confidant—having served in neighboring provinces as young Komsomol functionaries, they have known each other for about thirty years. The new foreign minister thus has a potential for influence. Much will depend upon the succession at the Central Committee's International Department and at the Ministry of Defense. If young and well-connected politicians take over from the current old and inept officeholders, both Shevardnadze personally and his ministry may have to share some of their present power.

Like the Foreign Ministry, the military reports directly to the Politburo. There is no military department on the CC Secretariat. The Main Political Administration of the Soviet Armed Forces has the formal status of a CC de-

[20]Reported in *Pravda*, December 17, 1985.

partment. But its responsibilities are limited to morale, indoctrination, and discipline of Soviet military personnel, and it is directly subordinate to the Defense Minister. In dealing with arms control, it is only the military—the Defense Ministry and the General Staff—which possesses full information regarding Soviet deployments and operational requirements. Although the Foreign Ministry is in a position to evaluate U.S. proposals, defense industrialists and the R&D community may speak about Soviet technological capabilities, and the State Planning Committee is expected to address budgetary constraints, only the military has the unique combination of expertise and information required to offer the leadership an evaluation of the consequences of American defense programs and, conversely, of arms control initiatives on Soviet security.

Nevertheless, it is difficult to be sure how influential the military is with the leadership these days. For the first time since 1973 the Defense Ministry is not represented on the Politburo by a full member. Ustinov's replacement, Marshal Sokolov, was in charge of administering the Defense Ministry's machinery for eighteen years, and he clearly lacks Ustinov's stature as well as his extensive connections in the CC apparatus. Sokolov, the sole top official promoted to the Politburo level position under Chernenko, was awarded only a candidate (nonvoting) status by Gorbachev. Anyway, because of his age he is perceived as a transitional figure. Shortly before Ustinov's death, moreover, the Soviets dismissed Chief of Staff Marshal Nikolai Ogarkov, a highly regarded and assertive military leader. He was succeeded by a deputy, Marshal Sergei F. Akhromeyev, who, while also reputed to be quite competent, definitely does not yet have Ogarkov's clout.

The Soviet involvement in arms control with the United States allowed the military to acquire a more sophisticated appreciation of America. Inside the General Staff, the Legal and Treaty Directorate—the military's "mini foreign ministry"—has gained considerable prominence. Currently headed by Colonel General Nikolai Chervov, the directorate performs three main missions. First, its generals and officers serve on Soviet arms control delegations. Second, the directorate, and particularly General Chervov himself, takes an increasingly visible part in public elaboration of Soviet arms control approaches to Western audiences. Finally, Soviet sources claim that the directorate provides an independent evaluation of U.S. and other arms control positions to the General Staff chief and the Defense Minister, and through them to the Politburo.

The Foreign Ministry, the military, and the General Secretary's personal staff are the focus of Soviet decision making on the United States. Needless to say, there are many other relevant players, such as the KGB, the economic planners, foreign-trade institutions, and the defense industry with its influential design bureaus. But their involvement in the policy-making process seems to be of a limited nature, usually restricted to their specific areas of responsibility, even in the case of the KGB. Despite its preoccupation with intelligence and counterintelligence operations against America, the KGB does not appear to be a crucial voice in determining Soviet policy vis-à-vis the United States. But, particularly when the domestic implications of this policy are involved, this voice should not be discounted either, especially since the new KGB chairman, General Victor Chebrikov, was promoted to full Politburo membership in April 1985, shortly after Gorbachev became General Secretary.

What about the foreign policy research institutes of the Academy of Sciences, especially the two most preoccupied with the United States—the Institute of the United States and Canada and the Institute of World Economy and International Relations (IMEMO)? There is a growing tendency in the United States to treat the institutes with contempt, primarily as propaganda outfits lacking any real influence in Moscow. A few Soviet insiders have contributed richly to this image. The Soviet ambassador in Washington, Anatoly Dobrynin, is known to have advised U.S. officials against taking the U.S. and Canada institute director, Georgi Arbatov, too seriously.[21] Shevchenko has the same perspective, claiming that Arbatov had no access to Gromyko and was not told about Soviet arms control positions.[22] Finally, Arbatov's own former subordinate, Galina Orionova, who defected during a trip to London, argued that his institute was at best of marginal importance in the formulation of Soviet policy toward America.[23]

These accounts probably are essentially correct, but they are somewhat incomplete. The institutes are indeed next to irrelevant to the operational conduct of the USSR's diplomacy. Striving to be perceived as independent and well-connected while portraying Soviet policies in the most favorable light is undoubtedly a priority for the institutes. But under Gorbachev, public diplomacy is a key component of Soviet foreign policy, and those who engage in it cannot be dismissed lightly. Arbatov was *seated* next to the General Secretary during the *Time* magazine interview.[24] And the IMEMO director, Aleksandr Yakovlev, was put in charge of the crucial CC Propaganda Department. In that capacity he was a ranking member of the Soviet delegation in Geneva, clearly enjoying an impressive closeness to Gorbachev. Yakovlev's successor at IMEMO, Yevgeniy Primakov, is still not in the same league politically. But this former *Pravda* correspondent in Cairo is a knowledgeable foreign policy specialist as well as a shrewd bureaucratic infighter. Chances are that he will manage to keep IMEMO on Moscow's political map.

Another function of the institutes is to contribute to an assessment of fundamental trends in American society and policy. Located on the periphery of the institutional structure, the institutes are not well equipped to provide

[21]See Zbigniew Brzezinski, *Power and Principle* (New York: Farrar, Straus & Giroux, 1983), p. 153.

[22]Shevchenko, *Breaking with Moscow*, pp. 208–11.

[23]See Barbara L. Dash, *A Defector Reports: The Institute of the USA and Canada* (Delphic Associates, May 1982), pp. 211–20.

[24]*Time*, September 9, 1985, p. 22.

much input into everyday decision making, and in crisis situations they probably are not consulted at all. Yet it is precisely their role as relative outsiders which allows the institutes to speak with a degree of detachment from the political requirements of the moment. They (in the highly centralized Soviet system "they," in practical terms, refers to the institute's directors and other leading officials) enjoy sufficient access and prestige to have an impact on the USSR's evolving perception of its superpower rival.

The Leadership Factor

Two general observations about Soviet policy making are in order. First, although the Soviet political process is heavily institutionalized, personalities and personal relationships are extremely important. The current bureaucratic setup in Moscow is connected with the distribution of power inside the small leadership circle. The recent and unprecedented influence of the Foreign Ministry, for example, was to a great extent a function of Gromyko's personal prominence coupled with Chernenko's uncertain hold on power and the absence of a senior and secure CC Secretary (with a seat on the Politburo) with responsibility for international relations. As Gorbachev emerges as a strong party leader, the present diffusion of power will be considerably reduced.

Second, with the ascendancy of the Gorbachev generation, the Soviet leadership is developing a longer-term foreign policy perspective. For the last decade, and probably even longer, the Politburo has been preoccupied with little more than the requirements of the moment. As an illustration of this attitude, Shevchenko tells the story of a failed effort to create a genuine policy planning office in the Foreign Ministry. The office survived but degenerated in a way not entirely unfamiliar in Washington into a "garbage can" for diplomats on their way out.[25]

Imagination and experimentation are not standard bureaucratic virtues anywhere. The Soviet system offers an extreme example, because no compensating inputs come from outside the institutional framework. The Soviet themselves tend to admit that most of their previous assumptions about the direction of the international process proved to be false; specifically, the Kremlin has ceased, at least for the time being, to claim that the correlation of forces in the history-shaped competition with the West is steadily shifting in its favor. The new official Soviet line is more modest—namely, that the Soviet Union is strong enough and determined enough not to lose ground under pressure from its imperialist opponents. Yet this newly defensive attitude has not been transformed into a major policy reassessment. Such a reassessment may become possible now, with the consolidation of Gorbachev's authority. There is already abundant evidence that the conduct of Soviet foreign policy has been improved under his stewardship. The Kremlin acts faster and

[25]Shevchenko, *Breaking with Moscow,* pp. 160–61.

with a greater imagination, fitness, and flair for public relations. Gorbachev and his associates still have a lot to learn. It was, for instance, probably a serious error on Gorbachev's part to insist during a joint press conference with President François Mitterrand on engaging the French and British in negotiations (separately from the United States) on intermediate nuclear forces limitation in Europe. Mitterrand's opposition to the proposal was on the record, and the General Secretary left his host no choice but a public rebuttal. Similarly, the Soviets' penchant for control during the Geneva summit often made their massive public relations operation less than effective.

But such tactical mistakes can be avoided as Gorbachev's team gains experience, and particularly if new, more sophisticated and sensitive advisers are brought to positions of influence. It is going to be much more difficult for Gorbachev to undertake a fundamental policy review that would address the root causes of Soviet international setbacks. Drawing appropriate conclusions on the basis of such a review and implementing them in a practical policy is going to be a most formidable task. Whether Gorbachev is up to it remains to be seen. Meanwhile, he may be able to claim some accomplishments short of a genuine change in foreign policy directions.

The presence of a strong, secure leader helps the foreign policy bureaucracy have a greater impact, especially when politically neuralgic issues are at stake. If a man in charge is able to disregard the reservations of his colleagues, he can pay more attention to the professional advice of his lieutenants. Thus Khrushchev proceeded with major foreign policy initiatives only after he had crushed opposition in the Presidium. Similarly, Leonid Brezhnev signed treaties with the Federal Republic of Germany and moved to improve relations with the United States only when his preeminence in the leadership was largely assured. Both cases involved a reexamination of some ideological dogma and a readjustment of approaches to some emotional issues. In contrast, Khrushchev was still consolidating his base and had to share power with others when the Soviet Union signed the Austrian peace treaty, reached an agreement with Finland, and established diplomatic relations with Japan —all important steps, but not ones that touched upon serious domestic concerns.

Gorbachev's highly acclaimed performance notwithstanding, the Soviet Union continues to muddle through in the world arena. But, for a change, it is working its way up rather than down. In comparison with the pitiful picture seen in recent years, even that much is definite progress. In all likelihood, however, the Gorbachev leadership will discover in two to three years that this progress will stay limited and may prove to be short-lived unless some far-reaching foreign policy reassessment takes place.

America on the Soviet Foreign Policy Agenda

Still, even a much more formidable leadership would probably fail to make Soviet policy toward America entirely consistent and highly sophisticated.

Consistency comes hard to superpowers, which have a variety of conflicting interests and are subjected to pressures from many different directions. And sophistication would require nothing short of appreciating the intricacies of the U.S. political process—a difficult test for any foreigner.

As far as the relationship with the United States is concerned, the Soviet leadership has to find a place for it among other foreign policy priorities. This place has never been permanently settled. True, American abundance, technological advancement, and power have always been, to Soviet rulers starting with Vladimir Lenin, a model to be replicated. An "equal" relationship with the United States is a symbol of status and a source of legitimacy for the Soviet leadership.[26] And since World War II, Washington has continuously acted as a major constraint on Moscow's international ambitions. Moreover, the United States is the only power with the capability to threaten the Soviet Union militarily and indeed to destroy it altogether. In the late sixties and early seventies Soviet policy makers had some concern over the Chinese potential for making trouble. But in military terms the concern was not over China per se but rather over what China could do in alliance with the United States.

In addition to the United States, however, there are many other pressing factors that the USSR has to take into consideration. The security and maintenance of the Soviet empire, particularly in Eastern Europe, is on top of the agenda. America is certainly not about to help the Kremlin consolidate its hold over this troubled region. Conversely, no U.S. administration ever made a serious effort beyond rhetoric to loosen Soviet control there. When indigenous developments make things tough for the Soviets in Eastern Europe, the Politburo may tend to overreact to a perceived American meddling. And, of course, American interference is a convenient excuse for saving the East Europeans from themselves. On balance, however, the preservation of the status quo in Eastern Europe is not significantly affected by the United States.

The Soviet leadership, as a rule, is similarly reluctant to pressure allies and clients on behalf of the American adversary. Richard Nixon and Henry Kissinger did not get very far in trying to persuade the Politburo to make the North Vietnamese more amenable.[27] In the Middle East the Kremlin preached caution while supplying arms to the Arabs. Moscow wanted to avoid an open confrontation with the United States, but it was not prepared to jeopardize ties to Cairo and Damascus by displaying excessive moderation.[28] In the late 1960s the Soviets were openly unhappy with Fidel Castro's efforts to export revolution to Latin America,[29] possibly because in the after-

---

[26]For more details see Dimitri K. Simes, "Soviet Policy toward the United States," in *The Making of America's Soviet Policy,* ed. Joseph S. Nye, Jr. (New Haven: Yale University Press, 1984).

[27]Richard Nixon, *The Memoirs of Richard Nixon* (New York: Grosset & Dunlap, 1978), p. 391.

[28]See Mohamed Heikal, *The Road to Ramadan* (New York: Ballantine, 1975), pp. 172–73.

[29]See, for example, *Pravda,* June 4, 1966.

math of the Cuban missile crisis, Leonid Brezhnev and his associates wanted to avoid needless provocation of the United States in its own backyard. Also, Cuba was completely dependent upon the Soviet superpower's sponsorship and economic assistance; unlike the Egyptians, it could not switch alliances to America. And unlike the North Vietnamese, it was neither willing nor able to manipulate the Sino-Soviet rivalry to gain more room for maneuver.

The Soviets' fundamental commitment to support national liberation movements is also non-negotiable, a point that Gorbachev made quite clear in Geneva.[30] The political legitimacy of the Soviet regime is contingent upon a periodic demonstration that it is riding on the tide of history, and for this purpose an association with successful Third World radical factions and governments is of great importance. Certainly there is a profound difference between Soviet determination to maintain the status quo in Eastern Europe and its ambitions to change the status quo outside its own sphere of influence. In the Third World it is more a sense of momentum than specific victories in remote regions which appears to matter to the Soviet leadership. The particular locations and forms of Soviet involvement are influenced by local circumstances as well as by a new fear, that of being overextended. And here the American policy of imposing constraints and offering inducements can and already does affect the USSR's behavior. But a more general decision to abandon national liberation movements would have far-reaching ideological implications, would require a major reassessment of Soviet policy, and is unlikely to be undertaken merely to satisfy the United States.

The impact of ideology on relations with the United States is both profound and complicated. It is complicated because the contents of ideology do not remain static. Also, starting with Lenin, the Bolsheviks have traditionally been able to combine single-minded ideological commitment with a great deal of operational flexibility. Nothing would be more erroneous than to assume that the Politburo's American policy is guided by Marxist-Leninist texts.

On the other hand, the ideology provides an intellectual prism through which the Soviet leadership looks at the United States and the world in general. It does not direct the USSR's policies, but it shapes the elite's basic predispositions, which in turn inevitably affect the Kremlin's thinking about international affairs. Soviet ideology today is a peculiar blend of traditional Russian nationalism, with its well-documented messianic tendency, and a highly competitive and even more messianic Marxist-Leninist vision. The ideology can be meaningful even in the absence of a powerful drive on the part of its adherents. In the Soviet case it contributes richly to an exceedingly suspicious and hostile view of the West and to the feeling that in the long run, the relationship with the West, and particularly with the United States as a rival superpower, cannot be anything but a fundamentally competitive one.

Conversely, the Soviet Union has little alternative to approaching America

[30]*Pravda,* November 21, 1985.

as a principal partner in managing the East-West relationship.[31] In the late sixties the Brezhnev leadership made an effort to build a separate detente with Western Europe and Japan. The effort was fruitless, and the United States had to be included. It could not be otherwise. How, for instance, could the problem of West Berlin be dealt with if the United States, one of the occupying powers, were not involved? And the West Berlin settlement was a key to improving relations with the Federal Republic.

Gorbachev's team has manifested an interest in dealing with Western Europe and Japan on their own merits. But simultaneously, it has recognized that the community of industrial democracies cannot easily be split, that an open effort to drive a wedge between the allies is likely to backfire. A relatively painless deployment of U.S. missiles in Europe, despite heavy-handed Soviet pressure has, once again, driven this point home for the Kremlin. The Soviets publicly admit that one reason they seek rapprochement with Western Europe is to use it to influence the United States to accommodate Moscow's demands. The Geneva summit and the way it was portrayed by the USSR as a historic event should put to rest fears that somehow, if the Reagan administration fails to satisfy Gorbachev, the new General Secretary may adopt a policy of not-so-benign neglect of America.

Implications for U.S. Soviet Policy

The domestic context of Soviet policy making virtually assures that nothing the United States can realistically do would fundamentally change the competitive nature of the relationship with Communist Russia. Nor would it be fruitful to yield to the temptation to influence political dynamics inside the Soviet Union, despite their great bearing on the USSR's international behavior. Americans know too little about what is going on behind the Kremlin walls, are too impatient and moralistic as a political culture, and have too few instruments at their disposal to affect Soviet political struggles in a desirable direction. Anyway, considerations other than relations with the United States are likely to heavily affect the Kremlin's critical choices.

Yet within the broad limits imposed on both superpowers by their conflicting aspirations and interests on the one hand, and their fear of nuclear conflict on the other, U.S. policy can make a difference. What the United States can successfully affect, and in fact has affected on many occasions, is how the Soviet Union defines some of the choices it faces. Working to structure these choices in a way that would be simultaneously beneficial to America and acceptable to Soviet policy makers should be a constant preoccupation in dealing with the USSR.

To hope to do so successfully, however, requires that American priorities

[31]*Literaturnaya Gazeta,* November 27, 1985.

be clear. Understandably, no administration can hope to pursue a policy vis-à-vis the Soviet Union which will be shaped exclusively by reason and calculation: both the mechanics of the U.S. political process and the deep-rooted American aversion to *Realpolitik* ensure this. Yet at a minimum, it is essential to recognize that Soviet responses will be shaped not by the image Americans hold of their own actions but by the way those actions are perceived by the Politburo and its elite constituency.

Such a recognition puts a premium, in particular, on maximum clarity in communicating U.S. objectives to those who formulate Soviet policy. The need for clarity encompasses both action and rhetoric, and it can accommodate both toughness and sensitivity. But to be meaningful, it should incorporate knowledge of both the Soviet political mindset and the political organization of Soviet society, for the clarity of the message is in the eyes of those on the receiving end.

As an element of U.S. containment policy, clarity assures Soviet caution about encroaching upon areas of vital American interest. The converse also applies: the Vietnam and Watergate traumas produced uncertainty about Washington's will to check Soviet geopolitical advances. As a result, the Kremlin, rather out of character, engaged in provocative ventures in Angola and Ethiopia. In retrospect, Soviet analysts admit that a sharp American reaction—at least on the rhetorical level—came as a surprise to the Politburo. If the Soviet leadership had been aware in advance of how seriously the U.S. body politic would take these African engagements, Moscow's calculations could have changed.

But the need for clarity works both ways. While it is indispensable to let the Soviets know where America would draw the line, it is also helpful to avoid giving the impression that nothing the Soviet regime can realistically do (in the context of its domestic preoccupations and international commitments) would satisfy American objectives and concerns. For if the Soviet regime comes to the conclusion that an unalterable objective of U.S. diplomacy is to put it on the "ash heap of history," undermining its domestic stability and its hold over Eastern Europe in the process, it will feel little incentive to make incremental concessions in order to accommodate the United States.

The key Soviet preoccupation is the stability and security of the regime; when the United States engages in human rights diplomacy, therefore, it touches on the most sensitive nerve in Moscow. Concessions on internal matters require the approval of the whole leadership, including provincial leaders ignorant of the outside world who would be inclined to interpret American interest in the most sinister fashion. If an assertive U.S. human rights policy acts to provoke domestic-oriented sectors of the Soviet elite, it thereby contributes to a climate in which the national security establishment has less flexibility to conduct business on all other matters.

It is, of course, both appropriate and, in light of the American political process, inevitable that the United States should put human rights on the diplomatic agenda with the Soviets. Moreover, the relaxation of Soviet emigration policy prior to (though not after) passage of the Jackson-Vanik Amendment by the U.S. Congress suggests that the Kremlin may, under certain circumstances, be prepared to make concessions even on internal matters. The Soviets' acceptance of the Helsinki Final Act, despite their dismal record of complying with its terms, stresses the same point. The key factor is the manner in which U.S. human rights policy addresses Soviet domestic practices. The historic record suggests that the Soviets understand and respect the concept of leverage, providing it is applied realistically and tactfully. But they turn to hostile polemics when they sense that American officials are trying to teach them decency or, more important, to impose alien and threatening norms of internal conduct.

Also, senior Soviet officials tend to have long tenure and even longer memories. They are annoyed by U.S. requests to renegotiate agreements when a new administration takes office. U.S. administrations that want to achieve ambitious deals with the Politburo may be better off building upon previous —even if imperfect—arrangements than starting a negotiating process anew. Moreover, U.S. and Soviet political processes run on their own cycles. The sharp turns characteristic of new U.S. administrations are uncomfortable for the Kremlin, which operates on its own schedule.

Attempts to circumvent this or that Soviet agency or leader usually backfire. The attempt by the Carter administration in March 1977 to go directly to the Politburo in order to avoid military opposition to U.S. SALT proposals proved to be counterproductive. The Soviet decision-making process is an orderly one and is resistant to crude outside manipulation.

Finally, it is important to be aware that with Gorbachev's consolidation of power, the Soviet Union has at last acquired a formidable leader. The good news is that the General Secretary appears to be intelligent, creative, and decisive. These are qualities that may allow him to become a promising partner for America when superpower interests overlap. The bad news is that the very same qualities make Gorbachev a dangerous rival. And in the course of his first year at the helm, he has not shown much of an inclination to change those basic directions of Russian policy which put Moscow and Washington consistently at odds. Accordingly, the difference Gorbachev will make as long as the relationship is dominated by competition is, at least in the short run, not necessarily to America's advantage.

It makes little sense to second guess Gorbachev's ultimate intentions. He may not be quite aware of them himself. After all, the position of ultimate authority, especially in the field of international affairs, is still new to him. The United States would do well to focus on pursuing its own interests and communicating them to the Soviet leaders in terms they can comprehend. As long as Gorbachev and his colleagues are still in the process of shaping their foreign policy strategy, the Reagan administration has a unique opportunity to contribute to Soviet deliberations. Although it should not be exaggerated this is an opportunity to which we must be alert.

III

The Next Phase: Issue Areas in U.S.–Soviet Relations

7

U.S. – Soviet Trade and East – West Trade Policy

ABRAHAM S. BECKER

"East-West relations," Edward Heath instructs us solemnly, "are connected with politics, diplomacy and military activity; North-South relations are concerned with economic and social affairs."[1] So much for scribblers on East-West economic relations (and for analysts of North-South political-military matters). Was it then a "nonsubject" that for at least two years in the early 1980s was tearing the NATO alliance apart? But Heath does have a point: the heart of the matter in East-West relations is military power and the political objectives of the participants. It is not economics but politics (understood broadly to include security, of course) that will determine the main lines of East-West relations in the foreseeable future. Nevertheless, economic interests will continue to help shape the patterns of East-West involvement and the internal-external rationalizations adduced for such involvement. And East-West economics maintains its potential for complicating relations in the West, where the alliance's consultative structure to this day can only awkwardly encompass anything outside its pristine military purpose.

What utility does economic policy have in the West's efforts to cope with Soviet pressures? This chapter contends that U.S.-led attempts to use Western economic strength to affect Soviet policy and behavior have been notably unsuccessful; that to the extent such efforts have not been simply demonstrations of opposition to Soviet purposes but were intended to influence Soviet decisions, they have misconstrued or ignored both the requirements for success and the effective possibilities of the West; and finally, that a more realistic assessment suggests that economic policy can have only a modest role in future Western strategy. East-West relations during the rest of the 1980s are not likely to concern economics much because the West seems incapable of developing the political consensus required.

[1] Edward R. G. Heath, "East-West and North-South Relations," Seventh Annual David R. Calhoun, Jr., Memorial Lecture, Washington University, St. Louis, January 30, 1984.

The Pattern and State of U.S.-Soviet Trade

Ask Americans what U.S. economic relations with the Soviet Union are all about, and if they live in the farm states of middle America they will, one imagines, mention grain sales first. Elsewhere, many others would probably think first of exports of technology. It is doubtful that more than a handful of respondents would be able to name the chief U.S. imports from the USSR. This image of Soviet-American economic relations is composed of both fact and stereotype. U.S.-Soviet trade is largely one-way, to the USSR, and grain is the staple export, but technology transfer is a fairly minor element of that trade. Total U.S.-Soviet trade has rarely been a quantitatively significant element of Soviet economic intercourse with industrially developed countries.

The United States has never been the major Soviet trade partner. The value of two-way trade between the two countries was below 100 million rubles at current prices, with the single exception of 1964, from 1949 until 1969.[2] Turnover increased sharply from this very low base thereafter, but even in the peak year, 1979, Soviet trade turnover with West Germany exceeded that with the United States by 50 percent. French and Italian two-way trade with the USSR were each higher than that of the United States in five of the ten years of the 1970s, Japan's in seven of the ten. In the latter seventies Soviet trade with the developed capitalist countries fluctuated around 30 percent of its total trade (at Soviet valuations—which tended to understate the relative importance of trade with hard-currency countries), but trade with the United States covered only about one-tenth of that subtotal. Even in the peak years of the 1970s, of course, trade with the Soviet Union was quantitatively insignificant for the United States, accounting for 1 or 2 percent of total U.S. exports.

Prominence given by the media to examples of equipment that the Soviet military has openly or covertly extracted from the West, and the debate over the proper scope of export controls to stem the flow, have generated a public image of large commercial shipments of U.S. machinery and equipment to the USSR. That image is a distortion of reality. In only the briefest interval at the heyday of detente did the United States play a significant *quantitative* role in Soviet machinery purchases from the noncommunist world. Only in 1975 and 1976, according to Soviet data, was the U.S. share in that aggregate as much as 12 and 14 percent, respectively. The shares declined quickly thereafter, and in the last year of the Carter administration U.S. sales accounted for less than 7 percent of Soviet purchases from nonbloc countries. Throughout the latter seventies Soviet purchases from West Germany were generally two and three times higher than from the United States.

In contrast, the United States was the major source of Soviet grain imports in the 1970s. Like its czarist predecessor, the Soviet Union was traditionally a

[2]Except where indicated otherwise, Soviet trade data in this chapter are from various issues of the Soviet statistical yearbook, *Vneshniaia torgovlia SSSR*.

net grain exporter. Only in the 1970s, under the pressure of several poor harvests—but equally important, after a leadership decision to pursue sharp improvement in the national diet—did Moscow become a net importer of grain on a steady basis. The U.S. share of total Soviet grain purchases by value increased, with a single year's exception, steadily until the embargo year of 1980.

In the early 1980s Soviet-American trade fell off considerably. Turnover in 1983 was down one-third from the peak level of 1979, even in current prices. Soviet exports to the United States were near the 1979 mark, but the amount concerned was less than $500 million. It was the much larger Soviet imports that bore the full burden of the shrinkage. The grain embargo slashed Soviet imports almost in half; the recovery of both 1981 and 1982 was set back in 1983 as a result of a 25 percent fall in Soviet imports, reflecting a five-million-ton cutback in grain purchases. In 1984 grain imports jumped sharply, bringing total Soviet imports from the United States above the 1979 level (all at current prices, of course). Nevertheless, Soviet-American trade flows remain relatively small. The United States accounts for only 8 percent of Soviet trade with industrially developed capitalist countries, as against a 19 percent share in 1979. Moscow's most important capitalist trade partner is still West Germany, with whom trade turnover is 2.5 times that with the United States. Two-way trade between the USSR and France, Italy, and Japan (until 1984) also exceeds that with the United States.

In part because of increased vigilance in Washington, but probably much more because of Soviet decisions regarding the overall level and geographical distribution of purchases, U.S. sales of machinery and equipment to the Soviet Union have declined during the Reagan administration—by Department of Commerce estimates, from $301 million in 1981 to $149 million in 1983 and $110 million in 1984. The USSR buys less machinery and equipment from the United States than it does from Austria, the United Kingdom, Italy, the Federal Republic of Germany, Finland, France, Switzerland, Japan, or India. Soviet purchases from the Federal Republic are more than twelve times and from Finland eight times higher than from the United States. Department of Commerce figures show machinery and equipment accounting for only 3 percent of U.S. exports to the USSR in 1984; more than three-quarters derived from the category "food and live animals" (grain, essentially); "inedible, non-fuel crude materials" and chemicals contributed another 13 percent.[3]

Thus American trade with the Soviet Union has always been relatively small and largely involved Soviet imports. Agricultural products are the bulwark, and machinery and equipment lag far behind. Soviet trade with West-

---

[3]The share of machinery and equipment was higher in earlier years, but the peak, in 1981, was only 13 percent; agricultural exports were 68 percent of the total in that year. The relative weight of materials and chemicals fluctuated in 1981–84 between a tenth and a quarter of total U.S. sales to the USSR.

ern Europe and Japan has almost always been quantitatively more significant than U.S.-Soviet trade.

Trade and Foreign Policy

Despite this seemingly unpromising quantitative base several U.S. administrations have attempted to manipulate U.S.-Soviet trade flows for foreign policy purposes.[4] In each case, policy makers thought they perceived a Soviet trade dependence, and therefore a U.S. position of strength, that could be used to advance a U.S. goal or frustrate a Soviet purpose. The perceptions of Soviet dependence were half-right, but the conclusion about U.S. bargaining strength was optimistic. Too often the policy was inconsistent and the implementation maladroit, particularly in relation to other Soviet trade partners. Results were therefore disappointing and frustrating. The political and economic circumstances surrounding U.S. policy decisions make it doubtful, however, that tangibly different outcomes could have been expected. That finding suggests a sobering conclusion regarding future policy options.

Before reviewing the foreign policy use of trade relations we need first to develop some distinctions among policy purposes and measures. Consider the class of economic measures intended for *suasion,* to move the policy of a foreign state in particular directions. It may be believed that the purpose can be achieved by *benefaction,* using economic instruments to confer benefits on the recipient, to accelerate the growth of its economy, or to improve the welfare of its population. *Denial,* in contrast, would seek to impede welfare improvements or economic growth, either of the economy as a whole or of particular sectors (usually the military). The denial effort may be all-encompassing at one extreme or highly selective at the other, with corresponding differences in the level of impedance of gains sought. Because it is out of fashion to pursue total impedance—at least with regard to the USSR—most discussions of denial policy concern partial impedance, particularly with regard to Soviet military resource allocation. The constraints considered may involve selective denial (specific Western exports of militarily useful goods and services) or general denial (limitations on aggregate resource supply to the USSR in order to reduce allocations to the military). Finally, a strategy that employs measures of either benefaction or denial, but with the intention of directly affecting the behavior of the target state's leadership, is here called *leverage.* Leverage is thus distinctive both in its direct emphasis on the alteration of behavior, as opposed to the indirect behavioral effects of benefaction and denial, and in its readiness to grant benefits or to implement threats of denial as circumstances warrant.

[4]The basic argument of this section is elaborated in A. S. Becker, *Economic Leverage on the Soviet Union in the 1980s* (Santa Monica: Rand Corporation, R-3127-USDP, July 1984). Source references are given there.

Technology Transfer

The closest thing to a constant policy concern in U.S.-Soviet economic relations during the postwar period has been the appropriate set of controls to
be imposed on exports of machinery, equipment and knowhow—technology
transfer—to the USSR. Reflecting the spirit of the Cold War, the Export
Control Act of 1949 sought to constrain the "economic potential" of the
USSR; its controls were correspondingly broad. Detente mandated a liberalization of trade controls, and the Export *Administration* Act of 1969 rejected
its predecessor's goal in favor of limiting trade's contribution to communist
"military potential." (Interestingly, that is also the general objective of the
Reagan administration's trade control policy.)

At the height of detente not much attention was paid to the relation between Western technology transfer and the growth of Soviet military power.
But in the latter 1970s growing public awareness of the duration and cumulative scale of the Soviet buildup brought the relation to the policy forefront. It
has become an even more salient issue under the Reagan administration. In
this context the policy problem concerns the desirability of different forms of
a strategy of denial for partial impedance. But limitations on technology
transfer were discussed in another context during the Carter administration,
as a tool of human rights policy: export controls were to serve in a strategy of
leverage to secure an improvement in the civil rights of Soviet dissidents. Not
surprisingly, policy became entangled among these different motives and
strategies, pressured by various groups with a stake in the preservation of
detente. In the last years of the 1970s both human rights and impedance of
the Soviet buildup seemed to take a back seat to the administration's primary
goal, securing the ratification of SALT II. The invasion of Afghanistan and
the Iranian hostage crisis altered both President Carter's perspective and the
domestic U.S. political balance.

That export controls should be used to impede Soviet military buildup has
found a consensus in the United States for more than thirty-five years. But
apart from the years of the Cold War, the consensus has been superficial. No
one advocates selling missiles to Moscow (although President Reagan did
suggest eventually sharing "Star Wars" technology with the USSR), but controversy continues on controls applied to "dual-use" technology, technology
that has both civilian and military applications. This is, of course, the heart of
the problem. The controversy concerns both domestic and international
channels of control and therefore involves both domestic and alliance politics.
Simultaneously it is a problem of "turf," involving jurisdictional disputes
among agencies of the U.S. government. Also the legislation embodying domestic controls extends beyond trade with the Soviet Union or Eastern Europe and, in particular, involves China, generating a different set of economic, political, and ideological issues. Under the combined pressures of
domestic interest groups, allied governments, and other interested parties,

the extension of the Export Administration Act was bottled up in Congress for more than two years before finally passing in mid-1985.

The dual-use problem is made to order for continuing controversy, because the judgment on military use and the relative significance of that use must be made on a case-by-case basis. The Reagan administration has contended that Western technology contributes significantly to the Soviet military effort, and while the magnitude of that contribution is evidently hard to quantify, the general argument has been widely accepted. The situation underscores the importance of arriving at agreed definitions of goods subject to control, but it does not provide the solution. The only important conceptual contribution to the debate in recent years was the Bucy Report's proposal to focus control on "militarily critical technologies" rather than on particular end products. The Bucy approach was incorporated in the 1979 Export Administration Act, but it only moves the debate on dual-use to another level of the input-output hierarchy, focusing controversy on what is truly critical.

Domestic U.S. criticism of the technology control program has come, as one would expect, from business interests, which complain about red tape and delays in securing export licenses, frequent shifts in U.S. policy, and damage caused to the competitiveness of U.S. producers in foreign markets. Other observers cite Soviet problems in absorbing and diffusing Western technology and argue that the danger to Western security is overstated.[5]

Moscow's purchases of machinery and equipment in the capitalist market, notwithstanding the high quality of U.S. technology and its attractiveness to the Soviet Union, are predominantly from Europe and Japan. The U.S. strategy of selective denial thus encounters further difficulties, in securing and enforcing international controls not only by allies but also by "neutrals" (and even the "non-aligned"). The primary international controls are the voluntary agreements reached in COCOM, the alliance's Paris-based Coordinating Committee (which also includes Japan). The Reagan administration has sought to tighten prohibitions, extend the list of products controlled, and strengthen the machinery of COCOM.

How successful is the selective denial campaign?[6] It is of course difficult for an outsider to judge, but even for those actively involved in the effort, assessment of results cannot be simple. The problem is to estimate how much escapes the control net. The ultimate criterion is the level of absorption in Soviet military production, but that, at best, can be evaluated only after a considerable time lag. Judging from press reports, it seems likely that the con-

---

[5]For example, Marshall Goldman, "Why Not Sell Technology to the Russians?" *Technology Review* 87 (February–March 1984).

[6]For statements of the Reagan administration's position on technology export controls and its evaluation of the success achieved, see Richard Perle, "The Eastward Technology Flow: A Plan of Common Action," *Strategic Review,* Spring 1984, pp. 24–32, and "East-West Relations and Technology Transfer," an address prepared by William Schneider, Jr., under secretary for security assistance, science and technology, U.S. Department of State, Bureau of Public Affairs, *Current Policy* no. 568, March 29, 1984.

trols, especially abroad, remain porous despite the great efforts of the Reagan administration and some increased cooperation from the allies. Opposition to further tightening seems quite vigorous. U.S. security-mindedness is confronted by considerably stronger economic interests in East-West trade in Europe and Japan, as well as by strikingly divergent views of the desirable course of relations with the USSR. The two factors are not unrelated, of course.[7]

The Grain Embargo and Its Aftermath

The grain embargo of 1980 and the sanctions against Poland and the USSR levied in December 1981 and June 1982 were the most dramatic examples in recent years of denial measures used to exert economic leverage on communist countries. Of the two episodes, the grain embargo was a purer case of denial-for-leverage because, as will be indicated below, there were mixed motives in 1981–82. Both cases have been judged failures by most observers, although an important qualification must be made in the case of the grain embargo. The U.S. government is now committed to a totally different policy of unfettered, dependable, and maximal levels of grain sales to the USSR; the use of grain exports for leverage has been forsworn.

President Carter's effort to deny Moscow seventeen million tons of grain was only about one-third successful, because Argentina, Australia, Canada, and the European Community were willing to fill the gap. Soviet meat supplies (the target of the embargo) dropped only marginally, and the Kremlin refused to listen to demands about withdrawal from Afghanistan. President Carter probably had in mind deterrence of further aggression rather than immediate Soviet withdrawal, but while Moscow did not invade Iran, it did aid and abet the Polish counterrevolution of December 1981. In any event, the embargo was pronounced a failure. Moreover, it was alleged to have hurt U.S. farm income; data on production, sales, and income in 1980 make this claim seem doubtful, but the charge was politically powerful. President Reagan rescinded the embargo shortly after assuming office and thereafter promoted agricultural exports to the USSR.

As a consequence of the repudiation of the grain embargo and under the pressure of the U.S. farm lobby, agricultural exports to the Soviets are now protected with a triple guarantee.

Legislation of 1981 requires extensive compensation to producers in the event of a future restriction on export of an agricultural commodity for reasons of national security or foreign policy, unless the restriction is imposed on all U.S. farm exports.

[7]See, for example, *Wall Street Journal,* July 24, 1984, and *New York Times,* January 1, 1985. For recent German views, see Heinrich Vogel, "Technology for the East—The Tiresome Issue," *Aussenpolitik,* 1985/2, pp. 117–26, and Klaus Ritter, "The Critical Issue of the Transfer of Technology," *NATO's Sixteen Nations,* July 1985, pp. 40–43.

Legislation of 1982 denies the president the right to restrict export of any farm commodity under an export contract at the time of restriction, if delivery is to take place within nine months.

Finally, the long-term agreement concluded with the USSR in August 1983 guarantees annual sales of nine million to twelve million tons of grain for five years, with additional amounts subject to negotiation, and forswears the right to curtail sales of the guaranteed amounts for any foreign policy purpose.

As one Department of Agriculture official put it after signing of the 1983 agreement: "It would have to be a very serious thing, a national emergency, a severing of diplomatic relations, almost a state of war for the United States to curtail supplies."[8]

Denial of grain sales for impedance or for leverage is effectively barred for the next few years, very likely for the rest of the 1980s. The mood of the administration also appears to reject the possibility of benefaction for leverage. President Reagan willingly (and apparently without much negotiation) raised the ceiling on Soviet grain purchases for the year 1984–85 to 22 million tons, which was also the maximum allowed for 1983–84.[9] There has been no hint since 1981 that the administration was even considering using grain sales as a carrot to elicit more acceptable Soviet behavior at home or abroad.

That the 1980 embargo was in its own terms a short-run failure seems a fair conclusion. Renewed U.S. efforts to secure greater cooperation from other producers might have been to some avail, but with the election of President Reagan the embargo was clearly a dead letter barely a year after its institution. The embargo had the important effect of accelerating Soviet diversification of its foreign grain supply base through the conclusion of a series of bilateral agreements, some annual and some multiyear, with Argentina, Australia, Brazil, and Canada, as well as with the United States. The dominant American position in the Soviet grain trade has been seriously weakened: in 1979 the United States provided 69 percent of the value of all Soviet grain imports, but by 1983 that share had fallen to less than a quarter. It was still only 39 percent in 1984.

Critics of the embargo have, however, ignored its unforeseen, longer-term success. By Soviet admission the embargo helped sustain the momentum behind the Brezhnev "food program," which involved a continuation of heavy investment in Soviet agriculture despite the USSR's clear comparative disadvantage in food production. Kremlin confidence in the stability and reliability of Western supplies would have curtailed so costly an effort to develop near self-sufficiency in food production. In a period of dwindling growth rates and sharply competing demands for investment resources, the embargo at least complicated Soviet decisions about resource allocation even if it did

[8]Quoted in *New York Times,* August 26, 1983.
[9]*Wall Street Journal,* September 12, 1984, p. 36. The Soviets actually bought 15 million tons in 1983–84.

not actually cut into the military's share. Paradoxically, then, Carter's failed embargo had longer-term effects that seem consonant with the Reagan administration's own view of Western interests.[10]

In the heat of the debate on East-West economics in 1981–82, many Europeans criticized the American government's position as hypocritical, because it sought to curtail exports important to Europe (capital) but rescinded the ban on exports important to the United States (grain). The administration countered by citing Western Europe's undercutting of the 1980 embargo, but it also argued that U.S. grain exports "sopped up" Soviet hard currency. European exports, on the other hand, contributed to the generation of Soviet hard-currency earnings (particularly the gas pipeline), which could be used to aid the military buildup.

Regrettably, analysis of the American "financial drain" argument does not suggest a clear conclusion. On the economics, it is evident that Soviet grain imports expend hard currency, but they also save domestic resources that can be used for purposes less favorable to the West, perhaps. The Kremlin's fear of external dependence, however, limits the scope of resource savings. Unwilling to subject itself to future embargoes, Moscow continues to invest heavily in Soviet agriculture. The 1980 embargo, ironically, has helped neutralize the contribution that unrestricted American grain sales make to the Soviet economy. As important as the economic are the political effects of alternative U.S. policy courses, but they are much more speculative. Who would benefit on balance from Soviet consumption gains, assuming uncontrolled Western sales? Who, alternatively, would benefit from strict belt-tightening, if that were how Moscow responded to an effective embargo? Apparent economic-military advantages may in practice be political disadvantages, and vice versa.

Ultimate assessment of any leverage strategy will also depend on the appropriateness of the match between the economic instruments and the political objectives. This factor is discussed below, but it may be said here that the failure of the grain embargo with respect to its direct purpose reflected a mismatch between a weak economic tool (partial and temporary curtailment of U.S. sales) and a highly valued Soviet operation (maintenance of a Soviet-controlled regime in Afghanistan). Although such a disjunction is not inevitable in possible uses of the grain export instrument, the policy environment of the mid-1980s makes further discussion seem academic.

Polish Martial Law and the Siberian Pipeline

In reaction to the Jaruzelski coup of December 13, 1981, President Reagan levied economic sanctions against both Poland and the Soviet Union. Those

---

[10]It has been claimed that the embargo was also largely responsible for the loosening of restrictions on the private plot in the USSR. Terry McNeill, "Mikhail Gorbachev—Just Another Apparatchik?" Radio Liberty RL 464/84, December 10, 1984, p. 10.

against the Soviet Union primarily affected exports of American equipment for the oil and gas industry. Ostensibly because there had been no movement in Poland to return to the status quo ante, these energy equipment sanctions were extended in June 1982 to cover equipment manufactured abroad under U.S. license and by subsidiaries of U.S. firms. The president thereby linked American sanctions against the Polish declaration of martial law to U.S. opposition to the Urengoi-Uzhgorod gas pipeline between Siberia and Western Europe. A denial-for-leverage policy targeted on the USSR was absorbed and obscured by an act that, in fact if not in intent, exerted leverage against Washington's European allies. The consequences were predictably unfortunate.

With only one possible exception, forcing default on the Polish debt, the range of sanctions considered by the U.S. government could not be expected to dent Warsaw's or Moscow's determination to pursue the reestablishment of the Polish Party's authority. It was argued at the time that the December sanctions were also intended to deter further repression and possible Soviet invasion. Soviet invasion was in fact made unnecessary by the imposition of martial law—and that was one of its purposes. Whether the sanctions effectively deterred additional repression is arguable; in the event, new repression was also made unnecessary, by the partial success of the Polish military pacification.

Whatever hope existed of effecting change in Poland surely rested on a united Western reaction. With some hesitation, a joint NATO position on sanctions against Poland was reached in January 1982, but the United States was alone in trying to punish Moscow as well. The expansion of equipment sanctions into "extraterritorial" controls directed at the Siberian pipeline provoked a crisis in the alliance and underscored the isolation of the Reagan administration.

Opposition to the pipeline began in the Carter administration but became a serious alliance issue only after the Ottawa economic summit in mid-1981. The initial basis for U.S. concern was the possibility of reverse Soviet leverage operating on European dependence on Soviet gas. But in the second half of 1981 and thereafter the focus of the Reagan administration's opposition shifted to prospective Soviet hard-currency earnings from gas exports in the latter 1980s and the command over Western technology that such purchasing power would make possible. Here, for the first and last time, Washington's continuing policy of selective denial of militarily relevant technology suddenly appeared to be part of a strategy of generalized resource denial. It was still targeted on the Soviet military buildup, but angry Europeans openly questioned whether concealed behind the expressed goal of only partial impedance lay the real goal, total impedance of Soviet economic growth ("economic warfare").

No critique of U.S. policy, however graceless the policy may seem, can itself justify the gas pipeline deals concluded between the West Europeans and

Moscow. It strains credulity that in the largest project in the history of East-West economic relations the Europeans failed to act in concert even for their own economic benefit, let alone political leverage. The wasting of that opportunity was not an accident. It reflected European disinterest in leverage and a view of East-West relations sharply different from the one developing in Washington at the same time. This perceptual gulf is one of the basic factors conditioning East-West economic relations in the near and middle term.

The Polish Debt

Once a rarity, rescheduling of a nation's external debt has become commonplace. It was Poland that triggered the landslide in March 1981, with a formal declaration of moratorium and a request to its Western creditors for rescheduling. Liberal Western credits, recession among Poland's hard-currency trade partners, and Warsaw's misguided economic strategy had brought Poland to an economic crisis. The country seemed to depend heavily on the West to avoid catastrophe. When martial law was imposed at the end of 1981, the Western debate on Poland's plight changed from a discussion of the costs and benefits of supplying aid to a consideration of the opportunities for exerting leverage on behalf of the restoration of the status quo ante. Efforts in that direction were, however, inconsistent, beset by self-doubt, and riven by controversy. Inevitably, the results were disappointing.

In early 1981 the West was still sympathetic to the Polish request for help although troubled both by the scale of Poland's needs and by the possibility of Soviet intervention to crush the Solidarity movement. A rescheduling of Poland's official debt falling due in 1981 was arranged almost immediately, in April 1981, and on favorable terms. Former secretary of state Alexander Haig has revealed that in the summer of 1981 the United States favored admission of Poland to the International Monetary Fund and urged Warsaw to make application, a sharp contrast to the position Washington took after martial law was declared.[11] The Western banks were somewhat harder-nosed, and negotiations dragged on until March 1982. By then the NATO governments had gone on record as refusing to reschedule official debt falling due after 1981 or to provide any new credits, as a sanction against martial law. The banks, however, went ahead and negotiated additional reschedulings with the Poles in 1982 and again in 1983. In 1984 they decided to save themselves future effort and rescheduled all debts falling due in 1984–87 *en bloc*. Moreover, the terms of the bank rescheduling became progressively softer. In particular, despite the NATO governments' declaration and their own 1981 guideline, which had demanded full payment of interest arrears before rescheduling of principal, the banks yielded to Warsaw's demand that part of the interest

---

[11]Alexander M. Haig, Jr., *Caveat: Realism, Reagan and Foreign Policy* (New York: Macmillan, 1984), p. 246.

owed be recycled. The share was set at 50 percent in the November 1982 agreement and 65 percent in the November 1983 agreement. The 1984 agreement abandoned the recycling arrangement in name but maintained and extended it in fact, by providing Warsaw with $700 million in new credits for 1984 and 1985.[12]

What were governments doing in the meantime? For more than a year they stood pat on the January 1982 NATO declaration and refused to enter rescheduling negotiations with the Polish government. But they did not press their banks to adhere to national policy. No new government credits were extended to Poland, it is true, but neither was any interest collected on the existing debt. Poland was granted a "holiday" on interest payments, which probably was an important factor in Warsaw's ability to repay its interest arrears to the banks. (Few Westerners commented on this income transfer from the public to the private sector.) As the Jaruzelski government became increasingly able to cope with its domestic opposition and manage some economic recovery, the leverage potential in the combination of Polish dependence and the financial power of Western governments evaporated. Negotiations between Warsaw and the Western governments were reopened in 1984, and an agreement to reschedule the 1982–84 debt arrears was finally achieved in July 1985.[13]

The basic leverage issue in the United States in early 1982 was whether to declare Poland formally in default. Assuming that a U.S. government action would have triggered a wave of corresponding action by other governments and the banks, leading to generalized default for Poland, Warsaw would have been denied reschedulings and new credits indefinitely pending agreement with its debtors. There were, however, technical reasons to doubt the automaticity of a chain reaction following a unilateral U.S. government declaration or even the likelihood of forcing U.S. banks to trigger default. Many observers argued that the drying up of credits to Eastern Europe in 1981–82, which created conditions of near-default with characteristics similar to those of default itself, provided the necessary leverage without the potentially high costs of default. Indeed, a great deal of concern was raised in banking circles that triggering Polish default would threaten the stability of the international monetary system. Moreover, Washington's allies were all solidly opposed to default.

Default-for-leverage had two major purposes. In the first rationale, leverage was directed at Poland to impose a penalty for the imposition of martial law, secure amelioration of the martial law regime, and deter further repression. The second and more popular position hoped to force the Kremlin to

[12]On the 1984 agreement see *Financial Times,* April 28 and 30, 1984, and *East-West* no. 339 (May 22, 1984), pp. 5–6.
[13]*Financial Times,* January 17, 1985; *East-West* nos. 367–368 (July 25, 1985). The U.S. government has withdrawn its objections to Polish membership in the IMF (*New York Times,* December 15 and 18, 1984), opening up a major channel of access to new loans.

unfurl the Soviet "umbrella," to take charge of and discharge Poland's obligations to the West. For most proponents of this position, the goal was analogous to that of the argument directed against Poland—imposition of a penalty and deterrence of other inimical action. Others saw an additional benefit. If Moscow were forced to shoulder the huge debts of Poland, and perhaps of other Eastern European countries as well, it would have fewer resources to use on its military buildup and on perpetrating mischief abroad—in short, an argument of generalized resource denial was added to the denial-for-leverage base.

Would a triggered default actually have forced open the Soviet umbrella? Little evidence favored this supposition, unfortunately, and considerable logic opposed it. Moscow had regarded the Polish economic strategy of the 1970s with considerable misgivings, and ordinary Soviet citizens grumbled that Poland was already living at their expense. It was hard to see why the Politburo would want to bail out an errant Poland on behalf of Western bankers. Soviet actions on balance tended in the opposite direction. Although there was direct Soviet aid to Poland in 1980–81, Moscow then apparently reversed policy. It ceased to allow Warsaw to run a generous ruble trade deficit, which was cut 60 percent in 1982. Polish terms of trade with the USSR deteriorated a further 3–4 percent in 1983 after 6 and 8 percent declines in 1981 and 1982.[14]

Rather than shielding Poland, Moscow seemed to be insisting that Warsaw pull the nation up by the bootstraps. A Western declaration of default might have played into Soviet hands, helping to establish the image of a Western conspiracy and providing a stronger rationale for stringent belt-tightening. Perhaps more significant, a default declaration might have brought on a reorientation of Poland's trade to the East greater and more lasting than what was already taking place under conditions of near-default. The policy of no default did not seem to have a tangible impact on Polish events or on Soviet risk assessments, but a declaration of default might have both failed to accomplish its basic purpose and produced disconcerting longer-term consequences.

One basic problem of the debate on leverage in the Polish debt crisis was the concentration on denial to the total exclusion of benefaction. It was difficult to believe that the promise of indefinite continuation of sanctions would give either Poland or the Soviet Union an incentive to modify its behavior. Nobody in the United States, however, was arguing for an extension of aid to either country. Conditions under which sanctions might be raised or lifted were rarely made explicit but had to be inferred from the particular commentator's denunciation of Soviet and Polish behavior.

U.S. policy in the Polish debt crisis pretended to exercise leverage on the

---

[14]Wharton Econometric Forecasting Associates, *Centrally Planned Economies Current Analysis* 4, nos. 11–12 (February 22, 1984).

fulcrum of Warsaw's acute need for extensive refinancing. After the December 1981 coup a State Department memo declared: "We believe our economic leverage on the Poles is maximized if they must contend with meeting their Western debt obligations."[15] The department further argued that "the suspension of consideration of negotiations on rescheduling 1982 Polish debt allows us to pursue the collection of those debts."[16] In fact, however, the suspension of rescheduling negotiations provided the Poles with an unsanctioned moratorium for payments of both principal and interest on their official debt. The banks pursued their own interests and made the Poles' task of meeting their Western debt obligations on private account successively easier. Fear of disrupting the international monetary system and the firm opposition of the allies stayed the Reagan administration's hand in calling Poland in default. But default might have been counterproductive, and the absence of positive incentives to Warsaw or Moscow strengthened the likelihood of an unpromising outcome.

United Western policy that applied a full range of sanctions to both Poland and the USSR, complemented with positive inducements, might have had greater success. Many analysts argue that the firm retention of Poland in the Soviet bloc was a priority for the Kremlin, and no economic carrots and sticks could have induced the Politburo once more to run the risk of a pluralist Poland slipping out of Soviet control. They may be right, but the failure of a balanced and concerted allied policy, internally consistent and persistently applied, would have been no greater, and it would certainly have been more honorable, than the defeat of the actual policy.

Political Dissension in the West

The United States, as indicated earlier, has never enjoyed a dominant position in Soviet trade with the developed capitalist world. The initial U.S. political dominance of the NATO alliance has long since eroded and is unlikely to be restored in its original form. Washington thus cannot manipulate trade with the Soviets for security or other foreign policy purposes on its own; success depends critically on the cooperation of its allies. In both international crises of the early 1980s, however, Afghanistan and Poland, and in the various efforts to effect leverage or resource denial, cooperation was poor or absent. Other suppliers, including the European Community, helped the USSR circumvent the American grain embargo; European NATO members refused to join the United States in levying sanctions against the Soviet Union as a penalty for the imposition of martial law in Poland; Western Europe bridled at Washington's effort to thwart completion of the Siberian gas pipeline; allied

[15]Quoted in *Wall Street Journal*, January 7, 1982.

[16] "Treasury and State Department Background Paper on Poland's Financial and Economic Situation for the European Subcommittee of the Senate Foreign Relations Committee," January 27, 1982.

opposition was an important factor in dissuading the Reagan administration from declaring the Polish government in default on its official debt. The administration has had somewhat more success in securing multilateral agreement in COCOM to tighten export controls on technology;[17] the alliance may now be more sensitive to the role of subsidies in Western credit arrangements for the Eastern bloc; perhaps there will be a more concerted effort to extract better terms from Moscow should another gas deal be offered in the 1990s. But recent history suggests that alliance cooperation to exploit Western economic strength to "lever" Soviet policy is unlikely.

There are surely many explanations for this situation.[18] Economic interests on both sides of the Atlantic are asymmetrical: despite the low share of trade with the USSR in the aggregate trade volume of any of the developed industrial countries, that trade is much more significant for several West European countries, especially the Federal Republic, than it is for the United States. Geography and history are probably more important than economics, impelling Germany in particular to regard "normalization" of relations with the East as the only way to assure coexistence on the same continent with the Soviets. Obviously not all Europeans think like the left wing of the German Social Democratic party, just as far from all Americans share the views of the platform committee at the 1984 Republican party convention. But in the early 1980s a yawning gap was revealed between the modal European view of where East-West relations ought to be headed and the view of the Reagan administration, which was in turn widely supported in the United States. Europeans longed for a return to the cooperative second track of the alliance's dual-track political strategy, formulated in the 1967 Harmel Report. Washington felt strongly that the first, military, track had been badly neglected and needed urgent attention. A bifurcation in perceptions of Soviet power and goals, and of the appropriate strategy for East-West relations, was apparent to all.

Soviet Dependence and Vulnerability

U.S.-led efforts to effect denial or leverage with regard to the USSR were notably unsuccessful. One might ascribe that failure to the characteristics of the effort—disunity of the West, uncertainty of purpose, inconsistency and inconstancy of policy and execution. But what of the intended target? What contribution did the Soviets make to the frustration of the Western attempt? Was an alternative outcome possible—that is, were the Soviets vulnerable to a more aptly managed Western strategy of suasion?

[17]In the summer of 1984, for example, COCOM agreed on a new set of controls on computer exports. See *Financial Times*, July 16, 1984, and *New York Times*, July 17, 1984.

[18]See my "East-West Economic Relations: Conflict and Concord in Western Policy Choices," *Atlantic Quarterly* 2 (Spring 1984), pp. 12–39.

It is useful to distinguish three concepts of Soviet involvement in and sensitivity with respect to foreign economic relations—trade participation, dependence, and vulnerability. The scale of Soviet involvement in international trade, its *trade participation,* can be measured on a comparative basis by normalizing total trade values—dividing trade by the value of aggregate national output (gross national product or gross domestic product or the like). We have been brought to recognize that the Soviet import participation ratio measured in domestic prices is much higher than the same ratio at "world market" prices (foreign-trade-ruble values translated into dollars or other hard currencies at official exchange rates), and the USSR is actually comparable to several of the major trading nations of the West (lower than EEC countries or Sweden but higher than either the United States or Japan). This situation resulted from the dramatic growth in Soviet trade in the 1970s, itself a reflection of the watershed change in Soviet policy regarding economic interchange with the outside world.[19]

Soviet aggregate import participation was about 15 percent of GNP in 1980. This figure includes trade with Eastern Europe, other Soviet allies, and the Third World; excluding trade with these countries would reduce the participation rate by perhaps one-half. But the economic importance of trade, the degree of the nation's *dependence* on trade, is measured only crudely by participation rates. Dependence should be measured in terms of the opportunity costs of reducing trade participation, that is, the costs of substituting domestic for imported goods. Direct, quantitative measures of dependence are difficult to come by, but on a rough estimate Western equipment was the source of perhaps one in every six or seven rubles of Soviet investment in machinery.[20] The evidence from macroeconomic studies is still inconclusive and controversial. Case studies of technology transfer, however, have given clearer messages about the utility of imports for particular industries. For a time in the 1970s, at any rate, Soviet leaders seemed to view the importation of Western technology as an important means of accelerating Soviet produc-

[19]The major contribution here is by Vladimir Treml and Barry Kostinsky. See their Bureau of the Census report, *Domestic Value of Soviet Foreign Trade: Exports and Imports in the 1972 Input-Output Table* (Washington, D.C., October 1982), and Treml's earlier "Foreign Trade and the Soviet Economy: Changing Parameters and Interrelations," in E. Neuberger and L. D. Tyson, eds., *The Impact of International Economic Disturbances in the Soviet Union and Eastern Europe* (New York: Pergamon, 1980).

[20]An authoritative Soviet source declares that imported machinery "at present" accounts for about 35 percent of the machinery component of Soviet investment, compared to 15 percent in 1970. V. Sel'tsovskii, "Rol' vneshnei torgovli SSSR v reshenii narodnokhoziaistvennykh zadach," *Planovoe khoziaistvo,* 1984/7, p. 123. In terms of foreign trade rubles, the socialist countries account for about 70 percent of Soviet machinery imports. The socialist to nonsocialist ratio is likely nearer six to four in domestic ruble prices (inferred from Treml and Kostinsky, *Domestic Value,* p. 23). Sel'tsovskii provides no information on the price base of his numbers nor any indication of how quality differences in imported machinery are handled. The West's share of Soviet investment in machinery is augmented by East European imports that find their way ultimately to the USSR.

tivity. And Western food imports became a mainstay of the regime's program to stabilize and improve the national diet.[21]

Future levels of Soviet dependence are unlikely to be substantially reduced. At the end of the 1970s Soviet imports of Western machinery and equipment fell off, and some opposition was voiced to high levels of dependence on trade with the West.[22] In the 1980s purchases of machinery and equipment from the West have grown far less rapidly than those from the socialist countries. Nevertheless, Moscow may at some point wish to resume buying Western technology on a substantial scale. If Soviet annual growth rates fail to rise above the level of 2–3 percent in the next few years, it will be because the regime is unable to raise productivity sufficiently to compensate for the low (and even declining) rates of growth of labor and capital inputs. Western technology in Soviet hands did not spark a miracle in the 1970s; aggregate productivity growth was not accelerated. But it may have kept matters from getting worse. The Kremlin may be reluctant to increase its dependence on the West, but it also shows awareness of the large and often growing gaps between East and West in the technological level of many industries, especially those connected with electronics and computers. Gorbachev's economic program depends heavily on harnessing the engine of science and technology to pull the Soviet economy out of its low-growth rut.[23] It is not yet clear whether he believes he can do that without external aid, but the Western observer may be permitted to doubt that he can.

The magnitude of Soviet imports will, of course, depend also on Soviet ability to buy in hard-currency markets. Here the probable stagnation of Soviet oil production in the medium term—the long-heralded decline in Soviet output may now be starting—will present an important barrier. Sales of crude oil and products accounted for close to half of all Soviet exports for hard currency in the early 1980s. The solution to this problem may involve not only measures of conservation and cutbacks of supply to Eastern Europe, as well as substitution of more easily available natural gas, but also the resumption of substantial borrowing from the West. The Soviet net hard-currency debt—about $10.4 billion in 1984[24]—is very low by international standards, and Moscow's creditworthiness in Western banking circles remains fairly high, despite the less rosy picture for energy exports.

[21]In an unpublished paper for the Bureau of the Census, Vladimir Treml estimates that net imports accounted for 20–25 percent of Soviet daily food consumption in calories per head.

[22]Sel'tsovskii is among those Soviet writers who take a distinctly more positive view of the utility of imports ("Rol' vneshnei torgovli SSSR," pp. 123–24). See also Philip Hanson, "Soviet Advocate of More Technology Imports," Radio Liberty RL 231/84, June 13, 1984.

[23]On Gorbachev's economic program, see my *Soviet Central Decisionmaking and Economic Growth: A Summing Up* (Santa Monica: Rand Corporation, R-3349-AF, December 1985), sec. 3.

[24]CIA, *Handbook of Economic Statistics, 1985* (Washington, D.C., September 1985), p. 73. The Soviet debt service ratio (payments of interest and principal divided by all hard currency earnings) is still only 18 percent.

But what political price is Moscow prepared to pay to maintain these flows? Soviet *vulnerability* to external pressure is more difficult to measure than trade participation or dependence. It is a function of many variables of internal and external relations, political and economic. It depends on the structure of foreign trade markets, but most important it depends on the will to resist of the political leadership. In the early 1980s the potential existed for increasing Soviet vulnerability through coordinated action in all of the major arenas of East-West economic interaction—grain supply, technology exports, credit extensions and renewals—but, as we have seen, these opportunities were rejected, neglected, or dissipated. Had they been skillfully exploited, however, it is not obvious that the ultimate outcomes would have been much different. The crucial difference is Soviet political will. In a closely regulated society, where the regime is largely successful in shaping national perceptions about the intent of the outside world, it is the political will of the leadership that mainly determines the state's response.

This bring us back to the price the Kremlin is willing to pay. If the answer in the early 1980s emerged from rational calculation, then the Politburo's analysts must have estimated the resource costs of swallowing or, if possible, circumventing particular sanctions. These costs are finite, limited by the size of the economy and the diversity of its resources, and limited also because major adjustments take place in the short and medium term. The political costs and benefits of yielding or remaining obdurate are no easier to quantify in Moscow than in the West, but they probably receive primary attention in the Kremlin despite their inherent uncertainties. This reasoning suggests that the likelihood that the Politburo will yield to external pressure will be greater where the political disutility of yielding is judged to be substantially smaller than the economic costs of resisting.

Such a conclusion carries an obvious corollary: a combination of high-value political stakes and weak economic sanctions virtually guarantees Soviet noncompliance. Regrettably, such a combination seems to characterize the leverage experience of the early 1980s. Nor will it be easy to invert that combination in the future. In general, American public support for a sustained program of trade manipulation with modest political objectives would be difficult to obtain. Moreover, the most potent weapon in the American arsenal, grain sales, has now been withdrawn from active service. The use of other trade instruments is even more dependent on the cooperation of third parties, who for the indefinite future are likely to view East-West economic relations in a very different light from Americans. The West has been unable in the recent past to transform higher levels of Soviet dependence on Western trade into equally high levels of Kremlin vulnerability. It is unlikely to attain greater success in the future.

This discussion has considered the implications only of direct relations between the Soviet Union and the West. But an analysis of Soviet vulnerability to Western economic pressure must take some account of the role of Eastern

Europe, in its relations with the West on one side and the USSR on the other. The Soviet Union, if we can credit the estimates of various Western analysts, now pays a substantial economic price to maintain the integrity of the communist bloc, in terms of implicit subsidies on Soviet energy sales to and machinery purchases from Eastern Europe.[25] The terms of trade have been turning against Eastern Europe, however, as Soviet energy prices increase and Moscow insists on better quality in the machinery it imports from Eastern Europe. At some point this process will substantially reduce the value of the Soviet trade relationship to Eastern Europe. These countries are in any case interested in increasing their trade with the West, in order to accelerate their internal growth and improve their national living standards. They are being held back at present because of the high opportunity cost of Western energy—except for Poland and to a decreasing extent Romania, Eastern Europe must import its energy sources—and the production inefficiences that the tie to the Soviet Union has fostered in the East European manufacturing sector.

If Moscow continues to try to limit the economic burden of its hegemony in Eastern Europe, it risks augmenting the bloc's economic difficulties, leading possibly to greater political instability. An opportunity may thus arise for the West to exploit the Soviet dilemma and, at some economic cost, through widening East European access to Western markets (e.g., by increased concessional lending) to draw the East European states gradually out of the Soviet orbit. The resemblance such a scenario bears to the 1970s can hardly be missed, either in Moscow or in the Western capitals. Remembering the debt problems of Poland, Romania, Hungary (or Yugoslavia), as well as the political consequences, the West might hesitate to repeat the experience. The Kremlin has its own reasons to contemplate the prospect with distaste—including, of course, its opposition to subversion of the Eastern alliance.

If it appears necessary Moscow will presumably undertake a larger burden than it now seems willing to shoulder in order to protect its vital political stake in Eastern Europe. Would the consequent resource cost imposed on the Soviet Union (a penalty that could outweigh the effect of Western overt acts of denial) be sufficient to bring the West to resume large-scale lending to Eastern Europe?[26] But the very question presupposes a Western willingness to engage in political games which is belied by the painful history of efforts to wield leverage and denial in recent years. Eastern Europe is likely to pose a difficult policy problem for the West as well as for Moscow, but it seems unlikely that Soviet vulnerability will be significantly affected.

[25]The best known of these estimates is Michael Marrese and Jan Vanous, *Soviet Subsidization of Trade with Eastern Europe* (Berkeley: Institute of International Studies, University of California, 1983).

[26]Some in Western Europe, particularly in Germany, see economic and political reform in Eastern Europe as a channel for influencing social-political change in the USSR and as a path to revitalizing detente. For them, subsidizing greater East European trade with the West offers its own reward.

Prospects

What are the prospects, then, for Soviet-American economic relations?

Regarding trade flows, we may ignore Soviet exports to the United States, as unlikely to change dramatically,[27] and consider Soviet imports of food (mostly grain) and of technology separately. In the short and medium term U.S. grain sales are likely to continue, at least in moderate volume, under the protections of the Long-Term Agreement (LTA) and legislative acts discussed above. President Reagan raised the ceiling on Soviet grain purchases for 1984–85 to 22 million tons, the same maximum allowed for 1983–84. The Soviets brought only 15 million tons for delivery in 1983–84, but this amount was just short of the record level set by U.S. sales in 1979.[28] In 1984–85 Soviet purchases apparently reached the 20-million-ton mark.[29] Continued poor performance by Soviet agriculture could help maintain this level of U.S. grain sales in the latter 1980s. Indeed, a prudent forecast would see, in the absence of other disturbances, indefinite continuation of Soviet needs for U.S. feed grains on a low to moderate scale despite the maintenance of high rates of Soviet investment in food production.

It is conceivable, in the strictly limited sense of a logical possibility, that Moscow may decide to break the LTA before its appointed expiration date in 1988. This would surely not take place because the Soviets had managed to achieve a bumper harvest or two; the Kremlin could hardly have any illusions about the stability of Soviet weather and would not want to confront harvest failure after having burned its trade bridges with the United States. Breaking the LTA would most likely be a political act, one of retaliation or perhaps of warning after a "hostile act," in an attempt to deter some more damaging action in the offing. The Soviet Union has not been innocent of exploiting its economic relations with other states for political ends; contracts and agreements have been broken in the past. Nevertheless, Moscow has not used overt economic sanctions of this sort in recent years, and it has never done so vis-à-vis a major Western power. On the contrary, it has made an effort to demonstrate the credibility of Soviet promises and the steadfastness of the USSR as a trade partner.[30] So important is American grain to maintenance of Soviet consumption levels that severance of the LTA would be considered, one suspects, only in an environment of sharp deterioration of East-West relations.

The scale of Soviet imports of machinery, equipment, and knowhow from the United States depends on several factors. The general tenor of East-West

[27]Despite optimistic notes sounded in the 1985 meetings of the American-Soviet Trade and Economic Council.

[28]*Wall Street Journal,* September 12, 1984, p. 36.

[29]*Journal of Commerce,* August 26, August 28, September 3, and September 27, 1985.

[30]There have been a few cases of winter interruptions of Soviet energy supply to Western Europe. The Soviets explain them on technical grounds, but some European observers suspect they may reflect an attempt to firm up prices.

relations is probably of major importance, conditioning the entire set of economic relations. Other factors also play a role: the nature and scale of Soviet needs, of course; the state of relations between the USSR and other industrially developed countries, particularly Western Europe and Japan; and the state of relations among members of the Western alliance system, to name only the more important. While many combinations of these factors are conceivable, only a few seem generally plausible and internally consistent. Five are worth noting.

The first, Cold War–Stagnation, combines persistent stagnation in the Soviet economy (say, less than 2 percent annual growth in GNP) with intensified cold war in U.S.-USSR relations. Such an environment might put a premium on Soviet efforts to enlist the aid of Western Europe and Japan in stimulating Soviet productivity, a campaign that would evidently have great political significance. The United States could be expected to oppose a marked increase in trade and aid to Moscow, and the Soviet campaign would thus aggravate conflict within the Western alliance. U.S.-Soviet trade would shrink to minimal levels. In such an environment the LTA might be broken or not renewed in 1988.

The second scenario, Neodetente-Stagnation, retains Soviet economic difficulties but postulates something like a regulated state of coexistence between the superpowers, developed tacitly or perhaps even formally, through negotiated rules of the game which had more meaning than those developed in 1972–73.[31] Relations between the USSR and Western Europe and Japan would inevitably be even warmer. Domestic and allied pressures for expansion of trade contacts, as well as liberalization of credit and exchange relationships, would be high and difficult to contain even if Washington were so inclined. The cocom and U.S. export-control frameworks might remain in place, but the American drive to limit the flow of Western high technology adaptable to Soviet military uses would be increasingly vulnerable.

Both scenarios assume steady Soviet demand for Western imports in the now traditional categories—particularly food and capital goods—as a function of Soviet inability to climb unaided out of low-level growth. They assume, therefore, that Soviet leaders perceive a link between Western technology and increased, perhaps even accelerating, Soviet productivity. They assume further that Moscow is willing to court the political risks of higher dependence, either because Soviet leaders discount the ability of the West to exploit Soviet dependence or because they believe the political risks of failing to enlist outside aid surpass the costs of greater vulnerability. But such assumptions may be wrong. The new Soviet leadership may somehow manage to pull the economy out of the doldrums (bringing GNP growth to an annual

---

[31]Presumably the November 1985 "Fireside Summit" would be followed by U.S.-Soviet encounters at various levels which would somehow bridge some of the gaps only discussed in Geneva.

level of, say, 4 percent or better),[32] thereby weakening the felt need for Western aid. Even without such a strong recovery, moreover, the leadership may become more concerned about the political risks of greater dependence than about the costs of continued poor performance. Trade policy would then be modified autarky. It could accompany either of the East-West regimes outlined above, creating two further scenarios, Cold War–Modified Autarky or Neodetente-Modified Autarky. The former seems plausible in part because it evokes historical precedent; the latter seems less credible because it involves a conflict between a "warm" East-West environment and a "cold" Soviet trade policy. One might expect at the least a further modification of modified autarky in favor of greater trade with Western Europe and Japan. The combination of modified autarky and Cold War certainly suggests low levels of economic intercourse with all parts of the West.

Finally we must mention, for the sake of completeness if not of probability, the 1970s Refurbished: a combination of renegotiated rules of the East-West game plus a smart recovery in Soviet economic growth which leads to substantially higher trade flows.

Readers will prefer different scenarios. Some may want to reenact the 1970s, others may opt for an easing of East-West tensions but also a continuing limit on Soviet economic capabilities, at least for a while. There are grounds, however, for fearing the possibility of one or the other Cold War scenario. The first could bring an exacerbation of intra-West tensions focused on the level and character of East-West trade; the second might signify enhanced Soviet capabilities to support inimical purposes. Both are likely to imply low levels of U.S.-Soviet trade in anything other than food. Neodetente-Stagnation and the 1970s Refurbished would mean enhanced trade flows. But current trade patterns and current political realities make it unwise to promise American machinery manufacturers a vast new market in the USSR.

In trade policy, finally, there is likely to be a sharp divergence between the policy suggested by a sober recognition of history and contemporary reality and the policy that will actually be followed. To this observer of America's past attempts to turn its economic muscle to advantage in the East-West contest, the lesson seems clear: the U.S. trade position is too weak for unilateral action. The political process in the United States and in its major allies, and alliance differences in basic attitudes on East-West relations, preclude effective concert to wield the tools of international leverage. Selective denial to impede Soviet military buildup will probably be pursued under Democratic and Republican administrations, although with differing levels of intensity and dedication. Strengthened controls to prevent the leakage of militarily relevant technology, limitation of the subsidies involved in credits, perhaps even the rudiments of an alliance energy policy to avoid another Siberian gas pipe-

---

[32]The twelfth Five-Year Plan draft (1986–90) calls for an annual rate of increase in net material product of 3.5–4.1 percent, compared to a claimed 1981–85 average of about 3.2 percent per year.

line controversy—these seem feasible policy goals. But they represent only a marginal use of economic instruments relative to the far-reaching leverage and denial efforts of the recent past. Such, regrettably, appears to be the limit of the alliance's capability.

It is more likely, however, that the Reagan administration or a successor will ignore the record and on the occasion of some future Soviet act that offends U.S. values and sensibilities will reexamine the options for economic retaliation. One should not be too critical of such a reaction; in a world where military measures may be too dangerous to be contemplated, the arsenal of usable responses is pitifully meager. As an expression of moral outrage, such gestures have both internal value and external significance. But we should have few illusions about the effects likely to result from our periodic lashing out. Intermittent passion is not an effective substitute for long-term, reasoned alignment of means and ends.

8

U.S. – Soviet Interactions
in the Third World

Francis Fukuyama

While a great deal of attention has been focused recently on the question of nuclear war and arms control as the centerpiece of U.S.-Soviet relations, the Third World is the only arena of the competition in which the United States has actually engaged in major military conflicts since 1945, and in which Americans, Russians, their friends and allies have died in large numbers. Developments in the Third World—particularly in Korea and Vietnam—virtually defined the Cold War in its first two decades, and Soviet and Cuban activities there bore major responsibility for undermining the detente of the 1970s. The Third World remains the most likely venue for future U.S.-Soviet confrontation, and the Persian Gulf holds an all-too-real potential to spark nuclear confrontation between the superpowers and return us full circle to the nuclear question.

This chapter begins by outlining the general structure of U.S.-Soviet conflict in the Third World in the first three postwar decades, analyzes the several important changes that occurred during the mid-to-late 1970s, and concludes with the implications of those changes for the balance of the 1980s and beyond. In U.S.-Soviet interaction in the Third World, the future will look like the past in many respects, with the Soviet Union and its allies seeking to change a status quo backed by the United States. This chapter will argue, however, that in certain key respects the United States and the Soviet Union are in the process of reversing roles in the Third World. As a consequence, superpower interactions are likely to become quite different from what we have come to expect.

Characteristics of Postwar U.S.-Soviet Interactions

U.S.-Soviet conflict in the Third World in the roughly three decades since the end of World War II manifested a fairly consistent pattern: the United

[198]

States sought to maintain the status quo while the Soviet Union, its clients, and associated national liberation movements sought to challenge it. Like all generalizations this one is subject to numerous qualifications and exceptions, but it accurately characterizes both major wars in the period, Korea and Vietnam, as well as a host of smaller conflicts and crises—including those over Iran in 1947, Suez in 1956, Lebanon-Iraq in 1958, the Cuban Revolution, Laos in 1960, Algeria through the early sixties, Angola in 1975, the Horn of Africa in 1977–78, Afghanistan in 1978, and Nicaragua in 1979. It should be no surprise that the Soviet Union has generally supported challenges to the status quo, for the Soviet state was founded on the basis of a certain dynamic concept of history and much of the Third World began the postwar period either as colonial dependencies or as newly independent states struggling to cut ties with former colonizers. When the USSR made its first major venture into the Third World with the Egyptian-Czech arms deal of 1955, Moscow had virtually no friends or clients in the Third World; indeed, it had almost no physical access to the outside world as a result of the system of interlocking defensive pacts erected by the United States around its periphery. Change of almost any sort could only benefit Soviet interests and the United States was consequently likely to view it with suspicion.

Soviet foreign policy in the Third World was chiefly concerned with how best to bring about revolutionary changes in the status quo, in ways that both were effective and did not unduly damage the interests of the USSR as a state. The issues included the readiness of a country (given its socioeconomic level of development) for national liberation or revolutionary change, the role of armed struggle versus more traditional forms of political activity, collaboration with non-Communists in broad popular front organizations, and the role of peasants and bourgeois intellectuals in working-class organizations. Soviet policy makers brought to these questions a very rich background of theory and practical experience. Their debates with the Chinese in the 1950s and 1960s over such questions as guerrilla war and with the Cubans over the *foco* theory echoed the discussions of earlier years, within the Bolshevik movement before the Revolution and subsequently in the Comintern.

Many of these issues ultimately boiled down to tactics regarding the appropriate pace and risks to be undertaken in promoting revolutionary change. The Soviet Union, as an established state and a nuclear-armed superpower, generally tended to worry about premature bids for power which might at a minimum lead to the destruction of the local movement, and at a maximum provoke Western intervention with the threat of military confrontation and ultimately nuclear war. Soviet policy, drawing on its highly developed doctrinal background, demonstrated considerable flexibility, both in identifying and exploiting opportunities and in scaling back support and urging caution. Both Khrushchev and Brezhnev spoke of the need for peaceful coexistence and began a movement toward the regulation of relations with the United States which culminated in the detente of the early seventies. While Soviet spokesmen began talking to Western audiences about the need for mutual superpower restraint in local conflicts, however, to their own ideological sympathizers they emphasized that detente between the superpowers on a state-to-state level did not mean an end to the struggle for national liberation or social change. And indeed, Soviet behavior in the Third World became if anything more activist with the coming of detente.[1]

U.S. policy in this same period complemented Soviet policy. It was primarily concerned with how to deter or defend against Soviet threats to the status quo. The threat, as a result of American experiences in Europe and Korea, was conceived of in the 1950s as primarily a conventional military one. The U.S. response was to try to extend the protection of its nuclear superiority, through the doctrine of massive retaliation and the signing of formal mutual defense treaties modeled on the NATO alliance, to countries in the Middle East and Southeast Asia. As it became clear that such a strategy was not effective against the predominant threats that emerged in the Third World, internal instability and guerrilla warfare, U.S. emphasis shifted toward counterinsurgency and military assistance. Vietnam was in many respects the archetypical Third World crisis, with the application of massive U.S. military power to suppress a communist insurgency.

American policy had a political dimension as well. It sought to find a workable democratic middle ground between repressive authoritarianism and the sort of revolutionary change supported by the Soviet Union. Hence the United States encouraged decolonization in former Dutch, French, and British territories, supported land reform in Vietnam and more recently El Salvador, gave out generous amounts of economic assistance to promote long-term economic growth, and in the late 1970s tried to lay increased emphasis on human rights. In this sense U.S. policy supported, strictly speaking, not the status quo but moderate political reform. In practice, however, the development of democratic Third World alternatives remained more a goal than an actuality.

There were, of course, significant exceptions to this overall pattern. The United States made its own challenge to the status quo and sought to roll back Soviet gains in Korea and Vietnam; individual American clients, for example Israel, made gains at the expense of Soviet allies.[2] The Soviet Union for its part faced the problem of maintaining the status quo in areas where its policy had been successful, and it spent considerable effort trying to hang on to such clients as Egypt, Indonesia, Cuba, and Somalia. Nonetheless, U.S. actions against Soviet positions in the Third World (crossing the thirty-eighth parallel in Korea or bombing North Vietnam) were, generally speaking, tac-

---

[1]See Leonard Shapiro, "The International Department of the CPSU," *International Journal*, Winter 1976–77, pp. 49ff.

[2]There were, in addition, some cases of attempted and on occasion successful rollback as a result of covert intervention, including Iran in 1952, Guatemala in 1954, Syria in 1957, and Cuba in 1961.

tically offensive responses to prior, Soviet-supported initiatives. The United States remained on the strategic defensive. Challenges to the Soviet-supported status quo, moreover, came about mostly as a result of high-level shifts on the part of client state leaderships, not from broadly based domestic opposition movements.

Changes in the Third World Environment

By the end of the 1970s a number of changes had occurred in the Third World. Those changes had an important effect on the relative positions of the United States and the Soviet Union.

The first of these changes was the growth of Soviet military power and other instruments of leverage. On a strategic level, the Soviet Union had achieved parity or better with the United States by the early 1970s. While it is doubtful that the growth of the Soviet strategic arsenal can be translated directly into meaningful political leverage in local crises, that growth has succeeded in deterring the United States from any consideration of resort to nuclear weapons in response to Soviet-sponsored challenges,[3] particularly in peripheral Third World theaters. (Strategic superiority never has had the deterrent effect in the Third World that was hoped for in the Dulles era, but it is possible to document at least one instance when fear of U.S. nuclear escalation restrained Soviet behavior.)[4] On a conventional level, Soviet acquisition of substantial power projection forces and the bases to support them has permitted much more active intervention than in the past. At the time of the Suez crisis in 1956, for example, Soviet defense minister Zhukov is said to have responded to a demand for intervention by President Quwatli of Syria by asking "How can we go to the aid of Egypt? Tell me! Are we supposed to send our armies through Turkey, Iran, and then into Syria and Iraq and on into Israel and so eventually attack the British and French forces?"[5] By 1970, when the USSR sent nearly twenty thousand air defense troops to Egypt to defend the interior against Israeli deep-penetration attacks, it could no longer plead lack of capability for failing to intervene in Third World crises. Each of its subsequent major involvements, the October War of 1973, Angola, the Horn of Africa, and Afghanistan, demonstrated the effectiveness of these new capabilities.

The second change has been the emergence of Soviet proxies as major actors in the Third World. There is by now a de facto division of labor to sup-

[3]The Persian Gulf may be one exception to this generalization.

[4]During the 1958 Lebanese-Iraqi crisis Khrushchev reportedly refused a request by Egyptian president Nasser to intervene on behalf of the new regime in Iraq by telling him "frankly, we are not ready for a confrontation. We are not ready for World War Three. . . . Dulles could blow the whole world to pieces." Quoted in Mohamed Haykal, *Nasser: the Cairo Documents* (London: New English Library, 1972), pp. 131–32.

[5]Mohamed Haykal, *The Sphinx and the Commissar* (New York: Harper & Row, 1978), p. 71.

port pro-Soviet regimes and national liberation movements in the Third World, which suggests a fairly high degree of organization and systematic mutual support. The same countries have been active in a variety of geographically remote countries, with Cubans providing military manpower, East Germans restructuring internal security services, Czechs and North Koreans providing arms and technical assistance, the Soviets providing overall logistical support, and so forth. The Cubans have provided clients with substantial numbers of ground forces (substantial, that is, by Third World standards) without provoking quite the strong American response that direct Soviet intervention would stimulate. They have moreover played an important role in identifying opportunities for action, in many cases before the Soviets themselves.[6]

The third change has been in America's willingness to intervene in Third World conflicts following its experience in Vietnam. The most clear-cut example of this change was passage of the Clark Amendment in December 1975, forbidding U.S. assistance to any of the contending groups during the Angolan civil war. The Reagan administration has followed a somewhat more activist policy in Central America, Lebanon, and the Caribbean, and considerable public approbation attended the intervention in Grenada. Grenada was popular, however, only because it was short, successful, and relatively costless. The protracted guerrilla war in El Salvador is much more representative of Third World conflicts, and it is clear that the American Congress and public opinion will not support greater U.S. involvement there.

These first three changes have led to a fourth, namely, a major change in the nature of the Soviet client base. To some extent the difference is simply quantitative: while the Soviets have lost some major clients, Egypt and Somalia among them, a decade of intense activity in the Third World has produced a net gain in numbers and an upgrading of Moscow's position in other Third World allies (e.g., Vietnam).

More important, however, the difference is also qualitative, in the internal character of the new client states. In 1964 the Soviet Union had only three self-proclaimed Marxist-Leninist clients in the Third World: North Korea, North Vietnam, and Cuba. Twenty years later not only have these regimes remained in power, they have been joined by thirteen others: Angola, Mozambique, Ethiopia, the People's Democratic Republic of Yemen, Afghanistan, Nicaragua, Laos, Kampuchea, Madagascar, Guinea-Bissau, Cape Verde, Benin, and the People's Republic of the Congo.[7] Of these countries the first six are fairly important regionally and in terms of the U.S.-Soviet global competition.

The sudden proliferation of new Marxist-Leninist states since 1975 is no ac-

---

[6]The best example is Nicaragua, where up to 1979 the Soviets were counseling the pro-Moscow Nicaraguan Socialist party against premature attempts to overthrow Somoza.

[7]This list does not include the Marxist-Leninist regime in Grenada, overthrown by the United States in October 1983.

cident: the Soviet Union, Cuba, and other bloc allies have been instrumental in bringing to power or subsequently sustaining almost all of them. The fact that these regimes are willing to declare themselves adherents of "scientific" socialism sets them off clearly from Soviet clients of an earlier generation.[8] In the 1950s and 1960s Moscow's major Third World allies were a heterogeneous collection of left-wing nationalist states that found common ground with the Soviet Union primarily in an anti-imperialist foreign policy. Egypt, Indonesia, Guinea, India, Algeria, and Iraq explicitly rejected orthodox Marxism-Leninism in favor of a variety of syncretic doctrines that combined vaguely socialist programs with a healthy degree of local nationalism. The latter element tended over time to make these states highly unreliable allies, which Soviet commentators had already begun to point out by the mid-sixties. Of these left-wing bourgeois nationalist states only Cuba adopted scientific socialism as an ideology, and several, including Egypt and Somalia, defected from the Soviet camp altogether.

Several observers have maintained that the impact of Marxism is very superficial throughout the Third World and that the Marxist-Leninist regimes established since 1975 are just as nationalist as those of an earlier generation. We will suspend judgment for now on whether these regimes are more Marxist or more nationalist in orientation: obviously, no state is exclusively one or the other, and the real question concerns exactly where on the continuum they lie. Nonetheless, the six more important Marxist-Leninist regimes have at least four common characteristics that set them off from Moscow's noncommunist clients.

First, internally, five of the six are governed by Leninist vanguard parties that have consolidated their own power and created a variety of highly centralized, top-down hierarchical state institutions.[9] All six have to varying degrees pursued socialist domestic programs involving nationalization of large parts of the national economy, collectivization of agriculture and industry, creation of powerful internal security organs, and so on.

Second, in terms of foreign policy each of the six has aligned itself closely with the Soviet Union. Five of the six have signed treaties of friendship and cooperation with Moscow;[10] all vote consistently with the Soviet bloc in the

[8] The criterion used here for identifying a Marxist-Leninist state is whether the leaders officially declare it as such. Actual implementation of a Marxist-Leninist program is not a useful measure. There is disagreement both inside and outside the socialist camp as to what exactly the program would involve. Moreover, no state, including the Soviet Union, has ever fully implemented scientific socialism. The Soviets acknowledge only Cuba, Vietnam, Laos, and Kampuchea as states of "developed socialism" on a level (politically, at least) with the regimes in Eastern Europe; the rest are labeled "revolutionary democracies" or states of a "socialist orientation."

[9] Formal establishment of vanguard parties took place in Angola and Mozambique in 1977, South Yemen in 1978, and Ethiopia in 1984. The People's Democratic Party of Afghanistan began as an orthodox Communist party, while the Sandinistn Liberation Front in Nicaragua remains a national liberation movement.

[10] The exception is Nicaragua, probably for fear on the part of both patron and client of unduly provoking the United States. See Zafar Imam, "Soviet Treaties with Third World Countries," *Soviet Studies*, January 1983.

United Nations and similar forums. These states have also created a complex network of ties with one another, with Eastern European bloc members such as East Germany and Bulgaria, or with other sympathetic noncommunist state and substate actors (e.g., Libya, Iraq, the PLO) participate in the larger socialist "collective security system." Each one has also lent generous support to like-minded national liberation movements seeking to come to power. Angola, for example, has supported the South West Africa People's Organization in Namibia and the Front for the National Liberation of the Congo in Zaire, Mozambique Robert Mugabe before he came to power in Zimbabwe and the African National Congress in South Africa, South Yemen the National Democratic Front in North Yemen and the Popular Front for the Liberation of Oman and the Occupied Arab Gulf, Nicaragua the guerrillas in El Salvador.

Third, in the military sphere the new Marxist-Leninist regimes have cooperated closely with the Soviet bloc and have permitted Soviet forces access to air and naval facilities on their territory. Indeed, Marxist-Leninist regimes in Angola and Afghanistan have been able to remain in power only with substantial military support from the Soviet bloc. The Soviets have anchorages and port facilities in the People's Democratic Republic of Yemen and Ethiopia, a series of modern airbases in Afghanistan, and landing rights and port privileges in Angola. Other noncommunist Soviet clients, for instance Egypt and Syria, have cooperated with Moscow in similar fashion, but only after prolonged Soviet cajoling and the pressure of circumstances forced them to do so.[11] The new regimes, on the other hand, have cooperated with the Soviet and Cuban military from the outset and with much less evident reluctance.

Finally, each of the new regimes has demonstrated considerable weakness and lack of internal legitimacy, and each is the object of an indigenous guerrilla movement for national liberation. This weakness might be expected—a "natural" outgrowth of the sheer expansion of Moscow's client base—but the problems that these regimes currently face can be traced back to their underlying ideological orientation. Major Soviet clients of the 1950s and 1960s (India, Egypt, and Indonesia) were relatively well-established states with long cultural and historical traditions. Each had emerged from colonialism largely as a result of its own efforts, under the leadership of men who could claim stature as nationalist leaders: Nehru, Nasser, Sukarno. While the fortunes of these individuals rose and fell, the regimes they represented by and large enjoyed a broad popular support and nationalist legitimacy. The new Marxist-Leninist regimes, by contrast, either came to power with the help of the Soviet bloc or else required such help to stay in power. They were led by movements which expressed loyalty to internationalist ideals that were

[11]In a series of visits to Cairo in the mid-sixties, Admiral Gorshkov pressed Nasser for access to port facilities in Alexandria and elsewhere—a request consistently refused until Egypt's defeat in the June 1967 war.

overtly at odds with local nationalism, and by leaders with neither stature nor broad recognition.

Perhaps best known of the groups fighting the new Marxist-Leninist regimes are the Afghan resistance fighters, or mujahedeen, who began battling the regime of the People's Democratic Party of Afghanistan (PDPA) in mid-1978 and whose initial success provoked the massive Soviet invasion in December 1979. Clearly the PDPA is the weakest of the six new regimes and would be swept away were it not for the Soviet presence; in spite of poor organization and disunity the mujahedeen control most of the countryside and in selected areas such as the Panjshir Valley have set up their own administration. While some resistance groups have received outside help from the United States, China, and other Islamic and pro-Western sources, they derive the bulk of their supplies internally.

In Angola, Jonas Savimbi's National Union for the Total Independence of Angola (UNITA) controls and administers nearly one-third of the country's territory and operates freely in as much as another third, at one point reducing the governing regime's writ to the capital, Luanda, and its environs. Based on Angola's largest tribal group, the Ovimbundu, UNITA is more highly organized than the Afghan mujahedeen and administers a relatively well-disciplined guerrilla army and a large network of schools, hospitals, and so forth. Savimbi has for several years been receiving support from South Africa, but even his enemies admit that he is not a South African puppet. A charismatic figure who was trained in guerrilla warfare in China, Savimbi poses a threat so severe that it is doubtful the regime could survive without the presence of upward of twenty thousand Cuban troops.

In Mozambique the Frelimo regime has been opposed by the Mozambique National Resistance (RMN, or Renamo). Renamo was originally created by the white Rhodesian regime to retaliate against Frelimo for its support of Mugabe; after the Zimbawean settlement it was turned over to South Africa. Although its membership includes disaffected Frelimo supporters, tribal elements, and former Portuguese settlers, Renamo was to a much greater extent than UNITA a creation of Pretoria. As the organization has matured, however, it has begun to take on a life of its own.[12] Renamo has conducted terrorist and sabotage operations, chiefly against economic targets, in all but one of Mozambique's provinces and has succeeded in crippling several crucial sectors of the Mozambican economy.

The Sandinista regime in Nicaragua has been opposed by a number of groups collectively known as the Contras. The oldest of these groups, the Nicaraguan Democratic Force, was composed initially of former members of the National Guard. As the revolution moved further left, the Contras were joined by others, including the Misura Revolutionary Front and the Revolutionary Democratic Alliance, led at one point by former Sandinista Eden

---

[12]See Sean Gervasi, "South Africa's Terrorist Army," *Southern Africa*, December 1982.

Pastora and Alfonso Robelo, a member of the junta that deposed Somoza. CIA support for the Contras has been well publicized, and the issue has become highly politicized in the United States, making any objective assessment of indigenous support and power difficult. Nonetheless, the groups collectively have been able to field well upward of ten thousand guerrillas, compared to the nine thousand leftist guerillas said to be operating in El Salvador, a country with nearly twice the population of Nicaragua.

Ethiopia has been subjected to numerous separatist national liberation movements from its constituent ethnic groups. In addition to the Eritreans, the largest and most important separatist group, the Tigreans, Oromos, Somalis, and others have been battling the Amhara-dominated regime in Addis Ababa.[13] The three Eritrean organizations are fighting a Marxist regime and themselves claim to be Marxist.[14] They were initially supported by both the Soviet Union and Cuba as a means of putting pressure on Haile Selassie, and they continue to be supported by Cuba, which has urged the regime in Addis to seek a diplomatic solution to the Eritrean problem.

South Yemen has faced less severe internal challenges, though in the past it too has been opposed by a variety of tribal and other groups, including the Army of National Salvation and the National United Front, supported by Saudi Arabia and North Yemen respectively. Attempts by these two groups to overthrow the regime in Aden led to a brief border war between North and South Yemen in 1972, and other conservative states of the Gulf have since supported desultory efforts on the part of émigré groups to destabilize the south.[15]

The sixteen pro-Soviet, Marxist-Leninist regimes in the Third World do not by any means exhaust the totality of Soviet activities and clients there. Moscow retains strong relationships with important noncommunist states, and after Cuba and Vietnam, it is three non-Marxist regimes (India, Syria, and Libya) that have received the lion's share of Soviet military and economic assistance to and Soviet trade with the Third World. It is clear that where no better ideological alternative exists, the Soviets will cooperate with anyone willing to cooperate with them. Indeed, Libya and its like have proved to be more active participants in the socialist collective security system than many of the orthodox communist clients. Nonetheless, the proliferation of Marxist-Leninist states in the Third World constitutes a major development in the broader international environment, one that is likely to have systematic consequences.

Between 1974 and 1984, in sum, the Soviet Union and its allies developed

    [13]Ethiopia's leader, Mengistu Haile Mariam, is himself a Galla.
    [14]The Eritrean Liberation Front, the Eritrean Popular Liberation Front, and the Eritrean Liberation Front—Popular Liberation Forces.
    [15]See Laurie Mylroie, *Politics and the Soviet Presence in the People's Democratic Republic of Yemen* (Santa Monica: Rand Corporation, N-2052-AF, December 1983).

the political and military instruments to help put into place and sustain narrowly based Marxist-Leninist regimes, regimes that have proved to be more susceptible than similar regimes established earlier to Soviet influence and control but at the same time weaker and more vulnerable to internal challenges. These changes do not imply a net gain in Soviet influence in the Third World: expansion in the number of Marxist-Leninist clients must be balanced against their greater weakness and less favorable strategic position than those of an earlier generation. But these changes do suggest a qualitatively different environment for superpower interactions.

The Character of Future U.S.-Soviet Interactions

Soviets vs. Americans

In many respects, future U.S.-Soviet interactions in the Third World will look quite similar to the predominant postwar pattern. The Soviets will seek to expand their influence in the developing world by supporting challenges to the status quo, the United States will seek to contain those challenges. Moscow will continue to number bourgeois nationalist regimes such as those in Syria, India, and Libya among its most important clients, and it will seek to encourage others as they appear.

Two factors, therefore, will affect the extent and character of future Soviet-supported challenges to the status quo. The first is Moscow's inherent propensity to intervene and take risks, in the context of overall U.S.-Soviet relations. The second concerns the opportunities for Soviet and Soviet-bloc intervention provided by developments in the Third World itself.

Sorting out the relative impact of these two factors is extremely difficult. After the extraordinary burst of Soviet activism in the Third World between 1975 and 1980, Moscow has been relatively quiescent. Some have argued that this represents an autonomous change in Soviet risk-taking propensities—a deliberate restraint on the part of the USSR. Such restraint might be the product of several considerations, including the costs of assimilating past gains, caution in the face of an apparently tougher U.S. administration, economic constraints, concentration on European security problems, and preoccupation with such internal problems as the Brezhnev succession process. On the other hand, one could argue that the Soviets have not undertaken new initiatives simply for lack of opportunities. Soviet activities in Africa, after all, came only in response to the collapse of the Portuguese colonial empire after 1974 and were not themselves responsible for bringing that collapse about; comparable developments did not take place between 1980 and 1985.

Soviet quiescence, in my view, is better explained by lack of opportunities than by self-imposed restraint. At least, the case for restraint cannot be con-

clusively established on the basis of available information.[16] It is hard to see
how a Soviet leadership with higher risk-taking propensities would have responded differently to the major developments in the Third World of the
early 1980s: the Iran-Iraq War, the Falklands crisis, the Lebanon War of 1982,
the ongoing crisis in Central America. Beyond these crises, Soviet military
and economic support of its major clients (e.g., Cuba, Vietnam, India, Afghanistan) has continued at earlier levels and in some cases even increased.
Only in Mozambique could the case be made that the Soviets have done less
than they might to support their client, but even here the evidence is less than
conclusive.

If Soviet risk-taking propensities do in fact remain what they were in the
late 1970s, then the likelihood of further Soviet challenges to the status quo
will depend primarily on what opportunities arise in the Third World itself.
In many respects the U.S.-Soviet agenda of the future will resemble that of
earlier years, beginning with the Middle East.

The Arab-Israeli half of the Middle East, though it will continue to be a
major preoccupation for Soviet policy makers, does not appear to be a promising area for substantial Soviet gains. Soviet influence over the past decade
has suffered setbacks due to Israel's military predominance over its Arab adversaries and the strength of the U.S.-Israeli tie, Moscow's lack of viable
intervention options, and the unpredictable character of Arab politics. Moscow's principal client in the region, Syria, is representative of the older generation of noncommunist nationalist Soviet allies, having maintained a prickly
independence from its patron over the years. The Soviets have few instruments of leverage over Damascus other than their ability to provide enormous quantities of military assistance, which in turn has drawn them into
often unwanted confrontations with Israel and the United States. While unforeseen intra- or interstate instability could lead to future Soviet gains,
nothing currently suggests that Moscow's situation will improve; in particular, it seems quite unlikely that the Soviets will be able to deliver a solution to
the Arab-Israeli conflict of the sort its radical clients want.

Yet Moscow's ability to remain a player in the Arab-Israeli theater, despite
these evident weaknesses, is in many ways remarkable. Patient Soviet cultiva-
tion of Syria through traditional (and not terribly imaginative) foreign policy
instruments has had the desired effect: while Moscow has not been able to
shape political outcomes in ways it would have liked, it has been quite successful in blocking U.S. initiatives. Lebanon provides a good example of
Moscow's negative leverage: unable to defend either Syria or the Palestine

---

[16]There is some evidence of internal Soviet debate over whether to retrench in the Third
World following the death of Brezhnev, with some in the leadership arguing for a scaling back of
economic commitments to the Third World (or at least redirecting them toward Europe). See
Stephen Sestanovich, "Do the Soviets Feel Pinched by Third World Adventures?" *Washington
Post*, May 20, 1984.

Liberation Organization against the Israeli invasion in 1982, it nonetheless contributed to the blocking of an Israeli-sponsored settlement thereafter, through its military support of Syria.

The potential for Soviet advances in the Persian Gulf seems to be much greater. The acute concerns felt in the West over potential Soviet threats to the security of Persian Gulf oil in the wake of the invasion of Afghanistan have diminished somewhat in recent years, because of weaknesses in the world oil market and the absence of major crises. But while darker interpretations of Soviet motives—that Afghanistan was merely the prelude to a major move on the Gulf itself—have proved wrong, it would be a serious mistake to discount the dangers of U.S.-Soviet conflict in the region. The conservative, pro-Western states of the Arabian Peninsula remain candidates for instability, despite their success thus far in meeting the political and social challenges of rapid economic modernization. Western dependence on Persian Gulf oil remains high and subject to future, quite unpredictable shifts in the world energy market; and in any case, Soviet control over access to oil would have a political impact far greater than its economic significance might suggest. Any number of plausible scenarios could motivate the Soviets to intervene in the Gulf, one obvious one being instability following the death of Khomeini in Iran.[17] Moscow could act to secure not only the "offensive" gains implicit in control over Persian Gulf oil but also subjectively "defensive" ones, for example the protection of a sympathetic left-wing regime threatened by pro-Western forces in Iran or Saudi Arabia. The Persian Gulf remains the only Third World theater in which the stakes and the probability of instability are high enough to lead to direct, large-scale military conflict between the United States and the Soviet Union.

Soviet responses to the opportunities raised by a crisis in the Gulf are very difficult to predict. Potential gains may be great, but the risks of intervention will be enormous as well, particularly in view of Washington's efforts after 1979 to create a viable conventional capability to intervene in the Gulf. American policy, in turn, is likely to center primarily around raising the costs and risks attendant on large-scale Soviet intervention in the Gulf, as well as attempting to mitigate the underlying causes of an instability that might invite intervention (and over which it will have very little influence).

Central America and the Caribbean basin may well provide further opportunities for Soviet advances, given the endemic economic backwardness and fragility of political system there. Such is the imbalance of interests and capabilities for military intervention between the United States and the Soviet Union, however, that the Caribbean basin is unlikely to be more than an irritant to U.S.-Soviet relations and an issue for domestic American politics.

[17]For further discussion of such scenarios, see my "Escalation in the Middle East and Persian Gulf," in Graham Allison, Albert Carnesale, and Joseph Nye, eds., *Hawks, Doves, and Owls* (New York: Norton, 1985).

While testing the limits of U.S. patience on such issues as arms deliveries to Nicaragua, the Soviets do not appear to be willing to take large chances either to promote fresh revolutions or to support existing regimes.

Finally, there is a potential for instability and consequently for Soviet influence in entirely new areas, such as the Philippines. Currently the Soviets do not have strong ties with the pro-Chinese Communist party of the Philippines and its military wing, the New People's Army, which in any case is not representative of the broad spectrum of groups and social forces opposing the Marcos regime. Moscow's policy thus far has been limited to rather hypocritical efforts to woo Marcos at the expense of the United States. Should the Marcos regime or the military (or both) stay in power, however, the Filipino opposition may shift steadily leftward and at some future date seek Soviet support.

Americans vs. Soviets

Larger changes in the environment for U.S.-Soviet interactions in the Third World may also lead to something of a role reversal between the United States and the Soviet Union. The Soviet Union may find itself trying to defend the status quo, that is, while the United States, its allies, and associates challenge it. Of course, the Soviet Union has not always supported change: to the degree that Moscow successfully promoted the fortunes of clients and associated movements in the Third World in earlier decades, it developed vested interests in the status quo. What is new is the number and seriousness of the opportunities for American-sponsored threats to the status quo—and the possibility that such challenges could move to the forefront of the U.S.-Soviet agenda and become the dominant mode of conflict.

At first glance, it might seem, such an environment would be highly advantageous to the United States. It is generally easier for outside powers to support guerrilla wars than to help suppress them, and after several decades of steady Soviet expansion in the Third World the opportunity for the rollback of Soviet influence under the banner of genuinely popular national liberation movements will seem highly attractive. Yet both superpowers will be faced with a very unfamiliar set of problems. The United States in particular will face significant constraints, in adjusting to this type of environment and in managing this new mode of conflict with the Soviet Union in the Third World.

Future Issues for U.S. Policy

The chief issues for future American policy in the Third World will be how best to deal with Soviet clients (e.g., Afghanistan, Angola, and Nicaragua) and how to manage challenges to the Soviet-supported status quo. To some extent these issues have already been raised: the beginning of the Reagan administration's second term included considerable talk of an unofficial "Reagan doctrine" of U.S. support for anticommunist insurgencies in the Third World.

One possible reaction is to argue that the United States should not be in the business of supporting efforts to destabilize Soviet client regimes. Unfortunately, the issue is not likely to go away. One need not think about the problem simply in terms of destabilization, which is simply a means to an end. In many instances the objective of U.S. policy would be to wean Soviet clients from close embrace with Moscow or to change their external behavior and make it more compatible with American interests—objectives many Americans would find desirable. Moreover, the new Marxist-Leninist states tend as a rule to be rather egregious violators of human rights; many of the resistance groups opposing them have managed to attract broad popular support in their own countries and would have a great deal of appeal even to that segment of liberal opinion normally hostile to U.S. intervention in the Third World. Finally, future U.S. administrations, not just the Reagan White House, are likely to want to make use of the leverage that threats to the Soviet-supported status quo can provide.

Unlike the Soviet Union, however, the United States does not come to this problem with an elaborate doctrine for supporting wars of national liberation and guerrilla organizations seeking to overthrow legal governments. In fact, U.S. policy makers will be encumbered by cultural and historical preconceptions that serve as obstacles to the formulation of effective policies.

The first is the tendency of Americans at both ends of the political spectrum to regard force and diplomacy as mutually exclusive approaches to foreign policy. This cast of mind can be traced back at least to the Wilsonian view of a liberal international order: normal relationships between states are governed exclusively by law, and force is reserved as a punishment of last resort for states challenging the legal order. (It is a point of view which lawyers, so prevalent in the American foreign policy establishment, seem to find particularly congenial.) In dealing with revolutionary situations and Marxist-Leninist governments, liberals as a general rule tend to prefer negotiations and "peaceful solutions" while conservatives tend to prefer military pressure and outright force. Each camp thinks of its chosen path as alternative to the other's, and the result is arguments along the lines that, for example, in Nicaragua support for the Contras is incompatible with encouragement for the Contadora peace process, since no regime can be expected to negotiate under such duress.

The disagreement between liberals and conservatives regarding methods for dealing with Soviet client regimes reflects a more basic disagreement over the nature of the regimes themselves. Whenever a new leftist government, whether Marxist or not, comes to power in the Third World, U.S. public debate is at once polarized between two conflicting views about that government's nature (often virtually without reference to its actual character). Liberals, on the one hand, tend to insist that the new regime like most others in the Third World is much more nationalist than Marxist, that its socialist and anti-imperialist rhetoric is mere talk that will give way to more pragmatic policies once its rulers confront the problems of underdevelopment. If it receives assistance from Moscow or Havana, they will argue that the country has been forced to accept this aid only as a result of prior or continuing American hostility. Conservatives, on the other hand, tend to see the regime as a Soviet puppet that will follow ironclad rules of social development and turn into a carbon copy of the Soviet state. They are likely to dismiss evidence of the regime's gradual moderation or of its serious differences with Moscow.

Both points of view are partly right and partly wrong, and dogmatic adherence to either can lead to major failures of judgment and policy. Some specialists on Afghanistan, for example, characterized the Khalq regime that toppled Prime Minister Daud and seized power on April 27, 1979, as a group of "agrarian reformers" and "pragmatic nationalists" who would maintain Afghanistan's traditional nonaligned foreign policy. Those who saw more sinister implications in the takeover were still being attacked for their "Neanderthal" views long after the coup.[18] On the other side of the ledger, there were those who as late as the 1975 disengagement agreements dismissed Sadat's overtures to the United States as no more than a trick designed to elicit greater levels of Soviet support for Egypt. Both types of error can lead to serious policy blunders, a failure to recognize and respond to Soviet-sponsored subversion on the one hand and the missing of opportunities to negotiate settlements for disputes on the other.

An effective policy for dealing with Soviet clients must begin with an analysis, free from preconceptions, of the underlying character of those clients on a case-by-case basis.[19] Ideological self-conception is important, because Marxist-Leninist states tend to behave in consistent ways. But the analysis must go well beyond this level, because doctrine is interpreted and implemented differently from one client to another. Some communist states, Afghanistan among them, are so dominated by the Soviet Union that it is absurd to consider weaning them away from the USSR, while others, for instance Mozambique, have demonstrated a much greater degree of independence and are likely to be considerably more susceptible to U.S. overtures. Knowing where Soviet clients fall along this spectrum can only be determined empirically.

Whether aiming to wean the client regime away from Moscow or replace it altogether, the U.S. approach must combine diplomacy and force simultaneously. These are not alternative methods but two sides of the same coin.

---

[18]See Anthony Arnold, *Afghanistan's Two-Party Communism: Parcham and Khalq* (Stanford: Hoover Institution Press, 1983), p. 61.

[19]"Client" is used here broadly to signify any state retaining aid and trade relations, particularly in the military sphere, with the Soviet Union. It does not necessarily imply a high degree of Soviet influence over the local state.

Sandinista interest in the Contadora process or in direct talks with the United States, for example, far from being incompatible with U.S. support for the Contras, is in fact motivated by it. To those who think that diplomacy and force cannot be combined, I offer three instances when they were.

The first case is that of Egypt. Henry Kissinger had the perspicacity (or perhaps the luck) to recognize in 1973, at the time of the October War, that Sadat, in contrast to other Arab leaders, was interested in a long-term settlement of the Arab-Israeli dispute. The outcome was by no means predetermined, however, and it was brought about only by persistent U.S. efforts to act as an intermediary, through the two Sinai disengagements, Sadat's visit to Jerusalem, and the Camp David process. Some observers fail to recognize that Egypt's interest in negotiations resulted from four costly military defeats by Israel and the consistency of U.S. military support for Israel up to and including the signing of the final Egyptian-Israeli peace treaty. Sadat in his memoirs makes it very clear that his decision to pursue limited aims in the October War, and a negotiated settlement thereafter, proceeded not from any love of Israel but from his recognition that the United States would prevent Israel from being defeated militarily. It was the cost of continued armed struggle, and the war weariness it had engendered throughout the Egyptian population, which made negotations and eventual peace possible.

Egypt's case differs from those of the newer Marxist-Leninist clients insofar as the type of force used against it was Israel's conventional military power, not external support for opposition to the regime in Cairo. Though Egypt may not serve as an exact model for future Soviet clients, however, the case underlines the fact that even the most spectacular successes of American diplomacy in recent years were rooted in elementary considerations of power politics.

The second example is the Shah of Iran's support for Kurdish nationalists inside Iraq, support that ultimately led to the Algiers Agreement in 1975 and resolution of the border dispute between Baghdad and Teheran. The Ba'athist regime in Iraq had signed a treaty of friendship and cooperation with Moscow in 1972 and received a substantial arms buildup during the early seventies, supporting a wide variety of terrorist and subversive organizations throughout the Middle East, including several inside Iran.[20] The Kurdish war proved to be a continuing drain on Iraqi military and economic resources, however, and forced Baghdad to come to terms with the Shah. The Algiers Agreement did not change the fundamental character of the Ba'athist regime, of course, as its subsequent renunciation of the accord after the fall of the Shah proved, but it did considerably restrain Iraqi foreign policy for the nearly four years that the Iranian military and political system was strong enough to enforce good behavior.

---

[20] The Iraqis gave refuge to the Ayatollah Khomeini as an option against the Shah, a policy that would later return to haunt them.

The final example is South Africa's support for Renamo inside Mozambique. Unlike Egypt and Iraq, the Frelimo government in Maputo is a self-proclaimed Marxist-Leninist regime that received substantial help from the Soviet bloc while it was still a guerrilla organization fighting the Portuguese. It quickly established ties to Moscow after coming to power, accepted arms and help from Soviet bloc sources, and gave substantial support to various national liberation movements fighting the white settler regimes in neighboring Rhodesia and South Africa. Pretoria, however, exploited its leverage over Mozambique with great ruthlessness: not only did it provide Renamo with arms and sanctuary and establish the Voice of Free Africa radio in the Transvaal, but it could also threaten the earnings of the large numbers of Mozambican guest workers employed in South Africa—earnings that were critical to the Mozambican economy. South African military forces responded to operations by the African National Congress with large-scale reprisal raids against their bases inside Mozambique. This relentless military and economic pressure drove Samora Machel to sign the Nkomati ceasefire agreement with South Africa in March 1984. Mozambique agreed to end support for the African National Congress and other black nationalist organizations in return for Pretoria's agreement to stop assistance to Renamo.

The Mozambican case contains interesting lessons for both conservatives and liberals. To conservatives who might have thought that Frelimo was ideologically rigid and hopelessly ensnared in dependency on the Soviet bloc, the regime in Maputo has demonstrated that it is much more interested in its own survival than in Marxism. Maputo has done such un-Marxist things as seeking assistance from Western multinational corporations and counterinsurgency training from the Portuguese military. Rumors suggest, furthermore, that its collaboration with South Africa on economic and security issues may be much more far-reaching than initially thought when the Nkomati Accord was signed. But there are lessons for liberals as well. The agreement was not brought about by talking politely to Frelimo and showering it with economic assistance; it came from an extremely hardheaded policy of support for internal destabilization on the part of South Africa. Pretoria was interested not in overthrowing Frelimo per se but in neutralizing those aspects of its external policy which were most threatening to South Africa, and it combined both military and diplomatic means to achieve this result.

In dealing with Soviet clients, the United States cannot behave like the Shah of Iran or like South Africa. A widespread American policy to support changes in the Soviet-sponsored status quo, of the sort being carried out in the early 1980s to a limited extent in Afghanistan and Nicaragua, would encounter problems arising from the nature of the American political system itself. The first problem lies in the all-too-common inability of American administrations to establish strategic goals and long-term plans for policy. In the mid-eighties there are three broad alternatives. First, the United States could hope to impose costs on Soviet clients and the Soviet Union itself, thereby creating a disincentive for further adventurism in the Third World. Second, it could seek to overthrow client governments and replace them with regimes more sympathetic to the West. Third, it could try to build pressure on client states sufficient to force them to seek a political solution that would neutralize the regional threats they present and break them out of the Soviet orbit. Each of these possibilities presents specific difficulties.

If the United States is seeking merely to impose costs on the client and its Soviet backers, with no hope of ultimately changing the character of the regime, it will nonetheless incur moral obligation to support the resistance organization consistently and against possible Soviet or Soviet client retaliation. In the past the United States has unfortunately not consistently supported Third World clients, particularly when support proved costly or risky. Commitments made by one administration, particularly informal ones made to resistance groups, are all too easily broken by the next, or even by the same administration should it undergo a change of heart. In other cases U.S. support may provoke a strong Soviet reaction and even lead to the destruction of the pro-Western group. The Soviets have themselves faced this situation in the past, as for example when Stalin's advice to the Chinese Communists to form a common front with the Kuomintang led to suppression of the Communists by Chiang Kai-Shek in 1927.[21]

If the United States hopes actually to overthrow the regime in power, it must then bear responsibility for what follows. In the case of someone like Savimbi or in prior interventions like the Dominican Republic or Grenada, the result may not be so bad, but one cannot always choose the enemies of one's enemies. The prime example is Pol Pot's Khmer Rouge in Kampuchea, whose genocidal policies have presented an insurmountable obstacle to U.S. aid of any sort, much less actual restoration of the former regime. In other cases, for instance in Nicaragua, the United States might help to power an authoritarian, right-wing regime that may become a source of considerable subsequent embarrassment. While the Afghan mujahedeen have attracted considerable sympathy in the United States, individual commanders (e.g., Gulbadin Hekmatyar, who bears certain similiarities to the Ayatollah Khomeini) may not look terribly attractive as leaders of a post-PDPA Afghanistan. Moreover, while the Soviet Union has had many dealings with extralegal entities seeking to undermine legal governments, the United States is in prin-

---

[21]Some have questioned the morality of supporting the efforts of resistance groups like the Afghan mujahedeen where the chances of ultimate success are very small, prolonging a hopeless and costly struggle. My own view is that the fundamental moral choice has already been made by the groups themselves, who seek U.S. support and will continue to fight and die whether they receive it or not. In any event it is often very difficult to know when a situation is hopeless, since many long-shot opposition parties, including the Bolsheviks themselves, have succeeded in coming to power. In other cases U.S. support will take on the appearance of state-sponsored terrorism, of which the United States has accused the Soviet Union and denounced as a matter of principle.

ciple opposed to such practices. Such a policy contradicts other United States positions in countries like El Salvador, where the United States has taken a stand against power sharing on the grounds that insurgents should not be allowed to "shoot their way into office."

If the United States hopes to use anti-communist national liberation groups as an instrument of leverage to force Soviet clients to moderate their behavior, it will be subject to charges of selling out the movement it supported. Even though not directly responsible for the Algiers Agreement, the Ford administration received considerable criticism, including some from right-wing sources, for having condoned the Shah's betrayal of the Kurds. This type of agreement, common enough in diplomatic practice (witness the Molotov–von Ribbentrop pact), requires a flexibility and a cynicism that generally does not sit well with Americans. A principled and ideological streak in American foreign policy encourages Americans to divide the world into more or less permanent friends and enemies; it makes Americans suspicious of shifting alliances and dealings with dictators.

The potential conflict between strategies of weaning and overthrow is well illustrated by the situation in Angola following the lifting of the Clark Amendment in 1985. Direct U.S. support for Jonas Savimbi's UNITA,[22] which might one day overthrow the Marxist-Leninist regime in Luanda, undermines the policy followed by Assistant Secretary of State Chester A. Crocker to bring about a Cuban withdrawal from Angola by tying withdrawal to a settlement of the Namibia problem. In this case, the anti-Soviet insurgency proved too strong for Moscow's client to relinquish its Soviet-Cuban security blanket.

The final issue is whether these anticommunist national liberation movements will in all cases be better off with American assistance. U.S. management of military aid programs has often had a suffocating effect on its intended beneficiaries. Savimbi's UNITA has been prospering for several years without having received a cent of American assistance, whereas the Afghans, who evidently receive considerable assistance, continually claim that they are short of supplies. U.S. support may taint an otherwise credible organization, like Eden Pastora's Revolutionary Democratic Alliance in Nicaragua, and actually reduce its chances of coming to power.

In the end, domestic factors are likely to exert the greatest constraint on any U.S. policy designed to assist anti-Soviet resistance groups or movments. While causes like that of the Afghan mujahedeen engender considerable public support (indeed, Congress has sometimes led the Reagan administration on this issue), others like the Nicaraguan Contras continue to be controversial. U.S. policy makers need to consider very carefully the domestic reaction before undertaking to support the internal opponents of Soviet clients. The worst of all worlds is when the United States begins aiding a Third World cli-

---

[22]President Reagan publicly announced his administration's decision to provide UNITA with "covert" assistance in November 1985. *New York Times*, November 23, 1985.

ent or group and then pulls the rug out from underneath it for lack of adequate preparation of U.S. domestic opinion.

Managing the Soviet Empire

The Soviet Union will continue to exploit opportunities to expand its influence in the Third World as they arise. As a result of past successes, however, the new issues for future Soviet policy are likely to revolve increasingly around the question of managing its burden of empire in established positions. This has political, military, and economic dimensions.

In the political sphere the Soviets will have to seek ways to improve the staying power and reliability of their clients. This, I believe, has been the chief issue for Soviet Third World policy since the early 1970s—particularly since the fall of Allende in Chile and the defection of Egypt—and many elements of a solution are already in place.[23] In the case of the earlier generation of bourgeois nationalist clients, Moscow's principal problem was a lack of effective instruments of leverage to bring them into line. The Russians had to rely primarily on the promise of arms transfers, or in some cases the threat to withhold arms, to produce compliance with their wishes. This instrument proved to be weak at best: the Russians found themselves being drawn into unwanted confrontations with the United States (as in the case of the Arab-Israeli wars) or else supplanted by alternative suppliers (as in the case of Iraq and the French).

Since approximately the mid-1970s the Russians have sought to create more direct forms of leverage by much greater active involvement in the internal workings of client states. Their means have included large-scale deployments of Soviet, Cuban, and Eastern European combat forces and advisers to help in the management of external security, use of East Germans to restructure and supervise internal security, and development of centralized, Leninist state structures to control as much of the political and economic life of the country as possible. Encouragement of Marxist-Leninist national liberation movements and their transformation into elite vanguard parties has been an important element in this strategy as well, because if those parties came to power, they will as a general rule be less reluctant to cooperate closely with the Soviet bloc. They provide an institutional basis for a long-term relationship with Moscow. In this respect the weakness and lack of internal legitimacy of many of these new regimes, earlier noted as a liability, becomes an advantage for the Soviets: it ensures that the client will remain highly dependent on Soviet support for its survival. The effectiveness of this strategy may be seen in South Yemen. There East German and Cuban intelligence operatives and combat troops participated in the removal of President

[23]See Alex Alexiev, *The New Soviet Strategy in the Third World* (Santa Monica: Rand Corporation, N-1995-AF, June 1983), and my *The Military Dimension of Soviet Policy in the Third World* (Santa Monica: Rand Corporation, P-6965, February 1984).

Selim Rubai Ali in June 1978 when he appeared too zealous in his quest for detente with the conservative Arab Gulf states. It may be seen also in Ethiopia, where the military regime finally institutionalized its rule with the creation of the vanguard Worker's Party of Ethiopia on the tenth anniversary of its rule in September 1984. While Soviets and Cubans continue to work closely with noncommunist allies as well, we can expect future instances of active interference in the internal affairs of all clients.

In the military sphere, the Soviets and Cubans will face unpleasant and unfamiliar choices. For several years now they have had to fight or assist in fighting large-scale counterinsurgency wars in Afghanistan, Angola, Ethiopia, and Kampuchea. This type of warfare is not totally unfamiliar to the Soviet military, which has fought prolonged counterinsurgency campaigns within its own borders, against the Basmachi tribesmen in Central Asia in the 1920s and 1930s and against the Lithuanians after the liberation of the Baltic states in the late forties and early fifties. These earlier campaigns were costly but could be kept under control, because the guerrillas were operating on Soviet territory and did not attract significant outside political or military support. The damage caused to the Soviet international image by having to fight popular resistance movements in Angola and Afghanistan is significantly greater. No professional army, moreover, enjoys fighting a counterinsurgency war or does particularly well at it. The effects of such campaigns on internal Red Army morale, while less extensive than those for the U.S. Army in Vietnam, will be damaging and, in the case of Cuba, could have serious effects on the popularity of the regime itself.

The Soviets and Cubans may be forced to intervene more drastically than continuing peacetime deployments on behalf of certain clients to keep them in power. Such a decision has already been taken in the case of Afghanistan in December 1979. Even so, the intervention force is barely sufficient to control Afghanistan's cities and lines of communications. Further operations, to seal the border with Pakistan or to pacify and hold substantial parts of the countryside, will require a much larger commitment of forces, possibly upward of half a million men. Because Soviet leaders have evidently decided not to commit forces of this magnitude, they have in effect opted for a stalemate. They seem perfectly capable of hanging on for the indefinite future at the present level of costs and casualties, but higher levels of Western support for the mujahedeen could force the Soviets to take a more dramatic decision. Cuban troop strength in Angola has risen steadily from a low of approximately fifteen thousand to well over thirty thousand in 1985, in response to UNITA's successes, and may have to increase further still. While Cuban forces have up till now performed mostly garrison duties (thereby freeing up the ruling regime's manpower to fight UNITA), a serious threat to Luanda itself is likely to require a direct Cuban combat role. Nicaragua would become a sink for arms and advisers were it not for its geographical proximity to the United States, which would make any Soviet attempt to intervene costly and pointless.

While the situation of other Soviet clients is not quite as perilous, the security of any one could unexpectly deteriorate in the next decade to the point of requiring massive Soviet military assistance to survive.

Finally, there are the economic costs of empire. In the ten years since 1975 the Soviets undertook several expensive, new, ongoing commitments in addition to their $6 million-a-day subsidy of Cuba. These included Vietnam and the Vietnamese occupation of Kampuchea, Angola, Ethiopia, and the incremental costs of maintaining over one hundred thousand troops in Afghanistan. At a time when the growth rate of the Soviet economy has begun to slow considerably, Soviet economic planners must question the rationale behind some of Moscow's Third World commitments. To take one example, the USSR provided *North* Yemen with $750 million worth of arms following the brief border war with the People's Democratic Republic of Yemen in 1979, in an attempt to balance Saudi influence in Sanaa. There is evidence, as noted earlier, that some voices in the Soviet leadership have been urging retrenchment and greater selectivity in Moscow's Third World commitments.

Managing U.S.-Soviet Interactions in the Third World

A world in which both the United States and the Soviet Union are supporting challenges to the status quo is obviously going to be a dangerous one. The implication is that the superpowers will remain heavily involved in the conflicts that will inevitably arise in the Third World. That world will also tend to be more dangerous because the terrain will look less familiar. For U.S. policy makers, the typical question regarding Third World crises used to concern whether and how to intervene to stop subversion by various left-wing forces. The opposite question, how far to go before provoking Soviet intervention, came up in major issues in Korea and Vietnam and yet tended to be asked less frequently in the majority of postwar Third World crisis. This question U.S. decision makers will have to ponder closely as Soviet clients are increasingly challenged by forces seeking support from the West.

The United States severely misjudged Chinese willingness to intervene in Korea, but Soviet leaders have been relatively cautious about the use of force in the postwar era. U.S. concerns about provoking a major Soviet intervention in Vietnam proved in retrospect to be overdrawn. Nonetheless, the broad growth of Soviet military power over the last twenty years, and particularly the growth of Soviet power projection forces, may affect Soviet willingness to intervene in local conflicts.[24] Much depends on specific questions

[24]The actual question is much broader than the issue of power projection forces, which tend to get overemphasized in discussions of Soviet Third World policy. The Soviets have many ways of causing trouble for the United States in a variety of theaters, some of them far removed from the particular local conflict in question. They could, for example, send nuclear submarines to Cuba, mobilize along the Iranian border, encourage Vietnamese incursions into Thailand, fly re-

of stake and capability, in turn related to geography. The Soviets did not respond to the American invasion of Grenada because they did not have the means to do so, and because Grenada was a very minor client. Cuba is much more important, but it too is unlikely to receive direct Soviet military support in the event it is attacked any time in the foreseeable future. The same is not necessarily true in sub-Saharan Africa, however, where both superpowers operate at similar geographical disadvantages, much less the Persian Gulf and the Middle East, which are close to the center of Soviet power.

Pakistan presents perhaps the clearest case of how Soviet power might be brought to bear. Were the United States to increase its level of support for the Afghan mujahedeen to the point where Soviet casualties and other costs rose substantially, the Soviet Union could respond by conducting airstrikes or even ground incursions against Afghan resistance camps inside Pakistan, in the hopes of forcing Pakistan to deny the groups further sanctuary. The principal rationale behind the Reagan administration's $3 billion program of military and economic assistance to Pakistan was to bolster Islamabad's ability to stand up to the Soviets under precisely such circumstances. Should this aid prove insufficient, however, the United States would have to choose whether to increase its material support or assist directly in the defense of Pakistani air space with, for example, U.S. Air Force units. Despite the reestablishment of U.S.-Pakistani links in 1981, there is virtually no national consensus in the United States for the defense of Pakistan and plenty of opposition against further involvement with Islamabad for human rights and nuclear nonproliferation reasons. The most likely outcome is that the United States will refuse to intervene and cut back its support for the mujahedeen in the hopes of inducing the Soviet Union to back down. The same situation exists in Southeast Asia, where U.S. support (or increased Chinese assistance) for the Khmer People's National Liberation Front and other Kampuchean resistance groups may provoke a large-scale Vietnamese attack on Thailand. While the United States theoretically has the capability to defend Thailand, in practice, just as in the case of Afghanistan, domestic political constraints will undercut its ability to do so.

By and large, the risks that the Third World holds for the superpowers are those of getting drawn into long and costly interventions. The stakes involved in most Third World crises are too small to present the prospect of major, direct U.S.-Soviet conflict and escalation to general war, and with a minimal amount of prudence, things should stay this way. In the Middle East and the Gulf, however, the combination of high mutual stakes, continual local political instability, and the presence of strong military forces could lead to war between the Soviet Union and the United States. The regulation of

---

taliatory airstrikes into Pakistan, or even reopen the Berlin question in response, say, to U.S. activities in Africa. This type of behavior has been referred to as lateral escalation in the United States; consideration of Soviet options for lateral escalation suggest why such a policy may not be terribly advantageous for the United States.

U.S.-Soviet interactions in the Gulf presents a different order of problem from the ones considered in this chapter.

If the trends described here come to characterize the Third World environment of the late 1980s and early 1990s—and to some extent they already do—there is reason to think that we may be entering a period with greater opportunities for cooperative measures and bargaining between the United States and the Soviet Union. U.S. ability to challenge the existing, Soviet-sponsored order should, if handled correctly, result in greater overall leverage for the United States. Rather than being an overextended quasi-imperial power, perpetually responding to challenges all over the world, the United States might be able to take the initiative at times and places of its own choosing. The world would then be a rather mixed place, with the United States holding advantages in some theaters and the Soviet Union in others, or with each holding advantages in different countries in the same theater. The United States and the Soviet Union, or the U.S. and the Soviet client, would then have a basis for serious negotiations, on ending mutual intervention or totally neutralizing the area in question. It is such a situation which appears to be emerging in Central America now, where both El Salvador and Nicaragua are subject to guerrilla insurgencies. The mutuality of the problem gives hope for success to both the Contadora process and the direct negotiations that began between the United States and Nicaragua in 1984.

Looking even further ahead, it may be possible to negotiate more explicit understandings with the Soviet Union over spheres of influence or, perhaps, spheres of restraint, in which the superpowers would agree to suspend aid to groups opposing each other's clients. In theory, these tradeoffs need not occur within the same region but could be implemented in different parts of the world where both the United States and the Soviet Union have interests.[25] President Reagan, in his October 1985 speech to the UN General Assembly, proposed negotiations with the Soviet Union on five "regional conflicts," those taking place in Afghanistan, Kampuchea, Nicaragua, Angola, and Ethiopia. While the president singled out only conflicts involving challenges to pro-Soviet regimes, he left open the possibility of a broader regional dialogue that could eventually include such U.S. clients as El Salvador. Before we get carried away with such possibilities, however, it is necessary to point out two practical obstacles.

In the first place, however much the United States and Soviet Union may seek to become involved in Third World affairs, their influence over their respective clients remains limited. We are not, after all, living in a nineteenth-century world where local peoples are passive pawns of great powers. Superpower clients will strongly resist any attempts to reach deals behind their backs and usually will have the leverage to block such deals. One good

[25]Not all such deals are in the interests of the United States. One means of resolving the Sino-Soviet conflict suggested by several observers is Soviet restraint in its support of Vietnam in return for Chinese assistance in resolving the Afghan situation.

example in the historical record is Sadat, who feared that Washington and Moscow were conspiring to freeze the territorial status quo in the Middle East at their May 1972 summit. His response was to expel Soviet advisers from Egypt that summer and force the Soviet Union into supporting his launching of the October War. Similarly, Jonas Savimbi is not a force that can be turned on or off at will by outside powers; his power ultimately derives from his popular base inside Angola. The Rhodesians and South Africans, having created Renamo, are not necessarily in a position to curtail it; even without South African support the organization will continue to disrupt the Mozambican economy.[26] The cease-fires proposed by President Reagan in his UN address will be opposed by many local insurgent groups, like those in Afghanistan. While the United States and the Soviet Union may try to hatch deals about support for Third World clients, their ability to fine tune outcomes and ultimately deliver on promises is more apparent than real.

The second problem is a domestic American one. The idea of great power horsetrading over spheres of influence has always been alien to many in the United States, smacking of European cabinet diplomacy. Europe, for example, has in effect been divided into spheres of influence since the end of the war, but no U.S. administration has been able to admit the fact publicly. A universalistic strain in U.S. foreign policy makes it very hard for Americans totally to renounce interest in causes (for example, Polish independence) taken up as a matter of principle, however quixotic they may appear. U.S.-Soviet understandings on spheres of interest, therefore, while they may be possible on a very informal basis, would probably have to be kept out of the public eye. Whether this is possible in an age of congressional oversight and an active press remains to be seen.

Thus we come back to the question of unilateral U.S. policies. The United States will not be able to bargain away its problems simply by trying to exploit Soviet client vulnerabilities; it will continue to have to deal with Soviet expansionism and revolutionary challenges to U.S. friends and allies through the usual political and military means. Even if the United States is able to force Managua to end support for the left in El Salvador, only a small part of El Salvador's problem will have been solved. Besides the nations of the Caribbean Basin, a number of other countries—most notably the Philippines— may be subject to revolutionary upheaval over the next few years. Although the United States has had considerable experience with this type of situation, it has yet to come up with a satisfactory formula for reforming recalcitrant right-wing allies and encouraging in the Third World the development of liberal democratic societies that might serve as a more permanent basis for American influence.

---

[26]In the autumn of 1985 South African foreign minister Botha admitted that Pretoria continued to support Renamo even after the Nkomati Accord.

Belief in the possibility of moderate alternatives to right-wing authoritarianism for many parts of the Third World has, it is true, proved to be a naive illusion, one that has befuddled the thinking of past American administrations and caused them to acquiesce in the replacement of pro-Western dictatorships of the right with pro-Soviet dictatorships of the left.[27] The histories and cultures of some countries clearly give one no basis whatsoever for expecting the emergence of anything like a moderate democratic center. In such countries criticism of human rights abuses or attempts to democratize regimes serve only to undermine the client and bring about something much worse, both with respect to U.S. interests and in moral terms. Such was the case in Iran, I would argue, where belief that the National Front supporters around Khomeini would prevail blinded many American officials to the revolutionary dynamic at work there. In this type of situation, moreover, attempts to coopt the revolution seldom work. In both Ethiopia and Nicaragua the United States attempted to maintain good relations with the revolutionary regimes after they came to power, in both cases increasing military and economic aid over previous levels. Both regimes were uninterested in good relations with the United States, however, for reasons of principle which were little affected by U.S. behavior in the short run. They turned quickly to the Soviet Union and Cuba, not because they had nowhere else to go but out of inclination.

It is incorrect and potentially dangerous, on the other hand, to suggest that the Third World as a whole is an area of darkness incapable of building liberal institutions or democratizing its political processes through moderate means. Since the mid-1970s we have seen several examples of states in the lower tier of the developed world or the upper tier of the underdeveloped world (Spain, Greece, Portugal, Argentina, Turkey, and Brazil) move from right-wing military dictatorships to more or less functioning democracies. All of these countries are large and economically well-developed, with relatively advanced social systems and strong (if in some cases not particularly stable) institutional structures. It will not be possible to apply their experience to small and backward American client regimes like El Salvador, whose level of social development is of another century. But for others it will be possible, and as with Soviet clients one must evaluate these countries case by case. The Philippines, for example, unlike Iran, has had considerable experience with democratic institutions as a result of its long American tutelage; while timing is critical, it may still be possible for the United States to facilitate creation of a successor to the Marcos regime which is moderate and reasonably well-disposed to the United States.[28] For countries like the Philippines, and others like Argentina

---

[27] This of course was the argument of Jeanne Kirkpatrick in "Dictatorships and Double Standards," *Commentary*, November 1979.

[28] Chile, prior to the rise of Allende and the Pinochet coup, also had a long history of successful democratic institutions.

which have made the difficult transition back to democracy, the United States needs to formulate a much more creative strategy, a strategy for supporting and coopting social change before it is radicalized and the revolutionary process begins. In other cases, and Saudi Arabia is probably an example, Americans can only cross their fingers and and hope for the best.

9

U.S. –Soviet Nuclear Arms Control:
The Next Phase

ARNOLD L. HORELICK AND EDWARD L. WARNER III

After a series of intermittent, inconclusive talks in the early 1980s, U.S.-Soviet nuclear arms control negotiations have again resumed their familiar place at the center of the U.S.-Soviet relationship. But prospects for the Geneva negotiations remain highly uncertain. Despite the tabling of significant new proposals on offensive arms control by the two sides in the fall of 1985 and the impetus provided by the first U.S.-Soviet summit meeting in six years, the negotiations face the prospect of protracted deadlock. This is due largely to the mutually exclusive positions adopted by the two sides on the issue of space-based strategic defenses. Consequently, in 1986 U.S.-Soviet arms control negotiations stand, once again, at a crossroads. At stake are not only the chances for specific new agreements in this decade but the future of the imperilled arms control process as a whole and of its role as a key regulator of the larger U.S.-Soviet relationship.

This analysis of the nuclear arms control dimension of U.S.-Soviet relations begins with a review of the developments that led to the present situation. It then proceeds to examine the nuclear arms control agenda now before the leaderships of the two states and the altered strategic environment that they confront. It concludes with a consideration of prospects for future agreement.

Origins of the Impasse

Even in the best political circumstances the sharply divergent strategic interests of the United States and the USSR are extremely difficult to reconcile in arms control negotiations. In the political environment that prevailed during the 1981–83 intermediate nuclear force (INF) negotiations and Strategic

Arms Reduction Talks (START), a reconciliation seemed impossible and was not seriously attempted.

The climate of the U.S.-Soviet relationship had been increasingly troubled since the Angolan crisis of the mid-1970s. The Carter administration expended considerable domestic political capital in a vain effort to keep the SALT II arms control negotiations insulated from the adverse effects of unraveling detente during 1978 and 1979. But the prospects for improvement signaled by the signing of the SALT II treaty in June 1979 were decisively dashed by the Soviet invasion of Afghanistan at the end of the year, which caused the final slide of the relationship into the trough of the 1980s. In the ensuing postdetente environment neither superpower regarded the other as a sufficiently dedicated or reliable negotiating partner with whom to strike a bargain.

The election of Ronald Reagan, despite his harshly anti-Soviet election campaign, was not initially regarded with alarm in the Soviet Union. On the contrary, some in Moscow evidently had the Nixon model in mind for Reagan —a conservative Republican president with impeccable anticommunist credentials, invulnerable to attacks from the right, likely to be more interested than Democrats in trade and profitable commercial relations, a president with whom it might be possible again to have a "businesslike" relationship, including arms control negotiations.

Toward the end of Reagan's first year, however, when the expected "adaptation to reality" of the new president had still not materialized, the Soviet leaders evidently concluded that the new administration was so implacably hostile that it would not by choice deal with the Soviet Union on terms acceptable to Moscow. Revised Soviet expectations about Reagan were summed up in a statement by veteran Americanologist Georgi Arbatov: the Reagan administration "will be good only to the extent that it is not allowed to be bad, and safe only to the extent that it is not allowed to be dangerous."[1] Having concluded that the Reagan administration, left to its own devices, would be prepared to offer up little of interest in the arms control negotiations, Soviet diplomacy concentrated on other audiences. Moscow's diplomatic and negotiating positions were directed at those forces among America's European allies, in the U.S. Congress, and among the U.S. public thought to be capable of constraining the administration's freedom of action and of channeling its policies in directions less obnoxious to the USSR or possibly even acceptable to it.

On the U.S. side, the attitudes that prevailed initially in the new Reagan administration were decidedly unpropitious for successful diplomatic engagement with the Soviet Union. Senior officials in charge of national security matters assumed power believing that the military balances between the United States and the USSR had deteriorated to the point where the U.S.

[1] *Pravda*, July 26, 1982.

bargaining position, in regional issues as well as in arms control, had been gravely weakened. Serious negotiations had to await major improvements in the U.S. military position vis-à-vis the USSR.

For some in the administration this evidently meant restoration of strategic superiority, a goal so remote or unmeasurable that it might defer negotiations indefinitely. There was, moreover, a strong conviction in some administration circles that the arms control process per se was politically incompatible with the primary goal of rearmament. Some argued that arms control, by holding out the false promise of security through cooperation, was equivalent to moral disarmament and would sap the resolve of the Congress and the public to make the sacrifices required to sustain the needed military buildup.

By the fall of 1981, however, it had become clear to Washington that the maintenance of allied and domestic support for high-priority defense programs required the United States to reopen the arms control negotiations track in parallel with improving U.S. defense capabilities. Thus the administration was obliged, earlier probably than it intended, to initiate both intermediate nuclear force negotiations and Strategic Arms Reduction Talks.

Given the assumptions that each side brought to the table about the other's purposes and political strategy, neither superpower considered the other to be the primary audience for the negotiating stances it developed in both INF and START. For the Soviet Union, an appropriate arms control policy was one primarily intended to weaken Western support for the Reagan administration's security policies without reducing accumulated Soviet military advantages or constraining future prospects.

For the United States, conversely, the appropriate arms control posture was one calling for maximum reductions in perceived Soviet advantages while avoiding curbs on promising U.S. programs. This posture had also to preserve the support of the NATO allies for U.S. INF deployments and to maintain domestic support for unilateral initiatives, particularly military ones, to counter the Soviet threat. The fact that the other superpower happened to be on the receiving end of the arms control proposals that emerged from such calculations was almost coincidental. As it turned out, in the INF negotiations that dominated the arms control scene, the U.S. side judged better than the Soviet the arms control diplomacy required for West European audiences and played its hand more skillfully.

The Soviet walkout from the INF and START talks late in 1983 was triggered by the initiation of U.S. deployment of ground-launched cruise missiles (GLCM) in the United Kingdom and Pershing II ballistic missiles in the Federal Republic of Germany. But the walkout was foreshadowed by the stubborn Soviet refusal to sanction by agreement the deployment of even a single U.S. GLCM or Pershing II. Only a formula for fixing the size of a reduced Soviet SS-20 force in exchange for a similar cap on French and British nuclear arsenals was apparently deemed acceptable in Moscow. Failing agreement on these terms, the Soviet leaders had chosen to bank on the anticipated collapse of NATO political consensus or on civil disruption in Western Europe so great as to stop deployment or to make it the occasion for a possibly decisive alliance-splitting crisis. The juxtaposition of this intransigent Soviet stand and Washington's widely advertised conviction that Moscow would start negotiations "seriously" only after the first U.S. missiles arrived ensured the failure of the negotiations.

In turn, the collapse of the INF negotiations foredoomed the parallel talks on intercontinental strategic systems. Moscow had repeatedly insisted that the deployment of U.S. Pershing II and cruise missiles in Europe not only would destroy the basis for INF negotiations but also would constitute a circumvention of the SALT II agreement, which both sides had agreed not to undercut despite the Reagan administration's refusal to ratify it. More important, Soviet determination to stimulate an atmosphere of alarm, if not a war scare, in retaliation for the U.S. missile deployments, required suspension of the START talks along with the INF walkout.

From the Soviet viewpoint, U.S. proposals in the START negotiations had, in any case, offered faint hopes of producing an acceptable agreement, and there was nothing to lose from breaking them off. Some eighteen months of negotiations had failed to produce even a mutually acceptable negotiating framework to replace the one so painstakingly negotiated by Moscow with three previous U.S. administrations but unceremoniously scrapped by the Reagan administration in May 1982. The new U.S. proposal, prepared with less than deliberate speed in Washington, would have required the Soviet Union radically to restructure its strategic forces and to retire over half of its newly acquired fourth-generation MIRVed ICBMs. In return, the United States offered, at most, to scale back somewhat a few planned U.S. programs.

Moscow had no incentive even to consider such a new framework. The Soviets countered with a modified version of the original SALT II treaty, one that featured deeper reductions of 25 percent in the total number of covered strategic missile launchers and bombers, and in the various sublimits, but also new restrictions aimed precisely at the sea-based systems of primary interest to the United States. By the time the Reagan administration, in response to congressional pressure, began to modify its initial START position in the early fall of 1983, the Soviets were no longer paying attention. START had become a sideshow, its fate linked to developments in the then-primary arena of political struggle, INF.

The breakdown of the Geneva talks in November 1983 created a Catch-22 situation for Moscow. The Soviets had intended to use the INF talks to prevent the deployment of U.S. missiles in Europe. Having failed in this goal, Moscow had no incentive to resume negotiations that might appear to validate repeated U.S. public declarations that the USSR would not "seriously" negotiate until after the first U.S. missiles were deployed. As the initial deployments had not caused the sky to fall as predicted, Moscow's principal remaining leverage was the residual Western nuclear anxiety, fed the absence of arms control negotiations, by retaliatory Soviet missile deployments, and by a further worsening of U.S.-Soviet relations. Moscow was unwilling to forfeit such leverage by resuming negotiations without first extracting from Washington concessions that promised a satisfactory outcome and vindicated the Soviet stance. Thus the Soviet Union demanded that the United States withdraw its missiles or agree in advance to do so as a condition for reopening negotiations. The United States, on the other hand, refused to make any major concessions or to alter its negotiating stance in advance merely to induce the Soviets to return to the talks. Hence the stalemate.

Moscow's petulance served only to deepen the quandary in which Soviet leaders found themselves. In the absence of actions that Soviet leaders were evidently unwilling to risk, actions that might raise a real danger of war, harsh Soviet rhetoric and additional missile deployments (in Eastern Europe, in the USSR, and on submarines off the coast of the United States) failed to generate the pressures needed to halt U.S. deployments. Further, the contrast between repeated assertions of U.S. willingness to resume negotiations unconditionally and the Soviet demand that U.S. missiles had to be withdrawn as a precondition to such a resumption served more to underline Soviet intransigence than to build pressures for U.S. concessions.

In the final months of 1983 the Soviet leaders dealt themselves a poor diplomatic hand, weakening their position still further by callous mismanagement of the shootdown by Soviet Air Defense Forces of a Korean Airlines Boeing 747; and during most of 1984 the Politburo played the poor Soviet hand badly. In the face of a dramatic invitation by President Reagan early in the year to open a new phase in U.S.-Soviet relations and to resume arms control negotiations, Moscow clung to its clearly non-negotiable demand that the United States must first withdraw its missiles from Europe. It persisted in stale warnings about the apocalyptic consequences of U.S. failure to comply.

Washington's bid to resume the dialogue was received in Moscow by a Politburo in the midst of a deathwatch over its leader, Yuri Andropov, and facing the certain prospect of a second Soviet leadership succession in little more than a year (Brezhnev had died in November 1982). By mid-January 1984 Andropov was in the final stages of his long illness and was probably no longer involved in affairs of state. Under the circumstances, it is not surprising that Soviet policy at the time of Andropov's death was still being propelled by the momentum imparted to it earlier, when the outcome of the INF crisis was still in doubt.

The death of Andropov in February 1984 and the selection of Konstantin Chernenko to succeed him as General Secretary provided the Kremlin with an opportunity to use the symbolic cover of a leadership change for diplomatic reengagement with the United States at reduced political cost. But Chernenko, in poor health himself, lacked both the authority and the national security experience of his predecessor, and the process whereby the Soviet leadership under his direction dug itself out of the diplomatic hole that it had made for itself was slow and uneven. The key tactic in the evolving Soviet position was to shift the focus of attention from American missiles in Europe, which had since the beginning of deployment become politically inaccessible targets, to President Reagan's Strategic Defense Initiative (SDI) and antisatellite (ASAT) weapons, which not only were subjects of growing Soviet concern but also had become political targets more vulnerable than the INF missiles.

This shift was reflected at the end of June 1984 in a surprise Soviet proposal to open negotiations with the United States on a treaty to prevent the militarization of space, including a ban on antisatellite systems. But Washington deftly coupled an affirmative reply to this Soviet proposal with a statement of its intention to discuss offensive weapons as well (without any advance concessions on INF). The Soviet leadership, taken by surprise if not divided by the U.S. response, backpedaled on its own proposal in an effort to compel an explicit U.S. rejection and to pin the onus for failure on the United States. Washington, in turn, made every effort to show that Moscow, would not, as British foreign secretary Geoffrey Howe put it, "take yes for an answer."

By mid-July the episode had ended without agreement, but the experience may well have conditioned the next Soviet decision, taken even before the U.S. presidential elections: to begin seriously exploring the possibility of resuming the arms control dialogue in a new framework. The Kremlin could hardly have been surprised by the administration's refusal to make space weapons the exclusive subject of a new negotiation and to agree in advance to a moratorium on ASAT testing. Yet Washington's evident eagerness to resume the dialogue and its willingnees to discuss strategic defense in a broader arms control context had also been made manifest. It is quite likely that Moscow's experience with the abortive proposal to open negotiations on space weapons in the summer suggested the outlines of the fallback proposal that Chernenko finally made in a November 17, 1984, letter to the president. On November 22 Washington and Moscow jointly announced that the U.S. secretary of state and the Soviet foreign minister would begin discussing "new negotiations" on "the whole range of questions concerning nuclear and space weapons."[2]

At the Shultz-Gromyko meeting in January 1985 the framework adopted for the new negotiations was essentially an elaboration of the U.S. response to the Soviet Union's June proposal, plus bridging formulas to make the framework compatible with the divergent negotiating interests of the two sides on several key issues. Negotiations were to be conducted by a single delegation on each side, divided into three separate working groups to deal with strategic arms, intermediate-range weapons, and space arms. (Secretary Shultz carefully defined space arms to include those based or targeted on earth as well as those in space.) Questions concerning all three categories of

[2]*New York Times*, November 23, 1984.

weapons were to be "considered and resolved in their interrelationship." The nature of the interrelationship was unspecified, leaving open the full range of possible separate, linked, or comprehensively integrated agreements. Regarding space weapons, the objective of the negotiations was described as "preventing an arms race in space," an artfully contrived formula compatible in theory both with seeking to ban some or all space weapons altogether and with seeking merely to regulate their introduction or further deployment.[3]

Return of Arms Control

On the eve of the opening of the new Geneva talks in March 1985, the third Soviet leadership change in three years took place in Moscow with the death of Chernenko and his replacement by Mikhail Gorbachev, a young and vigorous leader but one with even less national security experience than Chernenko. During the first two rounds of the new negotiations the parties soon became hung up on precisely the issue that had been papered over by the ambiguous Shultz-Gromyko formula, "preventing an arms race in space." Soviet negotiators insisted that no progress on offensive arms control, much less on deep reductions, could be made until the United States agreed to ban space weapons. Meanwhile U.S. negotiators lectured their Soviet counterparts on the stabilizing virtues of strategic defense and the compatibility of immediate deep cuts in offensive forces with a future that might include greatly expanded space-based ballistic missile defenses.

By mid-year, however, the effects of Gorbachev's surprisingly rapid consolidation of power in the Politburo began to make themselves felt in arms control as well as on domestic Soviet political and economic issues. On July 2 Andrei Gromyko was "promoted" to the essentially ceremonial position of chairman of the USSR Supreme Soviet Presidium (titular president), relinquishing the foreign minister's position that he had held for more than twenty-seven years and from which he had come increasingly to dominate Soviet foreign policy making. One day after Gromyko's departure from the Foreign Ministry, Washington and Moscow simultaneously announced that President Reagan and General Secretary Gorbachev would meet in Geneva in November 1985.

Having taken the summit decision, evidently on a gamble that the U.S. president could be pressured to make concessions to ensure a "success," the Soviets almost immediately began to quicken the pace of their arms control diplomacy. During an early October meeting in Washington with President Reagan, Eduard Shevardnadze, the new Soviet foreign minister, presented the outline of a new, comprehensive Soviet proposal that featured 50 percent reductions in strategic weapons and their carriers, far deeper cuts than Moscow

[3]*New York Times*, January 9, 1985.

had previously hinted at or than Washington had expected. However, the promising new Soviet stance on offensive arms reductions was conditioned on U.S. agreement to abandon the SDI. Despite earlier hints by Gorbachev in a *Time* magazine interview of Soviet willingness to permit some limited research activity on space-based strategic defenses, the new Soviet offer repeated the maximalist Soviet position; it called for a complete ban on the "development, including scientific research work, testing, and deployment of space-strike arms."[4]

Moreover, as the Soviet side in the following days laid out the details of their new offensive arms proposal, the fine print revealed Soviet definitions of the "strategic" forces and weapons to be cut which were bound to make the Soviet proposal unacceptable to the United States. Thus Moscow proposed that in reducing "strategic forces" by 50 percent, each superpower had to include all of its nuclear forces capable of striking the territory of the other side. This was a reversion by the Soviets to an earlier one-sided definition of "strategic" forces. That definition they had unsuccessfully proposed during the early stages of both the SALT I and the SALT II negotiations in the 1970s, but it had not resurfaced during the INF and START negotiations with the Reagan administration in the 1980s.

According to the Soviet definition of "strategic" forces, the United States would have to reduce not only its central strategic ICBMs, SLBMs, and heavy bombers, which were limited in the SALT II treaty, but also its INF missiles deployed in Western Europe and its nuclear-capable fighter-bombers in Europe and Asia, as well as on all U.S. aircraft carriers, no matter where deployed. The Soviet Union, in contrast, would have to reduce only its intercontinental nuclear forces, because none of its far larger inventory of intermediate-range missiles, bombers, and nuclear-capable fighter-bombers are able to reach U.S. territory. This approach would require the Soviet Union to reduce its intercontinental launchers from 2,504 to 1,252 but would leave unaffected the USSR's entire intermediate-range force, estimated at around 2,500 missiles and fighter-bombers. The United States, on the other hand, would be obliged to cut its arsenal of "strategic" nuclear weapons carriers from 3,360 to 1,680, a ceiling under which both intercontinental *and* intermediate-range U.S. nuclear delivery vehicles would have to be reduced. To maintain parity in intercontinental delivery systems, the United States would have to abandon its theater nuclear forces, upon which the coupling of Europe to the U.S. strategic deterrent depends; or, if the United States chose to preserve its intermediate nuclear forces, it would be compelled to accept gross inequality in intercontinental nuclear weapons carriers, the ultimate deterrent.

The Soviet October proposal called upon both the United States and the Soviet Union drastically to reduce their inventories of "strategic" weapons to

[4]*Pravda*, October 17, 1985.

an equal aggregate of 6,000 nuclear "charges." As defined by the Soviets, "charges" include ballistic missile reentry vehicles, cruise missile warheads, and other bomber-delivered nuclear weapons. But as with weapon carriers, the Soviet category of "charges" included U.S. weapons carried on INF missiles and forward-based nuclear-capable fighter-bombers as well as American central strategic attack systems, while the Soviets had to count and reduce only the weapons carried on their ICBMs, SLBMs, and heavy bombers.

In an important new departure the Soviets also called for establishment of a "force concentration" rule that would permit no more than 60 percent of the 6,000 permitted "strategic" weapons to be carried on a single force element. The most important effect of this rule would be to prevent the Soviets from protecting their ICBM weapons against substantial reduction by concentrating the cuts on less capable elements of their strategic force.

On the offensive side the Soviet October proposal also called for a ban on the testing and deployment of "new" strategic offensive systems, defined as those ballistic missiles and aircraft which had not yet entered flight testing. It also included a ban on all long-range cruise missiles. The first ban would permit the Soviets to proceed with virtually all of their next-generation ICBMs, SLBMs, and bombers—which have already been flight-tested—while probably precluding U.S. testing and deployment on the "Midgetman" ICBM, the D-5 SLBM, and the advanced technology ("stealth") bomber—which have not yet been flight-tested. The second ban was apparently intended to halt and even reverse deployments of long-range air-launched, sea-launched, and ground-launched cruise missiles, even though the United States has already deployed all three types while the USSR has fielded one class of air-launched cruise missiles (ALCMs) and has substantial development and testing efforts under way in the other two areas as well.

Having transferred U.S. intermediate nuclear forces into the "strategic" category, the Soviet proposal had made no provision for limiting Soviet INF missiles, bombers, and fighter-bombers. Within a week, however, General Secretary Gorbachev, during an official visit to France, declared that the Soviet Union was prepared to enter into direct negotiations with France and the United Kingdom regarding reductions in their respective intermediate-range nuclear arsenals. The French and British governments both promptly rejected this offer.

At first the official U.S. response to the new Soviet offer was mixed. Administration spokesmen were quick to point out the blatantly one-sided and thus totally unacceptable aspects of the Soviet proposal—the total ban on SDI research, development, testing, and deployment; its inequitable counting of only U.S. intermediate forces; and its bans on cruise missiles and "new types" of strategic weapons which disproportionately penalized projected U.S. programs. At the same time, however, U.S. spokesmen expressed satisfaction that the Soviets had chosen at last to table a new, comprehensive proposal that contained some positive elements as well—a call for substantial reductions, limitations on weapons ("charges") as well as launchers, a willingness to accept in principle U.S. Pershing II deployments in Western Europe, and a force concentration rule that would guarantee a substantial reduction in the size of the Soviet ICBM force.

With the initiative in the public arms control maneuvering having suddenly passed to the Soviet side, Washington was prompted to develop a counterproposal. In early November, just three weeks prior to the summit, the United States presented its new offer at the Geneva negotiations. The proposal sought to build upon the positive elements of the new Soviet offer but without compromising long-standing U.S. objectives. Accordingly, the U.S. proposal contained no provisions affecting space weapons. Although it also called for a 50 percent reduction in the strategic offensive delivery vehicles of the two sides, the reduction was to apply only to the SALT-accountable intercontinental systems of both sides. The United States also proposed a reduction of approximately 50 percent in ballistic missile warheads, down to an equal ceiling of 4,500 such weapons for each side. Of the 4,500 missile warheads remaining after the cut, no more than 3,000 could be deployed on ICBMs.

In addition, the United States proposed a new limit of 1,500 on ALCMs. This limit, when combined with the 4,500 ceiling on ICBM and SLBM warheads, would, like the Soviet October proposal, produce an aggregate limit of 6,000 weapons, but with important differences. The U.S.-proposed 6,000 included neither weapons on U.S. INF missiles and forward-based aircraft nor short-range attack missiles (SRAMs) or gravity bombs carried by the heavy bombers of both sides. The former exclusion unambiguously registered Washington's rejection of the one-sided Soviet definition of "strategic." The latter exclusion reflected a U.S. aversion to treating SRAMs and gravity bombs as equivalent to ballistic missile warheads. It also reflected a desire to provide greater scope for maintaining a substantial U.S. bomber capability without having to "pay" heavily for it in a reduced ballistic missile weapon inventory. Consistent with these concerns, the United States proposed to establish a separate limit of 350 heavy bombers for both sides.

The U.S. proposal also included a ban on the testing and deployment of a new generation of heavy ICBMs and, unexpectedly, a ban on the testing and deployment of land-based mobile missiles. The latter prohibition on mobiles would compel the Soviets to halt deployments of their mobile SS-25 ICBMs and to dismantle those missiles already operational, as well as to forgo the anticipated rail-mobile version of the larger SS-X-24 ICBM already in advanced stages of development. It would similarly prohibit deployment of the small U.S. Midgetman ICBM currently in early stages of development in this country.

Finally, the United States proposed new limits on U.S. and Soviet INF missile forces. It called for an overall launcher limit of 140 on each side, equal to the number deployed by the United States at the end of 1985, and for a ceiling of between 420 and 450 missile warheads.

The Soviets barely had time to digest the new U.S. proposal when the two leaders met in Geneva on November 19–20. The summit produced no concrete change in the nuclear arms control positions of either side. Both President Reagan and General Secretary Gorbachev reportedly expressed in forceful terms their already well-known, starkly contrasting views on the role that space-based defenses might play in the Soviet-American strategic relationship. In the end neither appeared to have convinced the other. Gorbachev insisted that a halt in the development of space-based defenses was the absolute precondition for any reduction in offensive arms. President Reagan held firm to his hope that deep offensive reductions could be achieved while the sides pursued a vigorous SDI research effort without any constraints beyond those of the ABM Treaty. If successful, the space defense research effort would lay the groundwork for a long-term transition to a defense-dominant strategic posture, a transition that the United States has invited the USSR to conduct on a cooperative basis.

Having failed to make headway at the summit, Gorbachev sought in mid-January 1986 to recapture the diplomatic high ground by unveiling an omnibus three-stage plan calling for the universal elimination of all nuclear weapons by the year 2000. The new plan merely incorporated provisions of the October 1985 Soviet proposal regarding strategic weapons and space arms, but the Soviet INF offer was dramatically altered. Now the USSR proposed complete elimination within five to eight years of all U.S. and Soviet medium-range missiles in Europe conditioned on British and French agreement to freeze their missile arsenals and U.S. agreement not to supply strategic or medium-range missiles to other countries. Moscow subsequently indicated it was prepared to conclude such an INF agreement independently of the strategic and space weapons negotiations.

Erosion of Treaty Regime

Although the joint statement of the two leaders at the summit called upon the Geneva negotiators to accelerate the pace of their discussion in areas where common ground had been found, the failure of the sides to make the slightest progress in resolving their diametrically opposed positions on strategic defense left intact the largest roadblock in the path of agreement. Meanwhile the arms control regime defined by earlier treaties and agreements continued to erode. In the 1980s' atmosphere of great uncertainty about the future strategic environment, evidence has mounted of possible violations of existing agreements by the USSR. In addition, both sides are now pressing up against the limits imposed by the arms control agreements of the 1970s, and both are making extensive preparations for the development, testing, and eventual deployment of a variety of new offensive and defensive systems, which, if completed, would breach provisions of several treaties.

By general agreement, both among those persuaded that the Soviet Union has systematically and deliberately violated treaty provisions and those skeptical about those allegations, the most egregious Soviet behavior is the ongoing construction of a major radar facility near Krasnoyarsk in Siberia. This facility is located 750 kilometers from the nearest border to the south and 4,000 kilometers from the northern border, the direction toward which the radar is oriented. Its placement appears to be in violation of Article VI of the ABM Treaty, which limits the deployment of missile early warning radars to those oriented outward and located along the peripheries of the two countries. With regard to U.S. practices, Soviet charges of treaty violations, such as their complaints about U.S. plans to upgrade early warning radars in Scotland and Greenland and to build new ones in Georgia and Texas, have seemed to lack substance. More telling are Soviet allegations that the United States is undermining the arms control regime by refusing to ratify treaties already completed and signed and by conspicuously launching a major research and development effort looking toward deployment of a space-based antiballistic missile system that would directly contravene the ABM Treaty on several counts.

In addition, both sides are now at the point where their strategic programs are straining the limits of the SALT II treaty, which would have expired at the end of 1985 even if ratified but which each side has informally agreed not to "undercut" so long as the other exercises a similar restraint. The Soviets have now completed the modernization of their ICBM force with extensive deployments of the fourth-generation MIRVed SS-17s, 18s, and 19s within the constraints of the MIRVed ICBM sublimit of the SALT II treaty. They have long since been up against the SALT I ceiling on modern nuclear submarines (SSBNs) and submarine-launched ballistic missiles (SLBMs). They have brought new systems into operation by retiring older boats, some of which have been converted into attack submarines that may eventually be used to carry sea-launched cruise missiles; but this option may be less attractive to them as the future of the SALT arms control regime grows more dubious. Their fifth-generation ICBM programs continue to move ahead, including flight testing of the MIRVed SS-X-24 and initial mobile deployments of the controversial single-warhead, solid-fueled SS-25. The Soviets insist that the SS-25 is merely a modification of an older ICBM rather than a second unauthorized "new type," prohibited under the terms of SALT II, as the United States claims. Soviet telemetry encryption practices have, it is reported, progressively ignored SALT II strictures against encryption that would impede verification of restrictions on ICBM modernization and on the testing of new types of ICBMs.

Meanwhile the United States, whose own programs have until now not been significantly constrained by compliance with treaty provisions, has reached a point at which it has had to retire still serviceable Poseidon SLBMs on older nuclear submarines or MIRVed Minuteman III ICBMs, in order to make room for the deployment of additional new nuclear submarines carrying more advanced Trident I missiles. In the fall of 1985, as a new submarine carrying Trident I missiles entered sea trials, the United States chose to begin dismantling a Poseidon-carrying submarine, but administration charges of Soviet noncompliance threw U.S. willingness to dismantle additional submarines increasingly into doubt.

In addition, U.S. plans to arm additional B-52s, and possibly B-1s as well, with air-launched cruise missiles will soon outstrip the permitted "cushion" of one hundred and twenty such systems. Such plans will force further reductions in either Poseidon SLBMs or Minuteman III ICBMs to stay within the SALT II subceiling of 1,320 on MIRVed ballistic missiles and bombers equipped with air-launched cruise missiles (ALCMs). And the U.S. SDI, while it will not contravene the ABM Treaty before reaching the test phase for prohibited components, represents a conditional decision, assuming technical feasibility and fiscal manageability, eventually to seek permissive amendment of the treaty or to abrogate it. These multiple pressures on the partially expiring arms control regime created in the last decade make prospects for its survival seem bleak in the absence of a new treaty or a joint decision to extend the regime in the context of ongoing efforts to negotiate a new permanent treaty.

Moreover, both sides stand poised in their own strategic modernization programs or have already begun to deploy new systems that are not covered by existing treaty provisions but that will have major implications for the strategic balance. Significant recent expansions in the nuclear strike forces of the two sides (massive for the Soviet, still small for the American) have already occurred in intermediate-range ballistic missiles and ground-launched cruise missiles for which no arms control regime exists. The United States has made initial deployments of long-range sea-launched cruise missiles that are similarly uncovered, and the Soviets have already announced their intention to follow suit shortly.

Many of the new strategic systems, in varying states of development and testing or in the early stages of deployment, will pose difficult verification challenges. Some may already have gone beyond the point where high-confidence verification of a ban or limitations on deployment is feasible using national technical means, even when supplemented by extensive cooperative measures. Sea-launched cruise missiles are the most striking case in this regard. Arguably, bans on deployment or agreed limits that permit the deployment of low-altitude ASATs of the types launched by Soviet SS-9 ICBMs (tested periodically for more than a decade, but not since 1982) or by U.S. F-15s (successfully flight-tested against a target in space in September 1985) may also no longer be verifiable with high confidence. Land-mobile ICBM systems, such as the Soviets' new solid-propellant SS-25 and perhaps eventually also a rail-mobile version of the SS-X-24, as well as the still only notional U.S. Midgetman, will also pose significant problems if they are not designed and deployed with a careful eye to ensuring adequate verification.

Changing Superpower Arms Control Perspectives

In examining the likely future of nuclear arms control, one must take into account not only various pressures on the current arms control regime and the troubled state of U.S.-Soviet relations but also the superpowers' basic perspectives on arms control. Attitudes and perspectives on arms control in both Washington and Moscow have evolved considerably since their confluence in the early 1970s helped produce the SALT I agreements. At that time the United States sought to use arms control agreements as a means to cap the growth of Soviet strategic power and to stabilize a condition of deterrence based on mutual societal vulnerability. The Soviets, on the other hand, saw arms control as a vehicle for formally ratifying their attainment of coequal superpower status and for retarding further increases in U.S. strategic nuclear capabilities, thus protecting their strategic gains of the late 1960s and early 1970s. The United States particularly valued those provisions of the SALT I agreement which constrained further Soviet growth in launchers; the Soviets particularly valued the political benefits associated with the arms control process itself, including East-West detente and a dampening of U.S. competitiveness.

But by the end of the 1970s there was widespread disappointment on the U.S. side. Arms control had not stopped the growth of particularly threatening Soviet capabilities, embodied in the USSR's large ICBM force with its increasingly accurate multiple warheads carried atop the heavy throwweight SS-18s and SS-19s. Nor had it slowed the momentum of the multidimensional Soviet military buildup. Especially in recent years there has been growing pessimism and skepticism in the U.S. arms control and defense policy communities regarding the prospects for and utility of comprehensive arms control agreements of the SALT type. Conservative critics question the usefulness of the entire enterprise. The Soviets, they argue, will never accept meaningful limitations on their strategic potential and will seek to violate agreed limitations that become inconvenient. Moreover, they charge, previous SALT agreements had tolerated and even sanctioned a continuing shift in the strategic balance of power in favor of the Soviet Union. Those agreements granted Moscow significant advantages caused by asymmetries in the domestic and alliance environments of arms control policy making on the two sides. The very process of arms control negotiation is viewed in some quarters as counterproductive, because it is held to undermine public support in the West for the arms programs required to match or surpass Soviet strategic capabilities.

Many traditional supporters of arms control are also disillusioned. Some have declared that the era of comprehensive arms control is over. Agreements of this kind, they argue, take too long to negotiate, are too quickly overtaken by new technologies, and frequently serve to stimulate the procurement of new weapons whose development is justified as bargaining chips in the negotiating process. Some arms control proponents, pessimistic about prospects for achieving new agreements that meaningfully constrain or reduce strategic forces, have turned their attention to so-called strategic confidence-building measures, such as the creation of special centers designed to help manage intense superpower crises and prevent the initiation of nuclear war by accident or by unauthorized action. Still others continue to believe that the combination of equitable, verifiable force structure agreements that limit and reduce the strategic attack potentials of the superpowers with unilateral measures to improve the survivability of the residual arsenals can contribute significantly to the maintainance of a stable nuclear balance.

Despite these largely pessimistic crosscurrents, the necessity of continuing the strategic arms control process seems now to have been accepted by the Reagan administration, which had entered office with a skeptical view of the whole arms control enterprise. At a minimum, the need to respond to the nuclear anxieties of publics in democratic societies and the need to maintain public support for a strong defense are now widely seen as requiring a credible effort to pursue comprehensive arms control agreements with the USSR.

There is a widespread impression that while American views on the efficacy and desirability of the 1970s-type arms control process and the agreements it yielded have undergone substantial, even radical, change in the past half-decade, Soviet perspectives on arms control remain essentially unchanged. This is surely the impression that Soviet spokesmen, heaping blame on their unreliable, inconsistent U.S. negotiating partners, have sought to convey. But there is reason to question this assumption in the light of the sharply altered circumstances and prospects of the 1980s and beyond.

The Soviet approach to arms control has evolved through distinct phases in the postwar era in response to dramatic changes in the strategic positions of the United States and the USSR, in military technologies, in the larger global geopolitical context, and in the domestic and alliance environments of the two superpowers. More recent and ongoing changes in the environment of Soviet strategic policy making appear to be altering the Soviet perspective on arms control. Such changes are affecting Moscow's calculations regarding the kinds of results that may be attainable and acceptable in the coming decade and their political and military value.

The Soviet Union has been in the disarmament business since the earliest days of the Soviet republic, when the most far-reaching and clearly "non-negotiable" disarmament proposals were advanced by the Soviet government as instruments of political warfare against militarily superior opponents. This practice was renewed after World War II as a means to combat the U.S. nuclear monopoly. But arms control as a substantive political process in search of practical agreements, as opposed to arms control as an exclusively propaganda tool, became feasible and attractive to Soviet leaders only as the disparity between U.S. and Soviet strategic nuclear capabilities diminished in the 1960s.

By the late 1960s arms control recommended itself to the Kremlin as a means of helping manage the transition from Soviet inferiority to strategic nuclear parity more safely and less provocatively than might have been the case in a totally unregulated strategic environment. Arms control agreements appealed to Soviet leaders because they could contribute to the dampening of U.S. strategic competitiveness and as a means for gaining formal U.S. acknowledgement of the USSR's newly acquired coequal superpower status, an attainment to which Moscow attributed enormous political value. Arms control, however, was not the means whereby the Soviet Union overcame U.S. strategic superiority. That achievement grew out of the unilateral armament efforts of the Soviet Union during the 1960s and 1970s.

This was essentially the climate in which the SALT I agreements were negotiated, agreements that became the centerpiece of the U.S.-Soviet detente of the 1970s. For the Soviets, the arms control process that produced these agreements and nourished the atmosphere of detente was valued beyond any particular treaty provisions. Certainly they hoped to negotiate provisions that would constrain those U.S. strategic programs of greatest concern to them. On balance, however, when the choice came down to constraining the United States or protecting existing Soviet forces and ongoing programs, Moscow almost invariably opted for the latter. Even the largest and most important exception—the ABM Treaty—was only a partial exception. Although the Soviets consistently opposed the deployment of a countrywide ABM defense, they also generally insisted on retaining the system they had already deployed around Moscow. Apart from the ABM case, the choice between constraints on the U.S. side and protections for Soviet programs was not all that difficult for Moscow during SALT I negotiations, because the United States had few new strategic programs coming on line in those years. MIRV technology—the most important new development—was, for a variety of reasons, not on the table for bargaining.

Launcher limits established in SALT I and SALT II gave the Soviets sufficient leeway to continue those strategic programs of greatest value to them. Under the SALT I agreements they could proceed with the development, testing, and deployment of fourth-generation MIRVed ICBMs and of extended-range MIRVed SLBMs. And during a period of mutually agreed general compliance with the unratified SALT II treaty, they can move ahead with the development and likely deployment of two and possibly three fifth-generation ICBM systems, two new SLBMs, two new SSBNs, a new strategic bomber, an aircraft converted to carry cruise missiles, and a variety of ground-, sea-, and air-launched cruise missiles.

But the circumstances that shaped the Soviet Union's arms control perspectives in the late 1960s and 1970s are now changing, some of them dramatically. As a result, in the wake of the suspension of the INF and START negotiations at the end of 1983, the Soviets almost certainly reassessed their arms control positions. The altered circumstances go far beyond the more immediate challenge raised by the deployment of U.S. intermediate-range missiles in Europe and even beyond the long-term challenge of the SDI.

The first major change concerns the link between arms control and detente. In the 1970s arms control was the centerpiece of the U.S.-Soviet detente relationship, and arms control agreements seemed necessary periodically to punctuate the process and to maintain the momentum of superpower cooperation. Detente, in turn, was valued because it tempered U.S. strategic competitiveness, raised the threshhold of U.S. tolerance for Soviet assertiveness in the Third World, and provided a more propitious political context for extracting economic benefits from the West. Since 1979, however, when Zbigniew Brzezinski coined the phrase, the prospect has been one of "arms control without detente." This prospect tends to diminish for Moscow the political benefits associated with the arms control process and to place greater importance on the real balance of arms constraints associated with any putative agreement.

The second major change concerns the relationship between arms control and the probability that the U.S. government will prove capable of sustaining domestic support for its strategic weapons programs. As noted above, the Reagan administration's perception of the relationship between arms control and the U.S. military buildup has changed dramatically since President Reagan took office. In 1981 the administration's disinclination to resume nuclear arms control negotiations with the Soviet Union was palpable. Rearm first, negotiate later from a position of strength, was the preferred sequence. The Soviet Union meanwhile presented itself as the champion of arms control continuity and of immediate negotiations.

By the fall of 1983 these positions had been exactly reversed. On the U.S. side it had become clear to the administration that the Western arms buildup could not be sustained without a more credible arms control effort. The results of this altered environment have been evident in a variety of ways, particularly in the way in which the Congress has conditioned its funding support for several defense programs on adjustments in U.S. arms control positions, to make them more "negotiable."

By the time the Soviets broke off the INF and START negotiations, Moscow had concluded that an arms control negotiating environment was in fact helpful to the U.S. military buildup. Resuming talks with a U.S. administration that was unlikely in the end to negotiate acceptable terms would only help secure congressional support for military programs of concern to the USSR. Yet the Soviets also came to recognize that for them to be seen as unremittingly intransigent in the face of ostensibly reasonable U.S. proposals would also be counterproductive for Soviet interests in precisely the same respects.

Although the renewed arms control process no longer promises Moscow political benefits comparable to those of the detente era, other changes in the strategic environment make the military prospects for the Soviet Union *without* arms control considerably less promising in the years ahead than they were during the SALT years. The United States was not nearly as strategically laggard in the 1970s as is often claimed. Nevertheless, measured by almost any criteria, trends in size and capability of strategic attack forces—as in virtually all dimensions of military power—have generally favored the Soviet Union for more than a decade.

Beginning in the mid-1980s, however, a series of U.S. strategic modernization programs—the MX, the Midgetman ICBM, new longer-range and more accurate SLBMs, the revived B-1 bomber, the advanced technology (Stealth) bomber, and Pershing II, as well as ground-, sea-, and air-launched cruise missiles—will be yielding new, highly capable, deployed systems. Thus although Soviet strategic capabilities relative to those of the United States may today be at their highest point, the USSR now confronts trends that move in the opposite direction. These trends could, if not arrested, threaten important Soviet strategic gains. Added to this is the vigorous, high-technology SDI effort, which is being pursued, in President Reagan's words, to render Soviet ballistic missiles "impotent and obsolete."

The Soviets, of course, are also positioned to proceed with a host of new strategic offensive and defensive programs. Nevertheless, their extensively acquired advantages in prompt hard-target counterforce and long-awaited improvements in homeland strategic air defenses appear destined to disappear as the United States proceeds with its strategic modernization efforts. U.S. fielding of highly accurate ICBMs and SLBMs equipped with multiple warheads will increasingly place at risk the large, silo-based Soviet ICBM force, which is the very cornerstone of Soviet strategic nuclear prowess. And the still vague but menacing prospect of superior U.S. technology being harnessed in connection with President Reagan's Strategic Defense Initiative is bound to increase Soviet unease about the possible shape of the strategic balance in the years ahead.

A pessimistic Soviet assessment of the long-term trends in the strategic nuclear balance is thus coupled with a growing awareness of the high economic costs and risks that a more competitive U.S. adversary is likely to impose in an unregulated enviornment. The combination may well make Moscow more amenable than in the past to arms control agreements that require the USSR to accept substantial reductions in high-value forces in order to constrain the most threatening U.S. programs.

Ironically, a more *positive* Soviet assessment of other aspects of the military balance could reinforce Soviet interest in considering such tradeoffs at the strategic level. Advancing technology and tougher U.S. competition make the pursuit of strategic superiority, or of some politically meaningful edge, more difficult and costly for the Soviet Union. The perception that the USSR enjoys such an advantage, however, may now be seen as less vital than in the past for Moscow's grand strategy. The large-scale buildup of Soviet intercontinental nuclear capabilities has been accompanied by an even more costly modernization and expansion of Soviet conventional forces, especially for conducting rapid offensive operations in Europe and the Far East. Since the mid-1970s the Soviet buildup has also been marked by the acquisition of improved Soviet long-range and battlefield theater nuclear forces for potential employment in both major theaters.

As a consequence of the enhancement of long-standing Soviet conventional superiority and the trumping of U.S. nuclear options in the theater, the political and military burdens heretofore borne by Soviet forces designed for central nuclear war have been eased. To permit superior Soviet forces to prevail militarily in the theater, or, more to the point, to achieve dominance of the European security arena politically in peacetime, Soviet intercontinental forces now need only be large and capable enough to neutralize those of the United States.

Repeated Soviet attempts to gain Western adherence to a pledge of no-first-use of nuclear weapons are consistent with this perspective. The self-serving political purpose of the Soviet Union's unilateral pledge not to use nuclear weapons first are obvious; the doctrine of no-first-use may very well reflect also Soviet strategic preferences under the condition of Soviet escalation dominance at all levels below that of general nuclear war. To the extent this may be true, Soviet leaders in the future may be more willing to trade off some existing Soviet strategic nuclear advantages, likely in any case to be eroded in the years ahead, in exchange for constraints on the United States that would insure them against the rejuvenation and significant expansion of U.S. strategic offensive and defensive capabilities.

Common Ground and Divergences on Offensive Arms

In the new phase of U.S.-Soviet relations ushered in at the end of 1985 by the revival of high-level dialogue and the exchange of new arms control proposals, the governments in Washington and Moscow confront fateful choices. Overlapping elements in the proposals tabled by the two sides in the fall of 1985 and early 1986 could provide the framework for a comprehensive mid- to long-term agreement that would sharply reduce strategic offensive arms, including the most threatening components, and for an "interim" agreement on intermediate nuclear forces which would at least prevent an unregulated competition in that sphere. But progress in building on the common ground identified by Reagan and Gorbachev at the summit and bridging the still very substantial gap between the two positions on offensive weapons remains hostage to success in resolving the as yet totally irreconcilable differences between the two sides regarding space weapons, in particular the space-based elements of a multilayered ballistic missile defense system.

Soviet spokesmen have frequently asserted that U.S. agreement to a ban on space weapons would open the way to rapid progress on an offensive arms agreement. Even supposing the strategic defense issue could be successfully resolved, however, the obstacles to such an agreement remain formidable and technically daunting. The old START and INF issues remain: what to do about Soviet advantages in ballistic missile throwweight; how to handle sea-launched cruise missiles, the Soviet Backfire bomber, and British and French nuclear forces; how to cap the U.S. bomber potential. Also, the old problem of verification has been further exacerbated in recent years by Soviet violations and by the ongoing and projected deployments of new weapons for which verifiable limitations will be extremely difficult to devise.

The basic Euromissile issues remain technically unchanged since the breakdown of negotiations in 1983. But successful deployment of new U.S. missiles in Europe has resolved the major political uncertainty that had stalemated the negotiations and dictated the earlier grandstanding tactics of both sides. In January 1986 the Soviets indicated willingness to pursue an INF agreement without any linkage to the central strategic arms or space weapons negotiations. If there are sufficiently strong incentives on both sides now to single out INF for early progress, a compromise formula might be found. Such a formula could involve reductions to an equal ceiling in U.S. and Soviet missile launchers based in Europe. Alternatively, it could provide for complete elimination of all U.S. and Soviet INF missiles in range of Europe.

To be of real arms control value, a new offensive arms control agreement would have to yield substantial, equitable, and verifiable reductions in the total destructive capacities of the superpowers. Such cuts should reduce the actual and perceived capability of both sides to execute a disarming first strike while permitting and encouraging each side to deploy its remaining offensive forces in modes that are highly survivable in the face of the threats still posed by the other side. Some key elements found in both the Soviet and the U.S. fall 1985 proposals meet these criteria.

Both sides have proposed agreements to cut central strategic offensive arms which would result in substantial reductions below current force levels. The United States currently has approximately 11,100 and the USSR some 9,750 weapons on ICBMs, SLBMs, and heavy bomber forces. The Soviet proposal for a 6,000-aggregate ceiling on strategic nuclear "charges" could prove useful if the Kremlin ultimately agrees, as it has done twice previously, to withdraw its demand that U.S. intermediate-range systems be counted within this total. Without such a Soviet move, no offensive arms agreement will be possible. As in the past Moscow would surely seek "compensation" for excluding these U.S. systems and might hold back until the endgame and then seek to trade for U.S. concessions on defense. The Soviet 6,000 limit, if confined to central strategic forces, would include all of the ICBM and SLBM warheads on both sides, as well as the gravity bombs and air-to-surface attack missiles carried on their heavy bombers.

The U.S. November 1985 proposal, though it also included a limit of 6,000 on strategic weapons, would permit both sides to field significantly larger intercontinental strategic forces. The 6,000 ceiling in the U.S. proposal applies only to missile-carried weapons; each side could deploy up to 4,500 ICBM and SLBM warheads and 1,500 ALCM warheads. But both sides could also deploy an additional large number of short-range attack missiles (SRAMs) and gravity bombs on the 350 heavy bombers that were permitted in the U.S. proposal. The U.S. proposal placed no explicit limit on the number of weapons to be carried on the 350 bombers allowed for each side. But one could reasonably calculate that 75 of these bombers might be loaded with 20 ALCMs each to reach the 1500 ALCM limit, while the remaining 275 bombers could carry a load of eight to ten SRAMS or gravity bombs or both, a payload that conforms with operational considerations. This bomber loading of 1,500 ALCMs and 2,200–2,750 SRAMs and gravity bombs, when added to the 4,500 ballistic missile warheads allowed, would produce an effective overall strategic weapons ceiling of 8,200–8,750 weapons.

The much wider latitude for bomber weapons provided for by the U.S. proposal reflects both the strong American heavy bomber tradition and the U.S. position that weapons carried by U.S. bombers, which are much slower than ballistic missiles and must penetrate heavy Soviet air defenses, cannot be equated with the prompt, hard-target-killing warheads carried by heavy Soviet ICBMs against which there is as yet no defense. The Soviets, on the other hand, have strongly objected to the treatment of bomber weapons in the U.S. proposal. They have argued that under a sharply reduced ceiling for aggregate weapons, such a large U.S. advantage in "exempt" bomber weapons would be intolerable. This issue, too, is likely to be resolved only in the broader context of a comprehensive agreement that would provide scope for tradeoffs of various kinds. Despite these differences, the two proposals have laid the groundwork for serious bargaining, having both proposed aggregate limits on strategic weapons which are significantly below current, let alone projected, U.S. and Soviet force levels.

Ballistic missile throwweight, that is, the combined lifting power of each side's ballistic missile forces, is another key measure of potential destructive capacity. The United States has long been concerned about the enormous throwweight advantage enjoyed by the Soviet ICBM force in particular. That force includes 308 very large SS-18s and 360 medium-sized SS-19s—4.7 million kilograms of Soviet ICBM throwweight versus one million kilograms for the United States. Throwweight is an important element of attack capability, because it could serve as the basis for a sudden "breakout" expansion of Soviet missile-borne weapons: existing large missiles could, in theory, be rapidly retrofitted to carry a much larger number of smaller warheads. More important, this lifting capacity could enable the Soviets to deploy larger numbers of weapons with appropriate yields which could be used to mount lethal barrage attacks against either U.S. alert heavy bombers as they attempted to fly out from their bases or mobile missiles, if eventually deployed in the field, whose precise location was not known by the attacker.

Both the U.S. and the Soviet proposals tabled in the fall of 1985 included sublimits that would require substantial cuts in Soviet ICBM throwweight. The U.S. proposal would permit the Soviets to deploy no more than 3,000 ICBM warheads, less than half of the 6,420 currently deployed. The 60 percent force concentration rule in the Soviet proposal would translate into an effective ceiling of 3,600 Soviet ICBM warheads. In either proposal the resulting cuts in ICBM warheads would, by necessity, produce substantial reductions in Soviet ICBM throwweight as well. The more permissive Soviet formulation would likely translate into a reduction from the present 4.7 million kilograms of Soviet ICBM throwweight to approximately 2.5–2.9 million kilograms, while the lower U.S. limit would cut the Soviets to around 2.0–2.4 million kilograms, depending on the specific missile mix the Soviets might choose for their reduced ICBM force. Given the American preferences for a smaller ICBM component of its overall strategic posture, as well as the character of current and projected U.S. ICBM programs, U.S. ICBM throwweight under either proposal would probably remain near the current level of one million kilograms. Consequently, adoption of either proposed limit, or of some compromise between the two, would produce a deep cut in Soviet ICBM throwweight of between 40 percent and 60 percent thus greatly reducing both the USSR's ICBM breakout potential and the barrage threat to U.S. bombers or to mobile U.S. ICBMs.

The U.S. and Soviet proposals would, of course, limit the numbers of SLBM weapons which could be deployed as well. The U.S. proposal would allow no more than 4,500 warheads to be deployed on ICBMs and SLBMs taken together. The Soviet force concentration rule would permit no more than 3,600 warheads on SLBMs, and more to the point, the 6,000 ceiling on strategic weapons would compel both sides to trade off their SLBM warheads against ICBM warheads and bomber weapons within this aggregate. Differing traditional emphases in SSBN/SLBM deployments make it almost certain that the United States would maintain a larger SLBM component than the USSR within the agreed limits.

Whatever the ultimate choices—possibly 1,500–2,000 SLBM warheads for the Soviets and 2,500–3,000 for the Americans—both sides would find themselves with sharply reduced numbers of nuclear-powered ballistic missile submarines. The reason for this is simple: the newer SLBMs on both sides are equipped with eight MIRVs, and the most modern SSBNs designed to carry them have twenty to twenty-four launch tubes. As a result each large modern nuclear ballistic missile submarine contains 160 to 192 SLBM warheads. This means that the Soviets could maintain only ten to fourteen Typhoon and Delta IV SSBNs (down from sixty-two SSBNs today) to carry its 1,500–2,000 SLBM RVs; the United States would only require a force of thirteen to fifteen Trident subs (down from thirty-seven SSBNs today) to deploy its 2,500–3,000 SLBM weapons permitted under the fall proposals. This drastic reduction in the number of SSBNs on both sides would mean that even with relatively high day-to-day alert rates that placed on the order of 50–60 percent of SSBNs at sea rather than in port (the Soviets are at only 20 percent today, while U.S. SSBN patrol rates are already near the 60 percent level), each side would have, on the average, only five to nine ballistic missile submarines at sea in routine peacetime conditions. The fundamental strategic antisubmarine warfare challenge of successfully locating and attacking a submerged SSBN in thousands of square miles of open water would remain in principle unaffected. Such sharp reductions would, however, greatly reduce the numbers of submarines that would have to be found and destroyed by a would-be first-striker. This is an unintended consequence of the shift by both sides to very large submarines, ironically compounded by arms control reductions theoretically aimed at enhancing force survivability.

Despite such anomalies, it is clear that the restraints imposed on the strategic offensive forces of the two sides by either the U.S. or the Soviet proposals could produce a very substantial reduction in the strategic attack capabilities of both sides. The net impact of these reductions on the size of the retaliatory forces that could survive a first strike is not entirely clear, because survival would be highly dependent on the basing configurations and alert rates of the forces retained under any agreement. It should be understood, however, that neither proposal could restore and preserve the survivability of the fixed, silo-based ICBM forces on either side. Improvements in accuracy have outrun improved hardening techniques. And the numbers of highly accurate, silo-killing warheads available to both sides under each of the new proposals would be far in excess of the five hundred or six hundred needed to hold at risk the few hundred ICBM silos likely to remain on each side.

That is not to say that the survivability of the land-based ICBM force cannot be dramatically improved by a combination of arms control restraints and force modernization. The very substantial reductions in ballistic missile throwweight which would result from the limits on ICBM warheads would greatly enhance the prospects for deploying a highly survivable mobile ICBM force. A force of several hundred mobile missiles, particularly if they were deployed as blast-resistant transporter-erector launchers, would be highly survivable if the would-be attacker were compelled to mount a barrage attack over several thousand square miles.[5] Appreciating the improved survivability prospects for mobile ICBMs, the Soviets have already begun deploying the single-warhead SS-25 in a truck-mobile mode and are developing a rail-mobile launcher for the larger SS-X-24.

In light of these developments, both the U.S. proposal to ban mobile ICBMs, reportedly adopted largely out of concern about serious verification difficulties associated with mobile ICBMs, and the Soviet proposal to ban "new" as yet untested systems—a measure that would preclude U.S. deployment of the mobile Midgetman—would diminish the survivability advantages that would otherwise be realized for the land-based ICBM forces of both sides. The Soviets will in any case surely not accept a ban on mobile missiles now that they have developed and begun to deploy them in order to enhance the survivability of their otherwise increasingly vulnerable land-based ICBMs. Moreover, if acceptable provisions can be devised for verifying the numbers of mobile ICBMs deployed without compromising their precise location at any particular time, the United States may also choose to revert to the same strategic logic that impelled the Ford and Carter administrations initially to propose mobile basing for the MX. This same logic led the Reagan administration to adopt the 1983 recommendation of the Scowcroft Commission that the United States develop a new small mobile ICBM.

Given the reduced forces associated with the two proposals, both superpowers would also need to undertake a variety of efforts to preserve the prelaunch survivability and retaliatory effectiveness of their SLBMs and bombers. Sharp reductions in numbers of SSBNs that could be deployed would, as noted above, probably lead both sides to keep a larger proportion of their SSBN force at sea. Moreover, both sides would probably continue to deploy new, quieter Trident and Typhoon submarines equipped with long-range SLBMs, in order to make their missile-carrying submarines more difficult to detect when on patrol.

The significant reduction in the potential barrage threat to U.S. bomber flyout areas produced by the deep cut in Soviet ICBM throwweight would contribute to assuring the survivability of the U.S. alert bomber force during launch. Anticipated improvements in Soviet air defense capabilities, which would not be affected by any new agreement reducing strategic offensive arms, will pose a severe threat to the capability of the aging U.S. B-52 bomber force to penetrate Soviet airspace. It is precisely to improve base escape characteristics and penetration capabilities that the United States embarked upon the B-1B, Advanced Technology Bomber, ALCM, and advanced (stealthy)

---

[5]The Soviets, for example, would need at least four million kilograms of missile throwweight to deliver the weapons required to mount a full-barrage attack sufficient to neutralize a force of several hundred Midgetman ICBMs carried on mobile launchers hardened to resist up to 30 pounds per square inch of overpressure over a potential deployment area of 15,000 square miles. The U.S. small ICBM program is exploring Midgetman concepts along these lines with options to develop even larger deployment areas.

cruise missile programs. Therefore the United States will clearly not agree to the Soviet proposal to ban all long-range cruise missiles, thus precluding ALCMs with their improved penetration capabilities, nor to prohibit all "new" systems, thus precluding deployment of the Advanced Technology Bomber.

The November 1985 U.S. proposal, like its predecessors in START, included no provisions regarding sea-launched cruise missiles (SLCMs). Technology creep, the attractiveness of a highly accurate naval standoff weapon, and the quest for arms control bargaining leverage led successive American administrations to develop and begin testing SLCMs. Administrations did so despite a general understanding of the extremely difficult, if not insurmountable, difficulties for verification posed by a torpedo-sided weapon that can be deployed on a host of naval platforms in nuclear- and conventionally armed variants that are for all practical purposes indistinguishable. U.S. military planners and arms controllers failed to come to grips with this dilemma in good time, and now that deployments have begun on the U.S. side and are imminent on the Soviet side, there appears to be little prospect for limits on long-range SLCMs in any new offensive arms agreement. Ironically, the heavier concentration of high-value targets along U.S. coasts and the fact that U.S. deployment plans emphasize conventionally armed rather than nuclear-armed variants mean that unconstrained SLCM deployment may in the long run provide the Soviet Union with a net advantage in nuclear strike capabilities.

Although the Soviet October proposal included U.S. INF systems within its definition of "strategic," subsequent U.S.-Soviet exchanges raised the prospect of splitting off the INF missile from the central strategic and space arms issues. Splitting off INF could mean either a deliberate finesse with no explicit agreement, or the conclusion of a separate or "interim" agreement as envisaged by both Soviet and American proposals in early 1986. Such an agreement might simply cap the U.S. Pershing II and GLCM deployments at some point well below the NATO-planned objective of 572 missiles in return for reductions in Soviet INF missiles targetted on Europe and Asia. Or a more ambitious "zero option" agreement for Europe might be sought. In either case, the Soviets will continue to seek assurances that the British and French will not implement current plans to expand their INF capabilities greatly by deploying new multiple warhead missiles. Neither the British nor the French are likely to agree to such restraints. In addition, the United States will probably continue to demand a substantial cut in the Soviet SS-20s deployed in Asia, possibly down to zero as Washington proposed in mid-February, and the right to maintain "in reserve" in the United States a number of missiles equal to those retained by the USSR in Asia.

Whatever progress may be achieved in concluding a separate INF agreement, or in finding acceptable compromises on deep cuts in central strategic systems, no new treaty reducing central strategic systems is likely to be signed unless the two sides can also find a way to address what has become the overarching Soviet concern: the future of the American SDI program. Once President Reagan advanced strategic defense from a remote technical possibility to an active, high-profile technology program, with a conditional commitment to deploy a full-scale ballistic missile defense system if it proved feasible, strategic defense once again, as in the early 1970s, inescapably became a pivotal issue in strategic arms negotiations. This link between offense and defense in arms control was formalized in the January 8, 1985, U.S.-Soviet agreement that led to the current Geneva negotiations, and it was reaffirmed in the joint statement issued after the Reagan-Gorbachev summit in November. But the formula in those documents provides merely that nuclear and space arms questions are to be "considered and resolved in their interrelationship," leaving it up to the parties to work out the nature of the interrelationship during the negotiations.[6] The course of the U.S.-Soviet search for new agreements is almost certain to be dominated by an effort to find a mutually acceptable approach to defining that relationship.

"Squeeze" or "Deal" Strategies

The offense-defense link in arms control has become key to a debate in Washington between advocates of two alternative strategies not only for arms control but for dealing generally with the Soviet Union. Both strategies proceed from the common premise that a shift in favor of the United States is occurring in what the Soviets call the global correlation of forces. Different policy conclusions are drawn from this assessment, however.

One group supports a strategy of "squeezing" the Soviets, seeking to maximize competitive pressures on the Soviet Union. This strategy would attempt to press favorable trends still further in the hope of securing an even more substantial shift in the correlation of forces, eventually compelling Soviet retreats all over the globe or, if the Soviets exhausted themselves economically in an effort to avoid retreat, inducing an internal crisis in the USSR that would weaken the Soviet Union still further or even result in system transformation with revolutionary, long-term benefits for the West.

With regard to arms control, the squeeze approach would call for the United States to take an essentially uncompromising position on the whole range of issues at Geneva, making at most only marginal, essentially cosmetic adjustments designed not to enhance the negotiability of U.S. positions but rather to help manage domestic and alliance political concerns. Protecting the SDI from arms control constraints is the central concern of partisans of the squeeze position. Either they believe in SDI's great strategic potential for the United States, or they believe that withholding SDI from the negotiations is likely to preclude a compromise arms control agreement that would at best

[6]*New York Times*, January 9, 1985.

produce marginal benefits while squandering hard-won U.S. gains and momentum. SDI in this view should be used as leverage on Soviet force structure, not indirectly through enhanced arms control bargaining strength but directly, by compelling the Soviets to restructure their forces to compete in areas of comparative U.S. advantage.

A second group supports an alternative strategy of "dealing." It holds that the United States should take some initiatives in exploring ways to break the arms control deadlock. Partisans of this view generally believe that a sustained state of high tension between the United States and the Soviet Union is potentially dangerous and surely corrosive to the Western alliance if the United States is believed to be at fault. A credible attempt at arms control negotiations is held necessary to sustain public and congressional support for the administration's large-scale armaments program.

Advocates of this view tend also to believe (like those who favor squeezing) that the correlation of forces is indeed shifting against the Soviet Union. They prefer, however, to negotiate from that improved position now rather than gamble on the outcome of a totally unregulated arms competition of enormous and possibly unsustainable cost, incalculable risk, and indefinite duration. Soviet anxiety about an intensified new round of strategic arms competition is held to provide an opportunity for inducing the USSR to consider basic tradeoffs in strategic weapons negotiations—tradeoffs that would involve cuts in Soviet offensive forces of greatest U.S. concern in return for an easing of U.S. competitive pressures in areas of greatest concern to the Soviets.

It is important to note that there are, as yet, no indications that adherents of this viewpoint or others in the Reagan administration are prepared to constrain substantially, much less to forgo altogether, long-term options for space-based missile defense. Some may, however, be favorably inclined toward supporting a long-term exploratory technology program in this area while agreeing to restrict field testing for some years and to eschew so-called intermediate deployments of space-based missile defense systems. Conceivably, in this view, the imposition of long-term constraints on potential ballistic missile defense might in time become an acceptable option for the United States, in return for very substantial reductions in the intercontinental attack capabilities of both sides.

The leaders in the Kremlin will also have to confront serious choices as they consider their strategic arms control options. As noted earlier, they must first decide what value they place on the pursuit of strategic arms control given the prospect that revitalized arms control talks are unlikely to be accompanied by a return to 1970s-style Soviet-American detente. Moreover, the Soviets are undoubtedly aware that simply by continuing the negotiations they may well increase the chances that the U.S. administration will succeed, at least in the short term, in gaining congressional support for major weapons programs that could serve as actual or potential bargaining chips in the negotiations. And they can have no assurance that the Reagan administration will, in the last analysis, be prepared to depart substantially from demands—including a free hand on the SDI—that have been wholly unacceptable to Moscow in the past.

In addition, the Soviet leaders are likely to feel that their bargaining position is considerably weaker than it has been over the past decade. Although the actual military balance is, if anything, marginally better for the Soviet Union than it was in 1979, when SALT II was signed, Moscow has reason to view prospective trends in that balance as distinctly unfavorable. The next series of moves in the strategic arms competition will be marked by unprecedented emphasis on high technology, thus pitting U.S. strength against relative Soviet weakness. The new Soviet leadership can hardly relish tacking such a massive, costly, long-term effort onto the other serious domestic and foreign policy challenges it faces.

The Soviet leaders thus have a choice. They can make a maximum effort to retain marginal strategic offensive advantages that the United States is no longer willing to concede while at the same time risking an even more costly new competition in areas of American technological advantage. Alternatively, they can trade these hard-won Soviet strategic advantages for U.S. agreement to ease the pressure of a potential U.S. technology surge, thus heading off a new, unpromising phase in the competition. The second course of action would require the Soviets for the foreseeable future to abandon whatever ambitions they may have harbored for central strategic nuclear superiority, or at least for a militarily significant margin of advantage.

For the U.S.-Soviet arms control negotiations initiated in Geneva in 1985 to culminate in a new, meaningful agreement will require that both sides adopt, or at least be willing to explore the interest of the other in mutual adoption of a dealing strategy appropriate for the rather different circumstances of the two countries in the mid-1980s. As the exchanges during the November 1985 summit indicated, neither side will permit the other to have things all its own way. Both are determined to achieve some satisfaction on their primary concerns: the United States regarding deep cuts in strategic offensive capabilities, including a substantial reduction in Soviet ICBM throwweight; the Soviet Union regarding the looming threat to its strategic position posed by the SDI program.

SDI: Threat or Boon to Arms Control?

A solution to break the stalemate will require both sides to back off from their present maximalist and totally contradictory positions. Since 1983 the Soviets have persistently demanded a ban on all activities, including "scientific research," that are part of a military R&D program dedicated to space-based strategic ballistic missile defense. This criterion would ban virtually all U.S. strategic defense activities that have been organized under the SDI program, most of which in fact predated that program and to which the Soviets had previously raised no objection. At the same time the Soviet position would sanction all ongoing Soviet research, including research with potential SDI-like applications, because there is no public record documenting any Soviet intent to explore, test, or deploy defensive systems that would violate the ABM Treaty.

As there are fundamental differences between the way that the United States conducts its military R&D and weapons development processes within the constraints of the American constitutional system and the politically unconstrained way the USSR conducts these activities, the criterion of unverifiable "intentionality" implies a double standard that would penalize the United States for its open political process and reward the Soviet Union for its closed system. On these grounds alone the Soviet position is totally unacceptable to the United States. If the Soviet leaders seriously wish to negotiate constraints on ballistic missile defense activities not covered to their satisfaction by agreed interpretations of the ABM Treaty, they must propose a line to be drawn between permitted research and forbidden activities, a line that can be verified according to objective criteria applicable equally to both sides.

The United States, on the other hand, takes the position that any limitations on SDI research beyond those already included in the ABM Treaty would be both premature and unnecessary. In this view the promise of effective ballistic missile defense, no matter how distant or remote, is potentially so important that the long-term option for developing and deploying such defenses must be protected from any limitation. It is apparent, however, that important differences have arisen since 1983 between American and Soviet interpretations of precisely how the ABM Treaty applies to space-based technologies. And during 1985 even the U.S. view of these matters became unclear. Senior officials announced that according to a new official U.S. reinterpretation of the ABM Treaty, the treaty is now regarded as permitting all research, development, and testing activities short of actual deployment of ABM systems based on "other physical principles."[7] (One official stated that even deployment was permitted.) Although the Reagan administration subsequently announced that for the time being the United States would abide by a "strict" interpretation of the treaty which would ban testing of ABM system components, the interpretive waters have now become so muddied that mere reaffirmation of the ABM Treaty without clarification would not help much to resolve U.S.-Soviet differences.

A way out would require each side to address the paramount concerns of the other with respect to the linkage between strategic offense and defense.

[7]The phrase "based on other physical principles" appears in Agreed Statement D of the 1972 ABM Treaty and is meant to distinguish between ABM systems of a kind then existing and those that might be created in the future "based on other physical principles" and including components capable of substituting for ABM interceptor missiles, ABM launchers, or ABM radars.

The crucial importance for arms control of nationwide strategic defense, now that it has been dramatically introduced as a serious potential option, does not derive from any particular expectation about its effectiveness. A major strategic defense program featuring large-scale field testing of key components within the next several years would provoke a variety of responses by the other side because of the enormous strategic consequences of even a moderately effective ballistic missile defense, one that fell far short of being "leakproof," and the irreducible uncertainties about the effectiveness that could actually be achieved. Countermeasures would almost certainly include the development of means to disable key components of the adversary's defense system; measures to overwhelm or evade the defense such as the proliferation of missile warheads and decoys; the design of hardened and rapid-burn ballistic missiles; the expansion of bomber and cruise missile attack capabilities; and, of course, a major push by the "responding" side to develop and deploy a defensive system of its own.

Some American proponents of the SDI have expressed interest in a jointly managed, long-term transition to a "mutually assured survival" relationship between the superpowers. Such a relationship would involve a combination of extensive, extremely effective missile and air defenses and substantially reduced strategic attack forces on both sides, apparently the only arrangement that would permit the strategic defenses to reach significant levels of effectiveness. Yet given the vast uncertainties associated with what will necessarily be extraordinarily difficult and long-term efforts to develop such impressive defenses, if they can be developed at all, it is clearly premature to speak of "agreeing" to such a transition in the near or even mid-term future. By the same token, as others have pointed out, were the superpowers able to negotiate such a stringent and fine-tuned cooperative transition, they would also be able to conclude an agreement constraining strategic attack forces that was so far-reaching as to render strategic defenses almost superfluous. Whatever these long-term possibilities, the Soviets continue to insist on agreements now that would permanently preclude the development and deployment of space-based defensive systems, as the condition for a new agreement on offensive arms.

The Soviet side, however, has not sufficiently appreciated the extent to which the high-priority U.S. search for a long-term strategic defense option has been fueled by widespread disappointment and disillusionment with the results of arms control agreements thus far (and of Soviet strategic behavior under arms control constraints). In particular, the arms control process has failed to arrest, much less to reverse, the steady erosion of U.S. offensive force survivability on which, in the American view, the stability of the strategic deterrent depends.[8] U.S. incentives to develop and deploy extensive strategic

---

[8]Related to this also is disappointment with the failure of the United States to find an appropriate unilateral "fix" for its offensive force vulnerability problem through mobile, deceptive, or "dense pack" basing modes. That failure reflects societal and political limitations on strategic activities in the United States which do not obtain in the USSR.

defenses are therefore strongly affected by assessments made in this country of prospects for stabilizing the strategic balance and reducing the risk of nuclear war in the absence of defensive development.

On the other hand, the American side has tended to underestimate the concern of Soviet leaders about the risks of agreeing to deep reductions in their offensive forces precisely at a time when the United States is in the midst of a costly program to develop extensive defensive systems whose effectiveness would in large measure depend on the size and character of opposing Soviet offensive forces. The U.S. side has acknowledged Soviet concerns that a combination of deep offensive arms reductions, increasingly capable residual U.S. strategic attack systems, and a substantial U.S. advantage in strategic defense might present first-strike threats to the Soviet Union. But the anxieties of the Soviet side have not been appeased by presidential offers to share defensive technologies with the Soviet Union if U.S. programs should outstrip comparable Soviet ones, or to offer discussions (without granting Moscow "veto power") prior to deploying a system based on such technologies.

Accordingly, the Soviet demand for a flat ban on all U.S. research related to space-based strategic ballistic missile defense, a demand that would for all time foreclose the defensive option, is politically impossible, technically unverifiable, and strategically premature at the least. But the Soviet need for assurance against a U.S. strategic defensive breakout during the lifetime of any new, far-reaching, offensive arms reduction treaty is understandable. The United States itself has relied for more than a decade on ABM Treaty limitations and prohibitions to provide it with assurances against the threat of Soviet breakout, because of the USSR's continuing research on a rapidly deployable ABM system featuring conventional land-based ABM components, its construction of a series of large, phased-array tracking radars, and the upgrading of the permitted ABM system around Moscow.

The objective of an agreement providing the USSR with such assurances would be to secure Moscow's assent to an offensive arms control treaty that provided for radical reductions in ballistic missile warheads over the next several years while permitting both parties to continue to explore the feasibility of extensive ballistic missile defenses within agreed limits. Such an agreement would thus preserve the long-term option of transition to a more balanced offense/defense strategic mix. At the same time, it would ensure that neither side could so rapidly break out of defensive development constraints during the lifetime or soon after the expiration of the offensive treaty as to deprive the other side of the lead time required for countermeasures to protect its vital strategic interests.

Such an approach would require that both the Soviet Union and the United States move away from their long-standing maximalist positions of "no SDI research" and "no SDI constraints," respectively. The assurances against strategic defense breakout envisaged here could take a variety of forms. Possible approaches to an agreement that would be designed to draw a line between permitted research and forbidden activities pertaining to ballistic missile defense during the lifetime of a new offensive treaty might include:

1. a reaffirmation of the ABM Treaty, with clarifications to resolve ambiguities inherent in the treaty and exacerbated by the emergence of competing interpretations. (These clarifications might be negotiated in the Standing Consultative Commission without requiring that the entire treaty be reopened.)

2. a ban on the field testing (a) of weapons based in space against any physical objects in ballistic trajectories, in orbit, or on the earth's surface; and (b) of any weapons designed on "other physical principles," no matter where they are based, against physical objects in ballistic trajectories or in orbit;

3. an amendment of Article XV of the ABM Treaty extending the period of required notification of a decision to withdraw from six months to a period of several years.

The precise details, including the duration of limitations and prohibitions, would, of course, require a great deal of negotiation. They would clearly involve tradeoffs between the severity and duration of defensive limitations, on the one hand, and of offensive reductions and constraints, on the other.

Such an agreement might possibly slow down the pace of the SDI, depending on precisely where the line was finally drawn between permitted research and forbidden testing and for how long. Some SDI partisans have expressed concern that without periodic flight tests to provide dramatic demonstrations of progress in the development of new kill capabilities, political and funding support for the SDI would soon erode, threatening the entire program. But domestic support and allied tolerance of the SDI would amost certainly be jeopardized if the administration's refusal to constrain the program in any way were perceived as blocking conclusion of an otherwise available and highly desirable agreement to reduce intercontinental and intermediate-range nuclear arms. Indeed, in the context of a new treaty reducing nuclear offensive arms, continued U.S. conduct of a vigorous SDI research program within agreed constraints would provide the Soviet side with strong additional incentives to comply more punctiliously than it has in the past with treaty provisions.

By facilitating a radical reduction in the offensive nuclear forces of both sides, moreover, acceptance of constraints on space-based defensive development for the duration of an offensive agreement would make the environment for any future transition to defenses much more favorable than it would otherwise be. And if it ultimately turned out that space-based ballistic missile defense was not technically feasible or cost-effective, neither side would have missed an opportunity to strengthen the stability of the offensive balance at lower levels of nuclear weapons while finding this out.

IV

The Next Phase: Alternative Frameworks

for Managing U.S.–Soviet Relations

10

An Alternative Policy for Managing U.S.–Soviet Relations

MARSHALL D. SHULMAN

It is one of the mischances of history that the two superpowers are currently so out of phase with each other. The Soviet Union, under new and more vigorous leadership, is in a period of change, uncertain whether its priority efforts to modernize its economy can be facilitated by a moderated relationship with the United States or will be hampered by an intensified military competition. The United States, at mid-point in a conservative swing in its domestic politics and a nationalist phase in its foreign policy, is divided and uncertain on how to use its relative strength to coherent purposes.

There are always choices before the two countries, but the current state of affairs is unusually fluid, ambiguous, and unstable. The choices waiting to be made in Moscow and Washington in the period immediately ahead may be fateful for a long time to come, perhaps in some irreversible ways. It is useful to remind ourselves that relations between the two countries are not simply relations between two entities, as is often described in diplomatic histories, but involve an interaction between the complex political forces within each of them. It is in this interacting process that the choices will be determined.

For the United States, it is a good time to go back to fundamentals. Are U.S. interests better served by maximum pressure on the Soviet Union or by an effort to manage the competitive relationship at more moderate levels of tension and of military competition? These are questions unresolved in our government and in American public opinion. Matters are further confused by the fact that our public positions are not reflected in our actions.

Public policy on any subject is seldom a product of rigorous analysis, and this may be more true of policy toward the Soviet Union than of any other. The subject is shot through with emotions, areas of dark uncertainty, fears, prejudices, and primitive stereotypes, and most important of all it involves ultimate and complex questions of security and survival. As a consequence, our policy thinking has tended to rest upon widely accepted assumptions about

the Soviet Union which are in fact questionable and upon prevailing judgments about how to change Soviet behavior which may be 180 degrees off.
The combined effects of these assumptions and these judgments are pushing
the relationship in directions contrary to our own best interests.

What particularly requires our attention is the conjuncture of two elements
of the problem which are unusually fluid just now. One is the current situation in Moscow. The other is the changing state of military technology. The
clarity with which we understand and react to these two elements will determine whether they lead to singular opportunities or to heightened insecurity.

This chapter starts with a characterization of the present state of the U.S.-
Soviet relationship. It proceeds through an analysis of the main elements currently affecting each side of that relationship, to a discussion of what the objectives of our policy should be. It concludes with some main guidelines
better suited than current policy to these objectives and our own interests.

The Present State of U.S.-Soviet Relations

A starting point for thinking about the present relationship between the
Soviet Union and the United States is the deterioration that set in almost
immediately after the high point of the so-called detente in 1972. It is often
said that it was the Soviet invasion of Afghanistan in 1979 which destroyed
detente, but in fact relations had reached a low plateau even before that event.
Efforts at arms control had failed; the military competition had intensified;
trade, cultural, and diplomatic contacts had been reduced; cooperative programs had virtually ceased; and tensions had begun to mount. American attitudes toward the Soviet Union hardened in response to Soviet actions in the
Third World, Soviet military programs, and Soviet actions against human
rights, and these responses were intensified by a conservative and nationalist
tide in American politics.

In the course of 1984 a partial and ambiguous change modified the harsher
aspects of confrontation between the two countries, as each sought to deflect
away from itself responsibility before world public opinion for the dangers of
the confrontation. Diplomatic contacts were reopened, prompted on the Soviet side by concerns over the prospect of heightened competition in space
weapons and by the desire to probe the change toward a more conciliatory
tone in U.S. statements.

These probes did not lead the Soviet Union to encouraging conclusions
about the prospects for negotiations with the United States. But with the
succession of Mikhail Gorbachev as general secretary in March 1985 came the
long-heralded generational change in the Soviet leadership and a reinvigora-
tion of Soviet policies, both foreign and domestic. After long debate the new
Soviet leadership chose to accept the American proposal for a summit meeting, still skeptical but prepared to probe once again the possibilities for an

improvement in relations which it saw as the condition most favorable for carrying forward its domestic economic program.

The summit, held in November 1985, failed to make any progress on what the Soviet Union regarded as its central issue, strategic defenses and the competition in nuclear weapons. Despite this failure, Gorbachev made the tactical decision to emphasize the positive value of the civil dialogue that had been established and to express optimism about the beginning of a process that could be continued in subsequent meetings while treating the unreconciled differences on arms control frankly but in measured tones.

The result has been that the relationship, as of this writing, is in a state of unstable ambiguity. Notwithstanding the improvement in the tone of communications between the two leaders and progress on some secondary issues, the relationship appears poised, awaiting decisions on each side of the military issues. If the arms control impasse continues and the military competition continues to intensify, both qualitatively and quantitatively, it is doubtful that the other aspects of the relationship can be insulated from the mounting tension. The consequences will be serious for a long time to come. The projected increase in new weapons systems, less stable and less verifiable than those presently deployed, will increase apprehensions and insecurity on both sides and will make any arms control regime even more difficult in the future. The mobilization of effort and resources required by the Soviet system to keep pace with these developments will strengthen both intractability in Soviet policy and repressive practices within the Soviet Union. The risk of miscalculation and escalation in the event of unpredictable local conflicts will also be increased. Reciprocal effects of these developments can be anticipated within the United States, and strains within the Atlantic alliance will be intensified.

Whether the relationship will evolve in this direction, or whether the opportunity will be taken to direct events in a less dangerous direction, will depend upon choices now waiting to be made in Moscow and Washington. If the past is a guide, these choices may depend less upon rational calculations than upon clashes of interests and outlooks—parochial and broad, ideological and pragmatic, traditional and modern—and will be heavily influenced by perceptions of the intentions of the other side. There are too many uncertain variables to predict the outcome, but it is possible and useful to outline the conditions within each country which may affect its range of possible responses.

Factors Affecting Soviet Responses

The "objective situation" (to use a familiar Soviet phrase) presents strong incentives for the Soviet leadership to seek easement of further drains from its civilian economy into the military sector, if such easement can be found on acceptable terms. For fear of appearing weak and encouraging its adversary to seek advantages, the Soviet Union is reluctant to acknowledge these considerations, but the signs have been evident in recent Soviet behavior. Not only in the overtures of 1984 and the presummit proposals of 1985 but even earlier, during the negotiations on SALT II, the Soviet Union was prepared to make many more substantial concessions than was the United States to bring the negotiations to a successful conclusion. Several factors have created this "objective situation."

1. The long-term decline in the growth rate of the Soviet economy is the most pressing problem facing the Soviet leadership. This decline has been reflected in continued low productivity in agriculture and industry, a lag in the advanced technological sector, a decline in capital investments, a decline in the growth of the labor force, a decline in raw materials and energy resources in the European part of the Soviet Union, low labor morale, and widespread drunkenness, corruption, bribery, and theft. These are the problems to which Gorbachev has directed his immediate efforts, while foreshadowing more far-reaching structural reforms and ambitious economic goals to follow after the Twenty-seventh Congress of the Communist Party of the Soviet Union in February–March 1986.

The problem is made more acute by the continuing revolution in industrial and military technology. The current world transformation in industrial technology, involving the application of computers and electronics to the processing of information and to production, raises serious problems for many countries but most forcibly for the Soviet Union. The indexes of power are changing among nations according to the varying capacity of domestic institutions to adapt to the requirements of this advanced technology, and in this new phase of industrial competition the relative disadvantages of the Soviet economy are an increasing liability. The rigidities, the overcentralization, the built-in disincentives for innovation and initiative, the burdensome bureaucratization—all mean that in the absence of a radical transformation in the administration of the Soviet economy, the USSR's relative position as an industrial power will continue to decline.

Not only did the period of detente, which was intended to import advanced technology into the Soviet Union to ease these problems, fail to do so in sufficient measure, but the increased tempo of the military competition threatens to deepen them. The problem is more than a matter of the continued or increased diversion of resources from the industrial sector to the military sector. The emergence of an increasingly complex military technology inescapably links the future of a nation's power to the strength of its industrial technological base. Given the lag in Soviet industrial technology, doubts about the ability of the Soviet Union to compete with the United States in new and still more advanced military technology, without great internal costs or fundamental changes in the administration of its economy, reflect a painful dilemma for the system.

2. A related set of considerations may be found within the military sector itself. By diverting an estimated 12 to 14 percent of its gross national product to the military sector after about 1963, the Soviet Union succeeded in achieving strategic parity with the United States by the end of that decade. Although this achievement was reflected in a new note of confidence in Soviet military writings—that the Soviet Union had the capability to retaliate against a possible attack—Soviet military programs did not stop there. Whether because of the traditional Soviet habit of overinsurance, the strong influence of the military bureaucracy, the perception of U.S. advantages in the asymmetrical strategic balance, or the fear of U.S. technological superiority, the Soviet Union continued to develop and deploy new weapons systems. It found itself faced with a further modernization of U.S. forces which it had helped to stimulate.

The result is that the Soviet Union now faces the specter of an adverse trend in the correlation of forces, which means a still higher diversion of resources into the military sector at the expense of the consumer sector and the upgrading of its industrial technology. It also faces the requirement of restructuring its forces to reduce their vulnerability to new U.S. capabilities and the possibility of an enormous future drain: competing with the proposed U.S. space weapons program by countermeasures will require a further expansion of offensive weapons and research and development of its own space defense capabilities. Like the United States, the Soviet Union is preparing new generations of ballistic missiles, cruise missiles, bombers, and submarines. It faces the prospect that the astronomical costs will be able to yield no advantage other than avoiding the appearance of falling behind in the competition and becoming vulnerable to pressure or to the threat of attack.

3. These economic and military factors have been the central considerations addressed by Gorbachev's priority efforts to apply modern technology to Soviet industry. Consolidating his position more quickly than anyone could have foreseen, Gorbachev has moved swiftly to make personnel changes that have not only strengthened his political position but also brought to positions of political and economic responsibility officials who are younger, more vigorous, and more competent. By his personal style and the vigor of his reversal of the immobilism that had characterized the Soviet leadership during the previous decade, he has changed the tone of Soviet political life from its previous pessimism to one of buoyant expectation. Whether his leadership will succeed in overcoming the inertia and bureaucratism of the Soviet system, as well as the resistance of an essentially conservative society, cannot be foretold, but he has the benefit of support for his strong leadership from a population that has grown restive in recent years. It is at least possible that he may inaugurate a new stage in the Soviet Union's historical development and that his leadership may result in far-reaching changes, both intended and unforeseen, in the Soviet system and in Soviet society.

But formidable problems remain to be overcome. Demographic changes are resulting in labor shortages and in a shift from the preponderance of the Russian population over other nationalities, particularly the Central Asians. There is occasional evidence of restiveness among the minority nationalities, intensified in some areas by economic shortages, in others by religious repression. But although dissatisfaction is widespread, there are no indications of revolutionary sentiment, even among those who dare to express opposition to the regime. On balance, it would appear to be a prudent assumption that these problems are not likely to confront the Soviet system with a dramatic crisis in the near future.

4. In all directions, Soviet foreign policy faces problems, some of them serious, and few promising prospects. In addition to its central problem of costly and dangerous relations with the United States, the Soviet Union faces its most serious challenge in Eastern Europe. The solution of the Polish problem is not in sight. The German Democratic Republic is unexpectedly restive, with Hungary and Bulgaria showing a cautious readiness to follow its wayward lead. The increased economic drain of the bloc compounds Soviet economic problems. Questions lie ahead for the Soviet leadership concerning the balance between flexibility and tight control it will bring to bear to maintain the integrity of the bloc.

The Soviet Union has made persistent efforts to improve its relations with China, with positive results in the economic sphere and in the tone of the relationship, although it has not been able to meet Chinese conditions regarding Afghanistan, Kampuchea, or the withdrawal of Soviet forces from the Chinese border. Nor has it been able to prevent growing economic and military contacts between China and the West. Soviet military deployments reflect a growing concern about the security of the Pacific region, but Soviet diplomacy has been so heavy-handed in relations with Japan that it has not yet been able to deflect Japan from its relations with China nor from its security alliance with the United States.

In Europe, the Soviet Union has not been able to turn strains in the Atlantic alliance to its advantage, and its efforts to wean the Federal Republic of Germany from its Atlantic orientation have been impaired by a harsh revival of the "revanchist" line of attack. Despite its failure to mobilize West European antiwar sentiment to block the deployment of American intermediate-range missiles in Europe, the Soviet Union has not given up hope of fanning renewed concern in Europe, stimulated by the space defense issue. Its capability to influence these developments is, however, limited by a lack of support for its policies in Europe.

Soviet influence has further diminished in the Middle East and in Southern Africa. The only notable recent advance has been the willingness of Colonel Mengistu to establish a Communist party in Ethiopia.

Soviet foreign policy, in comparison with its relative activism in the 1970s, has been relatively quiescent thus far in the 1980s. This quiescence may be attributable in part to the preoccupation of the regime with its domestic problems and in part to the absence of opportunities to exploit at low cost and low risk. Given the unpredictability of the manifold sources of conflict within and between the developing nations, it is not possible to foretell whether crises may arise which will involve the great powers in conflicting interests, nor how the Soviet Union will react to such local conflicts. The Soviet Union has not acknowledged any awareness that its activism in the Third World during the 1970s contributed to the deterioration of its detente relationship with the United States, but that lesson would be hard to escape. Whether such awareness would be a factor of restraint in relation to local conflicts in the Third World might depend upon whether the Soviet Union nourished hope of improved relations with the United States or felt driven by the need to demonstrate that it was not weak or intimidated.

In the light of the foregoing factors, whose weight is adverse to Soviet prospects for an active prosecution of its competitive relations with the United States, is it possible to conjecture what choices the Soviet leadership may make in the period immediately ahead? Such conjectures are obviously central to U.S. calculations.

At the immediate, tactical level the Soviet leadership must decide whether and for how long to continue its postsummit posture of modulated optimism about the prospects for productive negotiations with the United States. This posture gambles that the logic of the American situation, including particularly the pressures of its deficit, may lead it to negotiate toward a moderation of the military competition; further, it gambles that common ground may yet be found to break the impasse on space defense weapons, thus opening the way to reductions in offensive weapons. Clearly this would be the most desirable outcome from the Soviet point of view, but to persist with this expectant posture has its costs. It gives the United States the advantage of propitiating domestic and West European public opinion, forestalling concerns about the danger of nuclear war which would otherwise attend increasing military programs.

At a more fundamental level it is likely that debates will continue in the Soviet Union about the political strategy laid down by Brezhnev at the Twenty-fourth Party Congress in 1971: Is it still valid, or has it been proved bankrupt? That political strategy rested upon the arguments that arms control negotiations with the United States were possible and in the Soviet interest; that relations of reduced tension would have economic benefits for the Soviet Union, which the Soviet economy required; and that the political competition could go forward side by side with businesslike relations with the United States.

If, however, the skeptics are proved right, the Soviet Union is prepared to turn toward a foreign policy less U.S.-centered than it has been following and to accept a higher level of military competition and of tension with the United States for as long as may be necessary. The available options are inescapably framed by the perceptions in Moscow of U.S. intentions and capabilities. To this extent, therefore, the debates may center around such questions as whether the United States is seen as unalterably committed to an effort to undermine the Soviet system and to acquire a position of clear military superiority or whether, if this be the present policy of the United States, it will prove transitory in the changing tides of American politics.

Is American policy, in sum, seen as leaving room for acceptable choices or only for capitulation? If the latter, the only possible answer can be defiance. This brings us to a discussion of the American side of the equation.

Factors Affecting U.S. Responses

The dominant political mood in the United States supports a strong policy of adversarial pressure against the Soviet Union. Although the United States is presently in a position of relative advantage in this competitive relationship, there is a danger that the current mood may lead the United States to press its advantages in ways that will be counterproductive from the point of view of our own long-term interests. Following are some of the main factors bearing upon present U.S. policy toward the Soviet Union.

1. From the mid-1970s a hardening of popular attitudes toward the Soviet Union resulted from Soviet actions in Angola, Ethiopia, and Afghanistan, as well as from Soviet actions against human rights and the continuing Soviet military buildup. These feelings were intensified by a backlash from the unrealistic expectations aroused by the so-called detente period, which was understood differently in the two countries. They were also intensified by a widespread sense of impotence stemming from this country's experience in Vietnam and with the hostages in Iran, and by the passing of the period of American military superiority.

2. Domestic political trends in the United States heightened these reactions. From the mid-1970s the United States experienced a conservative political tide and a resurgence of nationalism, expressed as a heightened patriotism. The external ideological focus of this mood is expressed as anticommunism as the main organizing principle for foreign policy; it reacts against what it characterizes as the weakness of the "liberal illusions" of the previous period by supporting policies of greater activism and military strength against a perceived heightened threat from the Soviet Union.

3. Taken together, these sentiments created powerful political support for a strong anti-Soviet posture, and they discredited policies directed toward arms control, reduced tension, and measures of cooperation with the Soviet Union. In what became the ascendant view, the Soviet Union was seen as having acquired military superiority; the arms control process was seen as disadvantageous to the United States; upheavals in the Third World were seen primarily as the results of Soviet intervention; and more fundamentally, the

Soviet system was seen as inherently and intractably committed to world conquest. It followed logically from this point of view that the main objective of U.S. policy should be to bring unremitting pressure to bear in order to compel fundamental changes in the Soviet system, a contraction of Soviet power from Eastern Europe, Cuba, and elsewhere, and a Soviet capitulation in the military competition.

4. The policies that flowed from this ascendant view of American objectives included:

forcing the pace of the military competition in order to overcome a perceived American inferiority, relying on the U.S. advantage in advanced technology, and drawing upon the traditional view of security through superiority rather than through negotiated limitations on weapons;

reducing economic relations with the Soviet Union, not only in advanced technology to staunch the "technology drain" but as much as possible (given political constraints) to maximize pressure on the Soviet system and to reduce its capabilities to shift resources to the defense sector;

applying political, ideological, and propaganda pressure against Soviet vulnerabilities in Eastern Europe, among minority nationalities, on the human rights issue, and so forth; and

stressing East-West aspects of local conflicts, and providing military assistance to governments and political forces identified as anticommunist.

Despite the change of tone in public statements since 1984, and particularly since the summit of 1985, these policies have continued to constitute the hidden agenda of influential elements within the government. Some confusion does, however, result from the presence within the administration, as was the case during the previous administration, of contending elements who would, in greater or lesser degree, modify these objectives and this policy agenda.

The assumptions on which the dominant policy rests are not clearly articulated, nor have they been subjected to examination or debate, but their widespread uncritical acceptance is congenial to the present mood in American politics and is a source of popular support. Some of these assumptions, however, are at best questionable, and the policies derived from them may have consequences quite different from what is anticipated. Among these assumptions, four are noteworthy.

It is widely assumed that Soviet expansionist behavior is so rooted in the nature of the Soviet system that such behavior can be modified only by bringing about fundamental changes in the Soviet system. The argument for this assumption rests upon the assertions that the revolutionary ideology remains in full force as a driving determinant of Soviet foreign policy; that the Soviet system needs to expand in order to hold its leadership in power, to claim legitimacy, or to validate its view of history in ideological terms; and that the messianic tradition in pre-Revolutionary Russian history and its continental expansion reinforce the ultimate aspirations of Marxism-Leninism. These assertions ignore the considerable modifications in Soviet foreign policy behavior since 1917, the attenuation of the revolutionary ideology in practice if not in rhetoric, and the pragmatic nation-state responses to the external environment which have been dominant in Soviet foreign policy for many years. In fact, containment has worked where it has been applied, and in fact, Soviet expansionist tendencies have been modified in practice where firmness, a balance of military power, and effective foreign policies have foreclosed opportunities for effective Soviet exploitation. The practical effect of a policy that seeks to compel fundamental changes in the Soviet system is to create in the minds of the Soviet leadership the apprehension that if the driving purpose of American policy is to undermine the Soviet system, there can be no alternative to a relationship of total conflict.

A second and related assumption is that the problems of the Soviet regime are of such a magnitude that external pressure could precipitate a collapse or compel the leadership to accept fundamental changes that would weaken its power. This assumption rests upon the arguments that there exists a revolutionary potential within the Soviet population; that external pressure could cause so serious a deterioration in living conditions as to activate that revolutionary potential; and that the response of the Soviet leaders would be to accept fundamental changes in the system in the direction of democratization at the expense of their own power rather than to resort to further mobilization and still greater repressiveness in the face of external hostility. It is difficult to see evidence for any step in this chain of assumptions and arguments. It is also difficult to see how this effort, if indeed it were possible to mount and coordinate such a campaign not only by the United States but by other industrial societies of the West (as would be required), would do anything other than drive the Soviet Union precisely in the wrong direction, toward a still greater authoritarianism. The assumption is wrong. Not only does it exaggerate the crisis proportions of problems facing the Soviet regime and lead to consequences contrary to its professed aim, but it ignores the more plausible probability that whatever prospect there may be for changes in the Soviet system in the direction of decentralization, less repressiveness and a more significant degree of popular political participation are more likely to come from forces for change within the system, under conditions of a nonthreatening environment.

Another assumption implicit in present U.S. policy is that the most effective way to influence Soviet behavior in the directions we desire is the unremitting application of pressure. As commonly stated, the argument runs that the Soviets understand only the language of force, that the Soviet leaders, being realists, will have to recognize the disadvantages of their situation and will capitulate or make concessions under pressure. It is no doubt true that, up to a point, the pressure that grows out of adverse prospects such as the Soviet leadership now faces can usefully discourage adventurous behavior; but it is also true that beyond a certain point externally applied pressure can become counterproductive if it puts the Soviet leadership in the position of being cornered with no way out except humiliation or bellicose defiance. There was wisdom in President Kennedy's handling of the Cuban missile crisis, creating a situation of strength in the area which obliged Khrushchev to withdraw but allowing him a graceful way to do so. We are more likely to move Soviet behavior in the directions we want by firm but nonbellicose measures, leaving room for the Soviets to protect their legitimate interests in acceptable ways.

Finally, in the management of the military competition with the Soviet Union, our prevailing assumption appears to be that our security is best assured by seeking to regain a position of superiority. This traditional approach to security, carried over from the prenuclear era, can lead under present circumstances only to a continuing unregulated increase in the level of armaments on both sides and a decrease in security for both sides. Given the scale of destructiveness of nuclear weapons, it is not possible for either side to acquire a militarily useful superiority. The only rational available alternative is a balance of stable weapons at more moderate levels, to be achieved through arms control negotiations. It is often argued that arms control has failed, but the fact is that previous efforts in this direction have been constrained by political necessity to stop short of measures that would limit our planned military programs. What has been lacking is a political leadership and a political constituency strong enough and committed enough to support a more rational management of the nuclear military competition. No one can say with assurance that the Soviet leadership would be enlightened enough to respond with equal rationality, but the United States cannot claim to have tested that possibility.

Earlier it was argued that Soviet leaders have strong incentives to seek an easement in the heavy drains of its military sector, if such easement can be found on mutually acceptable terms. But if the United States, instead of testing that proposition fairly, continues to force the pace in military technological innovation, there can be no doubt that the Soviet Union will keep pace with us, whatever the cost.

In sum, it seems apparent that the foregoing policies and assumptions, instead of leading toward greater security and a more tractable Soviet Union, are pointing in the contrary direction. We are, in many ways, the strongest country in the world, but we do not appear to know how to use our strength wisely. Is there not a way of managing our relations with the Soviet Union more rationally?

An Alternative Policy for Managing U.S.-Soviet Relations

First of all, to forestall misunderstandings, it should be made clear that the alternative policy discussed here is rooted within the broad center of the spectrum of American politics. It is not a "soft" policy; it is not based upon "liberal illusions," nor does it advocate weakness or a return to the so-called detente of the 1970s. It begins with a question: Given a realistic understanding of the nature of the Soviet system and of Soviet behavior, what responses on our part make sense in the light of our own best interests?

It accepts the necessity for strength and a military balance but asks, What kind of strength contributes to our security?

It makes a distinction between firmness and bellicosity.

It seeks to keep before the Soviet leaders a way out of their present situation which meshes their enlightened self-interest and our own.

Above all, it gives primary emphasis to the most urgent problem in the relationship—the rational management of the nuclear military competition.

No one can doubt that the Soviet system is authoritarian and repressive, or that the strong police bureaucracy within it behaves in a way that is repugnant to our values. Nor can anyone doubt that the Soviet Union sought, and seeks, to expand its power and influence wherever it thinks it can safely do so, or that its guiding purposes in international life are antithetical to our own. It has to be recognized at the outset that the relationship is a serious, competitive one. What requires greater clarity of thought on our part is the question of how to manage that competition so as to make it less dangerous and less destructive to our interests and our values.

Clearly the primary objective of our policy in the immediate period ahead has to be to protect our security, our interests, and our values in ways that reduce the danger of nuclear war, and to manage the competition at less destructive levels of tension. If we are successful in this, the way will be opened to a longer-term policy that should have an evolutionary purpose. It should be designed to encourage Soviet leaders to see that acting with restraint and responsibility, and enlarging the areas of genuine cooperation between the United States and the Soviet Union, would serve their own self-interest in the framework of the international system.

Two main and related imperatives flow from the implementation of these objectives. The first is to work toward a more stable and moderate level deterrent balance between the two countries. The second is to work toward a political relationship that makes these arrangements on the military plane possible and that also makes possible the forestalling or safe management of crises. We should have ever present in our consciousness, in the ways we address these two imperatives, that our long-term purpose is to encourage the relationship to evolve in a less dangerous direction.

What follows is offered as guidelines to an alternative policy and does not attempt, within the limited compass of this chapter, to flesh out the detailed implementation.

Managing the military competition

It might not have been predicted several years ago that the most troublesome issue in the arms control negotiations would become the prospect of a large-scale effort to develop space-based systems intended to defend the area of the United States from ballistic-missile attack. Appealing as the prospect of such a defense might be, the practical consequence of its introduction into the scene has been seriously to damage prospects for progress toward arms control in exchange for dubious prospects for realizing its stated purpose.

Once it is understood that the proposed defense-dominant strategy is not feasible, and that our persistent commitment to it will result in a destabilizing and enormously costly turn in the military competition, we should return to the realization that our security is better assured by a deterrent balance of offensive weapons. Our efforts should be directed to making that balance as stable and survivable as possible, at more moderate levels.

It is likely that some level of continuing research on strategic defense will be supported in the future, as in the past. That level has been determined in the past by the requirement to protect the United States against the possibility of a breakout by the Soviet Union, and the U.S. effort has been judged adequate and nonprovocative. It is possible that further research on ground-based terminal defense may reach the point at which the United States would wish to discuss the possibility with the Soviet Union of limited programs to offer some defense of some missile sites. This could be done within the framework of the SALT I agreement; it need not have the destabilizing consequence of the presently proposed Strategic Defense Initiative program, if it is made clear that there will not be flight testing or deployment of components of the boost-phase elements of the SDI program and that we are prepared to move seriously toward a ban on antisatellite weapons, which would be even more important to us than to the Soviet Union. Such a course would address the principal Soviet concern that the priority emphasis in the SDI program upon research on directed energy weapons in space, whether or not it succeeds in creating a defense system in orbit over the Soviet Union, will be more likely to produce space weapons capable of offensive use and a new stage of military competition in space.

In the absence of such limiting measures on the SDI program, there can be no doubt but that the Soviets will do what we would do if we were in their situation: launch intensive programs for countermeasures, develop hardened and rapid-burn ballistic missiles and increase their numbers as well as the numbers of missile warheads, expand production of cruise missiles and bombers, and expand research on strategic defense. Under these circumstances, they would not be receptive to proposals for a reduction in their arsenal of offensive missiles.

The alternative reflects the recognition that our security is best assured by a stable and survivable retaliatory balance at more moderate levels. It would involve making serious efforts to negotiate toward a comprehensive agreement that would, through a series of modest steps, reduce warheads and delivery vehicles in all categories, including missiles, bombers, and submarines, so as to balance equitably the asymmetrical force structures of the two sides. Meanwhile, in our own modernization program, we should emphasize survivability and stability of systems as a matter of our own interest and to avoid giving plausible substance to Soviet apprehensions that we seek to acquire a first-strike capability.

One bar that would have to be overcome is the shibboleth that it is against our interest to consider the negotiability of our proposals. The effect of not doing so is to advance positions so transparently one-sided that they are certain to be rejected, an outcome that is not unwelcome to those who, while professing to support arms control negotiations, in fact regard them as disadvantageous.

Another and more fundamental requirement is a more rational process of decision making on defense policy, one that looks beyond the immediate present to the adverse effects that proposed systems may have on our own security, as we did not do in the case of the multiple warhead missiles. This requires improved institutional provision for articulating an overarching national interest against the parochial interests and pressures that now drive decisions on weapons procurement and on defense policy generally.

Managing the political competition

The essential first step in managing the political competition in the Third World is for the United States to give greater emphasis to the local factors involved in Third World upheavals and to recognize that the Soviet Union is a complicating factor rather than a prime cause of these eruptions. Because of our ignorance of foreign political cultures and languages, we have not understood the local sources that have generated protest movements in the Third World. We have consigned all such protest movements indiscriminately to the Soviet camp without regard to the desire of local actors to avoid such a dependency. We have tended to treat local conflicts mainly as counters in the East-West competition. This has been our problem from Vietnam to Iran to Central America today and the effect has been to make our responses ineffective, to polarize local conflicts between equally unsavory extremes so that only military solutions are possible. We can compete effectively with the Soviet Union in the Third World. We have many advantages in that competition, but we have to overcome our parochialism and ignorance to understand the local sources of turbulence and upheavals throughout the Third World. We need to give appropriate and constructive attention to local economic and political conditions.

Regional conventional military capabilities may be required in some instances to guard against military intervention by the Soviet Union, but the United States should accept for itself, as it would ask of the Soviet Union, restraint against intervention by force to produce or prevent political change in the Third World. The U.S. government should not regard it as essential to our security to prevent every increase in the Soviet presence, provided that such increases do not threaten areas of vital interest to the United States or that they are not of such a magnitude as to threaten the independence of other countries. Containment need not be interpreted to mean that the Soviet Union should be prevented from peaceful expansion of its economic or political relations in nonthreatening ways.

It has not been productive to seek agreement on abstract formulas for limiting the political competition or on across-the-board "rules of conduct." It may, however, prove productive to seek tacit or explicitly agreed limits on levels and means of intervention in areas of conflict on a region-by-region basis, taking account of the relative intensity of interest of the two sides in particular areas, with the aim of reducing the risk of escalation. In a number of instances such agreements have been made through diplomatic channels, and the experience can be generalized through mechanisms established to forestall, manage, or localize regional crises.

It should be part of our purpose, consonant with our longer-range objectives, to persuade the Soviet Union that its self-interest requires acceptance of and support for the international system. To do so, however, would require that the United States recognize more clearly than it has done that the strengthening of the international system is also of cardinal importance to our own security and interests. We should not be tempted, in our competition with the Soviet Union, to violate international law or to flout the authority of such international institutions as the World Court.

The political competition with the Soviet Union also involves the industrialized nations. Our relations with the industrial democratic nations should be regarded as the vital central nucleus of shared democratic values and the rule of law in the international system, and they should be managed with attentive concern for our respective interests. This requires close consultation to harmonize our respective security, foreign policy, and economic interests. It has been all too easy to react with irascibility to the internal political and economic strains of our partners and the limitations they impose on their policies, but this manifestation of our currently ascendant nationalism is shortsighted and would deprive us of the central core of support for democratic values in the world. Such gains as the Soviet Union has made among the industrialized nations, in Western Europe and Japan—and they have not been notable—have resulted more from the shortcomings of our own policy than from Soviet adroitness.

Bilateral aspects of the relationship

Both constraints and incentives are required to influence the movement of Soviet conduct in desired directions.

Among the incentives, the most important instrument available to the United States is the prospect of an increased level of trade between the two countries. We observed during the period leading up to the Twenty-fourth Party Congress in 1971, when the matrix of Soviet political strategy for the recent period was established, how much the support for a policy of reduced tension flowed from domestic economic needs. There can be no difference on the point that items of direct military application should not enter into such trade. But a prudent measure of trade, projected to increase over time in the absence of egregious Soviet adventurism, can limit the risks of strengthening military capabilities while providing at least marginal constraints on foreign policy adventurism that would jeopardize such trade.

Academic exchanges, properly managed, have resulted in a quantum leap in the sophistication of American studies of the USSR, giving us insights into the range of Soviet political life not reflected in its printed materials. Some cooperative programs, along the lines of the eleven bilateral commissions set up in 1972–73 concerned with health, agriculture, the environment, and so forth, although marginal in their effects upon the central core of the relationship, give expression to the existence of common interests in some limited areas and to the possibility of an expansion of these areas of cooperation if and when the relationship moves in more productive directions.

It should be added that the conduct of our bilateral relations requires more adequate diplomatic communications, not only at the top levels of government but also in the day-to-day conduct of business. Management of the competitive relationship means that even during times of tension—and perhaps particularly during times of tension—adversary communication can help to establish boundaries within which situations of competition or conflict can work themselves out with less risk of an escalation that may be wanted by neither side but that can result from loss of control or miscalculation. In the conduct of these diplomatic communications, the tone is of the essence. Firmness and clarity in stating and defending our interests do not preclude civility, whereas posturing for domestic audiences reduces these communications to an exercise in propaganda to which the Soviets are all too ready to respond in kind.

Longer-term considerations

We cannot predict what choices the Soviet Union may make, but it is apparent that the Gorbachev regime will be examining its options for changes in domestic and foreign policies.

Although these choices are mainly in their hands, they will be influenced by their view of our policies in considering the range of choices open to them. It is in our interest that if they, in their own self-interest, move toward greater restraint and responsibility in the military and the political competition, we should be prepared to accept a more productive and less dangerous relationship. We should make it clear that we regard it to be in our interest as well as theirs for the Soviet Union to be more deeply involved in the world economy and to participate in and support the international system as a bulwark against international anarchy and violence.

This course necessarily requires a long-term perspective, and both patience and firmness, for a movement in this direction would be a great departure from habits of thought developed over many decades. But although its full realization may mature only over a long period, it is important that we make clear our readiness to be responsive to moves in this direction now, when the matrix of a new regime in the Soviet Union is being formed.

II

Dealing with the Russians:
The Wages of Forgetfulness

RICHARD PIPES

The Russian Revolution and the Soviet state that issued from it have been with us now for two-thirds of a century. A reasonable man might assume an experience of such duration to have yielded unforgettable lessons. There has to be some accumulated wisdom from sixty-eight years of relations with a regime that in so many ways has impinged on the destiny of Western nations: from the historic record of the Communist International, the Popular Fronts, the Nazi-Soviet Pact, the Cold War, detente. For only when those who conduct relations with the USSR assimilate such wisdom can we be certain that each successive generation does not start afresh, groping its way through dangerous territory that others have already surveyed and mapped.

Alas, this is not the case. The experience does not transmit, the wisdom does not accumulate. Each secretary of state, upon assuming office, seems to be driven by some secret ambition to succeed where his predecessors have failed, to discover new approaches to the Soviet enigma in order to realize at long last that ultimate objective of U.S. foreign policy, the Nirvana-like condition of enduring "stability." The professionals charged with formulating and executing U.S. policies toward the Soviet Union—that is, essentially, the Department of State—seem to possess virtually no institutional memory. Nothing illustrates this contention better than the astonishing fact that nowhere in Washington can one locate a complete set of the exchanges between U.S. presidents and their Soviet counterparts because on leaving office each president takes that correspondence as part of his baggage and deposits it in his memorial library. This means that the persons charged with the conduct of relations with Moscow lack ready access to documents of the greatest and most immediate relevance to the field of their responsibility. Such disregard for the lessons of the past manifests itself in other ways as well. In the 1970s, for instance, the Congressional Research Service brought out a splendid history of the U.S. record of negotiating with the Russians since 1917, as recreated by the participants and analyzed by scholars.[1] One could hardly conceive of a more useful guide to current U.S. negotiators than that provided by these documents. Yet the promised second volume of this study has never appeared, apparently for lack of demand. Is it surprising that in Washington's dealing with Moscow, each day is the first day of Creation?

In a speech delivered in October 1984 the secretary of state said that we must "fashion—and stick to—a long term strategy" toward the Soviet Union.[2] This is a familiar exhortation: probably every secretary of state since the end of World War II has called for such a strategy. The difficulty, however, has always lain in translating this appeal into coherent policy, into something other than the familiar melange of formulas—some obvious, some dubious, some in mutual contradiction—which has been the staple of U.S. foreign policy for decades.

The main theme of his address, as has been the case with his predecessors, was the "Yes, but" cliché. Yes, the Soviet Union is run by a self-perpetuating elite that represses free thought and frowns on free institutions. This unpleasant reality out of the way, there came the caveat. We must maintain a constructive relationship with the Soviet Union because it is powerful: "Its military strength, including its vast nuclear arsenal, is a reality that we cannot ignore." Since this formula was first uttered by President Eisenhower thirty years ago, it has provided the philosophical underpinning of Washington's policies toward Moscow. Except for the first two years of the Reagan administration, it has never been deviated from, even though its consequences have been detrimental both to U.S. national interests and to the broader cause of international peace. Such an approach is by its very nature counterproductive because once one concedes that it is nothing but Moscow's military power that compels us to acquiesce to its repression, aggression, and hostility, then Moscow cannot help but conclude that the more it enhances its military power, the greater will be the impunity with which to repress, expand, and sow hatred. The connection between cause and effect in this case should be readily apparent, the more so that the record of the past confirms it. Yet Republicans are replaced by Democrats, and Democrats, in turn, give way to Republicans, and the "yes, but" philosophy remains as solidly entrenched as if logic had not been invented and experience was of no account.

The practical effect of this approach is to decouple Soviet behavior from the Soviet nuclear threat, that is, to acquiesce to Soviet outrages (in every respect but words) so as to avoid a direct military confrontation. No wonder that Soviet observers express puzzlement over the American tendency to isolate military power, which for them is always an instrument of politics, from

---

[1] Library of Congress, Congressional Research Service, Senior Specialists Division, *Soviet Diplomacy and Negotiating Behavior: Emerging New Context for U.S. Diplomacy* (Washington, D.C., 1979).

[2] "Managing the U.S.-Soviet Relationship over the Long Term," October 18, 1984, U.S. Department of State, *Current Policy* no. 624.

politics in the broader sense.[3] For them, such decoupling makes no sense and can only signify either confusion of thought or lack of will, or both.

It is not possible to devise an effective policy toward the Soviet Union as long as it is believed that we share with it an overriding common interest, namely preventing World War III. It is quite true that both sides are most anxious to prevent their disagreements from exploding into armed conflict. This fear enables them to establish a condition of truce, but it does not and cannot create a communality of interest leading to a state of peace, which derives only from sharing common values and objectives. The desire to avoid a shooting war is an insufficient basis for the "constructive relationship" between the United States and the Soviet Union which Secretary Shultz desires. The Soviet definition of peace embraces neither the right of sovereign states to exist nor respect for law as a regulator of international relations. Its definition calls for controlled violence and aims not at genuine coexistence but at pacification.

It is for this reason that the extravagant hopes placed on arms control negotiations are so misplaced and so certain to lead to disappointment. Even if one allows, for the sake of argument, that the USSR has a genuine interest in an equitable arms control agreement, it is difficult to see how limiting or reducing one type of weaponry can influence Soviet intentions toward the West. Optimally, such accords hold the promise of limiting the damage in the event that relations break down completely and war erupts, contrary to the wishes of the superpowers. (Even so, how meaningful this would be is not clear given that the most ardent proponents of arms control see the existing arsenals as sufficient to destroy the world many times over.) What they cannot achieve is to change the conditions that lead to hostility and armed competition in the first place. To see weapons and not the mind set behind the weapons as the threat is surely to confuse effect with cause. There can be no harm in negotiations to control and reduce nuclear arsenals (or conventional ones, for that matter). But nothing in the past record of arms control, going back to the late eighteenth century, indicates that such negotiations, even when successful, affect relations between the great powers or promote the cause of peace.

Soviet behavior in the past several years suggests that arms control has become less than ever an instrument of regulating U.S.-Soviet political relations. The implied refusal of the Senate to ratify SALT II and the stiff conditions proposed by the Reagan administration in START seem to have persuaded the Russians that the days when they could secure unilateral advantages through the arms control process were over. Because the main Soviet interest in arms control has been to restrict and, where possible, to abort U.S. advances in nuclear technology, it has become pointless for Moscow to

---

[3]*SShA* no. 1 (January 1970), pp. 62–63, cited in Richard Pipes, *Survival Is Not Enough* (New York, 1984), p. 86.

take SALT and START seriously. There are indications that Moscow no longer attaches much importance to arms talks; the most significant of these is the current practice of the Soviet government of unveiling its strategic proposals through the media rather than through regular diplomatic channels. Experience indicates that when Moscow is interested in coming to terms, it does not act in this manner.

This is not the place to enlarge on the nature of the Communist regime, since our task is to spell out the concrete steps that should be taken to avert the twin dangers of capitulation and war. Suffice it to say that the Communist regime differs as much from the traditional national state as the traditional national state, at the time of its emergence, differed from the feudal one. It is a completely novel amalgam whose outstanding characteristic is the militarization of politics, that is, the thorough reshaping of civic society on the model of a combat organization. Communist theory treats the state as "organized terror" and the political process always and under all circumstances (except in areas under communist control) as a form of warfare, be it between classes or between states. Once this view is adopted, a variety of consequences follow. For one, success in politics is measured by the ability not to reconcile differences but to smash the other side, the more thoroughly the better. The entire state with its human and material resources is mobilized to that end. Another feature of such a state is that it does not strive for international stability, which would create an environment for engaging in peaceful pursuits; destabilization of other societies is, so to say, its principal business. For the Soviet Union to accept stability as a permanent condition would be to settle for a draw and thereby to admit failure, with all that this implies for a system that identifies its survival with expansion of power.

These considerations are fundamental. They also happen to be entirely outside the upbringing and practical experience of the businessmen, lawyers, and politicians who shape U.S. foreign policy. Such failure of the imagination can have catastrophic consequences, as the whole dismal record of Western dealing with totalitarian states demonstrates. Every U.S. secretary of state should have before his eyes at all times the dictum of Lenin's, which he pronounced in 1918 in a speech intended to persuade his party to approve a most disadvantageous peace treaty with Germany: "History suggests that peace is a breathing space for war."[4] Or: "We have the great experience of the Revolution and from this experience we have learned that it is necessary to conduct a policy of merciless onslaught when the objective conditions permit it . . . but we must resort to the tactic of temporizing, the slow gathering of forces, when the objective conditions make it impossible to issue appeals for a general merciless repulse."[5] This is the wisdom of the Founding Father of the Soviet State, the man whose writings dominate communist thinking not because

---

[4]V. I. Lenin, *Sochineniia* (Works), 2d ed. (Moscow and Leningrad, 1935), 23: 12–13.
[5]Ibid.

they are either wise or inspiring but because they have proven eminently successful in defeating "bourgeois" states.

A fundamental premise of any policy toward the USSR must be that by the
very nature of things the USSR is the active, dynamic force (in the morally
neutral sense) and the United States the reactive one. This point can be demonstrated on the record of sixty-eight years of East-West relations, notwithstanding times when U.S. reactions, shading into overreactions, gave the
contrary impression. Every major turn and twist in U.S.-Soviet relations has
been initiated by Moscow. This is unlikely to change in the immediate future,
which means that any realistic program of U.S. policies toward the USSR has
to be in large measure conceived on defensive and negative principles. It is often more by what we abstain from doing than by what we actively undertake
to do that we can exert the greatest influence on the course of events.

One political conclusion that flows from this premise is that there is no
need to engage the Soviet Union in frenetic "dialogues." The absence of
negotiations no more means that we are on the brink of war than involvement in negotiation means that we are moving toward peace. Granted that
negotiating is what the foreign policy establishment does best and that no
secretary of state is immune to the blandishments of the attention that the
media lavish on him whenever he meets his Soviet counterpart, the practice is
often futile and sometimes dangerous. It is futile because there are in place already enough regular channels of communication between Washington and
Moscow to serve their purposes whenever they wish to say something to each
other—channels sanctified by centuries of diplomatic practice. Public perception notwithstanding—and the public has been badly confused by the
media's identification of diplomatic contacts with spectacular summits—at
no time during the first term of the Reagan administration were the channels
of communication between Moscow and Washington frozen. If no agreements were concluded, it was for want not of means but of will, especially on
the side of the Soviet Union whose weak and confused leadership of the time
lacked the courage to make the compromises. Public "dialogues" can be dangerous because the Western public, whipped up by the media, confuses the
theater of summits with political realities and pressures its side to come to an
agreement at all costs. It is surprising how many people believe that East-
West strains are due to mutual misunderstandings (rather than to all too
good understanding) and assume that, as in family disputes, the mere fact of
talking things over signifies progress.

The November 1985 summit in Geneva is a case in point. The meeting proceeded without an agenda: it was essentially a "get acquainted" occasion at
which the two leaders hectored each other in private and smiled at each other
in public. Nothing of significance was achieved. Yet the public, which tends
to appraise matters of high policy by appearances, has been told by the media
that the summit was a great success for both countries. The result has been an
entirely unwarranted sense of optimism. It is realistic to assume that future

summits will require an agenda and for that reason produce much more acrimony and lead, quite unnecessarily, to public pessimism and anxiety.

Historical experience indicates that whenever the Soviet leadership needs a "deal," it puts the other party on notice quickly and in unmistakable terms: no long preliminaries, no atmosphere of goodwill are required. Such was the case in 1922 in connection with Rapallo, in 1939 when the Nazi-Soviet Pact was hammered out, and again in 1954–55 in the wake of Stalin's death. The next Soviet decision to negotiate yet another armistice with the West may come soon, it may come later, or it may never come: the only certain thing is that it will come if and when the Politburo concludes that its interests call for such a temporary respite in tensions and not because of incremental benefits or goodwill gained from East-West "dialogues." History also suggests that the factors that determine swings in Soviet foreign policy, from brute hostility to its more subtle variants, are determined not by the tenor of Moscow's relations with individual "capitalist" countries but either by changes in the internal conditions of the USSR itself or by its leadership's revised assessments of the international correlation of forces. Hence the time devoted to "dialogues" with Soviet diplomats, when indications are lacking that Moscow needs an agreement, can be put to better use reading history.

It is the author's conviction that the Soviet leadership is determined to win the contest with the West which it unilaterally provokes, but that it wants to do so without resort to general war. To that end it has developed an array of instrumentalities that are meant to shift the correlation of forces in the Soviet Union's favor. The most important of these are: 1) interference in the internal affairs of other countries for the purpose of creating divisions and supporting forces that on specific issues may serve Soviet interests; 2) shaping the vocabulary and content of the international discourse to Moscow's advantage; 3) exploiting Western economic assistance for the purpose of enhancing Soviet military capabilities. By militarizing, as it were, activities that, in the Western view, are antithetical to militarism—domestic politics, information, and economics—the Soviet Union compels the West to respond in kind. The traditional alternative of "peace or war," taken for granted by the West since the Renaissance as the norm in relationships between sovereign states, has little meaning when applied to a regime that treats peace as a form of warfare. Should the West persist in approaching relations with the USSR in its traditional dichotomous manner, then it will inevitably narrow its options to war or capitulation. Such a choice can be averted only by broadening the scope of the West's instrumentalities of foreign policy to correspond to those the USSR employs.

Soviet interference in the internal affairs of noncommunist countries takes two forms: manipulation of competition among democratic political parties, and direct or indirect military intervention in Third World countries where democracy is either weakly rooted or absent.

Democratic societies can prevent Moscow from insinuating itself into national debates on foreign and defense matters only in one way, and that is by adopting the principle of bipartisanship, defined to mean firm exclusion of the Soviet Union from their own policy disagreements. It should be entirely unacceptable for candidates for the office of president or for senators to meet with high Soviet officials either here or in Moscow. The Constitution vests the conduct of U.S. foreign policy exclusively in the hands of the president, and it is he and he alone who should engage in negotiations with Moscow, whether formal or informal. To adopt a different practice is to invite the Politburo to insinuate itself into policy disagreements among democratic parties and to throw its weight now behind one, now behind another, depending on where its interests lie. When Gromyko emerges from a talk with candidate Mondale smiling broadly but looks glum after an interview with President Reagan, he is telling the U.S. voter that a Mondale victory will lead to improved relations with the Soviet Union and a better chance for "peace." Such an opportunity should be denied him. Even less should the leader of an opposition party (e.g., Vogel of the German SPD) openly solicit Soviet support in forthcoming elections. The Soviet leadership has been taught by Lenin always to seek out and exploit the slightest "fissures" in the enemy camp and to form temporary alliances with even the most unreliable "bourgeois" groups. There is no need to assist Moscow in these maneuvers.

Many Western leaders suffer from an extraordinary blindness in dealing with Soviet aggression in the Third World. In order not to have to confront the issue, they have recourse to explanations of poverty and social injustice as the alleged causes of "wars of national liberation," although no correlation can be established between the two phenomena. Because the same indifference prevails in regard to direct Soviet military aggression in Afghanistan, where poverty and social injustice cannot possibly serve as explanations, one is justified in suspecting that the true reason behind such thinking is the shortsighted hope that as long as the Soviet Union dissipates its energies and resources on conquering backward colonies, it is less likely to cause trouble in the West. The view is shortsighted because the Soviet Union carries out its campaign of conquests in the Third World not to gain nonexistent economic benefits but to secure military bases for eventual use against the West. It is, therefore, greatly in the interest of the West to help the forces which resist Soviet aggression and to withhold economic and other forms of aid from Soviet surrogates in the Third World.

    1. The Afghan mujahedeen, while fighting for ideals and a way of life that may be alien to us, are in the literal sense of the word fighting for us. A Soviet victory there will mean Soviet rockets and planes permanently stationed that much closer to the Persian Gulf and the Indian Ocean. Soviet humiliation in Afghanistan, by contrast, may produce internal repercussions in the USSR and discourage further acts of direct aggression. For these reasons it behooves the West to intercede in the conflict more directly and energetically, supplying the mujahedeen with the weapons they require, bypassing neighboring countries. We should also wage an intensive

antiwar campaign among Russian occupational forces, using as a model
Lenin's defeatist propaganda of 1917 which contributed so much to the dis-
integration of the Russian army.

2. It is senseless to assist Soviet imperialist ventures by providing Soviet
dependencies with the financial help that Moscow finds it difficult to provide. It is scandalous that the Gulf Oil Company and U.S. banks should
furnish the Communist regime of Angola with the bulk of the revenues
with which to pay its Cuban mercenaries and maintain itself in power. It is
no less scandalous for European bankers quietly to extend loans to the
Sandinistas ($400 million out of the $465 million in foreign credits which
Nicaragua obtained in 1984).[6] Close coordination among the allies in regard to policies in the Third World is essential to the security of the West:
in such matters the NATO alliance cannot stop at the frontier of Eastern
Europe and the Atlantic north of the Tropic of Cancer because such geographic boundaries hold no meaning for Moscow.

Information policy or propaganda is the one field of endeavor where the
West can assume an active role. There exists general agreement that piercing
the walls of censorship with which communist regimes surround their societies is useful and deserving of support. Unfortunately, in Western societies,
ideological warfare has no interest groups to give it support. While the military buildup has its protagonists and economic warfare its antagonists, propaganda basks in public indifference. I can recall no instance during the two
years that I served on the National Security Council when this matter ever
came up for serious discussion. It is characteristic of our attitude that the director of the U.S. Information Agency is not even invited to attend meetings
of the National Security Council. Such improvements as are made in this field
almost always concern the technical side, namely modernization of transmit-
ting facilities, overcoming jamming, and so forth, but very rarely if ever the
content of the transmissions. These are allowed to drift. The Board of International Broadcasting seems in recent years to have adopted a policy of "let
a hundred flowers bloom," which means that its broadcasts reflect every
existing current of opinion (except, of course, a procommunist one), without
clear policy direction.

This lack of interest and policy guidance means that our propaganda,
whether carried by air waves or by the printed word, does not convey to citizens of communist countries a clear political message, which can only be the
superiority of free institutions and democracy's commitment to peace. The
"hundred flowers" approach leads sometimes to banalities and sometimes
to very antidemocratic messages being transmitted. When Alexander Solzhenitsyn is given the hospitality of Radio Liberty to broadcast his eccentric political messages to Russian audiences—such as that democracy means self-de-
structive chaos, that the United States is not a reliable ally of Japan, or that
U.S. generals are planning a genocidal nuclear attack against the Great Rus-

[6]*Wall Street Journal*, October 2, 1984, p. 34.

sian population—he is in fact lending support to communist propaganda with the assistance of the U.S. taxpayer's money. No less damaging is Solzhenitsyn's argument, broadcast over Radio Liberty as well as the Voice of America, that the Russian Revolution was brought about by external forces, namely Western ideas and machinations, in which Jews played a prominent role. Such historical misinterpretations not only make mockery of the evidence but help harden among Russians anti-Western and anti-Semitic attitudes whose only beneficiary is the communist regime.

Although recent practices in U.S. information policy directed at the Soviet Union have suffered from especially serious flaws, the policy of appealing to Russian nationalism is not new. It has long been an article of faith of specialists in the U.S. Foreign Service that Russian nationalism is a potent force (which indeed it is) that the United States should exploit to its own advantage (a proposition of doubtful realism at best). The effect of this approach has been, on the one hand, to make a futile and even counterproductive appeal to the chauvinism of Great Russians and, on the other, to maintain a neutral position toward the aspirations of the non-Russian half of the USSR's population. Neither policy can be recommended.

1. With rare exceptions, Russian nationalism has been traditionally anti-Western in spirit: it expresses not so much a healthy pride in one's country as suspicion and dislike of foreigners. This holds especially true of its popular manifestations—that nationalism which secularizes dark religious passions, rooted in Orthodox xenophobia. In recognition of this fact, émigré nationalists of the Solzhenitsyn school have been attempting to win a following in their country by accusing the Soviet regime of being the product not of Russian history but of an artificial implantation in Russia's soil of Western ideas. In so doing they find themselves in competition with the Soviet regime for the allegiance of Russian xenophobes, with the difference that instead of channeling the dislike of foreigners directly against the West, as in Moscow's practice, they do so indirectly by treating the Soviet regime itself as a byproduct of the West.

Nothing good can come of this competition. For one thing, any regime in power will always win such a contest by virtue of the fact that its people, whatever their personal preferences, must view their own destinies as linked to the fate of the regime: during World War II even German anti-Nazis whose sons fought at the front had to hope for a Nazi victory. For another, the two competitors outbid themselves in disparaging Western values, values that alone can heal Russia's wounds and help promote in Russia a viable social order. U.S. appeals to the Russian people should be addressed, above all, to the educated groups, for they alone are open to Western ideas and to the argument that patriotism may sometime require a person to assume a critical attitude toward his government. Our guide in these questions should be not Solzhenitsyn but Sakharov.

2. A similarly misguided deference for Russian nationalism conditions U.S. official attitudes toward the Soviet empire, the last vestige from the

days when colonialism was in style. It has been U.S. policy all along to ignore the colonial character of the USSR and to treat the non-Russian half of the population as if it consisted of a linguistic and cultural subgroup of the species *homo sovieticus*, devoid of political aspirations—something like the Spanish-speaking minority in this country. In its broadcasts to the non-Russians the United States has lacked the courage to go even as far as the Soviet constitution, which accords every Soviet Republic the right to secede. Curiously, we have shown no such respect in the past for the imperialism of friendly powers such as Britain, France, and the Netherlands, whose empires we helped to dismantle even though they performed a civilizing mission superior to that of the Russians. U.S. squeamishness in this respect is motivated by the misplaced hope of winning or at least not losing Russian nationalist sympathies, it being widely believed that Russians are exceedingly sensitive to the fate of their empire and would rally behind their regime if told that the Americans support the national aspirations of their subject nations.

This position can be faulted on at least two grounds. First, there is no evidence that the majority of Russians care much one way or another about the Caucasus, Central Asia, or the other borderland areas; indeed, many of them believe that they are being unfairly taxed to subsidize these areas and maintain their allegedly indolent inhabitants at a standard of life higher than their own. Second, the Soviet regime does not require proof to charge the United States with malevolent intentions whenever such charges serve its interests. If it really felt that it was to its advantage to tell the Russian people that the Americans show sympathy for the national aspirations of their subject nations, it would do so without hesitation regardless of whether or not such accusations were true. As a matter of fact, it does nothing of the kind: no one has ever heard such Soviet accusations. The likely explanation is that Moscow fears lest suggestions that foreign powers sympathize with them might inflame the nationalism of the minorities and exacerbate relations between them and the Russians.

The United States need not call for the breakup of the Soviet empire, but it surely can and ought to express no less sympathy for the Ukrainians than it does for the Poles and do no less for the Uzbeks than it has done for the Indians. The major non-Russian groups of the Soviet Union are not "ethnics"—they are dynamic nationalities with as valid a claim to self-determination as the excolonial peoples once ruled by the West. U.S. broadcasts to them should reflect this awareness.

When all is said and done, however, the most effective way in which the United States can influence the course of Soviet development lies in the sphere of economics. There is a great deal of ill-informed opinion abroad that the Soviet Union is economically self-sufficient and, if pressed, can readily dispense with foreign credits and technology.

In reality, from the late seventeenth century on, when it initiated the policy of forced industrialization, until the present, Russia has never been able to dispense with Western technology and capital. The civil war was barely over when the Bolsheviks invited German assistance in reconstructing their shattered industrial economy. In the first five-year plans, Western knowhow played a critical role, and the same held true of Soviet industrial expansion after the death of Stalin, when every major branch of Soviet industry benefited from Western aid. Unlike Japan, which studied Western techniques, and then adapted them to its own uses, Russia, both czarist and Soviet, has never been able to emancipate itself from dependence on Western aid.

These facts are a matter of record, but they are either ignored or downplayed by groups that have a vested interest in extending to the Soviet Union technical and financial assistance. These groups talk and act as if the efficiency of Soviet industry and the might of the Soviet military were entirely unrelated phenomena; as if the USSR, like Western societies, drew a sharp dividing line between the "civilian" and "military" sectors of the economy so that assistance extended to the former has no effect on the latter. In fact, such a distinction hardly exists in communist countries given that their entire raison d'être is to serve military purposes. It is known that the State Planning Commission (Gosplan) has had on its board since the 1920s a powerful military contingent representing the interests of the General Staff which enjoys a decisive voice in investment allocations. Its decisions obviously are guided by short- and long-term military considerations. It can be taken for granted, therefore, that the vast majority of industrial imports by the USSR are heavily influenced by considerations of such a nature, that is, whether they enhance the capabilities of Soviet military forces or contribute to the improvement of the country's wartime mobilization base.

If this is the case, then *any* industrial and technical assistance rendered to the USSR helps the Soviet military establishment. The United States, which spends 6–7 percent of its gross national product on defense, ought to protest most energetically that its allies (who spend one-half or less of that on their defenses), through trade, help the USSR and its surrogates build up their military capabilities. Under existing practices, the United States not only shoulders the heaviest burden of defense in the alliance, but its burden is made still heavier by the assistance extended to the Communist bloc by its allies in the guise of technology transfer and credits.

To be truly effective, the Western alliance should augment military cooperation in the event of war with economic cooperation under the prevailing conditions of "neither peace nor war." Given the indisputable fact that in modern times military power rests directly on industrial might—since the Napoleonic wars every major military conflict has been resolved in favor of countries with superior industrial capabilities—it is absurd for the West to enhance Soviet industrial potential while preparing at great cost to match its military capability. NATO should be complemented by an economic alliance that would closely regulate the transfer of technology and credits to the Communist bloc. Such regulations would entail the following:

1. replacing COCOM with an effective organization to monitor the flow of technology East, with authority to enforce its decisions;

2. abandoning the prevalent practice of backing credits to communist countries with state guarantees. Such trade as is licensed should be carried out at the risk of the firms and banks that expect to profit from it;

3. refusing to develop Soviet energy resources on the grounds that such action enhances Soviet hard-currency reserves, solidifies the Soviet hold on Eastern Europe, and delays reforms of the Stalinist economic system;

4. refusing to provide credits to Moscow's colonies and dependencies in the Third World so that the whole burden of its imperialist ventures falls on the strained treasury of the Soviet Union.

The West desperately needs to get away from the unrealistic view that the Soviet threat is exclusively or even primarily a military one and that matching the threat entails mainly military countermeasures. In communist thinking the distinctions between war and peace, or between military and civilian, are quite blurred: these phenomena, which to us are antithetical, for them shade dialectically into each other. Dr. Johnson used to say that to trade with the Indies one must have the wealth of the Indies. It is no less true that to cope with Soviet Russia one must learn to think like Soviet Russia. Nothing has contributed more to the political triumphs of the Communists since 1917 than their knowledge and understanding of the mentality of their opponents and the unwillingness of these opponents to repay the compliment.

12

The United States and the USSR: Rebuilding Relations

WILLIAM G. HYLAND

The Reagan administration's approach to relations with the Soviet Union can be divided into two phases. The first phase lasted through the end of 1983; it was dominated by the ideas and plans that the administration brought with it into office. The second phase was inaugurated by the president's conciliatory speech of January 16, 1984, following the successful conclusion of the Euromissile crisis. In the initial period the administration sought to put itself in a position strong enough to begin the second and more diplomatic phase, leading to a summit meeting in Geneva in November 1985.

The Reagan administration left little doubt that it had broken with the "soft" policies of the past—not only the policies of its immediate predecessor but those of the Nixon and Ford administrations as well. Its most telling phrase was "a decade of weakness and self-doubt," and it believed that the illusion of detente was in large part responsible for the decline of American power. A centerpiece of this illusion was a faith in arms control; but the SALT II treaty was fatally flawed, and the whole concept of incremental arms limitation agreements with the Soviet Union not only had failed to reduce numbers of weapons but, worse, had created unverifiable agreements that invited cheating and misled the public into believing that the process of arms control was reducing tensions.

In the Reagan scheme, America's response was to rearm, creating a position of strength from which a diplomatic strategy might evolve. Not only would Soviet-American relations have to await this change in the strategic balance, but the Soviets would have to earn their entry into the political process by an improvement in behavior. Thus the new secretary of state, Alexander Haig, concluded in his memoirs: "At this early stage there was nothing substantial to talk about, nothing to negotiate until the USSR began to demonstrate its willingness to behave like a responsible power. . . . The time was not right to give the Soviets something they wanted as passionately as they wanted a treaty on strategic arms."[1]

This was not some quixotic notion that grew out of a tumultuous election campaign. It reflected a deep conviction that the United States had become seriously weakened while the Soviet Union had built up its global position. This weakness justified a multiyear buildup of American military programs. The new administration, acutely sensitive to the inevitable shifts on congressional mood, understandably believed that the U.S. buildup had to be "front-end loaded"; a political program of negotiations with the Soviets would risk undercutting the buildup. (In this they were prescient; consider what had happened by 1984 to the MX missile program and the funding of the Strategic Defense Initiative in the Congress.) Nevertheless, the Reagan approach was a break with previous U.S. strategy, which had assumed that arms control actually helped gain bipartisan support for defense programs. The buildup in strategic weapons that followed SALT I, for example, was made an integral part of the ratification process, and in effect it was the price for continuing arms control. The Reagan administration turned this approach on its head: a major buildup would be the prerequisite for arms control, especially a program to reduce strategic weapons.

A second feature of this initial period was a matter more of events than of design. The problem was to deploy new, intermediate-range American missiles in Europe in accordance with the NATO decision of December 1979. The new administration understood in 1981 that this deployment was by no means assured and that, in fact, it faced significant and growing political opposition in Europe. The administration also understood that the failure of the program could become a major victory for the Soviet Union in Europe. Deployment thus became a test case. But two strains of policy were in almost constant conflict, as determination to stick with the scheduled deployments waned with the grudgingly recognized necessity of placating European opinion by ostensible concessions to the negotiating process. Hence the Reagan administration's reluctance to start arms control talks was breached. The result, however, was the November 1981 proposal for a "zero option" (made largely for public relations purposes) followed in mid-1982 by the bizarre interlude of the "walk in the woods"—when the outline of an agreement was worked out informally by the chief negotiators only to be rejected later by both governments—which suggested that a bargain may have been possible.

This struggle for European opinion, the American rearmament program, and the maneuvering over arms control, all fell within what might be considered the "normal" bounds of the American-Soviet contest in the wake of the

[1]Alexander M. Haig, Jr., *Caveat: Realism, Reagan, and Foreign Policy* (New York: Macmillan, 1984), p. 46.

invasion of Afghanistan. What seemed to fall outside these boundaries was the psychological mind-set of the new administration, as reflected in casual comments as well as in more formal statements and policies. It became increasingly clear—at least to observers outside the U.S. government—that the Reagan administration harbored a deep hostility toward the Soviet Union. U.S. policy in the early 1980s aimed, it appeared, to dismantle arrangements that accorded the USSR legitimacy as a superpower.

Whether intentionally or not, the administration created the widespread impression that it could not contemplate "normal" relations with the USSR. Instead, it would pursue a policy aimed at seriously weakening the USSR in the name of a vaguely articulated, long-term objective: forcing internal reforms and changes that would lead to a more conciliatory Soviet foreign policy. This general idea was manifested most dramatically in the quarrel with Western Europe over the Soviet gas pipeline. No matter that the United States undercut its own arguments by making its own massive economic concessions, in the form of irrevocable commitments to sell grain—the debate over the pipeline was in reality a debate over grand strategy, not narrow economics. The net result of the episode, however, was partial American defeat. It was following this failure that one could begin to see the glimmerings of the second phase.

The administration began to realize that it could not complete its entire first term claiming that America was still too weak to negotiate with the Soviet Union. If that were truly the case, then how could the Reagan strategy be justified? In the summer of 1983 the administration began to hint that its policies were persuading Moscow to accommodate itself to the "new realities." It was argued by the administration that once the American missiles were in Europe, the USSR would adjust to the new situation and would begin serious negotiations. This theory formed a consistent American theme throughout 1983. It was underscored with gestures designed to prove that the administration would not slam the door on postdeployment negotiations—which might perhaps even include a summit.

Some evidence suggests that the Soviets were indeed adapting to these tactics in the summer of 1983; there were minor gestures, such as permission for a group of Soviet Pentecostalists, given sanctuary in the U.S. Embassy in Moscow since 1978, to emigrate from the USSR, the new grain agreement, and some moderated rhetoric from Andropov, especially in his meetings with a group of U.S. senators in August 1983. Then came the Soviet shooting down of a Korean airliner and the coincident illness of Andropov. A crisis of some kind must have been precipitated in the Kremlin. The formal statement attributed to Andropov at the end of September seemed to repudiate any earlier hints of flexibility; "illusions" about Reagan were specifically denounced. The statement had about it the marks of self-criticism, because one who had held such "illusions" might have been Andropov himself. In any case, the statement of September 1983 marked a Soviet turn toward a much harsher, more rigid position of hostility.

Nevertheless, the Reagan administration proceeded with this new attitude, and phase two emerged full-bloom at the beginning of 1984. With the crucial missile deployments in Western Europe begun, the president, on January 16, 1984, held out an olive branch, on the assumption that the United States was at long last in a position of strength.

> I believe that 1984 finds the United States in its strongest position in years to es-
> tablish a constructive and realistic working relationship with the Soviet Union.
> . . . We've come a long way since the decade of the 1970s—years when the United
> States seemed filled with self-doubt and neglected its defense. . . . Three years ago
> we embraced a mandate from the American people to change course and we
> have. . . . 1984 is a year of opportunities for peace.[2]

Soviet-American relations did not, however, improve. Somewhat surprisingly, the change in leadership from Andropov to Chernenko did not revive a line of accommodation, at least not immediately. Relations worsened, dramatized by the Soviet boycott of the Los Angeles Olympics. The hard line seemed to be in the ascendancy in Moscow; meanwhile a more benign attitude in Washington was punctuated by recurring older themes, among them the denunciation of the World War II Yalta agreement, which in the USSR could only mean a revival of the assault on its legitimacy. Such interventions probably strengthened Moscow's conviction that Reagan's more conciliatory overtures were hypocritical. Yet the strange episode of negotiations about Star Wars, proposed on June 29, 1984, by Moscow and then rejected by the Soviets themselves when accepted by the United States in a broader context that included talks of offensive arms, suggested ambivalence if not confusion and indecision in the Kremlin. The Soviets claimed that the proposal was a test of the new Reagan line, and this claim is not implausible. The episode served to highlight continuing contradictions in American policy: enduring, deep suspicion of negotiations clashed with growing concern that the president should not be isolated as the war candidate in the coming elections. The shrewd U.S. response, however, may have drawn the Soviets into further exploration, including more direct overtures.

The net result was that by the fall of 1984 both sides may have sensed that matters threatened to go too far and that a reappraisal was in order. This led to a Gromyko-Reagan meeting, September 23. One observer summed up the situation:

> In terms of the world, Reagan has unquestionably increased visible American
> military strength and forced the Soviet Union to reconsider its relationship with
> the other superpower. What can be debated . . . is whether he has evolved any co-
> herent strategy for making that power serve the cause of peace and the protection
> of vital national interests, or whether he is embarked on a course that will inevita-
> bly destabilize the world.[3]

[2]Quoted in *New York Times*, January 17, 1984.
[3]David S. Border, "Is Reagan the Only Real Issue?" *Washington Post*, national weekly ed., September 3, 1984.

This was indeed the question. Could the United States turn a change in the balance of power to its advantage? Clearly it needs a strategy to do so. Soviet-American relations have reached a point where general, wholesale rebuilding is required.

The year 1985 saw the initial stages of improved relations. Both sides chose to interpret the Geneva summit, despite a lack of substantive progress, as a turning point. Before examining the components of current U.S.-Soviet relations, however, some generalizations are in order.

The United States was never as weak as portrayed by the Reagan administration in 1980, nor is it now as strong as the administration claims. Despite some mournful American rhetoric over the past ten years, the United States has maintained a strong position in every category in which power can be measured. There have been significant geopolitical changes, to be sure, especially the loss of Iran and the appearance of serious problems in Central America, but these are offset by Poland, Afghanistan, the Soviet economic malaise, and the crisis of the Soviet leadership. The USSR is beset by serious problems, but these problems are not yet reflected in a new foreign policy. Indeed, the underlying structure of relations between the two superpowers has been more stable than the rhetoric suggests. But the trend has become favorable for the United States. This change, of course, is perceived in Moscow though not accepted as a permanent shift. The United States has recovered from the shocks of the 1970s, and the psychological balance has been redressed. But the power relationship remains one of rough parity. The past five years suggest that neither side is likely to achieve a permanent strategic advantage.

One factor of uncertainty is the state of the Soviet leadership. It seems likely that with the deaths of Brezhnev and Chernenko, and Gorbachev's accession, the generational shift has run its course. But until the character of the Gorbachev regime has emerged more clearly, Soviet policy will be difficult to assess. Moreover, though the Reagan administration won a stunning victory in the presidential elections of 1984, it is increasingly clear that public and congressional support for the harsher line of 1980–83 has declined. On the question of relations with the USSR, public opinion seems to have swung from the frustrations of the Iranian-Afghan period toward a more centrist position.[4]

Finally, the relationship between the principal contenders, Moscow and Washington, and their respective allies is weakening, more so in the East than in the West. Neither alliance system is in danger of collapse, nor are radical changes likely in the near term. Nevertheless the two superpowers can no longer simply command allied support inside Europe or outside Europe. This growing uncertainty about alliance support is especially evident in East-West security issues. How the two superpowers adjust to this critical change will be fundamental to their evolving relationship.

---

[4]Daniel Yankelovich, "The Public Mood," *Foreign Affairs*, Fall 1984.

In sum, East-West relations retain a certain fluidity. The operational consequence is that the United States still has the time and the opportunity, as a new leadership takes hold and a new "general line" emerges under Gorbachev, to shape its relations with Moscow.

Theoretically, the United States has three basic options for the latter 1980s and beyond:

1. To do little or nothing, on the theory that the crisis in the East is grave enough to justify waiting. Waiting will actually be beneficial to the Western alliance; the Soviet predicament will worsen and, finally, a way will be sought to alleviate tension with the West. At most a policy of small steps will be required in Washington, largely to placate domestic opinion. The Geneva summit was consistent with this strategy.

2. To do as much as possible, to achieve a "breakthrough," on the theory that the situation being sufficiently fluid, both sides could entertain departures more significant than they could during the last five years. The Soviets themselves occasionally suggest that something along these lines is needed to avert a strategic crisis (looming over SDI). The option is also compatible with President Reagan's insistence that the United States is now in a favorable position and, as far as possible, should turn that position into a permanent gain. But it clashes with the view of those who believe negotiated settlements are impossible because of the nature of the Soviet system.

3. To do what is required to reactivate relations, on a broad basis and without waiting for internal changes in the USSR but also without expecting a fundamental breakthrough. This, the obvious "middle" option, was foreshadowed by the outcome of the Geneva summit of 1985.

The foregoing scheme is somewhat synthetic. The first two options always tend to the artificial, and their proponents would not argue or present them in so simple a fashion. Watchful waiting may indeed be a serious strategy, but reliance on a major breakthrough is a dubious one. It can be dismissed largely because there is no focal point for such a breakthrough; certainly no current geopolitical issue compares to *Ostpolitik* and the Berlin agreement of 1971. An arms control breakthrough, such as massive strategic reductions, is possible, but it is more likely to result from a prolonged negotiation than from one bold stroke.

There is much to be said for a policy of watchful waiting, for allowing the Soviet crisis to run its course. The major problem is that the policy is too passive; no administration is likely to retain public support for a posture that leaves it to history to bring the benefits of peace. The United States would soon find itself in the worst conceivable position, refusing to act out of conviction but then being pressured to act on issues at a time chosen by critics or by domestic and allied pressure groups. Watchful waiting, moreover, would be based on a tenuous reading of history and politics. The current crisis in the Soviet bloc is indeed serious but surely not indefinite. In a few years, it might be, trends will alter; new accommodations could be made by Moscow with

China or even in Eastern Europe. The Soviet economy is large enough to sustain years of erratic performance.

Waiting is therefore a risky option for the United States. The policy could turn out to be correct, but there is a good chance that it would have to be abandoned. No administration, political party, or partisan faction will hold power long enough to realize the fruits of a long-term strategy of outwaiting the Soviet Union.

The real choices fall within the third option: deciding how to proceed on the major issues, in what combination, and with what objectives. One apparent choice is between a narrow approach and a more comprehensive one, but even this difference may be theoretical. A modest approach, in arms control for example, need not remain modest if it encounters success. Nor does a comprehensive approach mean that all components must succeed, for a comprehensive strategy is not invalidated by a partial success.

What is involved in rebuilding relations between the United States and the Soviet Union? I outline the requirements in three crucial areas: arms control, the political relationship, and economic relations.

Arms Control

Over the past five years there has been a vigorous debate on the role of arms control in East-West relations. Proponents of arms control have continued to argue that an arms control solution exists to the basic problems of East-West security. Opponents continued to argue that a penchant for arms control agreements was at the root of American weakness in the 1970s. The substantive debate, however, seemed in the early 1980s more amorphous than usual, partly because the situation at the official level was also bewildering.

The status of negotiated agreements illustrated the general confusion. Despite the Reagan administration's public attacks on the SALT II agreements, it held to the official position that the United States would not undercut the agreements if the Soviets did not. But over the years the administration has in fact accused the Soviets precisely of undercutting the agreements by violating key provisions. Thus a strange situation developed: unratified treaties were being observed even though, officially, grounds supposedly existed for denouncing them. Matters reached an absurd point: the United States, for example, began the dismantling of submarine-launched weapons as required by an unratified treaty even though that treaty was to expire in about one year's time. The same situation applied to the threshold test ban treaties of 1974; the United States appeared to be abiding by the 150 kiloton ceiling on underground tests while accusing the Soviet Union of exceeding that threshold.

This novel situation led some observers to speculate that a new approach to arms control was taking shape, one that would rely less on formal, negotiated treaties or agreements and more on informal understandings or reciprocal actions. Such an approach to arms control received some high-level encouragement within the administration. However, the general climate was growing more critical of arms control. This new climate, fostered by the Reagan administration, led many other observers to conclude that the era of comprehensive arms control had passed. At best, it was argued, a few interim steps or agreements might be achieved, but they would deal with only the most time-urgent problems.

Finally, of course, there were two radically different and opposing ideas: the nuclear freeze and the Strategic Defense Initiative. These two conflicting positions had a common starting point. Freeze advocates united with President Reagan in questioning the durability, realiability, and credibility of the reliance on nuclear retaliation as a means of deterrence. But the freeze movement envisaged an arms control solution. SDI enthusiasts, on the other hand, saw a unilateral solution—unless by some chance the USSR would agree to the transition to a strong defense on both sides.

This ferment coexisted with official negotiations that showed a notable lack of innovation. The positions advanced on both sides were either stale variants of old positions or propaganda tricks, such as the zero option in the Intermediate Nuclear Force talks. The Soviet Union was trying to preserve the rough status quo while allowing for its own modernization programs; the United States sought to refurbish hoary proposals—"tradeoffs"—that would undo the Soviet advantage in heavy ICBMs.

The inevitable stalemate was made the more solid because the major contest was not at the negotiating table but in the politics of NATO and Western Europe: either the United States would succeed in deploying medium-range weapons or the USSR would succeed in defeating the deployment. Until this contest was settled, there was no real room for progress on the major strategic systems. When the Soviets walked out of the INF talks at the end of 1983, therefore, it appeared that the whole framework of arms control was at risk.

In a broad sense the situation was ready-made for new ideas and new procedures. What emerged, however, was still propagandistic—the Soviet proposal for a 50 percent reduction in certain strategic forces, but those forces one-sidedly defined by the USSR. And despite the obvious defects in the Soviet plan the U.S. response was also a public relations position: accept the goal of a 50 percent reduction but adopt an acceptable baseline, and add some variants to bring the proposal back toward the original U.S. goal of reducing the USSR's first-strike potential.

The motivating force for these maneuvers was not only the Geneva summit of November 19–20, 1985, but more basically the threat of a strategic revolution inherent in the president's SDI. It was this initiative more than any other factor which forced a Soviet retreat from intransigeance and the resumption of negotiations. The effect was to bring to the bargaining table, for the first time since 1972, questions of how to link offense and defense. In short, out of the uncertainties of the early 1980s came a major strategic issue and a challenge for arms control: to join aspirations for large strategic reductions to the growing sentiment in favor of some sort of defense.

In this period there emerged a road map to guide the superpowers through pitfalls inherited from a different strategic era. The President's Commission on Strategic Forces, known as the Scowcroft Commission, came to some sound and durable conclusions.

The commission took the sensible position that arms control was an element essential to national security and to American strategy. It further argued that channeling the modernization of strategic forces in what would prove over the long term more stable directions was a realistic and legitimate objective for U.S. arms control. The general approach that the commission recommended remains valid:

> Over the long run, stability would be fostered by an approach which moves toward encouraging small, single-warhead ICBMs. This requires that arms control limitations and reductions be couched, not in terms of launchers, but in terms of equal levels of warheads of roughly equivalent yields. Such an approach could permit relatively simple agreements, using appropriate counting rules, that exert pressure to reduce the overall number and destructive power of nuclear weapons and at the same time give each side an incentive to move toward more stable and less vulnerable deployments.
>
> Each side will naturally desire to configure its own strategic forces. Simple aggregate limits are likely to be more practical, stabilizing, and lasting than elaborate, detailed limitations on force structure and modernization whose ultimate consequences cannot be confidently anticipated.[5]

But the key to future arms control is strategic defense. It would be mindless for the United States to reduce its offensive forces and try to stabilize the balance if both sides were proceeding with major strategic defensive systems, especially if those systems were based on deployments in space. Neither side could feel secure in such an environment, whatever political protestations might be made about innocence of purpose. This does not mean that the SDI must be banned, though that ought to remain an option. It does mean that the United States needs to establish a linkage between the defense and the offense—an elementary point that is too often brushed aside in Washington.

At mid-decade it would be foolhardy to pretend that all the answers regarding defensive arms control can be found either in unilateral policies or in arms control agreements. Again the Scowcroft Commission, in its final report, offers a helpful guideline, namely extreme caution:

> Ballistic missile defense is a critical aspect of the strategic balance and therefore is central to arms control. One of the most successful arms control agreements is the Anti–Ballistic Missile Treaty of 1972. That fact should not be allowed to ob-

[5]Brent Scowcroft, letter to the president, March 21, 1984; reproduced in *President's Commission on Strategic Forces.*

scure the possibility that technological developments at some point could make it in the interests of both sides to amend the current treaty. In considering this issue, it is important to distinguish between defensive systems designed to enhance the survivability of offensive systems and those designed to put a shield over wide areas, or all, of the United States or Soviet Union. However, no move in the direction of the deployment of active defense should be made without the most careful considerations of the possible strategic and arms control implications.[6]

The commission thus raised a basic question: if the objective is merely protecting ICBM sites would the risks of instability arising from a revival of strategic defense be worth the gain? If the fixed-site ICBM is a waning asset, which seems likely, then opening the entire question of defense in order to give protection only to Minuteman or MX silos would certainly be questionable. The tie between a new ICBM, whether the MX or the Midgetman, and an "active" antiballistic-missile defense needs to be thoroughly debated in the United States. Thus far the administration initiated has no such debate. The tentative decision to bar mobile ICBMs, as proposed to the USSR in November 1985, is puzzling. It fits no recognizable theory, and it seems to run directly counter to concerns about ICBM vulnerability.

Mobility brings to the fore doubts about verifiability, it is true, but the question of cheating is also being manipulated by the opponents of arms control. Long lists of supposed violations are regularly leaked to the press or presented in formal documents. Senators and self-appointed experts comment endlessly on data that are not available to the general public. But no action is taken. So the United States has the worst conceivable outcome: it continues to abide by agreements that have supposedly been violated. Most so-called violations are in the eye of the beholder: critics see massive cheating where supporters see phenomena easily explained. The subject has become so exotic, however, that it cannot be assessed outside the dark corridors of classified reporting, which itself is open to widely different interpretations.

In sum, the United States needs to pursue comprehensive arms control programs, along the general lines recommended by the Scowcroft Commission, while leaving open for negotiation the ultimate disposition of strategic defense and without overly punctilious concern for verification. Arms control needs to be taken out of the realm of ideological polemics and restored to foreign policy.

Arms control obviously will not succeed solely on its merits, whether agreements are marginal, interim, or comprehensive. A change will be required in the political atmosphere. Though arms control is essential, it cannot bear the entire burden of an improvement in relations—a point well made by Stanley Hoffman: "Arms control is essential but also too complex and politically too fragile to be the only instrument of Soviet-American cooperation.

[6]Ibid.

For arms control to succeed, the general climate of political relations has to be better, and the extent of Soviet-American ties greater than it is at present."[7]

The Political Relationship

Changing the political relationship is far more difficult than working out technical formulas for arms control. It is commonplace to observe that the Soviet-American competition is global. But however true the observation may be, it does not mean that a global settlement is required. Churchill's epigram still applies: one does not have to settle all things to settle some things. What one does have to do, however, is to set some priorities to guide American policy and to serve as a basis for discussions with the USSR. And our psychological approach is important. If we see the problem as the narrow one of "managing," failure is inevitable. We need to think more positively about partial settlements. If the Soviets are entering a difficult period, then the United States may have some unique opportunities for progress.

Obviously, there are areas of the world where both sides have relatively modest interests or are not intensely competitive. Much of Africa falls into the first category. Some of Latin America falls into the second, if only because the Soviets do not really compete there. The difficult problems relate to two areas: those where both sides have vital interests directly engaged (Europe, the Far East, China and Japan, and perhaps Korea), and those where competition is fierce (the Middle East and the Persian Gulf). The contest in Europe has been well defined, and the rules there are established. Though both sides still recoil in mock horror from the idea of overt spheres of influence, it is indeed on such spheres that policy is based, no matter how many denunciations of Yalta are uttered in Washington. The United States, including the Reagan administration, long ago conceded the Warsaw Pact as a Soviet sphere; we have never really challenged that arrangement. Nor since 1962 has the USSR directly challenged the U.S. position in Europe. Indeed, the present Soviet-American arrangement in Europe is based on spheres of influence.

Ironically, however, both superpowers occupy declining positions in Europe as their respective allies grow in autonomy and strength. For the United States this change requires that a new policy be developed toward East Europe. The old policy of "differentiation" is obsolescent. Poland has raised new, fundamental issues. How should the United States respond to the crises that seem likely to characterize Eastern Europe over the next decade?

Maybe the United States should allow the West Europeans to take a leading position where their interests are more directly involved. What happens to, say, Bulgaria is of no genuine importance to the United States except as a function of pan-European politics. Our policy goal used to be to weaken the ties between Moscow and the Warsaw Pact. Those ties are weakening now without U.S. assistance (though detente played a larger role in bringing

[7]Stanley Hoffmann, "Detente without Illusions," *New York Times*, March 7, 1983.

about the Polish crisis than America's right wing will acknowledge). What American policy faces is a series of special situations, each of which will require an accommodation to gains as well as to setbacks. Our general posture ought to be one of benign interest and occasional assistance, even when, as in sending food to Poland, our actions seem to coincide with a Soviet interest. It may not be too much of an exaggeration to suggest that developments in East Europe will have a more far-reaching effect on Soviet-American relations than how many warheads are carried on ICBMs.

In the Far East the United States is predominant in Japan and South Korea; the USSR has important interests in North Korea, interests that the United States does not challenge. The USSR has not challenged the U.S. position in Japan but protects its interests by indirect pressures on Tokyo. (A new Soviet initiative seems to be in the making, however.) China's position is pivotal and need not be rehearsed here at length. Suffice it to say that China cannot be the subject of a U.S.-Soviet dialogue. But Sino-American relations do have an important bearing on U.S.-Soviet relations, and the present order in East Asia is based on a Sino-American rapprochement. American-Chinese military cooperation is another matter, and a prudent policy is clearly in order. The United States should not flinch from a Chinese military relationship for fear of Soviet reaction. Such a relationship should be limited, however, for our own self-interest. Political accommodation with China ought in any case to be limited, for China has little in common with the United States beyond its opposition to Moscow. If this is indeed the case, then to bear in mind legitimate Soviet concerns about the growth of Chinese power makes sense. A balanced triangular relationship remains the best American option.

In the Third World, U.S. and Soviet interests clash, sometimes dangerously, and the Persian Gulf and the Middle East are crucial. In both areas the United States and the USSR find themselves relinquishing too much control to second-level powers. Unless the superpowers find some method for dealing with the competition and the periodic flareups caused by third parties, crises may now be inherent in the structure of relations.

One way to deal with Third World competition is to agree on new "rules of conduct" similar to the principles negotiated by Henry Kissinger in 1972, but this approach is no longer appropriate: what seemed worthwhile at the outset of a new relationship is not suited to the current stalemate. A better approach would be to create some mechanism that operates in crises and, equally important, operates in normal times when conventional means, contacts through ambassadors or foreign ministers, seem not to work. It may be possible to create an institutional framework. Taking a cue from informal academic exchange programs, several U.S.-Soviet working groups might be established to meet periodically, and privately, in Moscow and Washington.[8] Ordinarily, one might think the idea simply another gimmick, likely to wither

[8]This is roughly what was mentioned in President Reagan's address to the United Nations, September 24, 1984; and it seemed to be confirmed by the joint statement issued after the Geneva summit on November 22, 1985.

away. But if we are mindful of repeated warnings that our current situation is analogous to that of 1914, then maintaining contact may well be the best device available. The regular working groups could be tied into periodic summits, an idea that seems to have been revived by Reagan and Gorbachev. Summits, after all, are better treated as the culmination of preparatory exchanges than as a vehicle for a supposed breakthrough.

Admittedly, none of the foregoing ideas explains how to solve the contest in Central America, the Middle East, or elsewhere. These suggestions simply emphasize the point that a political dialogue must be continued and, preferably, institutionalized. Sporadic meetings between secretary of state and foreign minister are of limited value as long as they remain sporadic, and unstructured summits are hazardous. Something in between is needed, to serve as a link. If crisis control centers are believed to be important (and the proposals of Senators Nunn and Warner, endorsed at the summit suggest they are), then the prevention or preemption of crisis is equally important. The two superpowers have in fact controlled major crises rather effectively; but they have done poorly at foreseeing and forestalling crises.

Economic Relations

There must be some economic component to East-West relations. The question is, What kind? If arms control suffers from a lack of focus, Western economic policy is sheer chaos. The United States makes massive grain sales to the USSR, East-West trade is steady, and there are special allowances for East Germany but there is also an uncertain, though strenuous, effort to stop the flow of technology to the East. And all of these strands coexist with occasional efforts to use economic power as a sanction or means of coercion —efforts that have proved thus far ineffective.

One option for the West and for the United States is simply to permit the present muddle to continue. This option has the virtue of placating various interests: American farmers, European allies, some East Europeans, and probably even the Kremlin. But policy, it seems obvious, could be organized with a greater sense of purpose, especially since the economic relationship has been the focal point for a long debate on how best to influence the future course of the USSR. One school argues vehemently that continued economic pressure will add to strains that, over time, will force major reforms inside the USSR. Yet it also holds, apparently, that the Soviet position could become so desperate that the Kremlin will give "active" consideration to lashing out.[9]

Thus another option is to increase pressure, which would involve, among other things, constant cooperation with Western Europeans. (This strategy would be designed to keep Moscow "off balance.") Not only is such a strat-

---

[9]Editorial, "Andrei in the Rose Garden," *Wall Street Journal*, September 17, 1984.

egy unlikely to succeed for lack of European regional cooperation, however, but it could cut across a policy of conciliation toward Eastern Europeans. The debatable impact on the USSR of current technology transfer policies suggests that greater stringency might not succeed in any case.[10] But above all there is domestic politics: Will the United States forgo hundreds of millions of dollars in grain sales? If the Reagan administration is any model, then the answer is "Probably not."

The United States might choose the opposite of greater pressure, the older policy of using economics as an incentive to stimulate more acceptable Soviet behavior. But the time for a liberalization of trade, revival of credits, and so forth has passed. It is very doubtful that such a policy could gain domestic support now in the United States. Moreover, the policy is based on a theory that is highly suspect—namely, that the Soviets can be bribed by economic inducements into changing their foreign policy. It also overrates the leverage that the United States, acting alone, can wield. Once general relaxation is offered, U.S. influence is diluted, because West Europe and Japan will fill part of the Soviet demand. Only on the leading edge of high technology (and in grain) would the United States still have leverage. And to compete by allowing trade in technology of potential military value would be eventually to produce a domestic backlash.

Once again, therefore, a middle ground seems advisable. Certainly, the United States needs to retain some control over its economic exchanges with the USSR. It needs to protect those technologies which have special military importance. But on the other hand, it is high time to admit that such protections are more therapeutic than punitive. The White House cannot proclaim that we do not aim to "alter" the Soviet system and continue to justify economic controls in order to force long-term changes in internal structures and external behavior. If, however, the aim is the more modest one of raising the price of Soviet military programs, then the policy is probably acceptable. Yet it is still badly undermined by grain sales, which have a far greater value than military technologies that, unlike grain, the Soviet Union can reproduce at home.

Within the bounds of a policy that controls technology while offering a blank check for grain sales, there is much to be said for allowing the market to operate and consigning trade with the East to commercial interests. After all, the "hardline" Reagan administration sold five times more to the USSR in 1983 than the "detentist" Nixon-Ford administration did in 1974. Indeed, a review of East-West trade suggests that commerce with the USSR will remain a small percentage of American trade but a somewhat larger share for West Europeans. The fluctuations over the past ten years fall within a well-defined pattern.

There is still, however, the negative side: the use of economic sanctions.

[10]Frederick Kempe, "Losing Russia," *Wall Street Journal*, July 24, 1984.

The two most recent cases—the declaration of martial law in Poland and the shooting down of a Korean airliner—suggest that economic sanctions suffer from two defects: an American reluctance to use the full panoply of sanctions (the grain weapon again was not used), and the absence of consensus in the West. These defects seem to argue for treating economic relations more as a commercial element than a source of political leverage.

In reconstructing its Eastern policy, in sum, the United States ought to make it clear, first to its allies but then to Moscow, what the main features of that policy will be: (1) no transfer of high technology; (2) but no further restrictions on general trade except for U.S. restrictions on credit financing; (3) continued grain sales as contracted for; and, in this light, (4) no preplanned policy of using economic sanctions.

Prospects

How will the Soviet Union react to a U.S. policy of rebuilding relations? Its response depends on the Soviet calculation of the balance of forces as they appear in the late 1980s.

The Soviet strategic position has indeed been declining. The USSR is faced with a broad, strategic encirclement by the United States, Europe, China, and Japan. It has made almost no progress in breaking up this coalition. It cannot bring itself to make the basic concessions that China demands; it cannot return the territory that Japan wants back; it cannot impose its demands on the United States or split the United States from West Europe. And so it faces stark choices.

One choice is to "break out" with more aggressive policies. It is not an idle suggestion; indeed, breaking out was one of several Soviet motives in Afghanistan. And that area along the USSR's southern flank, especially Iran and Pakistan, remains potentially vulnerable to Soviet incursions. Greater Soviet aggressiveness could also provide a rationale for tightening up internal policies.

The alternative is to explore American terms for a modus vivendi, which seems to be the option chosen by Gorbachev. For the United States this course of action imposes a familiar dual obligation: be prepared to resist Soviet advances and encroachments, but also be prepared to negotiate an accommodation. In the five years since 1980 the United States has put itself in a better position to carry out the containment side of its policy, but now it needs to organize the diplomatic side. If it does so on a narrow basis, with a policy limited to small steps, the result is likely to be a continuing stalemate. Indeed, the United States might even drive the USSR inadvertently into a corner, with results dangerous to all. But if the United States can outline a broad basis for resuming a strategic relationship, then it will maximize its chances of drawing the USSR into a relationship that is also safer. And that is, after all, what American foreign policy is all about.

CONTRIBUTORS

ABRAHAM S. BECKER is a Senior Economist at The Rand Corporation, Santa Monica. He was the U.S. member of the UN Experts Groups on Reduction of Military Budgets in 1974 and 1976, and he has been a consultant to several U.S. government agencies.

SEWERYN BIALER is Ruggles Professor of Political Science and Director of the Research Institute on International Change, Columbia University, New York City. He is a MacArthur Foundation Fellow.

ROBERT D. BLACKWILL is a U.S. Foreign Service Officer, currently serving as U.S. Ambassador to the Mutual and Balanced Force Reduction Talks in Vienna. His chapter was written while he was on sabbatical leave as Associate Dean of the John F. Kennedy School of Government, Harvard University, Cambridge.

FRANCIS FUKUYAMA is a member of the Political Science Department, The Rand Corporation, Santa Monica. He served on the Policy Planning Staff, U.S. Department of State, in 1981–82.

HARRY GELMAN is a senior staff member in the Political Science Department, The Rand Corporation, Santa Monica. He served from 1956 to 1980 as an analyst for the U.S. Central Intelligence Agency, most recently as Assistant National Intelligence Officer for the Soviet Union and Eastern Europe.

ARNOLD L. HORELICK is Director of the Rand/UCLA Center for the Study of Soviet International Behavior, a Corporate Fellow of The Rand Corporation, and Professor of Political Science at the University of California, Los Angeles. From 1977 to 1980 he was National Intelligence Officer for the Soviet Union and Eastern Europe at the U.S. Central Intelligence Agency.

WILLIAM G. HYLAND is Editor of *Foreign Affairs*. He was a senior staff member at the National Security Council, 1969–73; Director of the State Department's Bureau of Intelligence and Research, 1973–75; and Deputy Assistant to the President for National Security Affairs, 1975–77.

[303]

JOSEPH S. NYE, JR., is Dillon Professor of International Affairs, Harvard University, Cambridge. From 1977 to 1979 he was Deputy to the Under Secretary of State for Security Assistance, Science and Technology.

RICHARD PIPES is Baird Professor of History at Harvard University, Cambridge. He was Director for Soviet and East European Affairs in the National Security Council in 1981–82.

MARSHALL D. SHULMAN is Adlai E. Stevenson Professor of International Relations and Director of the Averell Harriman Institute for the Advanced Study of the Soviet Union, Columbia University, New York City. From 1977 to 1980 he was Special Advisor on Soviet Affairs to the U.S. Secretary of State.

DIMITRI K. SIMES is Senior Associate at the Carnegie Endowment for International Peace, Washington, D.C., and Professorial Lecturer at the Johns Hopkins University School of Advanced International Studies, Washington.

JOHN VAN OUDENAREN is a member of the Policy Planning Staff, U.S. Department of State. His chapter was written while he was a member of the Political Science Department, The Rand Corporation, Santa Monica.

EDWARD L. WARNER III is Senior Defense Analyst in The Rand Corporation's Washington office, having retired from the U.S. Air Force in 1982. His service assignments included Assistant Air Attaché at the U.S. Embassy in Moscow, 1976–78, and Deputy Chief of the Strategy Division of the Air Staff in 1982.

INDEX

Library of Congress Cataloging-in-Publication Data

U.S.-Soviet relations.

"A book from the Rand/UCLA Center for the Study of Soviet International Behavior."
"This volume had its inception in a national conference on U.S.-Soviet relations conducted in Los Angeles and Santa Monica on October 18–19, 1984"—Introd.
Includes index.
1. United States—Foreign relations—Soviet Union—Congresses. 2. Soviet Union—Foreign relations—United States—Congresses. 3. United States—Foreign relations—1981– —Congresses. 4. Soviet Union—Foreign relations—1975– —Congresses. I. Horelick, Arnold Lawrence, 1928– . II. Rand/UCLA Center for the Study of Soviet International Behavior. III. Title: United States-Soviet relations.
E183.8.S65U18   1986   327.73047   85-48274
ISBN 0-8014-1912-3 (alk. paper)
ISBN 0-8014-9383-8 (pbk. : alk. paper)

DATE DUE